W9-BZF-917

FROM A STANDING START

My Tennessee Political Odyssey

WINFIELD DUNN

MAGELLAN PRESS
NASHVILLE, TENNESSEE

Special Thanks:
I gratefully acknowledge the encouragement and support
of S. Jackson Faris and Samuel W. Bartholomew, Jr., in the
advent of this book."
—*Winfield Dunn*

Library of Congress Control Number: 2007936347

FOREWORD

Of the more than two hundred years of Tennessee history, only a few stand out as truly epochal, years that altered the historical trajectory of the state and turned it clearly in a new political direction. One that comes most readily to mind is 1861, when the Volunteer State chose to secede from the United States of America and join a different nation, the Confederate States of America. That action has affected the lives of Tennesseans from that date to the present. Another watershed year was 1970, when the political course that had been followed by the state for an entire century was abruptly and forever changed.

From 1870, when the last Reconstruction governor left office, until 1970, Tennessee had been a one-party state and a charter member of the Solid South, the former Confederate States whose allegiance to the Democratic Party could be taken for granted. Tennessee differed from the other state members of this club only in having a Republican Party at all, albeit one that seemed relegated to a permanent minority status. During that century, it elected only three GOP governors—Alvin Hawkins, Ben Hooper, and Alfred Taylor—and the election of each was an aberration. The first two of these were elected because the Democrats were seriously divided over controversial issues, and the third, some Tennesseans have always said, received the winning majority only because of the immense popularity of Taylor's dog, the most famous of Tennessee canines, "Old Limber." In any event, Republicans were just not expected to win statewide elections.

When the year 1970 began, Winfield Dunn, who had announced his candidacy, did not appear to experienced observers to have any chance of winning. He was a Republican, and it had been fifty years since a governor had been elected from his party. Moreover, he was a medical practitioner, a dentist, a profession without previous success in such elections. Even worse, he was a resident of Memphis, a city of ill repute with state voters and from which only two citizens had ever been elected Governor of Tennessee.

But when the votes were counted after the election in November, the magnitude of Winfield Dunn's victory was stunning. A sea change in Tennessee politics had taken place. Not only was Winfield Dunn elected Governor, but Bill Brock from Chattanooga had won election as United States Senator to join Howard Baker, who in 1966 had already become the first Republican ever to be popularly elected to the Senate from Tennessee. With the elections of Dunn and Brock, all three major state-wide offices in the state were now held by the Republican Party.

It may be trite but it is also true to say that Tennessee has never been the same. Simply stated, the state changed from one hundred years of one-party dominance into one characterized by two political parties of approximately equal power. In fact, during the thirty-seven years that have elapsed since Winfield Dunn's election, neither party has been able to hold the governor's office for two consecutive administrations. So close is the party division within the state that it can no longer be taken for granted that the state will support even a native Tennessean in national elections, as Al Gore, Jr., learned to his disappointment in 2000.

This sharp break with the past likely contributed to the remarkable honesty so evident during the Dunn era. Previously, with some variations and exceptions, political corruption at the state level was a recurrent theme throughout the history of Tennessee. Those who did business with the State routinely gave money to politicians in office and expected favorable treatment in return. These payoffs, made more or less surreptitiously, were often in the form of campaign contributions or the payment of campaign debts of winners of elections. And, during these pre-Watergate years, the practice may not have been strictly illegal and certainly received little notice by the press. It was simply seen as part of the cost of doing business with the state. This changed after Winfield Dunn took office.

A salient characteristic of his administration was the large number of fresh faces among the executive staff. Conspicuously missing were seasoned politicians with knowledge of how things had been done in previous administrations, a situation that may have been both a handicap and an advantage. No doubt some time was lost during the early organizational period when basic lessons had to be learned by these beginners. (One aide later joked, "It was several weeks before we were even able to locate the pencil sharpeners.") But any initial delays were quickly offset by youthful enthusiasm and a willingness to work extraordinarily long hours. Carefully selected for their educational achievements, intelligence, and skill in personal relations, the members of the Dunn staff soon demonstrated an impressive level of efficiency within the executive office.

Moreover, when individuals who had previously done business with the state government came to these young members of the Dunn staff asking where to make contributions in exchange for state contracts for materials or services, they met a stone wall. The neophytes in the new administration were such amateurs in politics that they did not know it was customary to appoint a bagmen to receive "contributions," nor is there any indication that they ever did make such arrangements.

Dozens of interviews were conducted during subsequent years by the Oral History Research Office of the University of Memphis with campaign managers, administration staff, and journalists who covered the era included people in all parts of Tennessee. This extensive collection of historical material, now maintained in the Special Collections archives of the Ned McWherter Library at the University, was used by Winfield Dunn in the preparation of this autobiography and is available for use by all researchers. Not one of the participants and witnesses of the Dunn Administration who were interviewed in this project, however, could point to a single instance of dishonesty within the administration. Historians and other scholars may analyze and criticize any particular policy of this governor, but his was an administration notably free from scandal and charges of financial irregularity.

With the close of his gubernatorial administration, Winfield Dunn's life followed a different course. He changed his residence from Memphis to Nashville and also entered a new profession. Rather than returning to the practice of dentistry, he became a successful business executive, a career which continued for almost three decades— but that is a subject that would require at least another biographical volume. The one just completed required several years of careful research and writing. More than just personal memories, it has been enriched by painstaking review of official records, press and correspondence files, and the use of many oral history memoirs from the archives. This research has produced a high level of historical accuracy, given life in human interest terms by vivid recollection of events and people.

On a personal note, my own recollections of Winfield Dunn begin with the year after his election, 1971. Two special events are part of this memory. The first was the cold January day of his inauguration, an event conducted with conspicuous dignity and modesty. As a teacher of Tennessee history and a writer about the subject, I have attended the inaugural ceremonies of every governor since Buford Ellington, but the accompanying inaugural ball when Dunn took office was an especially memorable one, enthusiastically celebrated by a diverse group of people, many of whom likely had never attended one before—with the possible exception of any who might have been there at the last such Republican gala in 1921. All who were present surely remember the beginning, described in the book, when Winfield and Betty Dunn opened the ball dancing to the music of the "Tennessee Waltz."

The other memory of that year came shortly thereafter when the governor asked me to serve as a member of the Tennessee Historical Commission, another instance of his general practice of appointing younger and newer members to state boards and commissions. It was in this capacity that I learned, somewhat to my surprise, that the new governor had an extensive knowledge of history and a deep interest in the subject, particularly that of our own state. Later actions illustrated this interest. One was his approval, during the same year, of a law I had drafted and the General Assembly had approved requiring the teaching of American History in state institutions of higher learning. Another was his unrestricted approval, following his political service, of an oral history of the Dunn Administration undertaken by the school then known as Memphis State University.

An additional contribution to history is Winfield Dunn's decision to devote several years of his life to the labor of researching and writing this autobiography. Had every other Tennessee governor left such a book, those volumes would be of great value to those who teach and study Tennessee history. Unfortunately, only one other of the forty-eight governors of the state has done so, Ben Hooper.

Winfield Dunn not only made history in his state, he has also left an enduring record of that history that will be available for generations yet to come. This is a truly unique book. It is the story of a life, of a family, and of an era in the history of a fascinating state. It will provide amusement to some, nostalgia to others, and enlightenment to all who read it.

—*Charles W. Crawford*
The University of Memphis

PREFACE

During the years that have elapsed following my service as governor of Tennessee, I have met interesting people from all walks of life. Occasionally in meeting and getting to know someone for the first time, I have been able with some accuracy to predict a question from the new friend should a lull in our conversation occur. The question usually goes about like this: "How in the world did a dentist from Memphis ever get to be the governor of our state?"

My response is usually influenced by the time available and by my sense of the inquirer's genuine interest. In answering the question, I mention that I was born and brought up in a family environment where politics, political persons, and interest in government were matters frequently discussed. I explain that I have been interested in politics and government, to one degree or another, as far back as I can remember. And I note that many of the new friends I initially made in my adopted home of Memphis, Tennessee, had similar interests, particularly related to building a competitive two-party political system in Shelby County. As to my healthcare background, I was also quick to point out that a professionally trained person, no less so in dentistrythan in the law or medicine, could measure up to the demands of public service if political instincts and ability could get one to that point.

I have undertaken to tell the story of my political experiences because I can no longer resist a strong desire to get it done. The time has come to relate it "for the record." It will tell the reader how my family of five became an extended family of thousands of fellow Tennesseans who made a dream become a reality in less than one year's time. It will have a certain fascination for some readers because it is an out of the ordinary political happening in a state that has a colorful political history. It was a significant turning point for the state politically. It is the tale of a whimsical notion that became an idea. The idea became an adventure, and the adventure was uniquely real. It was not only real; it was also good. The goodness grew out of the nature of the people who were involved. I've said it before and I'll say it once again: Never in my life's experience did so many giving, unselfish, caring, and devoted people come together to do something that seemed more worthwhile. Their only reward was in the pleasure of hoping it could happen and in the accomplishment. And the fact that the dream did become a reality is simply one more example of the truth that people should never stop dreaming.

My hope is that in the years ahead the story may be of interest to some future members of my family who become curious about events that had such influence in my life and the lives of my immediate family members. I also write with the hope that an occasional student of the political history of my state might gain fresh insights into what I believe was a time of positive change. I, along with my family, was fortunate to play my part in the process. The story of my wife Betty's transition from dutiful mother and life's companion into an effective and impressive political advocate for her husband is unique within itself. Her beauty, charm, and intelligence were powerful factors in the outcome. I continue to feel that many who helped make this modest part of the state's history become a reality have never been adequately thanked for their efforts. There were so many good people involved. To each one of them I remain indebted. I deeply appreciate the privilege of being a Tennessean. To my immediate family including Betty; my son, Charles Winfield Dunn; and my daughters, Gayle Dunn Hurley and Julie Dunn Koss; and to my larger family of friends and supporters across the state, these words are lovingly dedicated.

TABLE OF CONTENTS

PART ONE

The Primary Election

CHAPTER ONE

SOME BACKGROUND

Evolving

Aristophanes of ancient Athens offered words of wisdom that have survived down through the ages. On one occasion he wrote, "Let each man exercise the art he knows." He later observed, "You cannot teach a crab to walk straight." Another wise and often humorous writer named Artemus Ward had this to say: "I am not a politician and my other habits are good." Aristophanes and Artemus Ward must have had folks like me in mind as their thoughts continue to resonate down the ages. Their words reinforce my belief that, when all is said and done, we human beings are, and continue to evolve into, just about what the original design called for. I feel that is true in my case.

Over time I've embraced the phrase "citizen politician" in seeking to explain or justify one of my strongest personal inclinations. I view the citizen politician as one who inclines toward the political process, not as a means of economic opportunity or survival, but as an entry, on a temporary basis, for deeper involvement in the public affairs of the people. Not unlike the common crab, my natural inclinations have consistently guided me in the direction of public affairs because my thoughts just naturally tilt in that direction. Unlike Artemus Ward, I believe it has been a good habit although I never viewed the world of politics or public service as an arena in which I could or should earn enough income to meet my responsibilities to my family.

I've always enjoyed the political process—that is, politics. It came upon me innocently enough, probably genetically in part and through a variety of other circumstances during my tender years. For instance, wandering into the old courthouse as a little boy in Meridian, Mississippi, looking for my dad, Aubert Culberson Dunn, who was Lauderdale County's district attorney in the early 1930s, was always an adventure that created memories.

The courthouse had a certain smell about it that was different from home, school, church, or Dad's law office. There were people odors; the pungent smell of tobacco dipped, chewed, or smoked; the scent of pine oil used to clean wooden floors; the smells of paper, roasted peanuts, coffee, and the noisy old steam-heated radiators along the walls. It was mysterious to me.

The main lobby was poorly lighted, and shadows added to the mystery. The doors to every room were heavy and wooden with a rippled glass inset bearing the name of the county clerk, the bail bondsman, the sheriff, or some level of the local judiciary. I never knew who I'd see when I opened one, but I always liked it when greeted by some nice lady who knew whose little boy I was. I didn't like to ride the creaky old elevator that was dark and small because it made weird sounds. I climbed the stairs to the second floor where the courtrooms were. There I'd often find my daddy.

Sometimes I'd follow Dad up to the third floor where the jail cells were located. He'd usually go there to speak with a prisoner. On those occasions, I stood by wide-eyed, but I found it difficult to look directly at the person behind bars. I imagined them to be a threat to any little boy, and I was probably right. I preferred the first two floors of the courthouse.

The variety of people in the courthouse was always a real curiosity for me. It included deputies with prisoners headed for the court-room, lawyers with clients of all makes and models, a judge I might gawk at or be introduced to, a legal secretary on a mission for her boss, a bewildered little country family seeking directions, a down-and-outer sitting on a bench, the blind vendor behind the notions counter, and others. It was always special to go to the courthouse.

I liked to listen to political talk between Dad and various people. Seeing a friend or some prospective voter, he'd always introduce me and expect me to put out my hand for a firm shake. He did a lot of handshaking. Candidates for the Board of Supervisors, mayor, sheriff, or some other office were usually the subjects of sage observations, biting or supportive comments, and sometimes baseless speculation.

Dad seemed to take some measure of pride in having me meet his friends. More than once, pausing in a conversation with someone, he would ask me to step up and make some kind of statement on a subject of my choice. I never refused, in spite of embarrassment, and my audience was always kind enough to compliment me. I'm certain that none of my buddies or schoolmates had the sort of exposure that came my way. I'm equally certain that those experiences had a lasting influence on me.

The only other political person in my family was the subject of my admiration as a small boy. He was my great-grandfather, William Wright Leggett, who was known by all as Pappy Leggett. Pappy was my mother's grandfather, who lived with his wife, Emma, in Magnolia, Mississippi. Even in his late years he was quite active and assertive. He was highly respected and popular in Pike County, where he served as sheriff during times when many people were hard to deal with and law enforcement was the main job of the sheriff. Later he was repeatedly elected mayor of Magnolia. In that role he served as magistrate, dispensing justice, marrying couples, and administering the simple business of the community government. Everyone, it seemed, loved Pappy Leggett.

My dad was very fond of Pappy and frequently took us on the long automobile trip over some paved and some graveled roads for visits. Of course, my mother, Dorothy Crum Dunn, loved those trips since it was a homecoming and the site of her birth. I remember that Pappy had a tall dressing chest in his bedroom where he kept his favorite brand of bourbon whiskey. He and my dad visited that chest often after making sure that Emma didn't know they were taking a nip. As a little fellow who followed both men around the house, one day I asked why they were drinking that stuff. Dad replied that it was really just medicine. I said they were sick an awful lot. They thought that was quite funny and they laughed. I really didn't mean to be funny. The two men "talked politics" quite a bit, and I was always an avid listener.

Meridian, Mississippi, was a fun place to grow up. My best buddies in the neighborhood were Ken Matthews and "Pee Wee" Feazell. We boys found so many ways to have fun, and most of that took place out of doors. Fishing in a nearby creek for perch; making rubber guns and pea shooters for "war;" making kites out of Sunday's funny papers, flour paste, and kite cord; climbing trees; and digging caves to hide in were among our more enjoyable pursuits.

In those formative years, I went to Sunday school, Baptist Young People's Training Union, and Royal Ambassadors, and I sang in the church choir. I was baptized at the age of ten. Sundays were always fun, but summer nights were most memorable. We'd play under the street light and eventually retire to the warm sidewalk leading to my front door. We'd lie down there and, with the cool night air upon us, listen to the conversations of adults sitting in lawn chairs nearby. It was easy to fall asleep, even on that warm concrete. I can still hear the tree frogs and katydids celebrating the nighttime.

Nothing could replace the memories of those wonderful, carefree childhood days. But unlike most of my friends, it's accurate to say that I grew up in a political environment. Large doses of Lauderdale County politics came my way. Those experiences increased as I became old enough and big enough to nail posters to light poles and trees when Dad ran for a seat in the U.S. Congress and won.

My family moved to Washington, D.C., in 1935 when Aubert Culberson Dunn was sworn in as a freshman U.S. representative in the 75th Congress. Those two years were most unusual for a little family from Mississippi. Many incidents occurred that left their marks on me at an impressive seven years of age. I met important political persons, some elected and some appointed. Among them was Speaker of the House Joe Byrns of Tennessee. On a visit to the House chambers with Dad, I was introduced to the Speaker. He picked me up and held me on his lap as he sat and presided. My congressman father loved to tell that story.

Life in Washington, D.C., was quite a change for a little boy from a small southern state. My father leased a fine home near Rock Creek Park for our first year in our nation's capital. My mother and two sisters adjusted to the change in residence and status very well. We brought along our maid, Willie Aaron, and our family handyman, whose name was John Woodard. These two fine people helped to make living in a much larger home quite comfortable for each of us. Each person had separate quarters in the house.

The big city and many wonderful buildings and memorials gave us opportunities for family outings at historic places. I remember vividly trips to the National Zoo and sled rides down the sloping streets of our neighborhood. During the second year of our stay in Washington, we lived in an apartment building nearer downtown. My first experience earning spending money came by assisting an older boy who sold newspapers on a busy street corner. I also found another way to earn money. It seemed that most people who rode the elevator in our apartment building had never heard a little southern boy speak. I rode that elevator frequently, speaking to people with my southern accent and earning tips from the amused listeners.

For a variety of reasons, including a lingering campaign debt, Dad chose not to seek reelection. We returned in 1936 to Meridian, where I continued to pursue a reasonably normal life. One of my greatest pleasures came from my mother's kitchen. She was a fabulous cook and I never lacked an appetite. Her hot, homemade rolls and biscuits were works of art. A platter filled with hot buttered biscuits smothered with blue ribbon cane molasses was regular fare for the appetite of a growing boy.

Back home again, I discovered new friends and interests. I enjoyed reading novels, including Tom Slade adventures and the stories of the Rover Boys. Sports on a more organized basis became very important to me. Football and tennis were two activities that I enjoyed. In my junior year of high school, our Meridian Wildcat football team won the conference championship. The position I played was left end. It might have been named "left out" because I wasn't the swiftest among my fellow athletes. We were invited to play Boys High of Atlanta in the Blue and Gray Bowl game in Montgomery, Alabama, on Christmas Day in 1943. We were the first high schools to be invited to play in that holiday bowl game because the Second World War had depleted the ranks of college all-stars. We lost that game, but in the process we made a little bit of history.

My teen years allowed me to discover that I was employable. At fifteen years of age, I received my Social Security card. My first job was as a car hop at a popular ice cream parlor. Salesmanship worked for me, and I did well later selling ladies' shoes at a local store. Delivering newspapers on a route, working for the state highway system, and clerking in a department store occupied me at various times. Those same teen years led me to discover girls. There were many pretty female students who caught my eye, and I enjoyed frequent occasions double-dating with other couples. Throughout much of that time I had one "steady" who remains, to this day, a good friend.

During the Christmas season of 1944, I applied for and obtained a job as a United States Postal Railway mail clerk. I was seventeen years old at the time. A wartime manpower shortage made it possible for me to be hired. The job required me to go to Shreveport, Louisiana. I rode a Trailways bus there and rented a room in a boarding house. Meals were served at a large table where all the boarders sat and helped themselves as the cooks brought in hot dishes from the kitchen. I remember how cold the bathroom was when I crawled into an old tub to clean away the accumulated railroad grime in the middle of the night. The job required me to be at the railroad depot at 5:00 a.m. and board the mail car of a short passenger train that traveled from Shreveport to Vidalia, a small community on the west bank of the Mississippi River directly across from Natchez, Mississippi. It was a six-day job concluding on Christmas Eve.

We loaded mail bags from the post office onto the mail car, and once underway, we collected additional bags full of letters and packages at each stop, sorting them out as we traveled down the rails. We unloaded the bags at Vidalia. We passed many communities without stopping, and to obtain their mail bags, we used a large metal hook that lay against the outside of the mail car attached to a wooden handle within the car. When the handle was forced downward, the big hook moved out. As we rolled along, often when it was still dark, my work mate, a regular mail clerk, seemed to know just exactly when to raise the hook. Sliding a door open with the hook in place and the cold air rushing in, I was always surprised when the hook snared a mail bag. A loud noise resulted from the metal hook hitting a bag. We'd haul it in, open it, and begin sorting mail. I could never figure out how he knew just when to get ready to snare a bag. He never failed. Those dirty bags smelled just like the interior of the post office back home.

At Vidalia, the steam engine was separated from the other cars. It was moved to a special set of tracks that slowly rotated, reversing the engine direction for the return trip. There was a delay while this was done. The engineer and conductor always suggested a poker game while we waited. I had played poker with match sticks as money in Meridian, and I thought I could hold my own with these fellows. During those six days, I won no more than two or three hands. In fact, I lost more money than I had with me. I didn't get paid until the job was over. When I returned home, I had to ask my dad for a few dollars that I owed one of those fellows. I felt terrible. Dad just laughed and gave me the money, and I mailed it on to Shreveport. It was a lesson learned.

In my senior high school year, I discovered that I had accumulated enough course credits to graduate at the end of the fall term in December. America had been at war with the Axis Powers for three years. At the age of seventeen years, five months, I persuaded my parents that I was big enough at six feet, three inches, to serve my country by enlisting in one of the military services. The U.S. Navy was my choice, and in January 1945, I was sworn in as a Hospital Apprentice First Class. I took my boot training at Great Lakes, Illinois. A boot company of 103 men was being put together to create what was then called the Navy's Blue Jacket Choir. I could carry a tune, and I was selected to join that group.

During my twelve-week training program, our choir sang on NBC's *Meet Your Navy Program* on Saturday nights. The emcee for that program was a young sailor named Durward Kirby. He was later to become a well-known radio personality in civilian life. On Sunday mornings we broadcast over CBS for the *Blue Jacket Choir Hour.* One night, April 12, 1945, after our boot company had hit the sack, we were awakened and ordered to march over to main side where we regularly broadcast. We were told that President Franklin D. Roosevelt had died. Our assignment was, at the appropriate time, to sing "The Navy Hymn," a favorite of the deceased president. For me, it was a dramatic and moving time. Roosevelt had been my only president for thirteen years. The Blue Jacket Choir experience was one I have always appreciated.

My special healthcare training was obtained in San Diego, California. I rode a fully loaded troop train for six long days before arriving in California. The train trip was unusually slow because we were frequently sidetracked and stopped while other troop trains with special missions were allowed to speed through. Later assignments were to take me to Virginia, Louisiana, and Pearl Harbor, Hawaii. Both Germany and Japan capitulated during my time in the service. I attained the rank of Pharmacist's Mate Third Class and found myself assigned many tasks that had nothing to do with the care of the injured and sick. I drove liberty buses, chipped paint to prepare for repainting, served as a medical warehouseman, and became the sailor in my unit in charge of the local athletic locker and weekly beer parties. The eighteen months I spent in the U.S. Navy were of great value to me. Among the many benefits I received was the GI Bill of Rights.

Following an honorable discharge in August 1946 back in Meridian, I enrolled for my freshman year at Meridian Junior College. It was good to be home. Many of my old friends were away on other campuses. I completed my college freshman year in May 1947 and spent the summer in Meridian working for the state Highway Department cutting brush along the road right-of-ways. During those days I heard great reports of college life at the University of Mississippi. I applied for admission, was accepted, and in September began my sophomore year there. It was a good decision.

My three years at Ole Miss were filled with many happy experiences and a very good formal education. I was enrolled in the School of Commerce and chose banking and finance as my major. I joined the Kappa Alpha Order fraternity and later was elected its president. I joined the Air Force ROTC program and was fortunate to be chosen cadet colonel of my class. I was inducted into the Omicron Delta Kappa honorary society. Delta Sigma Pi and the Scabbard and Blade Society were honorary organizations I was privileged to join. In my junior year I decided to run for the presidency of the School of Commerce. One of my most important campaign helpers was a fellow student named Betty Prichard. After a hard-fought campaign with a worthy opponent named Sonny Gunn, I was elected to that position. Good fortune continued to come my way, and I was chosen president of the Ole Miss Glee Club.

Before my campaign for president of the School of Commerce, my roommate, who happened to be the next editor of the Ole Miss annual yearbook, asked me to be the official escort for the annual Parade of Favorites. This was a group of approximately fifty young ladies who had been nominated by their sororities to compete in the selection of the five "Beauties" who would be featured in the yearbook. Earlier, Buddy Shaw, my roommate, had introduced me to a new girl on campus from Memphis named Betty Prichard. She was among the "Favorites" whom I escorted that evening down the stairway onto the stage before the assembled student body. I couldn't avoid noticing that she was the most beautiful of the group. Each girl was dressed in an evening gown. I was attired in a rented white tie and tails outfit, my first such experience, and I was sure I cut a handsome figure. Betty did say later that she noticed me as well. Out of that host of fine-looking ladies, she was selected one of the five campus "Beauties." She was chosen a campus "Beauty" again the following year. I began to see more of Betty whenever we could get together. That often occurred in the library. Being with her made studying more pleasant.

During our senior year, Betty and I saw each other frequently. One evening at her home in Memphis, I offered her my Kappa Alpha fraternity pin. She accepted, and because such an act was considered being "engaged to be engaged," I was a very happy man. On the day she and I graduated in early June 1950, with both our families in attendance, after getting her dad's permission, I offered Betty a very modest engagement ring that she accepted. After three intense years on that glorious campus pursuing a pre-law degree in banking and finance, a Second Lieutenant's bars in the Air Force Reserve, and a beautiful girl from Memphis who was a fellow student, I became a university graduate! My greatest honor came when I slipped that ring on Betty's finger. After having dated some very attractive girls on the campus, I won the big prize. What more could a fellow want?

I obtained my college education with the financial assistance of the GI Bill of Rights. By graduation time the balance of my GI benefit credits was very limited. I had been accepted for admission into the university's School of Law, but financial considerations made it necessary for me to choose between a legal education and a marriage that I did not wish to delay. I chose a marriage. That meant I needed a job. I applied for an interview with a nationally prominent business called the Aetna Casualty and Surety Insurance Company, which was conducting such interviews on campus. I was offered a position. With Betty's approval I accepted the offer and reported for work in July at the company's New Orleans office. Betty, meanwhile, had accepted a position as teacher of the second grade in nearby Turrell, Arkansas.

At the outset, my new position required an intensive twelve-week course of training in property, casualty, fire, theft, marine, and surety insurance at the company's home office in Hartford, Connecticut. During those lonely days in Hartford I had difficulty focusing on my training. My thoughts were on my bride-to-be. One evening I made a long-distance telephone call and asked if she would possibly consider moving our wedding date forward. She delighted me by saying yes, once more. We began to make plans for a late December wedding. We had originally planned for a wedding in June, but I was in no mood to wait longer. Betty's parents had to suddenly fit a December 30 wedding into their holiday plans. They did so as though they had planned for it all along. I completed the insurance course, Betty and I were married in a beautiful ceremony in Memphis, and we moved into a garage apartment at Bay St. Louis on the Mississippi Gulf Coast in January 1951. From that modest dwelling, our first home, I conveniently traveled to my office in downtown New Orleans on St. Charles Avenue.

Our social life in Bay St. Louis was limited because my travel schedule kept me away from home six days in each week. We had several college friends in the area that Betty enjoyed being with in my absence. Our tiny upstairs apartment was in the rear of a nice house that faced the beach. The lady of the house was Flora Maumus, a lovely woman who kindly looked after my young bride. In the rear of the garage a wilderness area was inviting during daylight hours but became a source of occasional strange sounds after dark. Betty's loneliness through the week brought her some discomfort at night when such sounds floated through the window. One Friday evening when I arrived home, she seemed unusually happy to see me. She explained that the night before as she busied herself in the kitchen, she had heard more such sounds than usual. She confessed that in response she retreated to the bathroom where she spent several hours with the door locked while she sat in the bathtub on a pillow, a kitchen knife for defense close at hand. Knowing my wife, I had no doubt that she would have defended herself adequately had she been called on to do so. I attempted to assure her that whatever wild animals were responsible for her unease might have been embarrassed had they known of her concerns.

My position with Aetna as a special agent required me to travel extensively in four states. My means of transportation was a Plymouth sedan my mother had given to me during my senior year at Ole Miss. In my travels for Aetna, I was reimbursed for my automobile at the rate of six cents per mile. The sum was hardly adequate. I loved that car, which I had named "Old Betsy." It was a loyal companion that served me well over many miles. My work consisted of making calls on local insurance agencies in various sections of the four states I represented. It was a good experience, and I met many fine citizens along the way. The only problems for me were the long hours away from my bride and the lonely nights in what were then called tourist courts.

Traveling over a network of roads and highways built in the 1930s and 1940s, I saw many interesting sights. Stray cattle roamed the countryside, often wandering up on the highway. It was a good experience getting to know the small communities I frequented. One of my most disappointing moments came as I sat in a small insurance agency and overheard a claims adjuster arguing feverishly with a wreck victim's mother concerning the cash settlement she might expect arising out of the serious injury of her child by a policy holder. I felt the adjuster who represented my company was not demonstrating the proper amount of sympathy. Enthusiasm for my company was temporarily diminished.

I enjoyed meeting new clients, but the pain of being absent from my new wife so much of the time persisted. We were prepared to accept that sacrifice because the promise of advancement within the company was very appealing. Time and time again I had been told by my superiors, as I am sure all other special agents were told, that there was a good possibility I would someday become the chief executive of the company. That was very inspiring. However, our plans and sacrificial attitudes were severely altered when we learned that Betty had become pregnant. A quick trip to Memphis to inform Betty's parents and to confirm the diagnosis took place. I am probably fortunate that I wasn't privy to conversations Betty and her mother must have had.

Our Mississippi landlord, Dr. Louis Maumus, was a dentist who commuted to New Orleans, where he enjoyed a very successful practice. During an occasional fishing outing with Dr. Maumus, I told him that my lawyer father had always encouraged me to consider dentistry as a profession rather than law. Aware of my unhappiness over being away from my pregnant wife so much of each week, Dr. Maumus encouraged me to consider leaving my work, becoming a dental student with his help at Loyola University in New Orleans, and joining him in his dental practice. The conversations with my dentist friend ultimately led me to consider not Loyola but the University of Tennessee's College of Dentistry because of an accelerated academic program it offered that could save me one calendar year in acquiring a new education.

After agonizing over a decision, receiving Betty's approval to make such a radical change, talking at length with Betty's father, who attempted to discourage me based on his experience that "the grass always looked greener on the other side of the fence," a decision was made. In late August, after only one year of employment, I severed the relationships with my company and my landlord. Betty and I headed for Memphis and a completely new life, a new education, a new experience as parents, and very little to support ourselves beyond the promise of help when needed from our parents. She was thrilled to be going home to Memphis. On our arrival there, we moved in for a temporary stay with her parents.

Betty and I agree that the birth of our son, Charles Winfield Dunn, on September 28, 1951, shortly after we moved to Memphis, was the single most important factor in assuring our eventual success in the new endeavor. He was the "glue" that helped us hold everything together during some difficult days that lay ahead. Betty and I loved each other very much, but our little fellow was our truest inspiration.

To prepare for my professional education, I was required to obtain one year of pre-medical studies. I enrolled at Memphis State University. Entry into the College of Dentistry would require passing tests and presenting qualifying transcripts. Dr. Frank Prichard offered to use his influence to help me gain acceptance. We had ambition and determination to succeed but little more. I wasn't assured of admission to dental school. I wonder what our families might have been thinking.

Arriving in Memphis with a little time on my hands and very little cash, I answered an advertisement in the local newspaper and obtained a temporary job with the Raleigh Company selling cosmetics and household items such as spices and cleaning compounds. I had a rather heavy sample case that I carried door to door. My route included old residences in and around Beale Street. I knocked on many doors and discovered that housewives were willing customers. During those days I earned modest commissions that helped our meager financial situation. Later, I found a part-time job taking blood from donors in a local blood bank. My earlier Navy corpsman training to tap blood veins came in handy. My blood bank donors consisted mainly of sailors from nearby Millington Navy base. Each was paid ten dollars for a pint of his blood. We located an inexpensive apartment near Betty's family. I used the remainder of my GI Bill benefits at Memphis State. The pre-medical courses were difficult, yet failure was out of the question. I worked, I studied, and Betty taught school as soon as it was feasible for her to do so. Her modest salary paid our way, and we skimped by.

As new parents, we had much to learn. Betty prepared baby formula with all the care and skill of a laboratory scientist. I quickly learned how to change diapers. There were no disposables at that time. I also became adept at burping the little fellow. The obstetrician and pediatrician we depended on, both friends of Betty's parents, refused to bill us for their great services. We were very fortunate.

I completed my pre-medical studies in August at Memphis State University. The Ole Miss undergraduate credits were approved, and in September 1952, I entered the University of Tennessee's College of Dentistry. Three years later, rather than four, thanks to the accelerated program adopted during the Second World War, I graduated with my Doctor of Dental Surgery degree. Those years of professional training were the most challenging, difficult years of my life. Without the encouragement and support of my wife and son, I could not have achieved my goal.

One day while working in the laboratory during my first quarter of dental school I glanced through a window just as several large automobiles pulled up to the curb. Out stepped a number of men, one of whom I recognized as Tennessee's Governor Frank Clement. I was interested to get a close-up look at the gentleman. I knew very little about Tennessee's governor, but I had been around politicians of one sort or another back home and knew them to be fairly ordinary folks. At the time, I was struggling to do well with my dental education. My mind was on anything but people in politics. I couldn't let Betty and my baby boy down.

I had established a good record in dental school, and I was proud of the new skills and knowledge that had been acquired. Somehow, with great encouragement from my family, I graduated with honors. Betty vowed she would never touch another iron. One of her big jobs was washing and ironing the dental smocks that I wore during clinic hours. Betty's mother, Ruby Prichard, was a blessing to us as she frequently cared for our little boy.

Betty's father, a highly respected dentist in Memphis, invited me to enter practice with him for at least a year. He suggested I would acquire additional knowledge that would prove valuable should I follow my original plan and return to Mississippi to practice dentistry. I gratefully accepted. He knew I could learn enough practical dentistry working with him to put me far ahead when I turned to a solo practice.

Although my graduation was in September 1955, I could not legally start practicing dentistry until I received my license in January 1956. I took state dental board exams and became licensed to practice in Tennessee and Mississippi. Beginning my work in Dr. Prichard's office meant going on a payroll and getting some experience in a fine dental office. Later, at his invitation, I decided to remain with Dr. Prichard in Memphis. Betty liked that, of course, and I felt only a few mild pangs of regret at not heading back home. It was an easy transition. I became a Tennessean by choice, but my Mississippi roots were alive and well.

CHAPTER TWO

THE INNOCENT BEGINNINGS OF
A REMARKABLE ADVENTURE

Starting a New Life

While I was in dental school, Betty taught second grade at Grahamwood Elementary School. I became employed as a lab technician at the Baptist Hospital. We were able to pay our bills with little outside assistance. My dear mother had loaned me money from her modest inheritance. I took great pride in repaying her those funds as soon as I could. Betty continued to teach in the Memphis public school system for several years as I assumed my professional life. Teaching was a natural experience for my wife. She was popular with the faculty and the parents of her students. She developed the firm conviction that the success of any public school depended first and foremost on having a strong principal to provide necessary leadership. My dental practice began to produce a growing income. In 1956 we purchased our first home. After I struggled through dental school, our lives began to assume a relative normalcy that we had never experienced in our years of marriage.

By the year 1969 I had practiced my profession for thirteen years. I was busy. My workload continued to grow, thanks to many good patients. I enjoyed the challenge of helping Betty raise our three children. I taught the Fellowship Sunday school class, sang in the choir, and served on the Board of Stewards at Christ United Methodist Church in East Memphis. We were charter members of that church and took great pride in its growth. We were members of Chickasaw Country Club. We enjoyed a special group of friends, many of whom were in Betty's bridge club. She was a stay-at-home mom and a wonderful wife.

I belonged to a social organization called the Phoenix Club, played a bit of golf, went fishing occasionally, and continued to be supportive of the Shelby County Republican Party. My loyalty to the Republican Party was strong. I had served as chairman of the County Executive Committee from 1964 to 1968 and believed deeply in what we citizen politicians were trying to do. Historically, all local and state politics were controlled by the Democratic Party. We wanted to build a real two-party political system in our county and in our state. That situation had not existed since the days of the Whig Party and the Reconstruction period following the Civil War.

Betty was an ideal mother, who was involved in all the activities of our children. We had sold our first home and moved to a somewhat larger residence in an area called Hedgemoor. She made our new house a wonderful home, was involved with the local Dental Auxiliary, and became active in the Hedgemoor Garden Club, where she served as its president. After teaching full time for several years at Grahamwood school, and later as a substitute teacher in the Memphis City Schools, she enjoyed being at home full time. She loved children and worked with the toddlers in our Sunday school.

I had recently been appointed a member of the Board of Trustees at John Gaston County Hospital and was active in the Memphis Dental Society. I served several years earlier as chairman of the Fluoridation Committee. The question of adding fluoride to the public water supply was a hot topic politically. It was a real challenge because the concept was opposed by a vocal group called the John Birch Society. Fluoridation was the right thing to do. Working closely with a man I admired, Dr. Eugene Fowinkle, director of the Memphis Department of Public Health, we were able to persuade the City Council to adopt the program. My appearance before the Memphis City Council as Fluoridation Committee chairman was my first before a governing body. I enjoyed the experience. As a result of much hard work by many dedicated professionals, Memphis children and healthy teeth became the beneficiaries of those efforts.

My wife and I were involved in many activities. Our days were passing swiftly. Betty and I were so proud knowing that our son, Chuck, a senior in high school, was thinking seriously about college. Gayle was an eighth grader, and our baby, Julie, was in the fourth grade. Chuck attended East High School while the girls were enrolled at Saint Mary's school. It was a good life in wonderful Memphis, Tennessee.

From the moment in 1955 that I went to work with Dr. Prichard, I benefited greatly from a professional point of view. Being conscious of the fact that I was now a Tennessean, not a Mississippian, was a process that occurred over time, mostly subconsciously. The intervening fourteen years leading up to 1969 had been happy and productive ones.

Included in our good fortune during those early years was the birth of our lovely daughter Donna Gayle Dunn. She was born on April 10, 1956, and immediately added a dimension to our lives more rewarding than we could have ever imagined. She was a beautiful baby, but I was concerned because Gayle came into the world without much hair. A high moment for me came when enough blonde hair grew to permit Betty to tie a little wisp of it with a pink ribbon.

Shortly after I began my dental practice in January 1956, I began to become more aware of the world around me. Freed from the very demanding pressures of dental school, I became increasingly convinced that Memphis was a great city. I enjoyed being a part of it. A friend encouraged me to join the Memphis Junior Chamber of Commerce. One leader in that group was an up-and-coming fellow named Tom Batchelor. He was lively, involved in the community, and quite impressive. He was a people person and had some notable connections, many of them political. We hit it off, and soon Tom had me signed up to be a parade marshal. Marshals were Jaycees who were assigned to work with crowds of people by courteously guiding them behind ropes stretched along Front Street to keep it clear during Cotton Carnival parades. I liked the mild distinction that came from having an official armband and a little bit of imagined authority. For several years, I enjoyed that responsibility and the people I met. The parades were always fun, and our children looked forward to them.

The weeks and months quickly merged into years. Betty and I were founding members of a new church in East Memphis, Christ United Methodist. Betty's parents were a part of the new church. She and her mother were very close. Dr. Prichard and I worked together very well and became good friends. When we bought our first home on Mary Ann Drive in East Memphis, Dr. Prichard loaned me the down payment, and I obtained a low-interest mortgage through the Veterans Administration. I came to know many of Betty's childhood friends, and the circle of friends, acquaintances, and patients grew. We frequently visited my folks in Mississippi, and life, in general, was normal and enjoyable.

On September 15, 1960, baby girl Julie Claire Dunn joined Chuck and Gayle to complete our brood. When Betty learned she was pregnant for the third time, we were completely relaxed regarding whether our third child would be a boy or girl. With one of each in the fold, we knew we couldn't lose. Beautiful Miss Julie filled the bill and added a dimension to our lives we could never have imagined, and we were a happy little group.

Early in 1960 my friend Tom Batchelor invited me to join him at a local political rally in support of a candidate for the United States Senate. I had been a Tennessee resident for little more than five years and knew nothing about its politics. Tom's candidate was Judge Andrew P. "Tip" Taylor, a Democrat from Jackson. He explained that the judge had run two years earlier in the Democrat primary for governor and had lost to Buford Ellington. Tom thought Taylor would make a fine senator. I respected Tom's opinion, and because I had always enjoyed the political process at a distance, I accepted the opportunity. I recalled helping my dad become a Democrat U.S. congressman from the Fifth District of Mississippi. The Democrat label seemed to me acceptable at the time.

Tom said that he thought I would make a great political worker. He wanted me to meet the candidate and get active in his campaign in Memphis. Hearing those comments from Tom Batchelor, I was flattered and accepted the invitation. At the rally, and after the speech, Tom introduced me to Taylor. As I shook the judge's hand, he looked me right in the eye and smiled warmly. His handshake, however, was not firm. I was somewhat surprised. I did not get deeply involved in his campaign. He was defeated in the August primary election by Senator Estes Kefauver. Since there was no Republican opponent, Kefauver returned to the U.S. Senate for another six-year term in 1961.

That was my somewhat tentative introduction to Tennessee politics. Frankly, although I had chosen to practice my profession in Memphis, I still occasionally thought of myself as a Mississippian. What little political interest I had focused on the powerful influence that "Boss" Ed Crump exerted in the city of Memphis. People in general, and my father-in-law in particular, seemed to go along with the politics of Mr. Crump. I thought that was unusual. Whoever the Crump people supported politically in city and county government appeared to be completely acceptable to the people. There was little or no competition. Citizens voted his way consistently. That would not have been the case, for example, in a Board of Supervisors' race in my hometown of Meridian, Mississippi.

In 1960, some time after I had met Judge Tip Taylor, I learned of a book written by United States Senator Barry Goldwater of Arizona titled *The Conscience of a Conservative*. It had been published earlier that year and was referred to me as a runaway best seller. I bought a paperback copy to satisfy my curiosity because I was told, as the front cover of the book stated, "Every American who loves his country should read this book." I proceeded to do just that. It was a hit with me. Each word, sentence, and paragraph I read seemed to become riveted in my mind. I read the little book several times. As a result, I began to be unusually conscious of how much I did love America and how right Senator Goldwater seemed to be about social, economic, and political challenges we faced as a nation. The senator expressed particular concern about the threats to freedom posed by what he described as the Communist conspiracy.

At that time, America was at peace following the tragic Korean War, and Dwight D. Eisenhower was completing the last of his eight impressive years as president of the United States. A national campaign to choose the next president was underway. I was certainly curious as to whom that president might be. Vice President Richard Nixon appeared to be the Republican choice while Senator Lyndon Baines Johnson and Senator John F. Kennedy seemed the front runners on the Democrat side.

In those days it was increasingly obvious to many Americans that communism and its major sponsor, Soviet Russia, were becoming real threats to freedom-loving people everywhere. The Russians were forcibly expanding control over neighboring Eastern European countries. They were covertly seeking influence in the Western world. Winston Churchill had declared that an Iron Curtain existed between Western nations and the Communist Eastern bloc. A Cold War was underway, and communism seemed to be spreading like a virus in every direction.

Newspapers, magazines, books, and the airwaves were filled with stories, congressional testimony, and first-person accounts about the threat of communism across the globe. Even though I was busy seeing patients during my working hours, I couldn't ignore some frustrations

I witnessed each time I entered our dental lab. The dental technician, Jim Brassfield, listened intently each day to a radio evangelist named Billy James Hargis as he railed against communism and invoked fragments of the gospel to his audience. When Brassfield wasn't listening, he was ranting, even while he did his delicate lab work. He knew the Communists were coming, and he couldn't understand why everyone wasn't as concerned as he was. Brassfield wasn't well educated, but he understood the spoken word. I was impressed by his concerns. We frequently talked about the threat of communism and our government. I feel sure that my close relationship to our technician and the frequency of his comments about the threats to our government and way of life piqued my interest in the subject. I became attuned to the complaint that too many important people in the U.S. government were "soft" on communism.

On a thoughtful, well-reasoned, and rational basis, Senator Goldwater had proposed in his book a more conservative approach to our nation's problems and opportunities. I agreed with a great deal of what he said. He spoke loud and clear about the Soviet threat. He was convinced that socialism was taking too strong a hold in many of our national policies. He believed that ultra-liberal efforts to redistribute wealth in America through government programs and policies were undermining the strength and foundation of the nation as it had been designed to function by the framers of our Constitution. The "welfare state" as a descriptive phrase seemed ominous and threatening to me. There was too much power in Washington and not enough in the states. I found myself becoming somewhat of a Goldwater disciple.

In frequent conversations and discussions, I expressed serious concern about where our country was heading. The topic was discussed after Sunday school lessons at church. I often quoted Senator Goldwater. Although I grew up in the one-party Democrat-controlled state of Mississippi, I had no special partisan interest. Later, however, I grew increasingly sympathetic with Republican philosophies represented by Goldwater, Eisenhower, and Nixon. I had never thought of myself as Republican or Democrat, but the Republican label was easy for me to relate to. My political juices began to flow more consciously, even though my devotion to family, work, and friends remained reasonably focused and on track.

I began to view Tennessee politicians, primarily those we elected to national office, with a more critical eye. They were mostly Democrats. Republicans in the eastern section did elect congressmen regularly, but that was a part of our long, narrow state with which I was unfamiliar. As far as I was concerned, Tennessee was simply a one-party state. Although the state had been carried by Eisenhower in both 1952 and 1956 due to his great popularity as a World War II hero, that had no influence on my impression of the state's political identity. My adopted state was essentially controlled by the Democratic Party.

Betty was very tolerant of my new political consciousness. Knowing my family background as far as politics was concerned, and having helped me successfully campaign for a student body office while we were in college, she accepted my interest in politics as somewhat normal. I was not rabid on the subject, and it apparently didn't interfere with my production as the family breadwinner.

On one occasion in 1961 she and I attended a presentation at a small community church in Memphis. The speaker was Congressman Walter Judd, MD, a Republican from Minnesota. We were persuaded to be present by having read of his strong anti-Communist sentiments and his record on that subject. Dr. Judd had spent many years in China as a medical missionary where he saw the growing presence and threat to freedom that communism represented. He was making speeches wherever he had an opportunity to alert people to the dangers he knew about firsthand.

He was an excellent speaker, and we listened intently to every word. At the conclusion of his speech, we went forward to congratulate and thank him. I recall Betty asking what people like us could possibly do to help the cause he represented. The congressman looked at both of us and said, "Get involved in the political process. Elect good people and send them to Washington." That was all he said, but it registered with us.

My schedule for seeing dental patients was arranged so that I could have Wednesday afternoons free for other activities. During a round of golf with two friends, Dr. Bailey Prichard, orthodontist, and Earl Hays, insurance salesman, on a Wednesday afternoon in early spring 1962, the subject of communism came up. My part of the conversation surely centered on many of the points Senator Goldwater had made in his book. I expressed my growing feelings that we citizens needed to become more involved with those we elected to public office. Very probably I recalled some of what Betty and I had heard from Congressman Judd. My new interest in the subject of citizen involvement in the political process must have stayed with my two friends based on what happened several days after our golf game.

I received a phone call from Dr. Bailey Prichard. He was a distant relative of Betty. He said there were several friends that he would like me to meet, based on my "political awareness and strong feelings." He had told them about our golf game discussion and my interest in Goldwater's positions. I agreed that I would like to meet the people he described as prominent and involved in local Republican politics. They were, he said, members of a committee that was looking for individuals interested in the Republican Party. My curiosity was aroused, and we set a date to get together.

The next Wednesday afternoon, I met a small group at the University Club. There were three people present in addition to me. They were attorneys Lewis R. Donelson III and Harry W. Wellford plus a delightful lady named Gwen Awsumb. Each one of these individuals was to become a dear friend in the years ahead.

After usual pleasantries, one of the three began to explain that they represented a larger group of Memphis and Shelby County citizens who were interested in strengthening the Republican Party. They had heard complimentary things about me and my feelings regarding citizenship and political involvement. That could only mean Bailey Prichard or Earl Hays had spoken with someone. Our conversation continued with each of us sharing our feelings about local politics, public personalities, and politics on the national scene.

Our discussion began to focus on the status of the Republican Party in Shelby County. I learned that local Republicans had never been able to elect officeholders at any level. The party had very little political presence and was completely without influence locally. These people believed the time had come for the old one-party Democrat monopoly that existed in the most populous county in Tennessee to be seriously challenged.

It was then that I was given a surprising slant on just what this small committee was interested in. They explained that there was serious interest among local Republicans in supporting a candidate in the November general election for Congress from the Ninth

24

Congressional District. The incumbent Democrat congressman, Clifford Davis of Memphis, was a remnant of the "Crump Machine." At that time, Mr. Crump had been dead for several years. Davis was elderly and was not going to be seriously challenged for reelection by anyone in his party. My new Republican friends felt that he had been in office too long, was ineffective, and could be defeated by the right opponent. They also felt Mr. Crump's death had created a vacuum of local leadership.

One of the three explained that a potential candidate who was anxious to run in the race as a Republican had been identified. He was described as a very respectable, successful local businessman who had been quite outspoken about his political views. The group noted that he was an honorable person and might be just the man for the effort. However, there were reservations among some Republican leaders that he might not have all the qualities they were seeking in a candidate, as far as potential to be elected was concerned. Because of those feelings, this group had been designated to look around for one or more additional candidates. That was the reason they wanted to meet with me.

Frankly, I was amazed, and I told the group just that. After further conversation the meeting ended. I expressed my pleasure in having met the group and headed for home.

As I drove, I continued to think of the circumstances that had led me to such an unusual meeting. Thoughts of my father's experiences in politics came flowing back. I tried to imagine what he would say about me even sitting down to talk politics with serious people. His long-held opinion that a dental rather than a legal career would surely be in my best interests may have been based in part on a concern that attorneys often seemed to gravitate toward politics. I am certain he did not want that for me. With such thoughts running through my mind I soon turned into my driveway at home.

We lived in an area consisting of new residences that were rapidly developing in East Memphis. We were very happy in our new home located in a neighborhood with other young couples and their families. As I arrived home from that meeting, Betty was there to give me a hello kiss. I told her about my meeting with the Republicans, but I don't recall that she had any particular response.

Several days later I received a telephone call from one of my new Republican friends. The message was that the group had discussed what I had to offer as a possible candidate for Congress. They also spoke with others among their Republican friends. Their conclusion was that I should give serious consideration to becoming the Republican candidate to challenge Congressman Davis for the Ninth Congressional District in that election year.

What a strange turn of events! I was flattered, excited, and awed by the message. My mind began to race through one scenario after another as the reality of what had been suggested settled in. I did not immediately say to the caller that, while I appreciated their feelings, I absolutely could not consider such a thing. Rather, I began to fantasize. What could be done with my dental practice and my new dental office and equipment? I was suddenly intrigued with the thought that I might find myself in Washington, D.C., strapping on armor to battle for a righteous cause. Just as suddenly my thoughts shifted to Betty and the children. What would they think?

That evening, with supper finished and the children tucked away in their beds, I told Betty we needed to have a talk. Sitting on the couch in the living room, I proceeded to tell her of my earlier phone call and my belief that the folks I had spoken with were serious. I let her know how amazed I was at their feelings and that I had many serious reservations about attempting such a thing. Her initial response was not surprising. She promptly told me she thought it was foolish to even consider leaving a good dental practice and all the obligations I had. She didn't waste time letting me know her impressions of the little she knew about my father's political past. She wondered how in the world I could consider such a thing. I recall that I didn't immediately agree with her. We let the subject drop.

At home the next day, Betty greeted me with word that she thought we should discuss further the subject of a political campaign. After supper, as we sat down together, my bride produced a yellow legal pad, and I could see two columns of her handwriting. I said I was still curious about the matter. She said she had spent the afternoon thinking about it and decided to make a list of pros and cons. Her pro list was on the left, and her con list was on the right. The pro list was short. The con list filled the entire right side of the page.

Starting with the pro list, she thoughtfully expressed her feeling that I was a sincere, capable person who might become a good congressman. She felt there was a real possibility I could win an election. End of pro list.

As she launched the con side, I knew I was in for a long session. Item by item, line by line, she read from her afternoon's work. She obviously had worked hard. There was no doubt that right, might, truth, and common sense all were on her side. In summary, she let me know that to propose leaving my practice, giving up our income, and becoming a serious politician was total foolishness. I had little or no basis for argument. She had done a wonderful job of thinking things through, one of her many strengths, and I found no solid ground to stand on. Still, I was unable to dismiss the idea proposed by my newly found Republican friends. Our long discussion ended without an agreement that I should dismiss the idea.

The next day I learned that Betty had invited her father to come by our home for a visit and to offer his comments. Dr. Prichard and I had practiced in his downtown office for five years before I moved my office to East Memphis in order to be more conveniently available for my patients. At the time of this political discussion, we were practicing in different offices and did not see each other every day. He was a man of few words but many good deeds. I admired him very much.

He reminded me of the fact that Betty and I were not prepared to leave a steady source of income to undertake a political campaign. He was gentle with his comments but left no doubt in my mind that I should thank the Republicans and get on with my professional life. It was good advice, and I took it. The offer to get political was later declined in a conversation I had with someone from the Republican group. I put such thoughts out of my mind and got on with my life.

Things didn't remain normal very long. One day a few weeks later I received a call from a Republican activist inviting me to a meeting to discuss the status of the party. I knew that by accepting the invitation, I was putting myself in the camp of those who were willing to get involved. Curiosity and interest led me to accept.

The purpose of the meeting was to discuss a plan to challenge local Democrats in the upcoming fall political campaigns. For years, perhaps forever in Shelby County, those elected to local, state, and federal offices were members of the Democratic Party. These Republicans were interested in electing state representatives and senators, as well as the Ninth District congressman. At that time, members of the state legislature were elected from the county at large. There were no individual districts in which a candidate would run.

I learned that they had a serious plan, and their next job was to find Republicans who would qualify to run, be nominated in the August primary, and proceed to oppose every Democrat candidate for the state legislature in the November general election. In past elections, the only political excitement occurred when Democrats opposed each other in the primary. Once the winners of those elections were known, the candidates merely had to stay alive until they were elected in November unopposed. I had never taken a close look at the process, but my underdog instincts told me that it would be great fun to challenge the undemocratic way things were routinely done in Shelby County.

Once again, I was surprised when someone in the group turned to me. He stated that although I had been unwilling to consider the first Republican offer that came my way, I surely couldn't resist their request to be one of the legislative candidates on the party ticket that year. I did resist, however, saying that I would take the matter under consideration.

During the evening I met several people who had already committed to being Republican candidates. They were obviously first-class individuals: a prominent young attorney named John "Buddy" Thomason and a most impressive Memphis housewife named Peggy Spurrier. As I met more people, I liked what I saw. None fit my preconceived notion of what people in politics frequently were like. They were just good folks, fully committed to the idea that it was time to build a second, competitive political party to oppose the monopolistic Democrat crowd. None of those I met struck me as being interested in politics for their personal gain. The most appealing feature consistently was that these people had professions, jobs, and responsibilities ongoing. They simply wanted to make a difference and were willing to give their time and energy to the effort.

My knowledge and curiosity grew throughout the evening. I learned the Republican group I had been dealing with was called the Memphis and Shelby County Republican Association. It existed along with the legally established County Executive Committee. The president of the association was Lewis Donelson, one of my new friends. Chairman of the Republican County Executive Committee was prominent attorney Millsaps Fitzhugh.

Mr. Fitzhugh was nowhere to be seen at any of the meetings I had attended. He owned an office building at 1352 Madison Avenue where he made available office space for the association to operate. The political energy for what was happening obviously was coming from the recently formed Republican Association. Volunteers did whatever work was required.

As the meeting ended, I headed home. The thought of becoming a Republican candidate in company with such good people was very appealing. I focused on Betty and her list of pros and cons. In this case, there was no need to worry about having to devote full time to a campaign. We would hold meetings and rallies at nights and on weekends. Expenses would be minimal, I was told, because the group of candidates would campaign as a ticket and every person's name would be mentioned in every pamphlet or poster used to promote the cause. I was told money was no problem. I liked the idea of being a part of the challenge.

CHAPTER THREE

MY FIRST POLITICAL RACE

Learning

The most important thing to consider was the possibility that I might be elected and required to serve a term of two years as a state representative. Leaving my family and dental practice several days each week for a significant number of weeks to live in Nashville was a major consideration. I knew I could not afford to do that. I knew that Betty would not agree to it. The fact was that no Republican candidate for the state legislature could possibly be elected since each candidate ran in the county at large. There were not enough Republican votes to elect any candidate under the circumstances. My race would be purely a symbolic effort challenging a Democrat. It was with that understanding that I agreed to challenge a Democrat opponent. That would be unusual in the county. It was a comfort to know I would have Republican running mates.

Many questions regarding becoming a candidate must have crossed my mind. I wondered if I might become guilty of neglecting my dental practice. I knew I couldn't afford that. The thought that some patients might be unhappy with my identification as a Republican surely occurred to me. There was no concern on my part that taking on such an important commitment would negatively affect my responsibilities as a husband and father. They were number one in my life. Actually, events would prove that many nights away from home in the ensuing months did deprive me of time with my family.

Betty must have had reservations regarding politics. Even so, she was concerned about political life in our country and felt good people had a responsibility to be involved. At some point, satisfied that chances of my being elected were zero, Betty and I agreed that I would join the group of Republicans willing to be candidates for legislative positions in the upcoming elections. It would be a purely honest effort with absolutely no chance that I might win. If she had been unwilling for us to step up in that manner, I would have been compelled to decline and get on with life as it had been. I'm glad she didn't say no. Our lives at that point began to change ever so subtly.

As president of the Memphis and Shelby County Republican Association, Lewis Donelson would have been the one I advised of my willingness to be a part of the team. There was an air of excitement among those serving as party headquarters volunteers, members of the association, and other prospective candidates. The sense of a righteous crusade, the opportunity to speak out against a political monopoly, the chance to fuel an ever present indignation toward "politicians" as we viewed them, a platform to speak against socialism/communism, a philosophy that stressed the less government the better, and an apparently unlimited audience to feed growing egos were heady and exhilarating, indeed! I was not immune. Added to that was the pleasure of meeting interesting, honorable, and patriotic new friends. There, I discovered, was a recipe for much personal satisfaction.

If only one outstanding trait or characteristic could be attributed to my wife, that one would be her complete and unequivocal devotion to our three children. Fortunately for me, she has many outstanding traits and marks of a wonderful human being. As I learned with each passing day what would be expected of me as a candidate, I could only hope I would have her enthusiastic support and cooperation. She never disappointed me and was always ready to do what she could to understand and help. She recognized the fine character of many new people with whom I was involved, and that gave her some comfort. First and foremost in every consideration were the children. Those needs being met, Betty was available to stand by my side, ready to help.

Among the good people I met through my new Republican identity was a gentleman named Alexander W. Dann. Alex and his wife, Mimi, were devoted Republicans who deeply believed what we were about was right, proper, and needed in Memphis, Shelby County, and Tennessee. We were all enthused about building a permanent two-party political system! It was pleasing to me to learn that Mimi Dann and Betty Dunn had been friends as young girls.

Alex Dann was a prominent Memphis attorney who was well

versed in things political. He was asked to be my campaign manager by someone in the association, and he readily agreed. We met at his office several days before my announcement, and he made quite a few suggestions in preparing me for what was ahead. He had a strong, resonant voice, a terrific sense of humor, and a good feel for how I needed to express myself when I announced my intention to run for public office. He helped me with my prepared remarks and generally pumped me up. We remained friends for many years.

Several steps had to be taken at the appropriate time. I would have to file my papers seeking election to a specific legislative seat, declare my party affiliation, and do so by a certain date in May 1962. That process involved dealing with the county Election Commission, a body consisting of three members, one of whom was a Republican. Our strategy called for Republicans to hold press conferences individually or in pairs to announce our candidacy. The idea was to stretch things out and get as much newspaper publicity as possible. By the deadline for filing, all Republican candidates would have been designated by the association. Public announcements could take place at any time.

A friend and fellow church member named C. Phil Lowe and I chose to do a joint announcement. Phil was a successful insurance salesman and an enthusiastic Republican. I had filed for Position 8 in the state House of Representatives. Phil chose Position 3. There were several newspaper reporters in attendance the day we announced our candidacies from association headquarters. Quite a few Republicans were present for the occasion. I was on crutches because of an injury to my right knee while on a fishing trip to Arkansas. No comments were made as to my being a lame candidate, at least not where I could hear them!

The Shelby County Republican Association soon recruited candidates to fill each of the four Senate positions and thirteen House of Representatives positions. Without exception, the individuals designated were citizens of excellent character and repute. They were knowledgeable, enthusiastic, and full of energy. Four were women.

The leader of our ticket was our candidate for the U.S. Ninth Congressional District, Bob James. Bob and his wife, Pat, were a formidable pair. They were among the most dedicated, high-principled, patriotic individuals I have ever known. He was a very successful businessman who was destined to leave his mark on public life in Shelby County for years to come.

A highlight of that time was a one-half-page advertisement placed in the *Commercial Appeal* and the *Memphis Press-Scimitar* newspapers. It featured pictures of each candidate, the elective position sought, and a strong message to the public seeking its votes in the primary election to be held on August 2, 1962. This first tangible evidence of our determination was encouraging.

Following the August primary election, with each association candidate having won nomination, plans began to be made for the general election on November 6. Meetings were held, schedules for coffees hosted by supporters were planned, conferences with various individuals recognized as centers of influence were sought, and interviews with various media outlets were obtained. Soft drink or Coke parties were held in dozens upon dozens of residential backyards, and I was frequently dampened by a combination of perspiration and evening dew.

Groups of volunteers requested permission from the county clerk's office to examine voter registration documents in order to identify citizens who had voted in past Republican primaries. Employees of the county clerk had never seen this sort of activity. Lists were made, addresses were recorded, and over the months of September and October, neighborhoods in which persons so identified lived were visited.

Candidates, usually working in pairs, "cold-called," knocking on doors, introducing themselves, and urging people to be sure to be registered and to vote in November. Residents who were total strangers seemed to appreciate our efforts. Pamphlets were distributed containing literature about the candidates on the association ticket. Citizens of Shelby County had never experienced such political activity, and many were not only amazed but also positively impressed. Such political activity would never have occurred while Boss Ed Crump reigned in Shelby County!

With limited funds, the sources of which were the candidates and friends, various signs and banners stressing a vote for Republicans were obtained. For the first time ever in the county, store fronts and residential lawns displayed such signs of support. I was elated to see the first political bumper sticker adorning an automobile. It was, of course, a Republican sticker.

For weeks, Republican candidates visited every corner of Shelby County. On at least one occasion on a fall afternoon, the entire "ticket" boarded a chartered bus and traveled to a carefully planned series of rallies that gave each candidate opportunities to make speeches. It was a very exciting time for all involved, and the feeling of being on a real, righteous crusade throbbing with political fellowship was almost palpable.

The memory of seeing my wonderful wife pushing a stroller containing our baby Julie along on a sidewalk while I knocked on doors and asked for votes is one I will treasure. Betty got caught up in the excitement and was wonderfully supportive of the effort. We made the most of evenings and weekends with our politicking. During the weekdays I worked at my profession. I could not afford to take time away from seeing patients.

In late September, a memorable event occurred for me personally. I received a telephone call from Ira Lipman, an active Republican and a successful Memphis businessman. Ira was a new friend who had expressed his admiration for my political enthusiasm. Unknown to me, he had, through his connections with the Young Republican National Federation, of which I was a member, obtained an invitation for me to attend a Young Republican Candidates' Conference with our former president, General Dwight Eisenhower, on September 29 in Gettysburg, Pennsylvania.

That same day, I received a telegram from Len Nadasdy, director of the YR organization, confirming the invitation, notifying me that a letter with details would follow, and asking me to confirm by return wire. I did so. By that time I had discussed the matter with Betty and begun making plans with Ira.

The plan was that Ira, Betty, and I would fly to Washington, D.C., where rooms were reserved at the Statler Hilton Hotel. On the next day, I would journey with a group of Young Republican candidates to Gettysburg, where the president and Mrs. Eisenhower lived in retirement. Ira and Betty would visit sites in our nation's capital.

The plan proved to be perfect in every detail. Betty's parents agreed to look after the children in our absence, and my only duty in preparation was to cancel several dental appointments and explain to my staff what was happening.

Arriving in Washington, the city in which I had lived for some time while my father served as a congressman from Mississippi, Betty and I were thrilled. When I registered at the hotel, I was surprised to learn that the room rate was twenty-eight dollars a night! I honestly felt that was an unusually high price. Betty reminded me later that my comment was, "The price of dentistry in Memphis just went up!"

Early the next morning, our YR group boarded a bus for Gettysburg. The notes I made upon our return to the hotel that evening tell part of the story. I offer them here just as I wrote them on a sheet of the Statler Hilton Washington guest stationery:

9-29-62

> *Boarded bus at 7:15 for 80-mile drive from YRNF Headquarters, Washington, D.C., to Gettysburg, Pa. There to meet, along with 34 other Young Republican candidates, former President Eisenhower in a conference concerning the various elections this November. The President came into the meeting hall adjacent to Gettysburg Hotel. Looked to be in wonderful health, wearing dark blue business suit, dark blue tie and vest.*
>
> *We lined up and individually offered our greetings to "Ike," shaking hands and posing for pictures. We sat down in three curved rows, separated by an aisle, facing the President, who sat with Len Nadasdy, Chairman of the YRNF. Len made a statement, introduced us to the President, and described the varied local, state, and national offices being sought by the candidates. The candidates then questioned the President on various aspects of the political scene. Replying to a question as to how Republican candidates might best counter Democrat claims that they are the party of the people, Eisenhower was very emphatic. "Those claims are mere propaganda, as Democrats also refer to Republicans as the party of big business. In reality, what is business but the American people—the inference is that only the rich control the party, and this is mere propaganda." The basic aim of his (Republican) Administration was to improve the welfare of the American people, to ensure their progress and security. Business is everyone's life. The mere fact that, in large and growing numbers, younger people are busy working hard to take care of*

their families, providing for their future, and still going into politics is the very best evidence that the Republican Party is the party of the people.

As to campaign issues, President Eisenhower stated that the greatest duty of the Republican Party and American people is to fight for and preserve a constitutional diffusion of responsibilities all down the lines of government into every local level, as opposed to an increasing trend toward centralization of more and more governmental functions in Washington.

The President also stressed the need for government on a pay as you go basis. At this time we must spend ten billion dollars to pay the interest on our present and growing national debt before we begin to pay for the other expenses of conducting the affairs of our nation. He pointed up, as another issue, the urgency of trying to ensure the progress of the farmer back to a position of independence and progress in our economy.

In closing, that great American hero, the former President, emphasized his convictions that a dedicated people in the local levels of government can prevent the necessity of any federal invasion of our local and state duties and responsibilities. "Local offices," he said, "soundly based, can and will assure better Federal government."

The president departed, and we candidates boarded our bus for a tour of the Eisenhower farm. It was a beautiful setting in the country on a sunny fall day. We saw apple trees loaded with fruit. The surrounding fields contained mature hay or grain. The barn served as a garage and contained two large Chrysler sedans. We were guided all around and carefully kept a reasonable distance from the home.

Just as we were about to board our bus to return to Washington, a housekeeper emerged from the front door of the residence and asked us to wait a moment. To our surprise, Mrs. Eisenhower stepped out and told us the "General" had just advised her that we were a group of young Republican candidates from across the nation and that we had been given a tour of the farm. Her hair was in curlers, and she was wearing a housecoat. She urged the group to wait until she got dressed, for she would like to give us a personal tour of the premises.

In a few moments, she came out looking lovely and proceeded to take us more closely around the residence. She showed us the president's private golf green and pointed him out to us as he stood in the sunroom in front of an easel, painting. He waved to us, and we all waved to him in return. Shortly, the former first lady told us good-bye and we headed for Washington. Each person in the group nurtured his or her own impressions, but I think it's fair to say we all felt we had been entertained by the American version of royalty!

I shared with Betty and Ira details of my visit with the president and tour of the farm. They had a pleasant time seeing the sights of the city. We returned to Memphis overjoyed with our experiences. The visit confirmed my newly acquired Republican identity and my strong beliefs in its philosophy as espoused by Senator Goldwater and President Eisenhower. Two added benefits were a nice article about the trip in local newspapers and a picture of the president and me. I treasure the picture, as well as the experience, and I remain indebted to Ira Lipman for that never to be forgotten occasion.

As election time approached, it was obvious that our Republican campaigns were having a direct effect on the opposition party. Several times as I stood outside a factory or business entrance early in the morning, seeking votes and distributing campaign literature to employees arriving for work, I noticed one or more Democrat candidates doing the same thing! Unheard of in Shelby County!

Democrat candidates also chartered buses and traveled the county seeking votes. Historically, this had been unnecessary. A simple endorsement from Boss Ed Crump had been a sufficient stamp of approval, which satisfied the average voter. Since Mr. Crump had passed from the scene, all that remained of his influence was a political vacuum of sorts that had not yet been identified for what it was.

In the early stages of becoming a candidate for public office, I delivered a prepared statement seeking to explain the purpose of my candidacy. It was offered as follows:

> *My fellow citizens, I am a Mississippian by birth, a Tennessean by choice, an American by the grace of God, and a former Democrat who is now a Republican because the Democratic Party, through its national leaders, has completely abandoned me and the things I believe in. I have always believed, and still believe,*

as did *Thomas Jefferson*, that the basic principles of government which have guided this country through its development are just as modern and usable today as are the Ten Commandments.

I am a candidate for the Tennessee state legislature simply because I, as a responsible citizen, can no longer sit at home in frustration and watch as selfish, power-hungry politicians use my tax dollars to entrench themselves in office. I also resent their playing social scientists with my American heritage, which I wish to leave to my children.

I honestly believe we as a nation are as much at war right now as we have ever been in the past. This is a different war, however, a cold one rather than a hot war, but the stakes are the same. The main battlefields of this war include the United States Congress and the state legislatures. The only weapons we have are our votes. Unless we are willing to throw down our weapons and call it quits, we must make every vote count. Our votes can send a courageous, two-fisted, patriotic American to Washington, D.C., to help fight our battle, or our votes can lead us down the same old road of carelessness and indifference, which we have been led down before. My friends, we must elect Bob James to Congress, we must elect responsible Republicans to the state legislature; we must do our part to fight this deadly battle, or forever give up any moral right we have to complain about what is happening to this nation and state.

A new political day has dawned in Shelby County, and I am grateful to have a part in this successful effort to give every voter a choice at election time. We Republican candidates represent as wide a range of experience and qualifications as you could wish for. Since we are to represent you in Nashville, it should be encouraging to know that the experience of the candidates will be available to meet the problems of practically any citizen who might need help. From legal knowledge to the grocery business, from the problems of the housewife to the field of education, from medicine to the insurance industry, we conservative Republicans have the experience, the ability and the desire to do our part for better government.

Tennessee needs lawmakers who will take a stand for state sovereignty, for the basic rights of our state to meet and solve its *own problems without cringing at the feet of federal bureaucrats. Every time we go begging to Washington, palms outstretched, waiting for a handout, we give up a little more of our freedom. States' rights mean states' responsibilities, and I believe in both. No one knows the problems of this state better than Tennesseans, and no one can deal with these problems as well as the people of Tennessee. We need to learn to say, "No thanks, Mr. Federal Bureaucrat, we can handle this problem ourselves," and then handle it. We must, as state officials, assert our rights to regain lost state powers. This we conservatives will do.*

Ladies and gentlemen, I want you to vote for me, Winfield Dunn. I am a plain, ordinary citizen like yourselves, and I have the courage of my convictions. When you go to the polls, don't forget that the strength of this nation, and the promise of its future, are no greater than the quality and sincerity of the people elected to the state and national congresses.

In closing, remember this—we must, as freeborn citizens, stand up and be counted, or the time is coming when we will be counted out. A vote for Winfield Dunn and the other conservative Republican candidates is a vote for the American principles which will keep this country free, will keep our state of Tennessee sovereign, and will maintain our dignity as individuals.

These were the facts as I saw them in those days. Democrats held a political monopoly in the county for one hundred years. Every public office was and had been occupied by Democrats historically. Every member of the state legislature elected from Shelby was required by law to run from the county at large. There were no smaller geographic districts as they now exist from which to run. No candidate bearing a political label other than Democrat could possibly expect to be elected to state office. The Republican Association had decided that it was time to challenge the monopoly by forcing every Democrat nominated for legislative office to be opposed by a respectable, aggressive opponent. Forcing Democrat candidates to actively go before the public and give their positions on issues prior to the general election would be an historic first. Only serious opponents could make that happen, and local Republicans were ready to go to work with that objective in mind.

Personally, I took comfort that the race was not winnable, based on the political structure as it existed in Shelby County. Except in the most confidential terms to family and close associates, I never mentioned that fact. Had the prospect of winning been even slight, I would not have considered being a candidate. I could not have afforded to be a part-time dentist, considering my financial obligations to creditors and to family. I was simply motivated and energized by the principle that competition is essential in most activities of life. Certainly in politics that was the case. I wanted to see the Democrats have to work for their assured elections in November.

On the Saturday before Election Day the following Tuesday, one final publicity effort was made by the entire Republican Association legislative ticket. At 9:00 a.m. in front of the Peabody Hotel on Union Avenue in downtown Memphis, our seventeen candidates gathered, and at the appointed time we linked arms, forming a broad line in the center of the street. We began a jovial but determined march eastward. A generous group of supporters was in attendance, as were representatives of the press. The supporters held homemade signs and banners. There was little auto traffic to deal with, and we marched for several blocks before singling off to politick in business establishments on either side of Union Avenue.

We worked the entire day, knocking on doors, shaking hands, and asking for votes. The next day, in Sunday's edition of the *Commercial Appeal* dated November 4, 1962, a grand article featuring a picture of the group with arms linked appeared. The candidates and all the campaign workers could not have been more pleased with results from our effort. It was excellent free publicity for the Republican team! We had run our races, taken our stands, made new friends, and set the tone for a new political day in Shelby County.

No individual worked harder than the Republican candidate for the United States House of Representatives from the Ninth Congressional District of Tennessee, Bob James. He took a leave of absence from his business and spent every waking moment campaigning for Congress. His efforts led him and whatever legislative candidates might try to keep up into every section of the district. Up and down the commercial and residential areas, in and out of shopping centers, into the office buildings and recreational areas he went. He was relentless in his efforts. Bob's wife, Pat, was just as energetic and dedicated.

They were a remarkable pair by any measurement. Many times when privacy would permit, I observed him dropping to the floor, lying on his back and elevating his feet on the nearest object of furniture, catching a moment of rest. He earned the complete respect of everyone who observed him in action.

Election Day, Tuesday, November 6, dawned bright and clear. There was great excitement in Republican Association headquarters at 1352 Madison. The association had recruited a large number of poll watchers who were assigned to various voting locations throughout the county. We were determined to have an honest election. People had been designated to be drivers for any voters calling into head-quarters needing transportation to the polls. Telephone volunteers were calling from lists of known voters, urging them to get out and vote. Republican candidates were covering the county, visiting various polling places, and thanking the additional volunteers who were standing by with "Vote Republican" signs and placards.

An exceptional example of the good that came from our hard work was found in the *Memphis Commercial Appeal* that very day. On the editorial page were a prominent article titled "Our Ballot Guide" and a great political cartoon by the nationally recognized cartoonist Cal Alley, Jr. While the paper followed historic editorial policy by recommending votes for Governor Frank Clement and Congressman Clifford Davis, it also chose to recommend Republican candidates for the legislature. It was a "first" of major proportions. Two of the four state Senate candidates endorsed by the paper were Republicans. Five Republican candidates for the thirteen state House positions being filled were recommended! I was amazed and grateful to be one of those endorsed.

The political cartoon was titled "Make It V-Day!" It featured a strong hand with the index and next finger forming a V for Victory sign. The hand was labeled "2-Party System." In the lower right-hand corner was a small figure of a person looking at his hand with the index finger pointing outward and a question mark over his head. It represented the small concept of a one-party system. To me, that page of our most prominent newspaper signified the recognition of an honest political effort. I knew the editor, Frank R. Ahlgren, to be an honorable man. The endorsements and cartoon elevated him to a new level of appreciation in my thoughts.

At the end of a long day, Republicans gathered at association headquarters to await the results of the voting. The governor and legislature totals, not surprisingly, were in favor of the Democrats in every case. Several of the Republican candidates received very respectable votes. Leading our ticket in numbers of votes was a grand and game lady named Peggy Spurrier. She had run for a House seat. She was followed by attorney John "Buddy" Thomason, a Senate candidate and an outstanding gentleman. My vote total was respectable, and I was very proud of it.

The most exciting vote was in the congressional contest between Clifford Davis and Bob James. Throughout the evening the contest was extremely close. We Republicans were overjoyed to see that our candidate was in the race until the end. The final vote total put Democrat Davis in the winner's circle by 1 percent or less of the total votes cast. The message clearly was that the voters of the Ninth District, basically Shelby County, could be persuaded to vote other than a straight Democrat ticket. Although he was the most disappointed of our candidates because of the very narrow margin of his loss, he took heart in looking toward another Election Day. The James campaign had been managed by an intelligent and energetic local businessman named Dan Kuykendall.

I was completely satisfied with the effort we had made. A winding down process began for me and my family. The Thanksgiving and Christmas holidays were coming up, and a new year meant refocusing on family and professional responsibilities. The experience had been healthy in every way, and the many new friends we made would be valuable resources in the future.

CHAPTER FOUR

NEW CAMPAIGNS

The Same Goals

The new year, 1963, was one in which I continued to be interested in politics but basically focused on leading a relatively normal life. Although I had not neglected my dental practice, I was conscious of the need to be more of a stay-at-home dad. Betty encouraged that. My professional work was demanding, and time spent with the family was the other primary interest. I did attend occasional Republican Association meetings. Bob James had been chosen chairman of the Republican Executive Committee. He continued being very active as a political person, and there was no doubt that he intended to be a candidate for Congress in 1964.

Bob James was encouraged by the success of William E. Brock III of Chattanooga who broke through historic patterns by being elected to the U.S. House of Representatives from the Third Congressional District as a Republican. Unknown to most of us in Shelby County, a movement to build a two-party system was alive and well in the land of Lookout Mountain. We were very proud of Bill Brock.

Early in 1964, a presidential election year for the nation, Republican activity in Shelby County began to pick up. I learned that Dan Kuykendall, the district manager of Procter and Gamble who had managed Bob James's race against Clifford Davis, had decided to run for the United States Senate against the incumbent, Albert Gore, Sr. A young Republican lawyer from Huntsville, Tennessee, named Howard Baker, Jr., was in the process of making up his mind to run to fill the two years remaining in the term of Senator Estes Kefauver, who had died in 1963. Governor Clement had appointed Herbert "Hub" Walters of Morristown to fill the vacant Senate seat pending the 1964 elections. Walters had indicated that he would not be a candidate for reelection. Bob James was busy gearing up his next race for Congress.

Attending local Republican meetings, I continued to gather new information. I began to get a clearer picture of the status of the Republican Party locally and statewide as well. It was quite interesting.

During the eight years of the Eisenhower presidency, a small group of East Tennessee Republicans had been in control of patronage matters that flowed down to the state. Ike carried Tennessee in both national campaigns, and these state party leaders were very influential. Three of the most prominent were Congressman B. Carroll Reece, Congressman Howard Baker, Sr., and Guy Smith, publisher of the *Knoxville Journal* newspaper. East Tennessee was the hard-core Republican area of the state.

Throughout the Eisenhower years, two prominent Shelby County Republicans were identified with the "Old Guard" and the Lincoln League. These two groups worked hand in glove with East Tennessee-elected Republican leadership. Lieutenant George W. Lee headed the Lincoln League and controlled the Republican Party in the county with the blessings of both Boss Ed Crump and the East Tennessee leadership. He was a prominent black insurance executive, an eloquent spokesman, and the person who largely controlled what few party activities occurred locally. Lee had been a friend and understudy of another widely respected black Shelby County Republican named Bob Church. Mr. Church had passed from the scene by 1964. Millsaps Fitzhugh of the Old Guard played a prominent and influential supporting role. These two men, Lee and Fitzhugh, coveted their ability to have major input into statewide party and patronage matters relating to Shelby County and West Tennessee. Congressmen Reece and Baker effectively controlled the party in the state. It was a cozy, comfortable arrangement that leaned strongly against a "rocking of the boat" by anyone from outside that small group. These people enjoyed the absence of a vital, competitive state party. There were others, especially others in Shelby County, who felt quite differently. I learned much of that history from respected Republican friends such as Harry Wellford, Gwen Awsumb, Lewis Donelson, Alex Dann, Bob James, Peggy Spurrier, and others.

Each county had the option to organize every two years by political party and to hold or not hold a primary election. An overwhelming majority of counties in Tennessee did not hold Republican primaries. This was the situation in Middle and West Tennessee, especially. State law required that any county desiring to organize and conduct a primary election must go through a process of holding precinct caucuses, choosing delegates, and giving those elected delegates the responsibility of holding a countywide meeting to elect a party chairman and an Executive Committee. The results were submitted to the secretary of state, always a Democrat. Still, no county was required by law to hold a primary election.

With Lee as Shelby Republican county chairman and an Executive Committee under his control, the strategy had been merely to hold caucuses in twelve or fifteen predominantly black precincts where his influence was unquestioned. During the 1950s, he apparently was not challenged about local elections as far as the remainder of the precincts was concerned. Following the steps required by law, Lee easily maintained control of Republican county politics and patronage.

The new Memphis and Shelby County Republican Association and its dramatic, effective political work in 1962 should have been a signal to the George W. Lee group that change was in the air. I cannot recall him being any sort of force in our 1962 campaign. I did not know him. The Democrats had regained the presidency by electing John F. Kennedy in 1960. There would have been few, if any, patronage opportunities for Republicans in Tennessee beginning in 1961. I was disappointed that Richard Nixon failed to carry my state.

At the end of a Republican Association meeting one evening in early 1964 I was approached by Lewis Donelson. He told me that plans were being made to have a full-blown, countywide party reorganization. Attorney Leo Buchignani had been selected to be the candidate for county chairman. After agreeing to be the candidate, he had changed his mind and chosen to run for president of the Tennessee Bar Association. Mr. Donelson looked at me and said I was now the association's choice to seek the party chairmanship, if I would agree.

My possible involvement suddenly became a serious matter. The thought of being county chairman had never entered my mind. I agreed to think about it after being assured I would have total support from what was identified as the Republican "New Guard." This element of party activists consisted of various Republican clubs that had sprung up in the county and were supportive of the

Republican Association. The people, I came to understand, represented all walks of life and a wide variety of occupations. Some inherited their Republican leanings. Many were veterans of the military. Some were housewives, labor union members, independent businesspeople, corporate executives, professionals, and people from a variety of other callings. There were few black citizens involved. One notable exception was a black minister, Reverend C. M. Lee, who was devoted to the cause of building a two-party system.

Whitehaven, Raleigh, Millington, Germantown, and Collierville are communities surrounding Memphis that had either formed clubs or were producing impressive citizens who were glad to be known as dedicated Republicans. Each of these locations contained many of the precincts in the county. That was a refreshing change from other days.

While the Old Guard Republicans had few incentives to be active because there were no presidential patronage plums to dispense, the word was getting around that Republican Association forces were on the move.

The possible loss of party control by the Old Guard in the county was an obvious threat to that group. I learned how vital party control was in choosing delegates and alternates to the Republican National Convention. Control was essential if the association was to elect a county chairman. The same was true in electing other officers of the county organization including an Executive Committee and a presidential elector. Certainly, Lieutenant Lee and Mr. Fitzhugh did not want that historic power to slip from their grasp.

In February 1964, leadership by such strong personalities as Wellford, Donelson, James, Awsumb, and others began to be felt in the community. It was necessary that preparation for Republican precinct caucuses begin since the county convention was scheduled for March. Individuals representing the Republican Association throughout the county were identified, locations for caucus meetings were chosen, precinct leaders began to offer invitations to sympathetic activists to attend those meetings, and meeting times were established.

This organizational activity took place under the supervision of the Republican county chairman, Bob James, and all information was duly communicated to the Shelby County Election Commission. These efforts in predominantly black neighborhoods were negligible as far as the Association was concerned because of the influence of George W. Lee and his Old Guard allies.

With much encouragement from Association leadership, I agreed to be its candidate for county chairman. I saw no potential conflict in filling that position as far as my personal activities and obligations were concerned. Betty agreed. My role as family breadwinner would not be influenced. Our son, Chuck, had recently become a teenager while Gayle and Julie were ages seven and three. They would be great supporters to the extent they understood what was going on. I was the teacher of the Kingswood Sunday school class at Christ United Methodist Church. Many of its members were supportive of my political activity. There were church members I knew to be politically connected in the county, but I gave that no significance as far as what I was interested in doing. Being a citizen politician, it seemed to me, was a mark of distinction.

Participation in these events gave me great pleasure. It was downright exciting! I continued to be enthused about meeting so many good people in the community. My Mississippi roots were as firm as ever, but the thrill of being actively involved politically in my adopted state of Tennessee was genuine. Betty and I continued to enjoy all our social relationships such as her bridge club, my Phoenix Club, and the Chickasaw Country Club. Church life and participation there were basic to our religious commitments, and they continued uninterrupted.

Betty's mother and father were very important to our relatively normal existence. We kept in close touch with my family back home. My dear mother was always supportive of things in which I was involved. My father may have been somewhat skeptical of such activity based on his own political experiences and his interest in seeing my dental career advance. I don't recall hearing that from him, however. It was clear to me that the Tennessee politics I was learning about was distinctly different from all I had observed in my youthful Mississippi days.

As precinct caucuses were held and results studied, the level of excitement continued to build among those of us supporting the prospect of a new political day in Shelby County. We became aware that Old Guard activists were busy holding caucuses and selecting their delegates to the county convention.

The Shelby County Republican Convention occurred on Monday evening, March 16, 1964. Delegates, candidates, elected leaders, supporters, and the press convened in Christian Brothers College auditorium. Tension was high and the excitement grew in anticipation of challenges to the seating of some delegates. The county convention had taken on the air of a regular Election Day. Pretty girls wearing attractive costumes and carrying signs or posters paraded in the outer areas of the auditorium. Campaign literature was passed out for both the James and the Gold Ticket factions, and spirits were soaring.

The James forces were obviously a majority of the more than six hundred delegates present. After an invocation and the Pledge of Allegiance to our flag, the first order of business was Chairman James's ruling that limited any debate on the seating of delegates from several contested precincts. The lieutenant protested to no avail. True to rumors that had circulated prior to calling the meeting to order, Lee and his Lincoln League forces, 180 strong, stood up and walked off the convention floor. In the foyer outside the auditorium they held a brief rump session. We learned later that this group convened in another Christian Brothers College room and named their own set of party officers and national convention delegates.

Inside the auditorium two slates of candidates were to be voted on. One group was called the Gold Ticket, representing the Millsaps Fitzhugh Old Guard forces. A close associate of Fitzhugh's was prominent attorney Warner Hodges. Their nominee for county chairman was attorney Leo Cole. Leo had been one of the legislative candidates on our 1962 team that made the Democrats go to work. He had been our back-door neighbor for several years before we moved to a larger home. His daughter was my dental patient, and our families often socialized.

Unfortunately, at an earlier time we had had a mild confrontation because my back porch light was an irritant to Leo as he sat in his den. My house was at a greater elevation than his, and the light was frequently left on unnecessarily. Rather than simply advising me that the light bothered him or asking me to adjust my light, Leo mounted a spotlight on the fence separating our properties and aimed it in our direction. Discovering the spotlight, I walked out and removed it. Unpleasant words followed. Our relationship was never as friendly as it had been. I would not have expected us to find ourselves competing for the local county chairmanship several years later!

Soon it was time for the convention to vote. Happily, the results were strongly in favor of our Republican Association ticket. A fine group of citizen politicians was elected by a vote of 352 to 78. Taking on the job of chairman was a new and sobering experience for me. I understood myself well enough to believe that I could get along with the people I had come to know and learned to respect. My job was to be the leader of the New Guard. There was no doubt that we would have a topflight group of candidates to campaign for later in the year.

No plans had been made to challenge the Democrats as we had done two years earlier. There would be candidates for individual state legislative offices, but our main focus was on electing our "champion," Bob James, to Congress. Based on the closeness of his previous race, we considered it a matter of just doing it! I viewed that campaign as the main business at hand. We elected delegates to the National Convention to be held in California in July, and they were solidly in support of Senator Barry Goldwater. He was at that time running against Nelson Rockefeller of New York for the Republican presidential nomination.

The county convention lasted approximately three hours. Following the vote, motions were offered and passed designed to make the losing ticket feel accepted. The County Executive Committee was expanded from twenty-five to thirty members in order to include leading members of the opposition group. Leo Cole was not one of the five selected.

A next day newspaper account of the evening's activities quoted Bob James regarding my election: "We couldn't have found a better man if we had looked the country over. He has a great sense of the other fellow's position. I know he's going to be the best one we've ever had." I have always appreciated that comment, but I did wonder at the time if Bob knew the real me! I knew the job was going to challenge me. I had no previous experience, of course. My enthusiasm and belief that what we were about was a just cause gave me some confidence.

With the New Guard Republicans firmly in charge, political developments in the county seemed to occur at a faster pace. Dan

Kuykendall, who managed Bob James's campaign in 1962, began to make public what he had been quietly planning for some time. Dan felt he could run a strong statewide race challenging Democrat Senator Albert Gore, Sr. He made a good case to his friends locally that Gore was increasingly viewed as out of touch with Tennesseans. He apparently had been in contact with Republican leaders across the state, who had encouraged him. He certainly had the enthusiastic support of his friends in Shelby County.

Harry W. Wellford, our fine Republican ally, was enthusiastic about his friend, East Tennessee lawyer Howard H. Baker, Jr., who was seriously thinking about challenging some as yet unknown Democrat for the two years remaining in the late Estes Kefauver's Senate term. I did not know Baker, but Wellford was his longtime friend and strong supporter.

In my role as county chairman, I was to call meetings of the Executive Committee, talk to and encourage prospective candidates locally, and be a spokesman for the party. I fell into the process with no inconvenience other than an occasional political call to my office that would require me to step away from a patient and respond to the caller.

While being interviewed on one occasion by local press and television people following a Republican meeting, I was asked questions that gave me an opportunity to explain our efforts to appeal to a broad segment of the voters. True to form, I held forth at some length. Later it became clear that I stressed our interest in attracting more members of the black community to our cause and to our candidates, among other things.

That evening Betty and I watched the newscasts in hope that my interview was reported. It was covered, and there was ample time to get my "message" out. The reporter did a good job, and I was satisfied I had done well. Shortly after the interview was over, our telephone rang.

I answered the phone, and a voice said, "Can you say hero?" I answered, "What did you say?" "Can you say hero?" the lady caller asked again. "Who is this, please?" I asked. After a brief silence, the person said, "Well, if you can say hero, then you can say *Negro*," and hung up! That was the only call I got in response to my TV coverage that evening. From it I received one of many lessons I was to learn as county chairman. I realized that my Mississippi upbringing may have left me less than polished in my diction. In my interview with the media, I failed to say the word *Negro* as correctly as it should have been said. I'm sure the lady's call was prompted by my pronouncing the word *Nigro* rather than *Negro*. I learned. Times were changing, and I did want to be correct.

Political events continued to unfold. Betty and I met Howard Baker, Jr., during one of his visits to Shelby County. I thought he was a good person, and I admired the rich political heritage he represented. Family background and heavy East Tennessee Republicanism were great assets for his candidacy. It was obvious that Betty was attracted to the man, politics or not, and she became one of his most enthusiastic supporters.

In July the GOP National Convention in San Francisco was fast approaching. Senator Barry Goldwater was our clear choice for the presidential nomination. James, Kuykendall, and Baker were our congressional candidates for the House and Senate. There was great political interest among Republicans in Tennessee and especially in Shelby County.

Delegates, alternates, and other Republicans from the county attended the convention. I watched the televised proceedings with great interest from home. Lieutenant George Lee created a stir and received special recognition but not official recognition from the national chairman as he attempted to present his credentials to be a delegate from Shelby County. The GOP platform was reasonably conservative and easily adopted by the convention of delegates. Goldwater received the party's nomination and gave a controversial acceptance speech in which he referred to extremism as no vice and moderation as no virtue in some instances.

Shortly after returning from San Francisco, the delegates and alternates from our county reported on the convention during a backyard gathering at my home. There was a good crowd, ample media coverage, and a high level of enthusiasm about Republican prospects in the November general elections.

After the primary elections in August, campaign activity moved into high gear. As in 1962, Republican state legislative candidates had qualified for every position in Shelby County. I attended to my duties as chairman and devoted my free time to supporting all our candidates. Following the leads of the candidates, we enthusiasts roamed the area knocking on doors, speaking at Coke parties, coffees, and rallies.

I organized a group of young men that we labeled "The Bull Elephants." We obtained lapel pins consisting of a little gold-tinted metal elephant with trunk raised, indicating a fighting attitude. The group would gather in the early evening, be assigned neighborhoods to canvass by knocking on doors of residences, then regroup at a given time to report on results. We went on many missions, always leaving some campaign literature behind and usually feeling that we were getting good results from prospective voters.

There was considerable interest in how the Baker and Kuykendall races were progressing across the state, but I had no time to give to their efforts outside our county. I got all my information second-hand, not by traveling outside Shelby County to watch them in action. The James campaign was in full swing in the Ninth District. The candidate was relentless in his efforts, moving across the district nearly nonstop. He set an unbelievable pace and an example that would be followed for years to come. Occasionally, Bob would come by the house to have a strategy talk. He never sat in a chair. Rather, he would lie down on the floor on his back with his feet elevated and propped on a chair seat. That continued to be his technique for resting his body!

A huge surge of excitement swept through our party workers when it was announced that candidate Goldwater would come to Memphis in October. Advance people from that organization swept into town, chose the site for the speech, and began to direct us locals in preparation for what I felt would be a big boost to his efforts in Tennessee.

The large wooden platform from which he would speak was erected on a landing along the Mississippi River. The large sloping stone apron on which traffic normally moved would accommodate a big crowd, and we were determined to have one present. We knew Goldwater would draw from all across West Tennessee, as well as East Arkansas. The time selected for his speech was the noon hour in order to attract people from the office buildings downtown.

I canceled all my dental appointments for that day. My job was to be on site early as the crowd gathered there at the riverfront. I made sure Betty and the children had good seats in front of the speaker's platform. Dan Kuykendall and Bob James were assigned to welcome the Goldwater party at the airport and ride with the senator to the riverside. The nominee flew in from an appearance at Louisville, Kentucky. The program consisted of an invocation, the Pledge of Allegiance, and a rendering of the National Anthem by Metropolitan Opera star Marguerite Piazza, a Memphian. I was to preside as master of ceremonies. Before 11:00 a.m. on a clear fall day the crowd began to gather. A musical group performed as various participants arrived.

At twelve o'clock, the most tremendous gathering of humanity I had ever witnessed in Shelby County was in place. The speaker system was working well, and I busied myself making remarks, welcoming people, and offering enthusiastic comments about the victory we were moving toward in November. Shortly, the sound of sirens told us the police-escorted motorcade was about to arrive. I was in awe over the size of the crowd and surprised by my own level of excitement. People were hanging out office windows on Front Street and were strung out all over that cobble-stoned section of the riverfront. It was an exhilarating moment, and as events turned out, it was for me the visceral high point of the entire campaign.

Senator and Mrs. Goldwater stepped onto the platform to be greeted by me, Betty Dunn, Jackie Kuykendall, and Pat James, among many others. The crowd roared their welcome. First came the invocation, followed by the Pledge of Allegiance. I then introduced Marguerite who, with the help of the musicians, offered a beautiful rendition of "The Star-Spangled Banner." From where I stood, I could see that she was holding what appeared to be a piece of a Kleenex box on which she had printed the words of the anthem. She obviously was determined not to make a mistake in the wording of the song we all had known by heart since childhood. I admired that.

Senator Goldwater had received much criticism about his all too candid remarks concerning the possibility of a sale of the Tennessee Valley Authority to private interests. I was confident he had put that issue to rest in his Louisville speech earlier in the day and was anxious to hear him repeat his comments. After all, now in Tennessee, he was in the heart of territory where the TVA was literally worshipped by many.

After all candidates had been recognized and some had made brief remarks, the Republican candidate for president of the United States was introduced. Goldwater was a ruggedly handsome man, and he made a fine appearance. He spoke for approximately twenty minutes.

I am confident I never heard a less inspiring speech considering the level of expectations from the huge gathering. The disappointing nature of his remarks took a while to sink in to my thoughts, but I clearly kept waiting to hear what was never said. No mention, at all, of the flap over TVA. I heard familiar phrases that reflected his philosophy of limited government and a hard line on communism. They remained in my memory as a result of having read his book *The Conscience of a Conservative* a number of times. The burning issue of the day, however, was his position on the future of Tennessee's beloved TVA. No comment from the candidate for president regarding TVA was thunderous in its silence.

The Goldwater appearance was a major disappointment, but there was no time to dwell on it. The following week, at the same location in Memphis, the Democrat candidate, President Lyndon Baines Johnson, made an appearance and speech. Although I did not attend, I listened by radio from my office. Newspaper reports the next day indicated the Johnson crowd on the riverfront far surpassed our audience. He was on a roll and received an audience response I did not hear for Goldwater. I learned some months after the Memphis speech that Senator Goldwater, the morning of his appearances in Louisville and Memphis, had come to the conclusion that he had lost the race to LBJ. His performance bore that out.

We Republicans had not lost our enthusiasm, despite Goldwater's unimpressive Memphis speech. Neighborhood after neighborhood was canvassed repeatedly by our candidates. On election night after the polls had closed, stalwart supporters gathered at party headquarters to await the results. The evening was a mix of highs and lows with the lows ultimately taking charge of our collective attitudes. Each of our local Republican candidates lost his or her race. Bob James, our champion, was devastated by his Democrat opponent. The Baker and Kuykendall races were the most exciting of the evening, although both men were defeated. Not surprising, Barry Goldwater was plowed under by a Democrat landslide, compliments of Lyndon Johnson. I left headquarters deeply disappointed.

The most encouraging result of our efforts statewide was the fact that Republicans were capable of attracting heavy, though not adequate, votes from the people of Tennessee. At the time, that seemed little consolation. Another fact that emerged was the unusually heavy vote cast in the black precincts of Shelby County. Voter registration drives by local black leaders obviously had been effective. Mulling over such things, I settled down to dentistry and the more normal existence a husband and father should pursue.

Several weeks later I called a meeting of the Executive Committee of the party to assess our situation. We gathered in new offices because Mr. Fitzhugh, our former landlord, had invited us to move out of his building on Madison. He was obviously displeased by his failure to retain a position of prominence in the party. Attending the meeting were Bob James, Dan Kuykendall, Harry Wellford, and Lewis Donelson, among other leaders. I specifically invited Lieutenant George W. Lee and was pleased by his acceptance.

Following a brief review of our recent election experiences and the disappointing vote totals that showed Republican weakness among black voters, I turned to George Lee. How, I asked, could we begin to build political strength with black citizens? His immediate response was that the first thing we had to do was bury Goldwater! I responded it was very clear that the senator had just been buried by the voters of the United States. Yes, replied Lee, but we must now dig him up and bury him again! From that point on our meeting went downhill. It was obvious no help would be forthcoming from the distinguished leader of the Lincoln League! Very little was accomplished during the remainder of the meeting. We adjourned. Christmas was fast approaching, and there were things other than politics that needed my attention.

CHAPTER FIVE

THE WORK OF A COUNTY CHAIRMAN

My World Expands

At thirty-seven years of age, my life was full of interests and
activities that kept me busy and involved. My professional life was
rewarding and challenging. The staff who worked for and supported
me as a dentist were also good friends who made the working environment very pleasant. My new responsibilities as Shelby County
chairman of the Republican Party fell smoothly alongside other
activities. The political side seemed to add spice to many patient
relationships. For example, Mr. Paul Barret of Barretville, just outside
Memphis in Shelby County, was a prominent and old-line Democrat who, along with his wife, became my patient. A wealthy banker,
operator of cotton gins, and substantial landowner, Mr. Barret
exerted political influence far beyond the boundaries of Barretville.
We had many enjoyable conversations during their dental visits. I
learned a great deal about past county political activities and personalities. He had over the years been allied with many of the state's
most well-known and powerful officeholders.

Betty and I were busy with three great children, Chuck, Gayle,
and Julie. We were blessed by the love and interest of Mom, Betty's
mother. Chuck and I were into the Indian Guides program that gave
us opportunities to enjoy workshops, hikes, and overnight camping.
That was followed by Boy Scouts. Gayle was into the Brownies,
among other things, and baby Julie at four years of age was a first-class
busybody who kept all of us on our toes. We frequently played
bridge with good friends and remained quite active at Christ United
Methodist Church.

I was so pleased when Dr. Frank Prichard decided to cut back
on the intense dental practice he had pursued and join me in
my office on Poplar Avenue. We enjoyed being associated once

more, and for several years prior to his sudden death in June 1968, we maintained a strong personal and professional relationship. Dr. Prichard, through his substantial influence, had been instrumental in getting me admitted to the University of Tennessee's College of Dentistry in Memphis as an out-of-state student. He was admired by his colleagues in the profession and was revered by his patients. Having been raised as a country boy in Dyer County, Tennessee, he had a very simple and down-to-earth approach to people that was most appealing. He served a number of years as a member of the Tennessee Board of Dental Examiners, a position of prestige.

On the political side, 1965 was a year in which we Shelby County Republicans continued to be enthused about prospects for building a two-party political system in the county and state. I had moved fairly easily into the role of county chairman and found it to be an enjoyable experience. After nursing the bruises from defeats in the 1964 elections, the general feeling among active Republicans was that we were in good shape. Control of party apparatus had been permanently acquired by the Republican Association from Old Guard elements at home and in East Tennessee.

We were encouraged by the election of John Duncan in the Second Congressional District and the reelection of Congressman Jim Quillen and Congressman Bill Brock in the First and Third Districts. Added comfort came from a U.S. Supreme Court decision holding that state legislative populations had to be apportioned by district, thus assuring "one man one vote." For more than sixty years, that right guaranteed by the Fourteenth Amendment to the federal Constitution and the Tennessee Constitution to reapportion had been ignored in our state. Now that Shelby County was districted by the legislature, Republicans faced a realistic opportunity to elect more members of the state House and Senate.

Local party activity continued at a routine pace. Meetings were called on a regular basis, and I found that my ability to preside and be fair to all individuals was meaningful. I certainly enjoyed those responsibilities. I had no exposure to politics beyond the county, and only occasionally did I meet other Republicans from around the state.

On one occasion I was asked to fill in for a member of the Republican state Executive Committee from Memphis. A trip to Nashville for that purpose was planned, and I attended a two-day session held in the Hermitage Hotel. The one individual I vividly recall meeting was a gentleman named Harry Carbaugh from Chattanooga. We struck up a friendship that was encouraged by his interest in me as a young Republican from Memphis and my interest in him as a long-time Republican and successful businessman. I learned later that he and Harry Wellford were good friends. We had several conversations during the Executive Committee proceedings. He would be a very important person in my life in days yet to come.

In January of 1966 we learned that the popular U.S. senator and former movie star, George Murphy, could be scheduled to visit Memphis for a Republican fund-raiser. Plans were made for a dinner at the auditorium downtown on January 31, and tickets were priced at $100 per plate. The senator arrived on the appointed day from California and was met at the airport by Dan Kuykendall and me. It was a bitterly cold day.

Full of excitement at having such a popular Republican leader as our guest, we drove the senator to the Holiday Inn Rivermont and escorted him to his corner suite in the handsome new high-rise building. Promising to return for him at the appropriate time for his appearance at our dinner, we went to the auditorium where Republican ladies were scurrying to get everything in order.

Two hours after leaving Senator Murphy at his suite, Kuykendall and I returned to the hotel, called his room, and were ordered to come up immediately. We were met at the door by a half-dressed, totally irate visiting celebrity who demanded to know where we had been. It was obvious that his "Irish" was up! Partially dressed for the evening, he was draped in a blanket and had no trousers on. Somewhat in shock, I could not avoid noticing that he had garters holding his socks up on very muscular legs. Through my mind flashed the recollection that he was a tap dancer in several of his movies with Shirley Temple.

Dan and I were in awe at the circumstances. Just after we left him, he roared, a power failure in the new hotel shut down the heating system. For the better part of two hours Murphy had been trying to keep warm in the large suite with all-glass outside walls. The glass intensified the cold. Hotel management had been able to provide him only with blankets, which were insufficient for a Southern Californian. Outside, ice and snow continued to cover the ground. Obviously, no portable heating devices had been available. Our guest had no way of knowing how to contact us, and he had been miserably cold. With the senator finally dressed, we headed for the dinner.

Murphy's Irish temper had calmed somewhat as we approached the auditorium. The fund-raising dinner was a big success. The speaker criticized Secretary of Defense Robert McNamara and Democrats in general to our satisfaction, and we added to our Republican Party bank account.

Following the dinner we learned that the Holiday Inn hotel had corrected the power failure. That was the good news. The bad news was that the Memphis airport had been closed down and no air traffic was expected for forty-eight hours due to the cold, snow, and icing conditions. With the senator's frustrated approval, we moved him the next morning to a motel on the edge of town nearer my home. Driving my Volkswagen Beetle automobile, I was able to carefully navigate the ice-covered streets. Murphy remained isolated in the local motel that day, which was Monday. Worried, I went by to check on him. He was exiting his room in search of a local newspaper as I approached. He stepped onto sidewalk ice and did a complete flip, landing on his posterior. I couldn't believe what I saw, but it happened without injury apparently. After being sure that he was as well positioned at the motel as could be expected under the circumstances, I said good night.

On Tuesday morning there was no letup in the wintry conditions. The airport would remain closed. I'm sure the senator was in touch with his Washington office and his family. In the afternoon, Betty decided to fix a dinner at our home for our stranded friend. She busily prepared a typically delicious meal and was assisted by our next-door neighbor who baked a chocolate cake. Our daughter Julie, having seen a Shirley Temple movie featuring actor George Murphy, was beside herself with excitement pending his arrival. I drove to the motel, picked the guest up, and headed carefully back to our home, driving on solid ice. As we entered the front door, Julie stood by eager to meet Murphy. To his everlasting credit he said hello, bowed, took her little hand, and kissed it in a most gallant fashion.

We were all excited to have such a guest in our home, and he must have been thrilled, under the circumstances, to have a taste of home life. Just as I went to the bar to fix him his requested cocktail, the phone rang. The call was from an American Airlines manager who advised me that an American Airlines flight out of Little Rock had been cleared to land in Memphis and pick up the senator. With that news, the drink was forgotten, the lovely meal abandoned, hurried thanks extended, and the senator and I were on our way in the little green car, driving very carefully. Upon retrieving his clothes from the motel, we made our way slowly to the airport where I bade the good man farewell. Back home, I enjoyed dinner without a senator but with a great sense of relief. Betty and Julie, along with our cake-making neighbor, had mixed emotions. Such was the life of the county chairman!

In March, we Republicans began to make plans for the next series of county caucuses and the county convention. There was no threat from the Old Guard elements we had fought two years earlier. I agreed to serve another term as county chairman, and many of the people who had served with me were willing to run again. Prior to the convention that would be held at East High School, a number of local people were positioning themselves to announce for various legislative seats from Shelby County. That was encouraging.

Dan Kuykendall was deciding whether to challenge the Democrats for the Ninth Congressional District seat. Many people were anxious to hear that Howard Baker, Jr., intended to run again for the U.S. Senate. Soon after the county convention where I was reelected county chairman without opposition, Dan Kuykendall announced his intention to run for the Ninth District seat. He had run an excellent race for the Senate two years earlier.

Baker would not commit himself to another race at that time. My friend Harry Wellford was very close to him but did not, as far as I could tell, know what his plans might be for making another campaign. It was logical to assume he did not want to make another race unless he felt there was a good possibility he could be elected. He would not want to be a two-time loser.

One day I received a phone call from Ken Roberts of Nashville, who wanted to come over to meet Shelby County Republican leaders. Ken came to our home on a Saturday. We had a very good discussion regarding his expressed interest in making a run for the U.S. Senate seat at that time occupied by Ross Bass of Pulaski. Bass had defeated Baker in 1964, earning the right to finish out the term of the late Estes Kefauver.

Ken Roberts was a native of Kingsport who had attended Vanderbilt Law School and was living in Nashville. I had never met him. The very first thing that happened during his visit to our home was that our six-year-old daughter, Julie, fell in love with the tall, handsome, would-be candidate. He was taken with Julie, and they had a very pleasant visit before we got down to talking politics.

Ken was anxious to run and wanted my opinion as county chairman of his prospects to do well in Shelby County. We talked at length. My position was that if he and Baker squared off in the primary in August, I, as county chairman, would remain neutral. He left knowing that he had impressed us and that he had at least one totally committed supporter named Julie Dunn! I am sure he also knew that I was impressed with him as a possible candidate.

Howard Baker took his own good time deciding whether to run again. Roberts decided that he could wait no longer on Baker. He announced his candidacy and his total commitment to be the next Tennessee U.S. senator. Later, Baker decided to make the race, and as a result, a full-blown, highly competitive primary campaign between the two began to shape up.

Kuykendall was organizing and working hard early in the year. Baker and Roberts began to campaign in earnest, several Republicans announced for state legislative races, and the political season in Shelby County was soon underway. Many new and interesting individuals were surfacing and rallying to the Republican cause. I maintained my neutral position in all contested races. Betty could not resist her strong desire to support Howard Baker. She went to work for him as a volunteer, and I, as county chairman, tried to look the other way.

The year 1966 proved to be pivotal for Republicans in Shelby County and statewide. Dan Kuykendall was elected to the U.S. House representing the Ninth Congressional District. That was an historic event. After a friendly primary contest between Roberts and Baker that Baker won, he then defeated former Governor Frank Clement in November to become the first Republican to be elected to the U.S. Senate from Tennessee. At that point in an election year, Tennessee had produced four Republican congressmen and one Republican senator. We were quite proud of Shelby County's efforts.

The following March 1967, before I left my job as chairman, we were thrilled to learn that we would have a visit from another notable

Republican leader. Senator Everett Dirksen of Illinois, father-in-law of Senator Howard Baker, agreed to appear at a Shelby County dinner as part of a joint, statewide Republican fund-raiser to be held in the four major cities of the state. Notable Republicans would appear at the other functions, and we would be linked by radio broadcast that evening.

On Saturday morning, March 8, I met my friend and Sunday school classmate Doyle Johnson at the Memphis airport where we boarded the Conwood Corporation Learjet Number 100 X for a flight to Peoria, Illinois. Doyle was chief pilot for Conwood, and the Lear happened to be the first production model to come off its assembly line. It was a fine aircraft generously loaned to us by Martin Condon, CEO of Conwood. I had agreed to fly with the pilot and co-pilot to pick up Senator Dirksen and his wife. They were in Pekin, Illinois, his hometown, for the funeral of his brother. As the county chairman, I was excited at the prospect of being the first to welcome them to Memphis.

When we met the Dirksens in Peoria, it was obvious they were weary, and I sympathized silently that they had a political chore to do for us. Mrs. Dirksen settled down in a forward passenger seat where she could rest quietly. The senator and I sat abreast, he to my left, and we were soon airborne. We chatted briefly. I gave him a rundown on the events that would take place at the dinner, the recent history of Shelby Republican activity, and a few words about my role. He was genuinely interested and considerate of me. I explained that they would have a suite at the Chisca Plaza Hotel where our fund-raising dinner would be held. After a good night's rest, our plans were to enjoy a breakfast at the Memphis Country Club hosted by other Republican leaders. Following that, they would be off by Learjet to Washington, D.C., accompanied by Congressman Dan Kuykendall.

As we gained cruising altitude, the senator displayed a melancholy mood. He told me that he and Mrs. Dirksen would prefer to complete the evening's activities, then re-board the jet and continue on to Washington. I assured him that was possible, and I understood the desire to get home to their own beds. With that, we settled down. I noticed that Dirksen had a sheet with several corporate stock listings that he read and penciled in a few notes. It was so interesting to be with him on such a personal basis, for he was an extremely important political figure in our country.

When we landed and taxied up to the private hangar in Memphis, we saw a large group awaiting our arrival. In addition to Republican leaders and news people I caught a glimpse of Betty and seven-year-old Julie Dunn. Exiting the plane, the Dirksens were surrounded by well-wishers. I introduced Betty and held Julie up in my arms to say hello to the senator. He reached out, took her in his arms, and gave her a big kiss. As I took her back she said, "Daddy, he kissed me right in the mouth!" That was a little much for Julie.

Arriving at the Chisca Plaza Hotel, I escorted the Dirksens to their suite. Mrs. Dirksen immediately retired to a bedroom to rest. I pointed out several amenities provided for their enjoyment, including a local newspaper and a large bottle of Scotch whiskey. I was about to excuse myself when the senator asked me to sit down and visit a while. He fixed himself a Scotch and water and sat to relax. We chatted about numerous but not important things. The senator then fixed himself another drink as our conversation continued. At length, it became clear that I should excuse myself and go home to prepare for the evening's event. As I was about to leave, Senator Dirksen advised me that he had decided he and his wife would remain overnight rather than continue on to Washington. I was delighted.

Leaving the hotel with a promise to return at the proper time to escort them to the ballroom, I was somewhat pleased with myself. The Dirksens obviously felt comfortable with arrangements that had been made, including the Scotch whiskey. I was satisfied that we had made them feel quite at home! Our original plan could be carried out, including the breakfast at the country club.

The dinner was a well-attended success. We heard by radio from speakers in three other Tennessee cities. They heard from Dirksen. The senator by that time was in fine fettle. He bantered with Mayor Henry Loeb, stating that he knew the mayor's private business was waste management and sensed that when he first arrived in Memphis. That got a big laugh. He spoke for fifty-five minutes, praising Republicans generally and criticizing Democrats as to the size of the national budget and the calamity in Vietnam. He was a big hit, and we were all grateful that Dirksen's son-in-law Senator Howard Baker, Jr., had persuaded him to come to Memphis.

The next morning, Betty and I escorted the Dirksens to the Memphis Country Club where a festive breakfast was enjoyed by all. At that point we said good-bye, thanked them for coming to our town, and sent them on their way to Washington, compliments of Conwood Corporation and its jet. We Shelby County Republicans were very proud of what we had accomplished in terms of raising funds and getting good publicity.

My second two-year term as county chairman ended in May of 1968, and I was glad to be relieved of those duties. A spirited contest to choose the next Republican county chairman for Shelby developed. My friend Harry Wellford sought the chairmanship and was opposed by an active Republican Association member, James Harpster. I did my utmost to keep the waters relatively calm among our active members. Both candidates had loyal and energetic followers. Following intense interest in precinct caucuses, delegates from the precincts convened for the county convention. Harry Wellford won the contest, became the new chairman, and proceeded to provide great leadership. I was relieved that he won. From that point forward, Harpster and his followers represented a sort of loyal opposition within our New Guard ranks.

Although no longer GOP county chairman, I was appointed a delegate at large from Tennessee to attend the twenty-ninth Republican National Convention to be held at Miami Beach, Florida, beginning on August 5.

Betty and I, along with the rest of the Tennessee delegation, headed for Florida and a new experience. Richard Nixon had reconstituted himself as a viable Republican after having lost the presidential election to Kennedy in 1962. He and I had met in the Farragut Hotel in Knoxville when he visited there in 1966. In fact, in a small room with several well-known Republicans in attendance, he and I had shared sitting space on a small footstool as we discussed political prospects. Butt to butt, so to speak! Nixon was traveling around the nation visiting Republicans, assisting candidates, and creating relationships that might help him in 1968. As the convention loomed, he appeared to be leading the race for the presidential nomination against Nelson Rockefeller of New York. Nixon was favored by our Tennessee group.

We enjoyed the GOP convention at Miami Beach and met several prominent Republican leaders. We got our first real live glimpse of actor Charlton Heston, at that time an active Republican. I was introduced to the former presidential contender Thomas Dewey of New York. One interesting and somewhat ominous influence during the convention was the presence of militant protestors of the Vietnam situation. Nixon won the nomination for president and selected Governor Spiro Agnew of Maryland as his running mate. At the Miami airport on our return trip to Memphis, I met a young Republican leader from Nashville. His name was Hamilton "Kip" Gayden. Later, he and I would have an interesting relationship.

The year 1968 would be a good one for Republicans. Richard Nixon was elected president of the United States, and all Tennessee incumbent Republicans were reelected. Nixon carried Tennessee. During my four years as county chairman, a serious effort had been made by county leaders to build a strong ward and precinct organization. The objective was to enable the party to turn out regular and consistent Republican voters in local, state, and national elections. This was strategically necessary to counter a growing black vote for the Democrats in a racially divided city. Several Shelby County Republicans were elected to the state legislature. Among them were my friends Curtis Person and Donnelly Hill.

In 1966, Curtis Person had run for a legislative seat as a Democrat. He was defeated by Barbara Sonnenberg, one of our terrific New Guard leaders. Of course, I supported Barbara, as did all Republicans. In 1968, Curtis changed party and announced his candidacy as a Republican for the state Senate. I received a call from the candidate asking if I would serve as his campaign chairman. I was pleased to accept that responsibility. He went on to win in November.

A highlight for Betty and me occurred when we attended the Nixon inauguration in January 1969. Along with Katherine and Harry Wellford, we were invited by Alex and Mimi Dann to travel to their old farm on the south shore of Maryland for a pre-inaugural party, after which we would travel to Washington for the festivities. The Dann farm was beautiful, and the visit was memorable. Our first presidential inauguration was all we expected. The Tennessee group was housed in a Bethesda, Maryland, hotel. Katherine Wellford had a special hairdo, and more than once we heard her say, "Don't touch me, Harry!" Down through the years we have teased Judge Wellford about that.

CHAPTER SIX

STIRRINGS

My Inquiring Mind

Back home following the Nixon inauguration, my focus and energy continued to be directed toward my family and my profession. There was never a hint that my political involvement adversely affected the dental practice. As far as I was concerned, politics in Tennessee had brought me nothing but pleasure, challenges, and new friends. I didn't miss being county chairman. I was satisfied that I had reached a pinnacle of responsibility as a volunteer citizen politician in my county. I never seriously considered any future political activity beyond supporting candidates and helping to build the Republican Party.

Dentistry was good to me, and my practice continued to grow. There were moments, occasionally, when the past excitement of political activities loomed in my thoughts. I recall, more than once as I reflected on what I had chosen as my life's work, if the practice of dentistry was the ultimate role I could look forward to playing in the years ahead. The question didn't require an answer, but it did suggest that perhaps dentistry was not all I was looking for in life at age forty-one. I knew there was the risk that I could be in danger of becoming somewhat bored with my work. I was aware that others in the profession had experienced such feelings. Nevertheless, I knew what buttered my bread. My family's security and well-being left no doubt that my profession was fundamentally important to our futures.

The individuals who worked with me in my office at the Century Building on Poplar Avenue were fine people. They included Dr. Frank Prichard; Mrs. T. L. (Annie) Hill, receptionist; Patricia Murphy, dental hygienist; Glenda Smith, dental assistant; and Julie Fry, dental assistant. The entire dental office occupied a total space of six hundred square feet. There was no room to spare, but the flow of patients in and out for treatment went smoothly.

On June 18, 1968, Dr. Prichard stepped into my operatory and asked if I was ready to go to lunch. It was our custom to go together for a bite to eat when possible. I begged off since I had to repeat a procedure on my patient. My son, Chuck, was assisting us in the lab during time off from his school. He and I ran out for a snack and returned to the office within the hour. Dental assistant Julie Fry met me at the door, and with fear etched on her face, she said the office had received a call stating that someone identified as Frank Prichard had been admitted to the emergency room at John Gaston Hospital. Mrs. Fry and I rushed there, hoping to find Dr. Prichard in some stage of treatment.

The place was crowded with patients and others. We couldn't locate my father-in-law. We were eventually led downstairs to a special room, the morgue, where we identified Dr. Prichard's body. He had had a seizure or heart attack while at lunch in a local restaurant and was transported by ambulance to the emergency room. It was a terribly sad experience for all of us, employees as well as family. Dr. Prichard missed reaching his seventy-second birthday by two days. He frequently said he was anxious to reach age seventy-two when federal law would permit him to earn income without penalizing his Social Security payments. Bless him—he didn't quite make it. He and I had enjoyed a close relationship over the years. Both Betty's parents were wonderful friends to me. His funeral service and burial closed a valued chapter in my life.

Life moved on. The children were our main focus. Betty continued to be a precious wife and mother. I became the choice of many of Dr. Prichard's patients and in the process became increasingly busy with a heavy workload.

I remained very interested in things political as far as the Republican Party was concerned. On a visit to Dyersburg in the spring of 1969 to look over the Prichard family farm, I took time out to attend a Republican rally being held by Congressman Bill Brock from Chattanooga at a local motel. I didn't know Brock well, but I did know several Dyer County Republicans. A nice crowd was in attendance. It was well known that Bill was laying the groundwork for a race against U.S. Senator Albert Gore the following year. As we stood listening to the congressman, he was exhorting the crowd to get involved, citing big government, communism, and the economy as matters of great concern to all Americans. At one point he urged the crowd to produce more Republican candidates. He looked over his audience, pointed directly at me, and said, "For example, Winfield Dunn would make a great candidate for governor." He continued with his remarks, concluded, and remained in place to visit with people. I doubt if he ever remembered he had used me as an example. His focus was the Senate race against Albert Gore, Sr., in 1970. Brock had been planning ahead for some time, and he had developed an effective statewide organization.

When he made the remark about needing more candidates and referred to me, my heart skipped a beat. I left the meeting feeling complimented. His words, casually spoken, became riveted in my memory. Of course, nothing changed outwardly, but I began to fantasize occasionally about greater political involvement. It was stimulating to think about such things, but fantasy was the only appropriate word for those thoughts. I had my work cut out for me with dentistry and family, period.

On another occasion during that spring, my former roommate at Ole Miss, Buddy Shaw, was in Memphis on business. We arranged a visit. He lived and worked in Nashville as an executive at the Benson Printing Company. He held a warm spot in my heart because he had introduced me to Betty during our early days as junior classmen at Ole Miss.

As we visited, the topic of politics came up. Buddy knew how involved I had been in Shelby County Republican activities. He told me about his concern and that of many of his friends in Nashville regarding a lawyer and businessman named John Jay Hooker. I had never heard of Hooker. It was interesting that I had not become aware of him as a major Democrat candidate. I learned that he had opposed Governor Buford Ellington in the primary of 1966 for his party's nomination for governor and had been defeated. He vowed publicly to make another race. Buddy made no bones about the fact that Hooker was highly unpopular with many people in Nashville, who considered him brash, arrogant, and a very liberal political opportunist. He was sure John Jay Hooker would be the Democrat candidate for governor in 1970. I was impressed by Buddy's intensity and seriousness as he urged me to encourage the Republican Party to find someone to oppose Hooker in the next election. I wondered why I couldn't remember hearing more of Hooker.

Recent Tennessee political history was becoming something more than of passing interest to me. Frank G. Clement had won a hard-fought intra-party campaign for governor in 1952 and served a two-year term. Because a constitutional amendment altered the term of governor to one of four years, Clement was reelected in 1954 and served four additional years. His commissioner of agriculture was Buford Ellington. Ellington succeeded Clement as governor and served a four-year term. Clement was reelected in 1962 to a four-year term, followed by Ellington in 1966 for a four-year term. The two men alternatively held the office in gridlock, sharing an organization fed by their individual popularity, patronage, state officeholders, employees, and families. Their significant allies included Clyde York, head of the Tennessee Farm Bureau Federation, and Dr. Andy Holt, president of the University of Tennessee System. These men were very strong politically. Along with Democratic Party dominance in the state legislature and in the courts, these powerful influences helped the Democrat Clement-Ellington combination retain the governor's office.

From all I could learn, each man was a popular governor, and the Democratic Party political monopoly in the state served them well. Clement served a total of ten years while Ellington served eight years. Republicans at the state level demonstrated their political presence only in the legislature and through some patronage provided by East Tennessee federal officeholders. Hooker's challenge to Ellington in the Democrat primary of 1966 was the first serious opposition to what had become known as "leap-frog" government.

Later in the year 1969, Betty and I were in Nashville visiting Buddy Shaw and his wife, Gloria. We had dinner at the Belle Meade Country Club. In the course of the evening Buddy pointed across the dining room at a figure slouched in a chair. He told me that person was John Jay Hooker. I was reminded of his earlier comments about the possible future governor.

In the fall season of the same year I drove to Dyersburg to meet James T. "Little Buck" Ozment, a landowner, farmer, and contractor in Dyer County. Little Buck was an important figure in the area due to his financial status, his widespread group of friends, and his family background. I was there to make the final payment for land-clearing work Buck had done under contract with Dr. Prichard.

As I handed over a check drawn on funds from Dr. Prichard's estate, we continued to visit, and the subject of politics came up. Buck knew that I had been Republican chairman in Shelby County. He had strong political ties in the Democratic Party, although he had never been involved as a candidate. He was a businessman. To my surprise, he stated that many of his Democrat friends were very concerned because they felt John Jay Hooker was sure to be a candidate for governor the next year and they didn't want any part of that fellow. He talked at length about those concerns, about Hooker's unpopularity with him and many of his friends. Then, to my amazement, he asked me why I didn't consider running for governor next year!

I don't recall my words in responding to him, but they must have expressed the feeling that such a thought was totally unrealistic. He persisted with the idea, saying I might be surprised how many people would consider me an attractive alternative to Hooker. He earnestly asked me to think about it and suggested that I stay in town overnight. He had the idea that the next morning, a Saturday, he would "walk" me around the town square and introduce me to a number of his friends. I, in turn, was intrigued with the idea and agreed to stay over with Betty's aunt, Miss Jemmie Prichard, who lived in the old family home on Oak Street in Dyersburg.

I met Buck Ozment Saturday morning and, falling in step beside him, began to walk the square. My head was still spinning with thoughts of how silly it was to be so engaged, but my mind was also still mildly throbbing with the far-fetched, fanciful fact that I was even entertaining such an unrealistic possibility. At the time I didn't know if there were others thinking about running for governor in 1970.

We went to a number of offices that were vacant, but we did find several individuals at work. In each case, Buck introduced me and spilled out his thoughts of me as a prospective candidate for governor against John Hooker. I recall only one individual specifically among those we visited. His name was Rocky Palmer, a prominent lawyer in Buck's circle of friends. His reaction was positive, probably for Buck's edification, but it was certainly not profound. That is, Rocky didn't launch into a litany of examples as to how that idea might become reality! Leaving Mr. Palmer, I received several additional introductions, after which I told my host good-bye. I drove to Memphis with

Little Buck's encouragement ringing in my ears.

On the trip home I could think of little beyond my continued amazement that a visit to heavily Democrat Dyersburg to pay off a business obligation could lead to a modest fire being ignited in my thoughts regarding something as ridiculous as a race for governor of Tennessee. And as a Republican! In my relative ignorance regarding such matters, I didn't resist continuing to fantasize. Had I known, even to a slight degree, the enormity of such an undertaking, I would have promptly dismissed the idea. In my case, ignorance was bliss.

I was to learn later that there was substantial interest among some in fielding a strong Republican candidate for governor in 1970. That was so despite the fact that a Republican governor had not been elected in the state in fifty years. I recall seeing billboards along the highways with the message "Stan Snodgrass Would Make a Great Governor" and a large, colorful picture of that person. This occurred in 1969 and suggested real interest by that Democrat. Others in the Democratic Party looked to the flamboyant John Jay Hooker, who boasted of a close relationship with the more liberal Kennedy wing of his party. Hooker had been defeated by Governor Buford Ellington in the 1966 Democrat primary race for governor.

Many thought former Governor Frank Clement, an unsuccessful candidate for the U.S. Senate against Howard Baker, Jr., in 1966 but still popular in many circles, might be interested in returning to the governor's office. A tragic automobile accident earlier in the year resulted in his death and thus removed a potentially viable threat to Hooker's ambitions. Clement's absence from the political scene was obviously a reason for the interest that a Democrat of Little Buck's stature showed in an unknown such as I was.

When I arrived in Memphis from my unusual Dyersburg trip, I told Betty what had occurred. Since I can't recall any reaction on her part, I conclude that she was unimpressed for all the obvious reasons.

There was plenty to keep us busy with other thoughts, and our lives continued to move along normally. The children were growing, learning, and remaining the central focus in our minds. Our family pet was a wirehaired terrier named Christy. At some point she presented us with a litter of pups. Betty was a great midwife, and we all enjoyed the experience of watching our dog become a responsible mother. Things became a little tense at one point when we discovered the pups were teething by chewing on the wooden leg of at least one of our dining room chairs. Eventually, we gave the puppies away, and life went on.

One day in the fall of 1969 and in the aftermath of my experiences with Bill Brock and Buck Ozment in Dyersburg, my congressman, Dan Kuykendall, asked if I would meet him on a Sunday afternoon at my office to clean and check his teeth. I agreed to do so. I had continued to dwell on the series of coincidences that led me to begin thinking about the upcoming contest for governor. I didn't know enough about what would be involved in attempting to explore the possibilities of being a prospective candidate. The thought was increasingly intriguing. I don't recall mentioning my fantasies or the comments of others to anyone but Betty. I had done that rather delicately and with little feedback. I felt I needed to talk to someone, and Kuykendall was not only my friend—he was a political pro.

As the congressman sat in my dental chair, I had the advantage in terms of being the one who did most of the talking. Kuykendall had one of the keenest political minds I had ever experienced. His first race for the U.S. Senate against Albert Gore plus his successful race for Congress two years later gave him many opportunities to demonstrate his skills.

At a point in the prophylaxis process, without any explanation in advance, I asked Dan what he thought about me taking a serious look at becoming a candidate for governor in the Republican primary next year. He sat right up, spit out a mouthful of fluid, and exclaimed that that was the most refreshing thought he had heard in a long time!

We continued to talk about the subject until he was ready to leave my office. He had a number of ideas for exploring the possibilities, including putting me in touch with some of the key Republicans he had met during his Senate race three years earlier. He was genuinely enthused with the idea and promised to be back in touch with me very soon. To say the least, I was surprised but pleased by his positive reaction. My mind continued to be occupied by political thoughts, stimulated by the congressman's response to my idea.

A very good argument as to why someone from West Tennessee should be seriously considering a race for governor began to take shape in my mind. In political terms, "the word" had begun to spread that there were two people who had given serious signs that they were considering running for governor as Republicans in 1970. They were both from the only parts of Tennessee with real Republican strength, East and Upper East Tennessee. I knew little or nothing about either area. However, I had been told that a little known Republican had run against Frank Clement in the general election of 1962 and had received a respectable number of votes, most of which were simply anti-Democrat expressions.

I had not done enough analysis to make an estimated guess about how many votes might be cast in an election for governor in 1970, but it seemed certain to me that there were significant general election votes out there to be had by a decent Republican candidate. In my thinking, which had by that time advanced from pure fantasy to naive speculation, I thought I could be more than a respectable candidate, especially if my opponent was that fellow Hooker.

A significant part of my evolving argument was based on the fact that Congressman Bill Brock was an East Tennessean, Senator Howard Baker was an East Tennessean, and three of our four Republican U.S. representatives were East Tennesseans. That represented a potentially large Republican vote in the general election of 1970. Since Dan Kuykendall was elected to Congress from heavily Democrat West Tennessee, it was clear to me that West Tennesseans weren't necessarily opposed to voting Republican if the right conditions prevailed. Many had established their right to look elsewhere by voting for a third party in the presidential contest of 1968 between Nixon, Hubert Humphrey, and George Wallace.

I felt the right conditions would depend on who the candidates were and which parts of the state they were from. After all, Dwight D. Eisenhower had carried Tennessee twice in the 1950s. Richard Nixon had carried the state once in 1968 after having narrowly lost the race for president against John Kennedy in 1960. Eisenhower carried Tennessee by less than three thousand votes in 1952. He was the first Republican to carry the state in a presidential election since 1928. I was beginning to believe that if Bill Brock were to have a chance to carry the state, the best possibility would exist if there was a strong Republican candidate running for governor who was a West Tennessean. The more I thought about it, the more I liked the way that argument sounded!

During the month of September 1969, Kuykendall and I exchanged ideas many times. I became aware that other Republican friends in Shelby County had begun to hear comments about my interest and my argument. The word was getting out because Dan talked about it to his friends. Such close Republican friends as Harry Wellford, Bob James, Alex Dann, Keith Spurrier, and Gwen Awsumb were showing real interest in the thought of my possible candidacy. We began to discuss the prospects very seriously. Dan was genuinely enthusiastic with the political possibilities he imagined, and he did a lot of talking in Washington as well as at home.

I began to eagerly respond to people when the subject came up. It happened with growing frequency. Always, I laid out the idea of West and East putting their political muscle together because of interest in two good candidates who would be seeking the two highest offices up for grabs in 1970. Whether the candidate for governor from the West was to be me or some other better known Republican, the thought of a Republican candidate who could stir up some real political support from the part of the state with the largest city, Memphis, and the largest county, Shelby, just seemed to make good sense.

I had been teaching the Kingswood Sunday school class at Christ United Methodist Church for a number of years, and the class had grown to a substantial size. Often, in the course of a lesson, I used political activity, current officeholders, the threat of communism, and the public's apparent lack of interest in who represented them in government to make certain points about morality and citizen involvement in public matters that affected us all. This reflected my past experience as county chairman, not my future political interests. Any time such a topic was touched on, good interaction with the class members occurred. There were healthy opinions that Christian responsibility included concern about public policies.

Sunday school class friends began to ask questions about what I was thinking politically. After the lesson was finished, we frequently stayed in the room and talked about it. Two class members come to mind. Jim Briggs was a successful businessman who became very interested in me and my ideas. He was a strong Republican who liked the idea of a West Tennessee candidate for governor on the ticket the following year. The other was Jack Morris, a well-known Democrat with strong connections to the Democratic Party and Governor Ellington. He would linger after class and argue that such a notion just didn't make sense for someone with my limited political exposure.

Conversations with other prominent Shelby County Republicans began to occur. Harry Wellford, Lewis Donelson, Bob Schroeder, Dr. Kyle Creson, Jim Gates, Jack Craddock, Dorothy "Happy" Jones, Frank Liddell, and others, as they became aware of what Dan Kuykendall and I were thinking, shared their thoughts. Opinions and enthusiasm varied, quite naturally. The feasibility of a totally unknown person attempting something as challenging as a statewide race for a major office long controlled by the Democratic Party was completely without merit, according to some. Others, unrestrained in their optimism, thought it was worth looking at. I continued to think it made sense to explore the possibilities.

Sometime in October, there was a brief article in a local newspaper reporting the rumor that I was taking a look at the governor's race in 1970. I distinctly remember three telephone calls I received as a result of that article.

A former Shelby Democrat legislator named Jack McNeil called. Jack was a Memphis lawyer no longer in office but very interested in state and local politics. He wanted me to know that the idea of my candidacy did not seem out of order, and he wanted to meet with me to discuss how he might help. He was most impressed by my feeling that a Republican West Tennessee candidate for governor the following year made good political sense. That was encouraging, and I promised to arrange a visit.

Another day I was called by a prominent Memphis businessman named S. L. Kopald, Jr., "Kopie" Kopald was a leader of Temple Israel and a well-known Republican in the city. I knew him mostly by reputation as an officer of the Humko Corporation, a company founded by his father. He enthusiastically approved of my ideas regarding the governor's race and wanted to encourage and support me in any way he could. I was elated to receive that call from such a fine, successful man. Calls of that importance fueled my interest in more serious political involvement.

An invitation to a Republican function in Weakley County was received sometime in October. At that point I was not considered a prospective candidate for governor but rather was seen as a former chairman of the Shelby Republican Executive Committee who might have some words of advice to a small group of party faithful. In planning my trip, I recalled that former Governor Gordon Browning lived in Huntingdon, not far from Weakley County. On the spur of the moment, I placed a call to his residence and requested an appointment with the gentleman. I was granted a visit and drove to the governor's residence the afternoon of my visit to Dresden.

Having the governorship on the front burners of my mind, I was intrigued with the thought of paying a courtesy call to the only living ex-governor. On arrival, I was met at the door by a gentleman who was an aide. He led me into a sitting room and introduced Governor Gordon Browning. He thus became the first Tennessee governor I had ever met. He was in his early eighties and had become severely palsied. However, his mind was clear, and his speech was faultless.

We easily fell into a comfortable conversation. The governor was in a good mood and showed sincere interest in my brief recital of background and interest in the governor's race. Our visit lasted thirty or forty minutes, following which I expressed my gratitude for his hospitality. My parting comment was that if I became the next governor of Tennessee, he could expect me to call on him for advice. His response was that he hoped I would, for he would like nothing better than to set a Republican straight!

I was accompanied to the front door by the governor's aide. He was, I learned, a sergeant in the Tennessee Department of Safety, a Highway Patrolman, whose full-time assignment was to see to the needs of Gordon Browning! Interesting! I felt very satisfied in having made a decision to meet the governor.

In November I was contacted by Bob Schroeder, who represented the third call. We met, we talked politics, and he made me an interesting offer. Bob's wife, Shirley, had a cousin named John Diehl who lived in Johnson City, deep in the heart of heavily Republican Upper East Tennessee. Bob had discussed my political interests with John who had, in turn, offered to host a reception in his home for me to meet a group of his friends and associates. I would be his guest as a possible candidate for governor who wanted to test the waters where real Republicans lived. I accepted the good offer, and plans were made for me to go to Johnson City as soon as possible. I had never been in Upper East Tennessee other than to pass through the region once years earlier on my way to Connecticut.

On a Saturday morning I caught a commercial flight to Tri-Cities Airport in the extreme eastern section of Tennessee. My traveling companion was Kyle Creson, MD, an enthusiastic and dedicated Shelby County Republican friend. When he heard of my plans to visit the Diehls, he asked to go along. I was glad to have him do so because this was to be an entirely new experience for me, and I needed some support. Kyle and his wife, Jayne, had been strong Republican workers during my years as county chairman. He and I would be total strangers to our Johnson City hosts.

Schroeder had briefed me on the Diehl family. They were transplants from Ohio. John Diehl was a Republican. He was in the condensed milk production side of the dairy industry and operated a plant in Johnson City. Schroeder also told me that John's wife was a wonderful lady and a strong Democrat. He assured me that she would be a great hostess but that I shouldn't expect her to encourage my Republican ambitions. There were three Diehl children whom I would come to know and care a great deal for in days ahead.

Kyle and I were met at the airport by John, a man I immediately became strongly attached to. He was relaxed, laid back, and filled with good humor. He was warm, welcoming, and very enthused about the party he and Marge were hosting in my honor that evening. As we drove toward their home in Johnson City, John gave us details about the events planned. The Diehls' backyard neighbors were Herb and Barbara Schulman. They were very well to do, Jewish, and strong Democrats! Barbara Schulman, I learned, had agreed to help Marge with the preparations. I was somewhat mystified by the strong Democrat presence, but I was so excited about the evening's events that such information did nothing to dim my optimism. I began to feel that, while John Diehl was a dedicated Republican who liked the idea of my West Tennessee strategy and wanted to know more about me, the real reason we were so warmly received was because they wanted to do something nice for their dear cousins the Schroeders.

Arriving at the handsome residence, we were met by Marge and the youngsters, and we were immediately caught up in the warmth and kindness they offered. After a period of getting acquainted with the Diehls, we were shown to our bedroom where we were made comfortable and advised to get rested up for the evening's affair. I was touched by their kindness and attention because both seemed very genuine.

Looking back, I believe it was about that time that I began to sense a slight change in my relationship with people. It boiled down to the fact that, once perceived as someone different, such as a star athlete, a movie celebrity, or even a real or potential person of public importance, one was treated with slightly exaggerated respect, admiration, or awe whether deserved or not. For the person being so treated, I can attest, it is a heady experience. The danger lies in the person beginning to believe what others only imagine.

At the appointed time, the evening got underway, and I was amazed at the large number of friends who had accepted the invitation to come by and meet me. Marge and John Diehl entertained generously, and folks clearly enjoyed themselves. While enjoying drinks and food from a buffet table I spent my time glad-handing and attempting to explain my theory of a winning formula for Republicans. People were kind in listening and wishing me well. Sometime during that exciting and busy evening, I was introduced by John Diehl to a young man who was a reporter for the *Johnson City Press-Chronicle*, the local newspaper. He asked for a bit of time to do an interview. We adjourned to a quiet part of the house.

This would be my first interview with a news person regarding my interest in the governor's race. He asked reasonable questions, and I did my best to explain the events that led up to my coming to Johnson City. I talked at length about my belief that East and West Tennessee could do good things together for a Republican Party that wanted to elect a senator and a governor in 1970.

The interview did not last long, and I soon returned to the large group of guests who were enjoying the Diehl hospitality. At a reasonable hour, the festivities came to an end. Dr. Creson and I visited at length with the Diehls. It was a very special evening provided by very special people. That was the beginning of a long and enjoyable friendship with John and Marge Diehl.

The next morning at breakfast I discovered that something totally unexpected had happened. The young reporter who interviewed me had gone back to his newspaper office and had written a story that appeared in the *Press-Chronicle*'s Sunday morning edition. It was prominently featured and totally incorrect. The headline for the article stated that a Memphis dentist had come to Johnson City to announce his candidacy for governor in next year's Republican primary. It then proceeded to describe the prior evening's activities and gave a bit of my background as I had given it to the reporter. I was quite surprised, and my host and hostess were also. I explained to them that I had said no such thing regarding an announcement of my candidacy.

About that time the phone rang, and Marge, after answering the call, said it was for me. I don't recall the person's name, but it was someone I had met the evening before. He indicated that I had either misspoken during the interview or the reporter, who I learned later was a brand-new employee of the paper, had misunderstood my reason for being in Johnson City. I realized I should have had Dr. Creson or someone sit in on the interview. We all knew that my reason for coming to Johnson City was simply to meet people and get some response to my political ideas.

The caller suggested that I get on the phone and place a call to the First District U.S. Congressman, Jimmy Quillen, who could be reached at his home in Kingsport. He asked if I knew Quillen. I responded that I knew who he was but did not know him personally or anything about him. The caller obviously knew the congressman well and felt it would be politically wise to let him know the real nature of my trip, including the fact that the reporter was in error. There was a note of urgency in the suggestion that I took to heart.

John Diehl quickly agreed that such a move on my part would be wise. Although I knew absolutely nothing about the man, I readily became convinced that Quillen had a reputation for wanting to know absolutely everything of a political nature that went on in his district. Feeling totally innocent of any wrongdoing and wanting to be sure I didn't offend the congressman, I promptly made the call.

The congressman was available by phone, and we had an interesting conversation. I was completely unknown to him, and he wasted no time advising me that I had come into his district unannounced and without credentials as far as he was concerned. I did my best to have him understand exactly what the purpose of my visit was and my total dismay that the young reporter had misinterpreted it. There was absolutely no warmth or understanding in Quillen's words to me, and our conversation was soon concluded. I told John Diehl and Kyle Creson the essence of the discussion, and we agreed that was all I could do. My call to the congressman was the unusual beginning of a relationship I would have with him over ensuing years, which, in retrospect, could only be described as bizarre.

Kyle and I caught our flight back to Memphis later in the day. He had enjoyed himself immensely. The word *gregarious* surely characterized the good doctor, and he was a big help to me. I felt the trip was worthwhile. Aside from making interesting new friends, the Diehls, the reception of my ideas by others regarding the politics of East and West Tennessee was for the most part positive. I had a good feeling about the experience, and I shared that with Bob Schroeder and others who were interested.

Betty was curious about all aspects of the Johnson City visit. She and I had not had a serious discussion of my growing interest in a potential political adventure of such magnitude, but we did talk about it occasionally. Looking back, I think she must have felt that what I was doing was a way of getting the entire political notion out of my system. That would have made sense. I knew she loved me and wanted good things for me, but I understood her reluctance to get serious about such an undertaking.

CHAPTER SEVEN

IT GETS SERIOUS

Building Blocks

As December rolled around, Dan Kuykendall and I agreed that a trip to Washington, D.C., to visit with Republican members of the Tennessee delegation might be a good idea. Dan knew that the elected leaders of the party liked to be kept informed about any political developments that might be in the wind. I traveled to Washington and met several key officials, among them John Duncan, Jimmy Quillen, and Howard Baker. Details of the visits remain vague, but I felt the trip was worthwhile. On each visit, Dan was with me, and the conversations focused on our idea that a West Tennessee candidate for governor in 1970 made good sense. I don't recall being encouraged in what we were thinking, but I was treated courteously. Howard Baker was well aware of the work that I, as county chairman, and Betty as his enthusiastic supporter had done on his behalf in 1964 and 1966.

In January 1970 as my political curiosity continued to be sustained, Dan Kuykendall proposed an interesting idea. His political consultant friend in Washington, D.C., Raymond V. Humphreys, had responded positively to Dan's story of my interest in the governor's race. Ray Humphreys was a protégé of Ray Bliss, the nationally known chairman of the Republican National Committee (RNC). Humphreys suggested to Dan that a letter be composed introducing me, making the case for a West Tennessee candidate for governor, and asking for a thoughtful response from the recipient. We knew we could get a list of people who voted in Republican primaries. Living in all parts of the state, few of these voters would have heard my name. The letter would be mailed, and the hope was that any significant response could give us some feeling for what we were thinking. I felt it was a good idea, and we moved ahead rapidly, conscious that we were already in the campaign year.

With professional help from Humphreys, a letter was drafted and prepared for mailing to approximately four hundred Republicans across the state. The letter contained my letterhead and return address. It read as follows:

February 4, 1970
May I Outline a Thought
And Ask for Your Opinion?

You and I share a deep interest in Tennessee. We have each worked in our own way toward its betterment. On this basis I am writing to you to seek your opinions on a most timely and important matter: the 1970 gubernatorial race.

The time has come for Tennessee to have a Republican governor. I am giving serious consideration to seeking to be that man. We both know that modern communications and travel make geographic loyalties less crucial than they once were, but sectional appeal can still carry considerable electoral weight. Many leaders feel a Republican candidate with area appeal in West Tennessee building on the base of Republican strength in the eastern half of the state is a potent formula for success.

A brief description of my civic and political activities over the years is enclosed. I have chosen to send you this background information privately and confidentially hoping you will share with me your thoughts on my possible candidacy.

I would feel compelled to campaign to win with high principles, imagination and all other resources at my command. Such determination brought Republican governors to Arkansas and Kentucky and now even to Virginia. Surely Tennessee can do as well.

I am willing to undertake this battle if a representative force of our political and community leadership is behind me. Your views—favorable or otherwise—are earnestly sought, even on the back of this letter, if that would be most convenient for you.
Sincerely,
Winfield Dunn

Included with the letter was a card bearing my picture and information on my background. It read as follows:

> *Winfield Dunn, the son of a former U.S. Congressman, has led a life in which involvement and excellence have been the guiding themes. After enlisting in the Navy and serving until 1946, he pursued his education at the University of Mississippi, where he was President of the School of Commerce and Business, KA Fraternity President, a member of ODK leadership and scholastic honorary and a cadet colonel in the AFROTC. Upon receiving his degree in business administration, he attended the University of Tennessee and earned his Doctor of Dental Surgery. At Tennessee, he was honored with membership in the Dean's Society and OKU scholastic honorary.*
>
> *Dr. Dunn has been an active contributor to the civic, religious and political life of Memphis. His interests range from building young boys' lives through work with the local boys' club to helping improve health services through membership on the Memphis and Shelby County hospital board. Other community activities include the Junior Chamber of Commerce and civic clubs. A devoted member of his church, Dr. Dunn teaches Sunday school and serves as vice-chairman of the administrative board.*
>
> *Dr. Dunn began his political career in 1962 as a Republican candidate for the Tennessee State Legislature. Since then he has served in numerous capacities with the Shelby County Party and the Young Republican Federation. He was chairman of the Party in Shelby County from 1964 to 1968, during which time Memphis and Tennessee sent to Washington a new Republican Congressman and Senator. He was delegate to the Republican National Convention in 1968.*
>
> *A practicing dentist in Memphis for 14 years, Dr. Dunn is married to the former Betty Jane Prichard and the father of three children.*

Within a few days my excitement and expectations grew as responses began to come in. Messages from people I didn't know were an entirely new experience for me. I felt that those responding were sincerely offering me their honest opinions. Over a period of several weeks, a steady flow of letters came back. The writers were obviously people who took their politics seriously, and the messages I received were, for the most part, encouraging. I have kept them all, and upon reflection, there is no doubt in my mind that these letters were a major turning point in the steps I had begun somewhat timidly to take. The advice was genuine, steeped with good faith, and very practical. I was strongly encouraged that others across the state agreed that my ideas made sense. Dan Kuykendall and Ray Humphreys felt it was time to move forward.

Some of the responders felt that the West Tennessee strategy made good sense. Many expressed the feeling that it was time Tennessee had a Republican governor. A number of writers stated that they were county chairmen of the party and had to be neutral, but that they thought I was on the right track and had proper qualifications, and they would gladly help me if I should visit their counties. Some letters had gone to people who maintained they were Democrats but nonetheless wished me good luck. Several responders were politically involved dentists, each of whom offered me support and best wishes. I received well in excess of one hundred responses, some written on the backs of letters they had received, some on the backs of the biography cards, and many on sheets of paper or personal stationery.

This is a quote from the Roane County Republican chairman's response: "As you so aptly put it, a West Tennessee candidate with wide area appeal and building on the East Tennessee strength should make a formidable Republican candidate. . . . I believe that your candidacy from West Tennessee would indeed be welcome and that you would have an excellent chance for the nomination in August and election in November."

A prominent attorney from Bristol, Tennessee, had this to say:

I am glad to hear of your interest and aspirations for this high office and I assure you that your background and activity in the past should qualify you for such an office and prepare you for a formidable race in the political arena.

Although I have always been an independent, conservative Democrat, I still feel that our state is big enough and important enough to accommodate two strong parties. I profoundly believe that a virile two-party system will be in the best interests of all the people and the political establishment that must govern.

Please be assured that you have my best wishes in your aspirations, and with kindest regards—

A responder from Henning in West Tennessee put it this way: *"I am sorry that I have not answered your letter before now. I'll agree with you that we need a Republican governor of Tennessee and I'll support any Republican who is the nominee, even if you are the man I'll support you."*

A response from a non-voting age young Tennessean from Marion County read as follows:

I am deeply impressed that you are considering running for governor. Your past record gives evidence of the fact that you are highly qualified and capable of holding this post.

Yes, I agree wholeheartedly that it is high time that Tennessee has a Republican governor. Even though I am too young to vote, I am eager to work in politics: Republican politics, that is.

Sir, if I can help you in any way—please let me know.

After you are elected, I hope to see you stop some of the bites we get from Democrats by pulling their teeth. haha

Good luck and best wishes for a successful journey to Nashville.

P. S. I think that a candidate from the western part of the state has better chances of securing the governorship.

From Jackson came this very honest response: *"It is my opinion that Tennessee could not elect a Republican governor unless the candidate was one of the two or three best known Republicans such as Representative Brock or Kuykendall.*

"The best of luck to you in whatever your decision might be."

And from Nashville, *"I am a Democrat but I vote my convictions. I was for Nixon.*

"We need new blood in our state. And the Good Lord only knows how we don't need John J. Hooker.

"Being a fellow dentist, I would like to see you elected. Don't lose your shirt money wise."

From Morristown, *"What I hope to see become a reality is a gu-*

bernatorial candidate from West Tennessee, Dr. Winfield Dunn, and a Senatorial candidate from East Tennessee, Congressman Bill Brock.

"It is my judicial thinking that East Tennessee should not covet two United States Senators and a governor. We, the populace of East and West Tennessee, should work as a unit and let Middle Tennessee suffer as we have."

And this message from a successful businessman in Milan: *"Read your letter about you running for GOP nomination for Governor.*

"Am glad to tell you I will be for you 100%. Also, I am for Bill Brock for Senator. Would like to see both of you win big this year.

"Please get in touch with me when you come through Milan."

These responses, among the more than one hundred received, energized me greatly. The very few that discouraged what I was contemplating or maintained neutrality were taken into consideration, but they failed to dampen my growing interest in running for governor.

The dental practice kept me busy. My office staff consisted of a new, young associate, Dan Morgan, DDS, in addition to the dental hygienist, Patricia Murphy; chair-side assistant, Glenda Smith; and receptionist, Annie Hill. These were fine people who were dear friends as well as employees. Each was dedicated to the job at hand and sincerely supported me and my patients They were all interested in my political activities and, like me at the time, totally naive regarding the possible enormity of what and where my political interests were leading.

Several members of my Kingswood Sunday school class at Christ United Methodist Church became a small cheering section. We would meet after class and talk about what was happening in statewide politics and about my interest in the governor's race in particular. One friend suggested that they take up a collection to help me with expenses if I began to travel to various areas of the state. I didn't encourage that generosity but it occurred, and I gratefully accepted small amounts of dollars that were given along with encouragement.

A number of phone calls proved to be pivotal to the idea of my possible candidacy. One, in particular, developed into a relationship that reinforced my growing resolve to pursue an interest in the primary. Dr. W. H. "Bill" Rachels, a Memphis dentist who had become an insurance executive in his wife Betty's family business,

National Burial Life Insurance Company, learned about what I was thinking, and we talked first by phone. Bill, whom I did not know well at that time, but who had known my wife, Betty, and her family over the years, wanted to get together for further talk. That we did.

Bill had been interested in state political and governmental affairs for a number of years. This I learned when he and I met and discussed those subjects. I discovered in that gentleman a level of energy, enthusiasm, and knowledge that was stimulating and genuine. I laid out my embryonic thinking regarding the facts of Tennessee politics as I saw them. I told him about the exploratory letter I had written and its response. He added several new dimensions primarily related to active politicians and officeholders. Among them were his relationships with the late Governor Frank Clement and a possible candidate for governor, former Commissioner of Mental Health Dr. Nat Winston. Nat Winston was a very popular Upper East Tennessee Republican, widely acclaimed for his skill on the banjo. The Winston candidacy had not materialized by the time I became involved. Perhaps as a result of that, Bill began to take a strong interest in what I was trying to do. He became a source of real encouragement to me.

To his everlasting credit, as far as I am concerned, Bill offered me temporary office space in his business quarters located in a small building in East Memphis. He correctly felt that I needed some organized space away from my small and busy dental office. Incredibly, he also offered me the assistance of one of his secretaries, Carolyn Weins, who was tremendously helpful in my efforts to begin to organize and schedule my time. Bill Rachels earned my undying gratitude for his generosity and faith. I continued to practice dentistry, keeping regular office hours but using spare time to make phone calls and attempt to attract the interest of others in Shelby County.

I began to receive calls from important Shelby County Republican friends. By the middle of March 1970, key people such as Harry Wellford, Gwen Awsumb, Bob James, Carolyn and Jim Gates, Alice and Jack Craddock, Frank Liddell, "Happy" Snowden Jones, Alex Dann, and Peggy and Keith Spurrier had expressed sincere interest and encouragement for my potential candidacy. I met with all these individuals as well as Bob and Shirley Schroeder plus quite a few more that month.

The East Tennessee-West Tennessee theory was in a process of incubation that I didn't actually recognize as such. I am sure the results of the letters I received in response to my earlier letter to Republicans statewide expressing our thinking had been getting around, at least in Shelby County. The main ingredients in the process were the expressions of support, the gut-stirring excitement that was beginning to build in my mind, the absence of serious opposition from Betty, and the surprising sources of some contacts I received.

One contact I mentioned earlier was the phone call from Jack McNeil. Jack expressed a genuine interest in my possible candidacy and suggested we meet for an in-depth discussion. He noted that his legislative experience and numerous contacts with other officeholders at the legislative level across the state might be helpful resources. I fully agreed, and we soon sat down together for a talk.

Jack gave me his take on those in the current legislature that I might find either helpful or probable barriers to any initiative I might launch. He unreservedly expressed interest in helping me explore the lay of the land. One particular friend of his was a former legislator in Morristown, Jack Fishman, who was in the newspaper business and quite influential in his area of the state. Based on my desire to begin to meet such people as Fishman, and knowing very little about how to start the process, I agreed to travel to East Tennessee with McNeil to meet Fishman.

In the meantime, McNeil began to educate me regarding the political influence members of the legislature represented. He warned me of what I might expect in terms of possible support or opposition. Although I had learned that the current Speaker of the state House of Representatives, Bill Jenkins of Rogersville, was interested in the Republican nomination for governor, I knew very little about him. He was the first Republican Speaker of the House of Representatives in modern history. I had never heard of his hometown of Rogersville, in Upper East Tennessee. I was told that most Republican legislators were strongly in support of Jenkins's candidacy. That caused me to wonder how many of the Shelby County GOP legislative incumbents were on his team. Being from Shelby, I might have assumed they would all be for me if I ran. How naive! Jack suggested that a visit to Nashville when the House and Senate were in session would be a wise move on my part. I determined to do that as soon as possible.

In early January as the second session of the General Assembly was getting underway, Jack McNeil and I drove to Nashville in order to meet Speaker Bill Jenkins, to visit with the Shelby County delegation members, and to get to know as many Republican officeholders as possible. My good friend Curtis Person joined us as we made the rounds. We found Speaker Jenkins, the first Republican to hold that important position since Reconstruction, at his living quarters in the Capitol Park Inn. That inn was a stone's throw away from the state capitol building. It was my first opportunity to get so close to the seat of state power. I had never been inside the beautiful capitol just up the hill.

Bill Jenkins was as warm and friendly an individual as I might have wished to meet. He was cordial and curious. I discovered that he was quite aware of my political interests, probably having heard about me from members of the Shelby County contingent. He was very frank to say his desire to be the Republican candidate for governor in 1970 was strong. During that meeting I learned conclusively that two other Republicans were interested in the same objective. They were Claude Robertson of Knoxville, an attorney and former state chairman of the Republican Party, and Maxey Jarman, the retiring chief executive officer of Genesco, Incorporated, of Nashville. I knew nothing about either individual. I learned that Robertson had been the statewide campaign manager of Howard Baker's successful run for the U.S. Senate in 1966. I knew little about Genesco, but I was soon to learn the company had manufacturing plants across the state.

I indicated to Jenkins that I was merely exploring the possibility of a candidacy, leaning heavily on the persuasive argument that, with Baker, an East Tennessean already an incumbent senator, and Congressman Brock, an avowed candidate for the nomination to run against Senator Gore and an East Tennessean, a balanced slate of Republicans seeking the two major offices would benefit greatly from East and West Tennessee Republicans being energized by that balance. I explained that I thought much less interest would be generated statewide if all three major officeholders or candidates were from the same part of the state.

During our visit in Jenkins's apartment, several of the Speaker's legislative friends dropped by. As various conversations took place, someone suggested that a poll be taken featuring those currently interested in the Republican primary for governor. The idea was that the individual getting the greatest percentage name recognition in the poll would be the party nominee. I quickly said I didn't think that idea made sense. There were several who chuckled over my response. We parted company that evening with my enthusiasm intact. I had learned nothing about Jenkins's progress to date as a prospective candidate or who his supporters were. However, I liked him from the start.

I was generously treated during my visit to Capitol Hill by Senator Person and Representative Donnelly Hill, my good friends from Shelby County. I had served as campaign honorary chairman for Curtis in 1968 when he was elected the first Republican state senator from Shelby County. Donnelly Hill was the wealthy son of a man who had built a very successful plumbing contracting business, had died, and had left the business to Donnelly. He and Curtis Person were close personal friends. I was deeply grateful that those two were sympathetic to my ambitions. I can't recall being encouraged by any other members of the Shelby legislative group.

Among the several Republican legislators I met during my visit to Nashville, state Senator Fred Berry of Knoxville was one who showed a genuine interest in me. We had a lengthy visit in his suite at the Hermitage Hotel. Senator Berry was a longtime political activist, an undertaker and proprietor of Berry's Funeral Home, Knoxville. He was an enthusiastic proponent of the idea that East and West Tennesseans should get together politically. We enjoyed an immediate friendship, shared our mutual interests in political matters, and agreed to see each other again.

That visit to Tennessee's state capitol building in January 1970 was educational. I left Nashville filled with a sense of excitement. Nothing that occurred during the visit intimidated me. It was obvious to me that the political environment was very appealing, at least to the extent that I had been exposed.

Carolyn Weins, my newly acquired assistant, began the invaluable work of collecting names, creating card files, and accumulating information I passed on to her as I moved around visiting various political events and individuals. She quickly became one of the most valuable associates I was to have as the future unfolded. The time and energy she devoted to our efforts were beyond any price. A single mother of two young daughters, she somehow found the time to be available at all hours to help me along.

In late March, Jack McNeil and I traveled to Morristown for an appointment with Jack Fishman. He was a feisty, energetic, uninhibited, intelligent fellow with plenty of advice for me. He did not discourage me, but as he spoke, I began to sense the magnitude of the candidacy I, a complete unknown outside my county, was considering. He dwelled at length on the Republican voting strength of East Tennessee and the recent history of party leadership. That history revealed the bleak fact that Republican power brokers in the region had displayed little interest in building a statewide party. Dealing with the Old Guard Republicans of West Tennessee, offering patronage plums occasionally, but retaining solid control of national Republican relationships, seemed to be the order of the day for those east state politicos. The election of a Republican U.S. senator, Howard Baker, Jr., with unusually strong support from West Tennessee voters, Fishman acknowledged, supported to some degree my theory. However, he pointed out that Baker was, after all, an East Tennessean. Congressman Bill Brock's interest in the Gore Senate seat seemed reasonable to him since Brock, too, was an East Tennessean.

The visit with Fishman did not dampen my enthusiasm. He was a realist, and I thought he was fair. He named key Republican leaders I should get to know as rapidly as possible, considering that the election year was well underway and the August primary was looming only five months over the horizon.

I returned to Memphis more knowledgeable and grateful to McNeil and Fishman. Fishman made no commitment to my efforts, but he did offer to be of help as things developed and if I made a firm decision to run. By this time I had made a half dozen trips to various parts of East Tennessee. There was no doubt that any campaign to win the Republican nomination for governor would require many, many trips to that part of the state.

My lack of knowledge of Tennessee outside Shelby County was not discouraging. Each time I returned to Shelby County, I did so with lists of new friends I had met. Their interest and encouragement were stimulating. I recall arriving home late one evening after a trip somewhere east of Cumberland County. Betty greeted me with a question. "Honey," she said, "do you know what you're doing?" My response was that I thought so, and I could hardly wait to have her meet some of the wonderful people I had just met. The one thing I knew with certainty was that if I was to have a chance in a primary, I had to cover a whole lot of territory!

One day in midweek I was at work in my office seeing patients. I was interrupted by my receptionist who told me a Mr. Jarman was on the phone and wished to speak to me. Having just seated several gold inlays for a patient, it was convenient for me to leave the chair and take the call. In my office with phone in hand, I was greeted by a strong voice stating that it was Maxey Jarman talking. After brief pleasantries, Mr. Jarman launched into his reason for calling.

He stated that he was in his office overlooking Fifth Avenue, New York City, and that a St. Patrick's Day parade was passing on the street below as he spoke. That comment was made for some effect, I'm sure. He continued. Having heard a number of comments to the effect that I might be considering a race in the Republican primary for governor in August, he wanted to confirm to me that he was committed to the same objective. Further, he wanted me to know that he had taken a number of major steps in preparation for making the race and felt very confident as to the outcome. He indicated that he had heard complimentary remarks about me.

The purpose of the call was to introduce himself, he explained, and to urge me to give consideration to joining him in support of his candidacy. He proposed that, upon his election and service as governor, he would then be pleased to endorse my efforts to be the next governor and throw his support in my direction. He stressed that candidates from both Middle and West Tennessee in the upcoming election would adversely affect an effort to keep the nomination from going to an East Tennessean. He believed, as I did, that an all East Tennessee slate would discourage potential Republican voters outside that area from becoming fully engaged in the general election. Making his case slightly differently, he stressed his feeling that two or more candidates outside the eastern area would split any vote, leaving the nomination to an East Tennessean.

I responded that I was seriously considering running because of the circumstances that currently existed in Tennessee politics. My strong feeling was that a candidate from West Tennessee offered the ideal means of getting a significant vote out from both areas in a general election. I stressed the fact that I wasn't trying to launch a political career but rather was attempting to offer the best opportunity for Republicans to be successful in 1970. I told him I wasn't interested in a campaign four years later for obvious reasons.

Mr. Jarman was about to extend his reasoning when I realized I needed to get back to work. With a quick explanation that I had a patient reclining in my dental chair, cotton rolls and saliva ejector in her mouth, and needing my immediate attention, the telephone conversation ended with my comment that I hoped we could have another talk in the near future. As I returned to my work with apologies to the patient, I couldn't avoid wondering what that incredibly important Wall Street tycoon Maxey Jarman must have thought about our conversation. I feel sure that no one but his wife, whom I came to know and admire later, would have dared to be so abrupt with him!

Some days later, as "my political pot" continued to boil, I decided it was time to talk seriously with Betty. Probably after supper one evening in the month of March, I asked her what she thought about me becoming a candidate for governor. Up to that point I had kept her fully informed regarding the results of the letter we had mailed to Republicans, my visits with various leaders, and the numerous ways I had been encouraged to keep thinking about running. She knew what Dr. Rachels had offered in support, and she also was aware of those comments I received that were negative. I had fully reported to her on my trips to Morristown and Nashville. As best we can reconstruct the conversation, her quick response was to ask me why I thought I was qualified to do that. My answer was simple, and it was truthful.

I said I was prepared by having earned a college degree in finance and administration. I had built my business from scratch and could manage people. I was a trained healthcare professional who understood human nature reasonably well, who was sensitive to those who needed my care, and I fully understood my ethical obligations to people who were willing to trust me in treating their dental needs. She knew that I had a genuine love for people in general and that I was not mean-spirited. My previous experiences of knowing and being around political officeholders, from my early days as a young boy, and down through years of occasional exposure, allowed me to feel I could deal with such people and even be one! Beyond that I believed honesty, decency, and common sense were what I was capable of providing. I didn't think it was a complicated proposition.

She asked me how in the world I thought I could make such a thing happen. It was at that point my simple optimism kicked in. The people who had encouraged me, the people who accepted my logical argument that a West Tennessean made the most sense in a general election, the new friends I had met on my brief travels, all seemed to accept my willingness to make the effort as the right thing to do. I didn't try to explain that which I didn't know . . . that is, how in the world we would raise the money it would take to compete in the primary. She knew we didn't have personal funds to put into financing the effort. She also knew that I wouldn't go into debt for political reasons. I assured her that we could afford for me to take the time off from my practice to make it through the primary because we could pay our bills with collections from my professional accounts receivable.

The last thing either of us remembers me saying that evening was what a great opportunity it was to get to meet new people. Betty recalls me saying that such an experience could open doors for us we couldn't imagine. At the end, she didn't say no. Why, I'm not sure. What I was sure of was that she loved me and believed in me. That was enough. On the other hand, she didn't say yes, either! My feeling was that she would watch, wait, and help when she could.

At the time, if I had any knowledge concerning how much money Mr. Jarman had already spent laying the groundwork for his primary race, I feel sure I would have become seriously discouraged at the prospects before me. The fact was that I didn't know anything about his preparations, nor did I have any information as to what preparations Jenkins or Robertson may have made. What I did know was just what was happening to me, day by day, in terms of the kinds of reaction I was getting from people, mainly but not totally from Shelby County. It fed my ego and my sense of optimism.

No one that I can recall attempted to sit down and drive home to me the many basic facts of political life. Dan Kuykendall, who certainly should have known what I was letting myself in for and who, based on his statewide race for the U.S. Senate in 1964, should have been able to tell it to me straight, did not offer to do so. All he did was encourage me and give me the best tactical advice he could come up with. That included many key people he had met during his 1964 statewide race. Bob James, our unsuccessful candidate for Congress in two attempts, could have come up with many negatives. All I heard from Bob was what a great candidate I'd be and what a great chance I had to pull off a win.

My parents in Mississippi had known of my political activities as county chairman. They had been, as always, supportive and interested. Mother thought anything I did would be the right thing. My father seemed to understand my interest in politics and offered no discouragement as long as dentistry continued to be my principal interest. I think he understood me well enough to be less than shocked to learn that I was contemplating a deeper plunge into political waters. He was a master at expressing himself and using his own political experiences as a point of reference.

On several occasions Dad and I had talked about what I was thinking politically. Prior to making my official commitment with a press release in April, I received a letter from him that remains an Aubert Dunn classic to me. It was lengthy, filled with perorations that reflected his basic opinion of the political process as he had known it, and the admonitions that he was glad to share with any political aspirant—even his own flesh and blood. The message was typed, two-fingered style, on his official letterhead. Following are portions that reflect his genuine interest, his somewhat jaded attitude toward a political path, and his sense of humor:

Aubert C. Dunn
Tenth Judicial District
CIRCUIT JUDGE
Meridian, Mississippi 39301

Dear Winfield: If, indeed, you should throw your hat in the political ring, you have my sincere commiseration and tender sympathy, so these few lines hereinafter are sort of an insight into the road ahead, or perhaps I should say, an admonition or prologue-ish discourse on the high road ahead.

The first thing to remember is, "you are in the hands of your friends." Like Caesar, you may be swearing you don't want the crown, but you must never-the-less smile graciously upon those who are offering it. The more you modestly hesitate, the more they will press you to receive it and save your country from the proverbial ends of wrack and ruin. . . . You will be nervous and reticent at first. You innately fear the daggers of Brutus and Cassius. . . . And all the while your friends are tossing their hats in the air and shouting "Viva la Candidate," half of them having never seriously considered what it takes to get even a taste of the meat in the coconut.

. . . After the perfunctory aspects of a public announcement, the whispering vultures leave their perch, and in a seemingly joint venture with the heralds of angelic truth (the newspapers), will begin the historic and almost ritual task of skinning you alive. . . . They whisper that you have an empty attic above your manly shoulders . . . that you are deceitful and manifestly unreliable from head to foot. In short little less than a whipper-snapper feeding on the whimsies of your fellow-snappers. These carrion-hustlers will feed (most of them paid) upon a diet of words which they quickly convert into fleshy substance. . . . They will whisper directly or by indirect overtness, "God pity his home, his unconsenting wife and children far from the hearth of paternal benevolence at a time when their feverish and inexperienced father is out seeking the Holy Grail from the southern edges of Shelby county to the rocks and rills and templed hills of Knoxville."

And these are but the prelude to the rhapsody known as "hell-bent-for-the-ballots." At any rate, if your hide is sufficiently tanned and your butt is capable of dragging the heavy load of a candidate here, there and everywhere, then it may be, throughout, you can smile and fight, not with guns, but WITH WIND. . . . There are some sweet prospects, sweet birds and sweet flowers along the way. For instance there are thousands of churches just completed that need a new organ and the committee will soon wait on you for a donation . . . and of course you needs must (dear brother) shove out the dough. It's a fact . . . these things are as inevitable as time. Don't let anybody in your organization, (and they are not all beloved disciples) tell you these aren't mountainous and actuarial facts in the life of a *state-wide or district candidate.*

Now let's get to the heavenly declamations, eulogies, windfalls and heart-versus-mind oral calisthenics you must put yourself through in the flaming pyrotechnics, including eulogies a la Eisenhower, Nixon and Dirksen, at picnic occasions, dinner reverberations when your throat is clabbered and your nerves frayed and tight—when you must meet the deadline of extemporaneous talks with the vernacular of the immediate vicinity in which you speak . . . and remember, some of these extemp speeches will vary from tributes to Stravinsky to the corn husks of the melodic music of Johnny Cash and Jimmy Davis.

Then comes the other meeting where you engage in a flightful and eloquent layout of pure diatribe on the influence of women. What women? Why, all women of course. Set 'em all on the topmost blossom of aromatic honeysuckle and leave them there with the lush of a devil-born flattery simmering in their hearts and minds like hog-eyed gravy in a pot of Tennessee grits. . . . And don't forget the side-splitting and devious anecdotes for the men should they somehow pollute the gathering of the saints. Just be doubly sure if you tell a private twister to the "men only," be durn sure it hasn't been pasteurized and over-told before. If you tell it at all, make it man sized and forthright. They can't tell it to their friends, remember, without giving you credit for it.

In conclusion, let me say that one of the blessings in politics is to be able to know that you possess the hide of a rhinoceros, thorn proof and dagger defying. And remember that gratitude is often a lively sense of favors to come. At any rate, as I have intimated, somebody's got to save the country, Caesar or not.

In your speech practice, remember that one bilious simile and one well oriented metaphor are worth a pound of statistics, whether computerized or not. The romance of words is not always an intelligent appraisal of the value of truth. And another thing. The frog that croaks the loudest AIN'T always the leader.

Love to all.
[Signed] Dad
Summing up the emotions I was experiencing at the time, it all

came down to the fact that I was naive to a fault and optimistic beyond reason. I could not have denied any one of those observations. But I was eager to take the next steps. I sensed that Dad understood the frame of mind I was in. The letter was his unique way of offering reflections on his own political experiences, perhaps as a means of preparing me for whatever might happen in my venture. As the primary campaign advanced, he had the pleasure and satisfaction of coming to Tennessee, being a part of the "inside" of things, and meeting some of the best people he had ever known. I do believe he got a taste of politics at its best, as opposed to some of what he had experienced in the past.

I was getting increased input from my friend Harry Wellford whose Republican ties went back much further than mine. Harry had been nominated by Senator Howard Baker to become a federal district judge stationed in Memphis. He was qualified in every way for such a prominent position. The process by which he might eventually be confirmed was time consuming. In anticipation of eventual approval by the United States Senate, Harry had begun to wind down his active law practice. Valuing his judgment and opinion as I did, he was often on my telephone call list. Harry's wife, Katherine, was also a good source of advice.

Others who became very interested included many who were involved in Shelby County Republican activities or who were my personal friends. They included Jim and Carolyn Gates, Jack and Alice Craddock, Joanne and Bob Fleming, Bob and Pat James, Jayne and Kyle Creson, Ann and Rad Daniels, Isabel and Gene Strong, Bettie Davis, Charlotte and Bill Ruppelt, and members of Betty's bridge club. Each of these good people became devoted to the cause, for which I remain eternally grateful.

During January and February I had made a number of trips to East Tennessee following suggestions from Kuykendall and others to seek advice and support from various Republican activists and leaders. The visits were productive in that I obtained names and information that would be used as we later worked on a strategy for campaigning. There were other contacts in West Tennessee I was fortunate to make. Most of this traveling was done on weekends. I occasionally cancelled appointments and included Fridays in my travels.

In late March, my efforts were still relatively unorganized. I had not made a firm decision to announce my intention to become a candidate. My thoughts, however, were increasingly focused on a political venture. My new friend and assistant, Carolyn Weins, had begun to collect names, take phone calls referred to her on my behalf, and put together a schedule of sorts. Beyond the nucleus of friends that were close by in Shelby County, calls began to come in from other areas, primarily in West Tennessee, made by Republicans or other political activists who had begun to learn of my interest and my political reasoning as to strategy. Dr. Rachels, Jack McNeil, and Kopie Kopald continued to show strong interest.

Bill Rachels knew that a key ingredient was getting a start on raising funds, which would be absolutely necessary. At his urging, I accompanied him on visits to several friends of his in Memphis who had the resources to contribute to my efforts. I met these people, none of whom I knew personally, made my pitch as to what I believed could be done, and left it to Bill to press for financial support. I do not recall a single commitment being made on those visits, and I was happy to leave it up to the good doctor to follow through. During that period of time, someone, probably Bill, opened a bank account listed as the Winfield Dunn Campaign Fund. I'll never know who made the first deposit.

Looking for a change of pace, Betty and I signed up to take an overnight bus trip with a group of friends to Hot Springs, Arkansas, where the thoroughbred racing season was in full swing. The trip was sponsored by the Chickasaw Country Club, and we saw it as a good chance to get away and see some horse racing firsthand. On the bus ride over I fell into a conversation with Joanne Fleming. We sat together and talked about politics.

Joanne and Bob were dear and close friends who shared many interests with us. Bob is an architect, and Joanne is a creative, thoughtful, and insightful person. Being well acquainted with my past political activities and curious about my current interest in the governor's race, she asked me to explain in detail what I was thinking, why it made sense to me, and how I thought it could actually happen. I did just that at length, and following some questions and answers as we sat together on the bus, she asked me if I would write down what I had told her. She explained that she wanted to read what I offered, think seriously about it, and have it in hand to discuss with others.

That evening, following an afternoon at the races and dinner, I sat down in my hotel room, took hotel stationery and pen in hand, and began to write. Betty knew what Joanne had asked and gave me time to sit, think, and scribble.

The next morning, after a delicious breakfast enjoyed by all, walks around the old hotel grounds and, for many of us, a fabled Hot Springs warm bath, we boarded our bus and began the return trip to Memphis. I took my several pages of notes written the night before and put them in Joanne Fleming's hand. I had made my case reasonably well, and I hoped she could read my handwriting on the small sheets of paper.

Several years after that happy weekend in Arkansas, I received a package in the mail. To my surprise and delight, I unwrapped a styrene booklet containing on each plastic page an embedded sheet of the several pages of notes Joanne had asked me to write explaining my political hope for that election year. I have kept and treasured that thoughtful and unusual gift throughout the years. Joanne and Bob have remained our dear friends.

During the days following our trip, my political thoughts intensified and my meetings with closest friends including Kuykendall, Wellford, James, Dann, Rachels, Schroeder, and others became more frequent. This group provided valued input regarding possibilities and potential problems that would be encountered in such a political venture. One worrisome point made by Harry was that Lewis Donelson was expressing strong reservations. "Lewie" was highly intelligent and had good political instincts. He was also a good friend. I respected his opinion but was not deterred by his thoughts that it might be an impossible undertaking.

It was obvious that we were nearing the time when I had to make a decision. The first person to be considered in that process was Betty Dunn.

Our son, Chuck, was in his freshman year at Washington and Lee University. We had spoken about the process I was going through, and he was very interested in what I might do. I did not feel it was fair to him to be asked to join in the decision making, and I did not do so.

His mother, however, was pivotal in my deciding to become a

totally committed candidate. I had consistently reported my experiences, the excitement in meeting new people, and my growing confidence that being a successful candidate for the Republican nomination was doable. She had begun to see and hear the reactions of people to the idea, and I am certain that gave her some degree of confidence. I do not recall a time when she gave me the "official" go-ahead. I do recall nights when I arrived home very late and put my head down on the pillow next to hers. Her question might have been, "Honey, do you know what you're doing?" My answer was likely to be, "Sweetheart, let me tell you about the wonderful people I met today!" Those talks took place quite a few times.

Late in the month of March or early in April, I received a call from Maxey Jarman requesting a meeting to discuss the governor's race. I agreed. Along with Harry Wellford and Dan Kuykendall, I traveled to Nashville for a discussion with Jarman at the Hilton Hotel near the airport. The meeting took place in a typical hotel room.

Mr. Jarman introduced us to his close friend, political confidant, and stockbroker, a very nice fellow named John Hazelton, also a Nashvillian. After a few words of further introduction, Maxey quickly moved to the subject at hand. He repeated his earlier words to me in our telephone conversation that he was a committed candidate for the Republican gubernatorial nomination. He added that extensive groundwork had been laid for his effort, and he was totally confident he would win the nomination and the general election. His support for me in a future race for governor was assured. My prospects of being successful in the upcoming primary seemed to him to be zero. He wanted me to move out of contention and throw my support to him. He felt my candidacy would give him a disadvantage against the East Tennessee candidates.

Harry and Dan made comments about my prospects in the race and outlined the events that had led us to the position we now held. It was clear that each side was firmly convinced of its own logic.

I attempted to reinforce what they had said. I stressed the enthusiasm I felt about the role a West Tennessean could play leading to a Brock win in the Senate race and my own effort to win the governorship.

We were sitting around a small table as we talked. Rather suddenly, John Hazelton stood up, banged his fist down on the table top, and said, "G—dammit, Winfield, get out!" About that time, we all figured the meeting was over. I responded that I was in the race to stay. We said good-bye. I don't recall further conversation among my group as we journeyed back to Memphis, but I am certain we felt we had done what we had to do under the circumstances. Chalk up one more adventure.

I learned that Congressman Bill Brock was scheduled to appear before a Young Republican rally at the Peabody Hotel during the first week in April. I called and made an appointment to visit with him the morning before his address to the YR group. Eager to get to know him, at the appointed time for our meeting I went to his hotel, was given his room number, and proceeded to go there. I knocked on his door and he opened it. He was only partially dressed. Obviously irritated by my presumptuousness in coming directly to his room, he suggested that I return to the lobby where he would meet me shortly. I did so chagrined, only then realizing that I should have called him from the lobby to let him know I was in the building. My eagerness translated into thoughtlessness. Our meeting was brief, but I did advise him of my serious interest in the Republican gubernatorial campaign.

Several days later, we learned that Brock would be speaking at a rally in a community near Chattanooga. Dr. Bill Rachels had funeral home and burial insurance contacts in Chattanooga he wished me to meet. He and I agreed to drive to Chattanooga to meet his business associates and seek permission to attend the Brock rally. Both parts of the mission were accomplished. I met and made friends with Rachels's associates. They were enthusiastic about our plans. We were successful in our request to someone in the Brock organization to attend the rally being held for Brock. We found our way to the meeting site out in the countryside and enjoyed getting to know a number of Brock's friends and supporters. After the congressman had spoken about his plans to unseat Albert Gore, Sr., and why that made sense for Tennessee and America, I was introduced as someone from Memphis who was interested in the governor's race. I was invited to make remarks and did so. Later, Bill Rachels told me I got louder applause than Brock and set some tongues to wagging. I think he got feedback from his business friends who attended the rally. That was a good taste of the campaign trail, and I liked it.

Financing for any future political activities was a basic concern. I decided that we needed to build some credibility if we were to move forward. Recalling the enthusiasm Senator Fred Berry of Knoxville had expressed when we met and talked in Nashville, I made a decision to ask him if he would travel to Memphis on my behalf. Harry Wellford, Billy Rachels, Dan Kuykendall, Jim McGehee, and Kopie Kopald, among others, felt it was a good idea because the senator represented many aspects of Tennessee politics that were really unknown to Shelby Countians.

Senator Berry accepted an invitation to come to Memphis and agreed to give his thoughts on my possible candidacy to a group we would invite to hear him. Plans were quickly put in place. Thanks to the strong connections that Wellford, Dann, Liddell, my friend and dental patient Jim McGehee, S. L. Kopald, Jr., GOP County Chairman Bob James, and others maintained with many affluent people in Memphis, a substantial group of possible contributors was invited to a reception at a local club. The invitation called for meeting in the early evening, enjoying refreshments and snacks, meeting Senator Fred Berry of Knoxville, meeting Winfield Dunn, and hearing some interesting ideas about a new day for statewide politics in Tennessee.

At the appointed hour on an evening early in April 1970, a significant number of curious Memphians joined their Republican friends at the club. After the preliminaries, Congressman Dan Kuykendall introduced Senator Berry. I doubt that any of the invited guests had ever heard of the distinguished state senator. Dan focused on the region the senator represented, heavily Republican East Tennessee. He gave the basic reasons we felt a West Tennessee candidate for governor in 1970 made sense. Dan did an effective job, as usual. He then asked the senator to speak.

The senator was relaxed and bubbling with enthusiasm. His area of operations, Knox County, was so far removed from Memphis geographically and so remote in the minds of Memphians in terms of anything of real interest to them that he appeared initially to be merely an item of curiosity. His carefully groomed silver hair, his natty attire including a diamond stick pin prominently displayed from his necktie, and the fact that he was a successful businessman in the funeral industry added to the intrigue. It did not take our visiting dignitary long, however, to begin drawing his audience into his message.

With some eloquence, Fred Berry quickly identified the Republican legislators in the gathering and those absent, all from Memphis, as important new elements with a growing influence in the legislature. He suggested that the political power represented by the large population of Shelby County was rapidly getting the attention of important people in state government. The subject then shifted to interesting and unusual circumstances that currently characterized statewide politics.

Mentioning by name the announced and prospective candidates for governor thus far identified, Senator Berry commented on them individually. He listed strengths and weaknesses, referred to well-known attitudes held by certain political factions in both major parties, and emphasized the somewhat hidden potential for political power that he saw in West Tennessee and, more specifically, Shelby County.

He then turned to the Republican Party, noting the immediate fifty-year period just passed during which no Republican had occupied the governor's office. The senator pointed out the importance of Tennessee having elected Baker to the U.S. Senate, Brock and Kuykendall to the House of Representatives, and the signals those successes were sending as to a need and possibility for change.

Comments and questions followed regarding the strong race Kuykendall had run for the Senate in 1966, Brock's campaign for Gore's Senate seat that was well underway at the time, and again, those persons who had shown interest in running for governor on the Republican side. He stressed that, in his opinion, the candidates for governor were from the wrong part of the state.

The effective presentation then shifted to Senator Berry's strong belief that Winfield Dunn as a candidate for governor in 1970 could make a big difference in what happened in the race for both governor and senator. He stressed the importance of West Tennessee and the impact that an acceptable candidate from the area could have on both positions.

Finally, the senator stated positively that he would be very enthusiastic and supportive of a Dunn candidacy. Further, he felt there could be strong support from the eastern part of the state if such an event occurred. Many Republicans in his area, he stated, were anxious to build a real two-party political system and were ready to put the old politics of the past aside. He believed it was a time for change, and he felt West Tennessee could play a big part in making that happen.

I made the closing remarks, noting the fact that Shelby County had not had one of its own in the governor's office for several decades. That former governor was Malcolm Patterson. I repeated much of the West Tennessee logic and stated that I was nearing a decision as to my candidacy. I thanked the senator for his presence and the guests for taking the time to hear us. I also stressed how important it was to know that I had support from my fellow citizens in Memphis and Shelby County. No pitch for contributions was made at the meeting, but I know those who did the inviting followed up with individual requests for financial support.

All those who were helping me come to a conclusion seemed to feel that the visit by a sitting Republican state senator who came across as mature, knowledgeable, and honest in his beliefs did a great deal to move the process ahead. I appreciated what Fred Berry had done.

CHAPTER EIGHT

THE PRIMARY CAMPAIGN

Committed to Run

Shortly after the meeting with Senator Fred Berry as our guest speaker, I made up my mind to become a candidate in the Republican primary race for the nomination to be governor. That resulted in a series of additional actions that flowed from my commitment to be a candidate. I had to prepare my dental office staff to begin thinking about shifting greater responsibilities to Dr. Dan Morgan. Each person was enthusiastic and cooperated in every way. Betty and I had to prepare a personal budget with less income for living expenses. I knew some income would continue as we collected dental accounts receivable each month. I needed the support of our children. They were ready to go, it seemed. I had to be sure I could count on Betty. As ever, she was ready to help in every way. I had to be sure Betty's mother, Ruby Prichard, understood and would be supportive. She would have to help us shoulder the responsibilities of parenthood and the routine activities that had to continue with as much normalcy as possible. She proved to be everything we needed. Additionally, we were to discover how unbelievably well our friends would respond to my decision. They were always there for us both personally and politically.

I had a ready explanation for anyone who asked why I was undertaking such a large and seemingly futile task. It consisted basically of my argument regarding the one-party monopoly, the untapped numbers of citizens who didn't feel they could make a difference in our state government, my advantage in a statewide race by being a West Tennessean, and so forth. I couldn't reach inside and pull up other feelings that fed my optimism and excited my thinking. I knew what I was doing was a very big gamble. I also knew there were many aspects of such a journey of which I was unaware. I sensed a vacuum in the political process that I felt I could fill. I knew some of the risks, and they were unavoidable. In my gut I also knew there would be no conscious action on my part that would embarrass my family or friends. The financial risk would be small because, if I didn't succeed, we would just pick up where we left off and get on with a fine dental practice. To sum it up, there was just a peaceful sort of inner understanding that I was doing the right thing for the right reasons and, therefore, the downside would be minimal. The upside of an unsuccessful experience would be that our lives would be forever changed through the friendships that we made.

A series of meetings resulted in the rudimentary formation of a campaign. Harry Wellford stepped into the role of organizing our efforts. His willingness officially to manage the campaign was pivotal. I was grateful that Jim McGehee took on the job of campaign treasurer. I had treated members of Jim's family. Betty and I had purchased our home from him. He proved to be the best, most tight-fisted, and accountable manager of funds, as well as fund-raiser, I could possibly have wanted. He had great support from Bill Rachels and prominent businessman, Jim Harwood, Sr. They in turn had help from other friends, many of whom I did not know at the time. It's safe to say that, from the start, Harry relied on Dan Kuykendall, Bob James, Keith Spurrier, Gwen Awsumb, S. L. Kopald, Jr., Alex Dann, and Lewis Donelson for advice and guidance.

Thanks to the influence of Dan Kuykendall, two individuals joined our efforts with specific assignments. One, Steven Sharp, a protégé of Ray Humphreys, came to Memphis from Virginia to set up the means by which the campaign would communicate with the outside world. He would produce press releases to keep the media informed. He and Carolyn Weins would handle scheduling. Steven took up residence in our home, in a room next to Chuck's bedroom. We were unable to talk with authority about a salary, but that didn't deter Steve. He was caught up in the political process and had been convinced by Ray Humphreys that our crusade would be worthy of his best efforts. Steven was quite a character, an irritant to many because of his personality, but a needed resource who did his job well and relentlessly stayed the course.

Two, a young man named Rufus Powell came on board. Optimistically, we assured him a nominal salary and a bright future.

He, unlike Sharp, was married and had been employed as an optometrist's lab assistant. Rufus's duties were to stay with me, remember for me, carry my bags, tote my briefcase, and, in many other but at that time unimagined ways, help me make it through each day. He was short, stocky, and strong and had a willing heart. He was also to be my driver. Since Betty needed her car and my little car was inadequate, successful efforts were made to find a good used automobile for my campaign travel.

Two major decisions were made immediately. First, a site for an adequate campaign headquarters had to be found. That was done by renting empty space in a strip shopping center on Getwell Road in East Memphis. I don't recall how it happened, but furniture, equipment, and basic office supplies appeared. Carolyn Weins took charge of that effort.

The second important step was to plan for an official announcement of my candidacy. After much discussion, it was determined that I would make my announcement on Saturday morning, April 18, from the steps of the state capitol building in Nashville. That site was chosen because we wanted to stress our start from the seat of government, a place of interest to all Tennesseans and one that emphasized the candidate knew where he was going. It just made sense as an appropriate starting point for a big objective . . . that is, for me to win that nomination.

The first of many press releases to come was prepared from Headquarters, Volunteers for Dunn for Governor, 5625 Poplar Avenue, Memphis. (I am sure that was the address of Dr. Rachels's business office.) Contact information followed: Harry W. Wellford, 1701 First National Bank Building, Memphis, Tennessee, 526-0631. Here is the text of the release:

This is for release Saturday, April 11
MEMPHIS, April 11, (Special)—

Winfield Dunn, Republican aspirant for Governor of Tennessee, stated today that he will go to Nashville to make his formal announcement for the position on Saturday, April 25. [The date should have read April 18.]
"A few weeks ago, I cautiously initiated an in-depth

exploration of the attitude of Tennessee voters after a great many close personal friends had urged me to seek the governor's office. I have long felt deep convictions about public service and had made a decision to make any necessary sacrifices in order to be available.

"The startling results of my findings across the state are that the voters are searching for unselfish leadership which will think of Tennessee first and personal welfare last."

Dunn emphasized that he had criss-crossed the state repeatedly during recent weeks talking with party and community leaders at every opportunity and he said, "The hour is here for a crusade that will excite the young and the old, the well-to-do and the working people in the full development of opportunity in Tennessee.

"Next Saturday, when I speak out from the Capitol in Nashville, I will introduce the first chapter in a great mission and I will call for an army of Tennessee Volunteers to help me do the job."

And so, with that public dispatch, the process was transformed from a slowly evolving series of events, speculations, conversations, and human emotions into an eventual result that would substantially reshape the political life of Tennessee.

The time, energy, intellect, knowledge, and trust that resided in each of us began to take on proportions I could hardly have expected at the outset. The earnest, honest, and selfless desire on the parts of people I knew, and many I would never know, to be a part of the political process amazed me. That process and all the intrigues associated with it quietly, and sometimes not so quietly, were driving us. And all of that, as far as I was concerned and as far as those closest to the effort, my remarkable friends from Memphis, were concerned, was undertaken with naiveté and shallowness of knowledge that belied any suggestion of a desire to pursue political power and influence for selfish reasons. The words *citizen politicians* suddenly began to characterize one segment of political life in Tennessee that our Volunteer State had never experienced to such an extent. What was happening was historic in the purest sense of the word, though we hardly recognized that fact at the time.

Without demeaning the incredibly valuable influence those closest to me had on my thinking and my actions, it is accurate to say that Harry Wellford quickly became the pivotal person to whom I turned for advice, counsel, and guidance. He had agreed to head up my efforts, that is, to become the campaign chairman. No single decision made during those times proved to be more important. I, along with several other key people, asked, and he accepted. Harry represented, to me, the consistent, steady touchstone I needed.

Having been nominated for a federal district judgeship by Senator Baker, and waiting on confirmation by the United States Senate, he was subject to being pulled away from the campaign. I am sure Congressman Kuykendall and others made efforts in high places, including Senator Baker's offices, to slow the confirmation process. Harry was a tremendous resource. He had great confidence in a number of our mutual friends, as well as others I didn't know at the time. He was wise enough to turn to them for advice and counsel as we organized our efforts.

The press release of April 11 was my commitment to go—no turning back. It reminded me how much I needed the support of others. Without the love and reinforcement that came from Betty and the children, as well as the enthusiasm, encouragement, and relentless efforts of our friends, what eventually occurred during the weeks and months that lay ahead would surely be, if anything, a modest footnote in the annals of the state's political life.

Preparations for the announcement on April 18 became intense. The message had to be good, and we hoped it would receive reasonable attention. Arrangements had to be made to transport a group of Memphis supporters to Nashville by bus. Permission to use the capitol building as an announcement platform was required. Detail after detail was handled by those who were committed to the effort, most of whom had never been involved in such a thing. Steps were taken to advise media people of the event in the hope we would get some coverage by the press, radio, and television. A press release was issued as follows:

Volunteers—Dunn for Governor
April 14, 1970
TO ALL STATEWIDE MEDIA:

Gentlemen:

You are cordially invited to attend a state-wide news conference to be held by Winfield Dunn, potential candidate for Governor in the Republican Primary in August.

The news conference will be held on the steps of the Capitol Building at 11:30 a.m., Saturday, April 18, 1970.

The news conference will initiate a lasting impact upon Tennessee politics and will be of extreme interest to all concerned citizens.

We look forward to seeing you there.
IT MUST BE DUNN

Signed: W. H. Rachels
VOLUNTEERS FOR DUNN FOR GOVERNOR

Early on Saturday morning, April 18, Betty, Gayle, Julie, and I were driven to Nashville where we had several staging rooms reserved for our party at the Capitol Park Inn, just east of the capitol building and down a sloping hill. I recall seeing several of my new friends and supporters from parts of East Tennessee who had driven over for the occasion. We arrived more than an hour before the announcement, which was scheduled for 11:30 a.m., on the south end outside.

As the excitement in our group grew and as different people attempted to assist Betty and me to prepare ourselves, I felt a need to be alone with my bride. I took her hand and led her to a small balcony outside the room we occupied. As she and I talked, we glanced up toward the capitol building, a handsome and truly unique state landmark. I vividly remember nodding toward the capitol, then looking directly into her eyes, and saying, "I'm going to take you there." I obviously meant I would do so by becoming the next governor. It was a bold statement and certainly made on the spur of the moment. She remembers that moment, and I remember that she smiled.

When I made that statement, I had not the slightest inkling of all the events and circumstances that would have to occur in my favor for that to happen. I had not begun to think beyond the primary race for the nomination other than to continue to feel that John Jay Hooker would be my Democrat opponent. I did believe that Hooker was unpopular with many in his party because of the race he had run against Governor Ellington in 1966 in their primary. There was no way for me to gauge the intensity of those feelings, but I knew there were Democrats who just couldn't take him. I rather innocently continued to believe that I was doing the right thing for the right reasons and that we could make it all happen. That was nothing but pure faith and hope at work.

The time arrived for our party to go to the capitol building. A Shelby County Republican friend who had somehow become a state employee and knew his way around was designated to drive my car up the hill and onto the grounds. When we arrived, he stopped the car at the north end of the building, although we were scheduled to enter on the west side. He explained that he'd better let us out where we were because if he were seen driving us, he might lose his job! We exited the car as requested. I'm glad Betty was a witness because I might later have thought I misinterpreted what he said! I had to assume that's the way politics was played.

Our group numbered twenty-five or thirty individuals, most of whom had never seen the capitol building nor had been inside its walls, including my wife. We climbed the steps and entered the hallway of the second floor, that level being the one on which the governor's executive suite was located. Gayle and Julie were very excited. Chuck had driven to Nashville from Washington and Lee University at Lexington, Virginia. My heart was pumping a little faster than usual, and it wasn't from climbing the capitol steps! Having all my family present helped very much.

Inside, we mingled in the poorly lighted capitol halls as the hour of 11:30 a.m. rapidly approached. The appointed time came and passed. The busload of supporters from Memphis had not arrived. At some point, Steve Sharp notified us that the press people who were waiting outside where microphones and speakers had been set up were getting restless and anxious for something to happen. Saturday, for the press, was normally a slow news day, and these reporters were apparently anxious to get on with their personal interests. The anxiety level rose even higher.

Feeling we could delay no longer, our group exited the building onto the veranda where media people and a few curiosity seekers plus my friends gathered around the podium and microphones. It was a very small gathering. Among the curious was Maclin P. Davis,

Jr., a friend of Harry Wellford's. He later became a close friend. Congressman Kuykendall made some remarks and then introduced me. I stepped forward and spoke. The remarks were as follows:

> *It is appropriate that we should come here today to the heart of Tennessee's state government to launch our campaign, not only to win an election, but to talk about a plan to revitalize our state.*
>
> *The old politics of Tennessee has outlived its day. What do I mean by "old politics"? By old politics, I mean the process by which our state has remained divided while those in political power have played one section against another for their own personal political gain. For example, I know that the people in West Tennessee are just as interested in industrial development as the people in Middle and East Tennessee. I know that the people of Middle Tennessee are just as interested in practical and economical educational facilities as people in East and West Tennessee. And I know that the people in East Tennessee are just as interested in fast, safe highways as those in Middle and West Tennessee. I have traveled the width and breadth of this state and talked with the people who are living with these problems.*
>
> *I find this process of government unworthy of the people of this state and utterly without regard for the future. People have paid a high price and gotten little for it. In fact, our rich potential as a leader among the states has not yet been envisioned, much less achieved.*
>
> *The secret of the greatness of American government has been that men like Washington, Jefferson, Jackson, Lincoln, and Eisenhower invested their talents and vision in unifying, rather than dividing, our people. Most of our problems have come from the weakness in an assumption that one man, clutching at the reins of a small team of workers gathered closely around him, could get the job done.*
>
> *Let's face the facts. The political system as it has been operated in Tennessee is not meeting the demands of today. It is not offering us the promise which we have every right to expect from leaders of our government for ourselves and our children.*
>
> *We live in an area which has the natural and human*

resources and climate to make it a veritable paradise. And yet, these great assets are not being developed as they should be. In fact, we are barely holding our own in economic development and Tennessee ranks 45th of the 50 states in per capita income. Why? One reason is that the leadership of our state government has failed to stimulate our growth and development.

This review of our situation is hardly pleasant, but it is an honest and frank statement of our situation as I see it today. What can I as governor do about this situation?

We must strive to overcome the handicap imposed by our thinking that this state because of three distinct geographies should be considered three separate segments. With modern transportation and communications, this is backward thinking, and it cripples our great potential.

My first act as governor will be to issue an order to remove the signs that welcome visitors to the Three States of Tennessee from our borders and replace them with signs which welcome visitors to the Great State of Tennessee. We must be one Tennessee.

With the changing of the signs must come a change in the hearts and minds of the people of this state. I would further see to it that the state government takes the lead in projecting the new image of a united Tennessee to ourselves, our neighboring states, and the nation.

Having participated in building the new Republicanism of Tennessee which produced national leaders such as Howard Baker, Bill Brock, Jimmy Quillen, John Duncan, and Dan Kuykendall, I know from past experience that the same principles of sound organization and common sense can be applied to state government. When we do this we will create the climate that is so desperately needed to get this state moving on the right track.

The most essential act of the new administration will be to restructure our state government to make it more responsive to the needs of the people, and make it operate more effectively with the resources at hand.

We must constantly press for more rapid industrial growth and for development of those industries, services, and sciences which will provide a balanced economy and add to the quality of life. And we must employ the salesmanship necessary to attract new opportunities to all areas of Tennessee without favor.

Growth in the high level industries that create good jobs and good citizens is dependent upon an educational system which stresses quality at all levels of learning. Industrial and educational growth is fostered by the proper learning environment.

We hear a lot these days about pollution. The pollution of our environment, our rivers and streams—the very air we breathe. As governor I would immediately launch a program that would put Tennessee among the leaders in putting the president's anti-pollution programs into actual being. In my opinion, however, there is another kind of pollution that is more devastating than environmental pollution. I am speaking of the pollution of the minds and bodies of our children by pornography and drug pushers and the malcontent extreme radical element who are allowed to spew their venom of hate and irresponsibility at will. This type of pollution which is poisoning the minds of our children and youth is the responsibility of all fair-minded citizens and certainly a responsibility of state government just as environmental pollution is. As your governor, I intend to see that it is corrected.

It is my feeling that the breakdown of law and order and excessive permissiveness have allowed this to get out of hand. As your governor, I intend to see that this is corrected.

I recognize the limits of any one man. I know that the great task here is one that will require the skill and dedication of thousands of interested citizens. It would be my purpose to make this opportunity available to willing minds and hands. I would also give it the administrative direction as the occasion would suggest.

In keeping with my strong faith in the people of Tennessee, I would like to announce that I will immediately appoint a task force, a representative group of the most talented and skilled business, professional, educational, and labor leaders of this state to help me research the depths of our problems and come up with specific programs which we will unfold as the campaign develops. This is not a one-man job, and I intend to recruit an army of volunteers to help restore the Volunteer spirit of the state of Tennessee.

On these premises I announce my candidacy for governor of the state of Tennessee. In undertaking this great mission, I prayerfully ask for God's blessing and earnestly seek the support of all Tennesseans from the highlands of Bristol to the banks of the Mississippi River. Thank you.

The audience was much smaller than we had planned. The absence of our Memphis bus with passengers made a huge difference in what we had wanted the impression to be on this first political outing. My remarks lasted no more than ten minutes. Near the end or perhaps just after I finished speaking, the bus rounded the turn at the southwest corner of the capitol building and its occupants spilled forth. It must have been a confusing event for the media people, but it was a blessed event for me and those who had planned it. The vehicle displayed Dunn signs and victory messages. Those who made the journey were jubilant and excited. The bus was late because it suffered a mechanical problem that took some time to solve.

Following my speech, several reporters asked questions, which I answered as forthrightly as possible. A story in the *Jackson Sun* reported the event. In response to a question about a general election opponent, I stated that it would probably be John Hooker and I believed I would have the best chance to defeat him. Another question was, what was my reason for believing I could win? My response was that I would emerge on top because of my age, health, vigor, love for Tennessee, common sense, good judgment, faith in a higher power, and faith in the wonderful people of the state of Tennessee.

The event itself went well in spite of the early absence of a good crowd, and it was fairly reported across the state by newspapers and television commentators. Our team was pleased with the results. At the least, people in all sectors of the state had an opportunity to read of my intentions.

My dental office received phone calls from patients who wondered about my future availability to serve their dental needs. We did not send out an announcement of my pending absence from the practice. Dr. Dan Morgan and the staff prepared themselves to serve in my stead. There were a number of patients who were in the process of being treated. It was necessary that I follow through in meeting those needs. I saw my last patient early in May, at which time I seated two gold inlays. Everyone in my office was excited about the events taking place politically.

I didn't say good-bye to the profession. I must have thought, however, how grateful I was to all those who had helped me build a respectable and rewarding dental practice. Betty and I paid a huge price to get my dental education. I had never worked so hard to achieve a goal. Betty lived through every step of the way with me. She began beautifully to raise our baby boy, keep me in starched and ironed dental smocks, feed us, and incredibly, teach second grade at Grahamwood Elementary School. Those were demanding days, and we were relieved when they ended with my graduation and receipt of a Doctor of Dental Surgery degree. I took comfort knowing I could always return to my dental practice if necessary.

CHAPTER NINE

COMING TO GRIPS WITH THE TASK

A Strategy for the Times

In Memphis, organizational, fund-raising, and recruiting efforts for the campaign moved ahead rapidly. A simple strategy, well established in my mind but not yet put on paper, began to take shape. My campaign had to be basically focused on Shelby County–West Tennessee and East Tennessee. The middle part of the state was not fertile ground for me. Dan Kuykendall began to study past campaign numbers, and we talked about them consistently during our strategy discussions. Dan was an apt student of primary and general election results by the numbers. He reviewed past primary election results and began to set numerical goals I would have to achieve. Each of us involved in strategy realized Shelby County would have to produce an historically high primary vote.

One number that stuck in my thoughts was the nearly 100,000 vote total that Hubert Patty, the relatively unknown East Tennessee Republican candidate for governor, polled in the 1962 general election against Democrat Frank Clement. As I have mentioned, I knew those votes for Patty were pure Republican expressions of opposition to any Democrat. I was convinced that a strong Republican candidate for governor, nonexistent for fifty years, could do much better in November.

Kuykendall was aware of the votes Patty had received, and his mind was at work on other numbers. We learned that various estimates of the Republican primary vote for 1970 ranged from 175,000 to 350,000. Considering the history of Republican voting in heavily Democrat Middle Tennessee, where many counties did not conduct Republican primaries, we knew for certain I would have to do well in the East against my four opponents. We would certainly have to turn out a record-breaking Shelby Republican primary vote, and I'd have to get a big piece of it.

Telephone calls and messages from other counties began to flow into our headquarters. Offers of help, requests for visits, invitations to events, and questions about my candidacy were encouraging. It was obvious early on that the phrase "Winfield Who?" would be uttered often and printed in many news articles. It was a logical question, and I think it helped me to establish my identity because "Winfield Who?" was bandied about as a sort of motto.

Several friends who had close connections with professionals in the public relations business came forward. Photos were taken of me and my family, including Christy the dog. Mock-ups for pamphlets and brochures were created for careful examination and serious consideration. Funds were scarce, and nothing could be wasted. Words were carefully chosen to convey a short message and brief introduction of the candidate. The word *whirlwind* never seemed to be so appropriate in trying to describe the events that were taking place.

We discovered that the Dunn name could be used in a variety of ways for identification purposes. "It Can Be Dunn—It Must Be Dunn—It Will Be Dunn!" was a play on words someone came up with, and it stuck. The name was easy to spell and easy to remember.

One stroke of good fortune grew out of my friendship with a fine human being named Ward Archer. Ward had an established but still growing public relations firm. I went to his offices for discussions as to how he could be helpful to our efforts because he had expressed interest. Limited finances were a real concern that he understood from the beginning. Regardless, he agreed to do as much as possible with the understanding that payment for services rendered would happen if we began to have a flow of cash contributions. During the remainder of April and all of May, June, July, and August, Ward Archer and Associates became another of those blessed happenings that gave my candidacy the visibility it needed.

Planning and strategy were among the highest of priorities. Harry Wellford took charge, and we talked regularly. Harry was still winding down his law practice in anticipation of being confirmed a federal district judge. He devoted much of his time to the campaign. His wife, Katherine, was a source of good advice to each of us and to Betty.

My friend Jim McGehee took charge of campaign finances with the skill and intelligence that had led him to become a highly respected and successful mortgage banker and insurance executive in Memphis. No one word better describes Jim than the word *organized*. The fact that my ambitions aroused in him the commitment he demonstrated throughout the entire campaign has never ceased to amaze and gratify me. The same could be said of others, to be sure. The contribution of time and energy given by Jim was awesome. His role was pivotal. A letter he wrote to "MESSRS. RACHELS, KOPALD AND DUNN" dated April 16, 1970, bears that out. It read as follows:

Gentlemen:

I have on several occasions discussed with you individually several matters of concern to me. These matters relate primarily to finance and in my remarks to follow I will attempt to be brief but thorough.

Speaking generally, I feel that it is essential to immediately designate one, but certainly not more than two persons, who would assume responsibility for determining if a particular project is essential to Winfield's candidacy. Once this decision has been made then, and only then, is there a need to consider our financial condition. Thus far the reverse of this has been the practice in that I have received numerous calls from numerous well intended workers wanting to know if we have sufficient funds on hand to do thus and so. I have, frankly, attempted to hedge my answer and steer them back to those whom I considered to be in a better position to determine just how vital their project is to the overall effort. I guess what I'm trying to say is "let's get organized." No item of expenditures should be approved unless it has first been run through the campaign chairman who in turn must, of course, concur as to the value of the effort or the results hoped to be obtained through a particular effort. In the absence of the chairman it would perhaps be well to have a back up vice chairman who would act in the chairman's absence. If this firming up of our organizational structure is not done promptly it will in my opinion inevitably lead to duplication of effort and expense, neither of which we can afford. Accordingly, I will hope that our efforts could be a little more tightly structured administratively and organization wise. Further, in this connection, it seems essential that we have both a secretary and administrative assistant for Winfield in order that appointments, appearances, etc. could be coordinated during Winfield's absence. Without stenographic and administrative assistance something as simple as coordinating Winfield's visit to the National Bank of Commerce with Pete Norfleet becomes a needless chore.

Any information concerning our financial condition, contributors, etc. will be instantly available to any one of you gentlemen who has need of it. For security and other reasons, however, my office force is under strict orders not to give any information to anyone over the telephone unless I have first authorized it.

My office knows at all times how to reach me and I am seldom gone for longer than an hour or two at a time. In addition Kopie has made the suggestion that perhaps I open a second account with a separate depository in order that inquiries to the banks concerning our finances become somewhat more complicated. I would like to have the benefit of the group's thinking on this suggestion.

Finally, I would like to expand the next and all subsequent financial statements to include an item entitled "authorized but unpaid expenses." This obviously would require some close coordination in that as efforts or activities are approved and the expense estimated they would at that time be entered into the financial statement under the above item. This would eliminate the obvious problem of "float" whereby various efforts are underway simultaneously each with its own expense for which no advance budgeting has been done. These various items could be listed as a foot note to the financial statement in order that each of us could visually spot check them at all times.

I am available to discuss these thoughts at any time.

Cordially, [signed] Jim

The kind of insight and planning reflected in a letter from a solid businessman who had never been involved in any political excursion, much less one that began from "under the grassroots," was what made our efforts such a remarkable adventure.

Memphis Press-Scimitar political writer Null Adams, in his Political Notebook column, wrote the following: "GOP leaders are pointing out, with a great deal of enthusiasm, that this is the first year that the Republicans have had a primary for the Governor's nomination, and this time there are four candidates." He went on to point out that two of the gubernatorial candidates had budgeted $100,000 for the race. He named Hooker and Jarman. Interest was building.

It was firmly understood that I would need to spend a vast amount of the next ninety days in the Republican-rich East Tennessee region. I learned that a routine political practice called for the Republican chairmen of various counties to designate a local party leader to be the contact for each statewide candidate, if needed. That designated person, if acceptable to the candidate, would assist him in meeting the "right" people. After that, it was up to the candidate. I knew I promptly needed to contact each county chairman. I also needed to get to know that person and his wife or her husband, make my case, and do all I could to gain silent support. Chairmen were supposed to be neutral in the primary. That, I learned, was not always the case. I also eventually learned that if the chairman could not find a respectable Republican to take me in tow, he or she often selected just anyone who would agree to help me. More than once the person chosen was not even an avowed Republican!

The first three Congressional Districts at that time consisted of thirty-three counties. The region was commonly referred to as East Tennessee. However, I quickly learned that, in the minds of many residents, it was further divided into East and Upper East Tennessee. Upper East, as well as much of the remainder of East Tennessee, was historically considered overwhelmingly Republican in its senti-ments. That identity was a product of emotions and loyalties during and after the Civil War. Having been raised in Mississippi, I knew that most white and black people who cared about politics were not only Democrats—they were Roosevelt Democrats. I looked forward to being with folks who revered Abraham Lincoln, as I always had.

By the time I began to make my presence felt in counties where I was nothing more than a name, my three major opponents had already been there and either had been provided a party contact or had begun to organize with other associates. Bill Jenkins had the advantage of fellow legislators helping him get set up in their districts. He was already well known in Upper East Tennessee. Mr. Jarman, immediate past CEO of Genesco, had the benefit of his company's manufacturing facilities and retail outlets scattered across the state. That was a big help for him as he organized in the primary and signed up volunteers he already knew and trusted. His initial strength in Middle Tennessee put him out front there, but it was not numerically powerful in the primary because there were so few Republican votes. Although I had to start from "scratch" in the East, I was grateful that being a West Tennessean seemed to give me an advantage with people in that section of the state. My argument for East and West cooperation in races involving the U.S. Senate and the governorship seemed to make sense to many. Claude Robertson did not appear to have made much progress in the West, early on. He was popular in Knoxville and that immediate area. He also had an advantage in being supported by a number of Baker people across the state.

Gearing up to build an organization and gain some identification in East Tennessee, we were extremely fortunate to gain access to Memphis-based private aircraft transportation. Alex "Judge" Maddox was a dealer for Mack Trucks and had a network of business relationships in several parts of the state. He was an excellent pilot. His wife, Barbara, was a member of Betty's bridge club, and we were good friends. He flew a twin engine airplane, and he was to save me countless hours of travel time during the next three months.

Help also came from a Memphis friend named Ewing Carruthers, an insurance executive. He owned a twin Bonanza airplane that on occasion he offered for my use. There was no way I could have afforded to compensate these men for the use of their aircraft, and it was not expected. Each made flights across the state, and they made every effort to schedule their business trips to coincide with my planned travels. I will forever be in their debt.

Both Betty and I had obtained our private pilot licenses in 1968, and we understood what was involved in operating non-commercial aircraft. We were comfortable with that mode of transportation, and we placed great value on having access to that means of getting around. Commercial airline travel within the state was limited, but it became useful many times as we moved along.

From the beginning of the official campaign, travel scheduling and networking with a growing number of contacts in the West and East became the chief responsibility of Carolyn Weins under Harry Wellford's direction. She was assisted by friends who created a volunteer support staff to assist her. The campaign headquarters space was adequate to house a variety of work areas, and it literally became a second home base to me. We no longer needed Dr. Rachels's office. It had served a needed purpose for several weeks.

With a permanent location, our headquarters became a gathering place for a wide variety of people. Print, equipment, and novelty salesmen were ever present. Telephone technicians were constantly coming and going because we were adding new capacity at a steady pace. The most unique visitors were housewives, mothers, dental patients, Sunday school classmates, and family members of friends who came by to offer assistance. The beauty of such people wanting to be involved was that 99 percent of them had never been in a political campaign headquarters before, much less had their "own dog" in a political fight! From what I could gather as I came and went, these wonderful citizens were thrilled to have an opportunity to be a part of something political that they felt good about. There was an aura of excitement with what was happening, even in the start-up stages. It seemed to have the potential to be seriously contagious. It bolstered my spirits.

My visits to campaign headquarters were always brief. As the process evolved, a typical week for me began early, usually around 5:00 a.m. on Monday morning, when I was picked up by Rufus Powell. Becoming more organized in late April, Rufus would be given a schedule of events and meetings lined up through work the previous week by Wellford and Weins. Often we headed for the airport to fly to East Tennessee. Less frequently, but consistently, we drove to a destination in West Tennessee.

In addition to meeting key people in various counties, being ushered around meeting other people who had been lined up for such visits, speaking at some small gathering of Republicans or a civic club, we always made three other efforts. We drove to the local radio station seeking to gain a recorded interview to be played later as a news item or feature for local listeners. Occasionally, I was lucky enough to have a live interview on the spot. Small town radio stations often had much flexibility in their programming. We also visited the local daily or weekly newspaper publisher. I began to get a feel for the process. Quite often I'd get a picture taken for use with a story in the next edition or for placement in the publications files. And finally, we never failed to visit the courthouse and city hall where that was appropriate. Those kinds of visits were effective in helping me to become a part of the local "talk."

It was stimulating and exciting to meet new people and to offer them my justification for being in the race. My energy level was high. I never ceased to be grateful for people willing to get interested in what I was doing and for the time they gave me. The people who began to associate with our efforts represented a variety of backgrounds and standings in their communities. Frequently, we were referred to people in other communities by good friends or supporters in Memphis who felt such people had the ability to help me politically. Other times, we were referred to people by the Republican county chairman. These were designated contacts—a courtesy of the chairman. At times these designees worked out well. Often, however, circumstances would lead us in other directions to establish our contact people and supporters in a county. It was a hit-or-miss process. We took what we could get and were grateful for it.

Rufus and I, accompanied by some newfound supporter or a more established friend, often traveled countless miles within a county looking for just the right person to enlist in our effort. I learned that one person often influenced the voting habits of dozens of family members, employees, and friends. Time after time we found ourselves on a wild goose chase, either just missing the person we sought or being turned down for one reason or another. Occasionally, we hit pay dirt. I discovered there were many shakers and movers around. Some became solid friends and supporters, but many others were determined to keep their political powder dry early in the game. Often, little or no Republican organization had ever existed in the area. We were learning how to become politically organized, county by county.

Our objectives were clearly in mind. We wanted new friends. We needed new friends. It was a first-time experience for many of them as well as for us. Those initial contacts had to be cultivated after I moved on. We supplied campaign headquarters with names, addresses, and phone numbers. That was Rufus's job. It was the job of the folks in Memphis to keep the relationship alive, well, and growing, we hoped, into an organized effort over the next ninety days.

Very few entrenched, hard-line, veteran political types made themselves available. In West Tennessee, the Democrat label was too much a part of their lives. They were very cautious about any association with a Republican candidate for governor. Most often the backbone for what became a Dunn organization in a West Tennessee county consisted of people who were completely new to the political game. We met so many good, well-intentioned people. Their interest was usually kindled by the exciting thought of being close to a likable fellow who just might become a governor of the state. It was new, it was different, and it was intriguing. We were helping to create citizen politicians, the very best kind, I believed.

I began to discover that there were small pockets of Republicans scattered across heavily Democrat West Tennessee, many from old Whig areas. Most often, these people were descendants of Civil War Union soldiers who had chosen to settle in rural areas and who clung to their Republican or non-Democrat loyalties. They were devoted to their political heritage, just as the overwhelming number of West Tennesseans were devoted to their Democrat forebears. Mr. Carl Ballou of Milan in Gibson County was one of those. He became my friend and strong supporter. He was an elder statesman, a lifelong Republican, and a man highly respected by everyone who knew him. Mr. Ballou helped me greatly throughout the area.

Henderson County was a Republican stronghold with a long Whig heritage. I was invited to speak at the party county convention in the county seat of Lexington. It was a good and successful opportunity to make new friends and supporters. I learned that none of my opponents had as yet attempted to get organized there. Henderson County was surrounded by counties dominated by Democrat officeholders and voters. Many of its people were fiercely proud of their Republican or non-Democrat heritage.

As I met West Tennessee Republicans, I was told time and time again of the struggles they constantly experienced dealing with Democrats. All state jobs were filled by Democrats. County election commissions were dominated by Democrats. Courthouses and mayors' offices were filled with Democrats. I began to feel that their enthusiasm for me was as much or more a desire for a little political power, as it was to help me because I was such a nice, enthusiastic fellow Republican. Regardless of the reasons, we welcomed their help. I realized that being the only West Tennessee candidate made a big difference in their thinking. I also began to realize that I was going to have to get many of those Democrat votes, if not in the primary, at least in the general election.

In the East where Republican voters and officeholders often represented the same kind of political strength and longevity Democrats enjoyed in the middle and western sections, things were frequently quite different. Not all East Tennessee counties were controlled by Republicans, however. Many counties had a reasonable balance between the two parties, and power shifted from time to time. A large part of the electorate in a number of counties was labeled "independent." The Republican influence was strong as evidenced by members of that party occupying the First and Second Congressional District seats for years. No one but a Republican had ever represented the Second District. Since 1962 Republican Bill Brock had represented the Third District.

In 1970, the First Congressional District represented the strongest concentration of Republican votes but not necessarily the greatest number. It was also the district most forcefully dominated politically by one person, Congressman James Quillen, who was first elected in 1962. I discovered on my initial visit to Johnson City for the John Diehl reception that Jimmy Quillen was in charge. The telephone call I received from an individual who had read the erroneous newspaper report in which I announced my candidacy sent a strong message that I needed immediately to touch base with the congressman. Our subsequent conversation that morning convinced me he would not abide being ignored. The congressman's tone was cold and clear. I took note. Later, word came down through verbal messages that Quillen didn't want to see that smiling, lanky dentist and his sawed-off lawyer friend in the First District without prior clearance from him! That message was not in print, merely word of mouth. Harry Wellford, the other target of the comment, was not tall in stature, but he clearly overshadowed its source. We did not ignore the message, but we moved on undeterred and in high spirits.

Congressman John Duncan of the Second District was a man of

great character who was hugely popular among his constituency. He was also a person of good humor and a determination to be fair to all Republicans engaged in primary contests. The congressman had been first elected in 1962 after serving as mayor of Knoxville. His entire family were avid Republicans.

On one occasion early in the primary, the four major GOP candidates for governor were invited to a country picnic and rally in a county adjoining Knox County. The crowd was large, the food was good, and Congressman John Duncan was the center of attention. When the time for "speaking" arrived and with the candidates on a raised platform, someone decided that the candidates for governor would, in alphabetical order, make brief remarks. I was first, and I was also behind schedule to get to my next meeting.

I thanked one and all, announced my hope to be the winning candidate in August, and asked for their help. At that stage in the race I was not at all well known. I apologized for having to leave early for another meeting. Then, I had an inspiration of sorts. I complimented the people for their good judgment in electing such an outstanding man to be their congressman. I remarked that I admired him greatly. I especially admired his last name because, if it is repeated slowly, it says "DUN—CAN!" I shook hands all around, left the platform, and went out of the building to some laughter and good applause. The congressman and I chuckled over that incident many times in later years.

CHAPTER TEN

EAST AND WEST

Mixing It Up

My first experience with a Tennessee folk festival occurred in late April. I had been contacted by a young lawyer who lived in Loudon. His name was Bill Russell. He had heard about my candidacy and called Memphis headquarters because he was interested in supporting me. He had been active in the Young Republican organization and thought he could be helpful. It was my first contact with anyone from Loudon County, and I welcomed it. Bill suggested the Festival of the Ramp, a long-standing event held in the Cocke County community of Cosby on April 30, would be a good occasion for me to get in some East Tennessee politicking. The year before, he said, the festival honoring a wild leek called the ramp that made its appearance in early spring drew 13,000 people. Mountain people from the earliest days of the Appalachian settlers had used the ramp in cooking and for medicinal purposes. I was told that if a person consumed a ramp, the pores of the skin of that person smelled of the ramp for several days. It was part of the lore in the area that schoolchildren who had eaten ramps were frequently excused from school for several days to let the fragrance pass.

We scheduled the date, and I met Bill Russell at an appointed time in Loudon. We then drove northeast, getting acquainted along the way. Bill was a topflight person and easy to be with. We eventually arrived at the site of the festival being held on Kineauvista Hill. The day was rainy and cool. The countryside was mountainous and magnificent. A tent had been erected on a gentle slope of a hill that looked like a mountain to me. Cars were parked across the broad expanse of meadowland. There were many people present that morning. It was by far the largest gathering in one place I had attended up to that point. Barbecued pork and chicken were being cooked, bake sales were underway in row after row of booths, and folks were milling around in spite of the dampness. The mingled odors of fresh mountain air, large drops of melted fat falling on hot charcoals, freshly baked delicacies, and dew-dampened human beings flavored the excitement I felt. It seemed to stir my conscious awareness that I was in an almost mystical setting. As a "flatlander" I felt good being there. We immediately began moving into the crowd with Bill as my guide. I discovered that he didn't know many of the folks we were meeting, but as an East Tennessean, he probably felt pretty much at home. I shook every hand that was offered as I attempted to identify myself.

There were other politicians working the crowd. Bill Brock and I crossed paths several times. Candidate Bill Jenkins was moving around energetically. Several local and state legislative candidates were present. When the time came to recognize and crown the Ramp Princess, a local girl previously selected for that honor, I saw Congressman Jimmy Quillen standing by to congratulate, kiss, and crown the young Princess. The festival chairman acted as master of ceremonies. He was also the president of the local Ruritan Club that sponsored the event. All candidates were invited onto the platform to be introduced. My brief introduction was a high point because, although we were not permitted to make remarks, that was the greatest group exposure I had experienced up until that time.

Earlier, I had been offered a taste of the ramp with the promise of a local person that the "delicacy" held the revitalizing power of a spring tonic. Before I could summon the courage to take a bite, Bill Russell took me by the arm and, thankfully, led me away from the enthusiastic fellow who had no idea that I was an aspiring candidate.

Following the ceremonies, with a light rain persisting and a low temperature setting in, Bill Russell and I took shelter in a small building near the outdoor platform there on the mountainside. We sat down in chairs along the wall of a single large room that was poorly lighted. I was chilled, but I was excited by the great opportunity I had just experienced. People were friendly, and I felt at ease among them. My adrenaline was running at a high rate.

As Bill and I sat talking, I noticed two people directly in front and to my left who were engaged in steady conversation. The two men were seated on bar stools at a counter. The voice of one seemed quite resonant. Although the lighting was not good, it quickly became apparent that the man nearest me was John Jay Hooker. He had not appeared on the platform to be introduced, apparently arriving late. I was surprised to see him. I stood, waited for a break in their conversation, then lightly tapped him on the shoulder and said hello. Without turning to look at me, he extended his hand for a quick shake. It was almost automatic, I thought. I greeted him by telling him that I was Winfield Dunn and I had looked forward to meeting him. As I mentioned my name, he suddenly swung around and gave me his complete attention.

Hooker also gave me a big smile and said he had looked forward to meeting me. The moment I looked directly at him and put the voice with the man, I was in awe. His face was almost bronzed, seemingly just off the beach at some sunny resort, his features were handsome, and I was very impressed with what I heard and saw. He struck me as movie star quality. We chatted pleasantly for a few moments, then parted, each wishing the other well. From his immediate reaction to the mention of my name, I felt he might have given some attention to my candidacy prior to our meeting.

As Bill and I exited the building and headed for his Chevrolet, I glanced over to my right in time to see three long black automobiles, probably Cadillacs, exiting the grounds through a gate and onto the highway. It was the Hooker party. At that point, my awe melted into irony as I pictured myself, a practically unknown candidate for statewide office, getting into a modest car with my new young lawyer friend, watching the entourage of my probable opponent do what I thought was a grand three-vehicle exit. The stark contrast of that picture in my mind was not reassuring.

On the drive back to Loudon, Bill and I had much to talk about. He was not impressed by Hooker. He thought I handled myself well with people, and he fully committed himself to help in my campaign. I was very grateful and said so. I also shared with Bill my belief from early on that Hooker would be my opponent in the general election. Bill Russell, I concluded, had special qualities.

My thoughts were sober as I reflected on the Ramp Festival. There were several thousand potential voters in attendance. If I was to complete the race as I had committed to do, there was no way for me to allow myself to be discouraged by a possible opponent I was not even running against at that time. I had many, many miles to travel, literally and figuratively. Being in Cocke County, a good Republican stronghold, and not having a single person there committed to my campaign with the primary election little more than ninety days away, I knew there was much work to do. At that point, I clearly realized what I was up against. That first festival experience showed me the darker side of the venture I had undertaken. Even so, by the time we arrived back at Loudon and Bill had pledged his support and loyalty, I felt better. I could not, however, shake off my impression that Mr. Hooker would be a formidable opponent for anyone. I also felt good about Bill Russell and his potential to help me succeed in my quest. His was an area of the state in which I needed much help.

As the month of May rolled around, two of Betty's good friends proposed a game plan that fit perfectly into our efforts to get organized as soon and effectively as possible. There was so little time before the August primary and so much ground to cover. Following my announcement as a candidate, a number of invitations from rural West Tennessee came to Betty to attend meetings composed mostly of women. She accepted each one of the opportunities, although she was concerned that she might not do a good job. She decided that, while she wasn't knowledgeable about political matters, she could comfortably talk about her husband and what he stood for. My wife did a great job and became increasingly effective as her experience grew.

A game plan was developed for Sara Jane Scott and Isabel Strong to become Betty's co-campaign managers. They created the Betty Dunn for First Lady Committee. These wonderful friends set up their own organized effort to decide what invitations to accept, to encourage invitations to coffees for ladies only, to concentrate on West Tennessee, and to help my wife fill in for functions that I could not attend. Wherever Betty traveled, always by automobile, one or both ladies were with her. Often they went in caravan with a number of her other friends. They always worked closely with my staff of people, especially Harry Wellford and Carolyn Weins. That game plan allowed me to spend more time in the eastern part of the state where I had to get serious numbers of primary votes. Betty filled in for me time after time.

The month of May continued to be a time of trial and error in putting an organization together that would support the emerging, full-blown primary campaign. Many of the individuals that were a part of the effort have been named. Many, many others will go unnamed but not unappreciated. Without their efforts, their contributions of funds, energy, and advice, the level of intensity in campaigning that peaked in early August could not have happened. The activities I had pursued during my four years as county chairman resulted in support and assistance from a number of West Tennessee friends I never expected to call on.

Many people of Memphis and Shelby County were soon to become interested in the political process at a level of intensity that was highly unusual. Two Memphians had become candidates seeking the governor's office. Robert Taylor, a prominent attorney, had announced his candidacy in the Democrat primary. I, of course, was the other Memphian. Each of us was treated with respect and seriousness from the beginnings of our efforts by the mayor of Memphis, Henry Loeb, a popular, conservative, and somewhat controversial leader of city government. He endorsed me in the Republican primary. That recognition certainly helped. Everyone in my organization focused intently on Memphis and Shelby County. The New Guard Republican leaders with whom I had worked so closely for nearly ten years became a local force I could never have designed. They were there for me. Their influence, throughout the county, made a huge difference in what we were trying to do.

Bob James and his wife, Pat, were invaluable friends. Pat was a leader among the Republican women, and her skill in mobilizing volunteers to get jobs done, both in the headquarters offices and in the neighborhoods, was amazing. Bob had twice run for Congress. He knew the city of Memphis as well as anyone could, having canvassed practically every neighborhood in the county, door to door. The impact of their efforts in the campaign could never be measured.

Special meetings began to occur in Memphis, not by planning or design but spontaneously through the energy and interest of people who had never been involved in politics. Friends from the dental profession, our church, our social life, and our former political involvement became enthused over the idea of "one of their own" being a candidate for public office at the highest level of state government. The gatherings were sometimes called "start-up" meetings.

One such meeting at Billy Rachels's office included a discussion of the need for some youthful, enthusiastic "troopers" to campaign throughout Memphis, Shelby County, and West Tennessee communities. Several of the ladies present thought a group of lively twelve- to eighteen-year-old girls gaily decked out in patriotic colors would be an attention-getting means of supporting candidate Dunn. Pat James came up with the name "The Dunn Dollies." Joanne Fleming, a take-charge lady of the first order, was asked to head up this facet of the campaign. She was delighted to do so. Take charge she did, and the results were amazing.

Word spread about the idea for the Dunn Dollies, and soon, according to Joanne, we had seventy adorable girls from ages twelve to eighteen on hand. In no time at all, the group had grown to over 115 for the Dunn Dolly Memphis Chapter. The qualifications for participating were to love campaigning for this candidate, cheerleading, and singing jingles while distributing flags, balloons, literature, bumper stickers, and buttons.

During the months of July and August, several other chapters of the Dunn Dollies were formed in other cities. The girls supported themselves by purchasing their own uniforms . . . red, white, and blue, of course.

The Dunn Dolly organization became serious business to Joanne Fleming and her associates. The young ladies were directed to perform several dance routines by Barbara Somers. The girls elected officers and a sergeant at arms. Our daughter Gayle, age fifteen, was an enthusiastic participant. Our daughter Julie was too young but later joined a group called "Young Dunn Dollies."

As the number of participants grew, Joanne was wise enough to divide them into teams with captains designated to communicate quickly by phone. Many times, as the campaign progressed, they had sudden requests to make appearances at yard parties. They participated in fund-raising activities as well. Joanne recalls one event called "Dunn Dollies Dilly Dally," a fashion show held in the beautiful backyard of Barbara and Brewster Harrington in Memphis. The mark of Joanne Fleming was all over that one!

Saturdays became special campaign days for the Dollies, and they went in many directions as the weeks went by. They made all-day bus trips to Adamsville, Selmer, Ripley, Bolivar, and other communities in the Seventh, Eighth, and Ninth Congressional Districts and as far away as McMinnville. The Dollies would flood the town squares, greeting people with smiles and handing out "Dunn for Governor" materials. They were always warmly received. Many of their mothers helped by chaperoning on the trips out of town.

On days in Memphis, the Dollies scattered in large shopping centers such as Laurelwood and Southgate. It was a special experience for me standing outside department stores shaking hands and introducing myself as a candidate while the girls caught the attention of all as they did their dance routines and handed out buttons and bumper stickers.

The Dunn Dollies were a permanent fixture throughout the campaign. Chapters in Knoxville and Nashville were created with more mature ladies becoming involved. The original idea had a touch of genius about it. In Shelby County, there seemed to be a mystique that captured the imaginations not only of the girls, but also of parents, relatives, and friends across a broad spectrum of the population. The role Joanne Fleming played went far beyond the hopes and expectations of those of us who were attempting to mastermind the evolving campaign. People who had never dreamed of taking a hand in a political activity became intensely involved because of the Dollies.

The challenge before me was to keep focused on the importance of making headway in East Tennessee without appearing to be giving Shelby County less attention than it deserved. Both of these vote-rich areas warranted all the time I could spend there. The work that was done by loyal supporters at home, plus the exceptional results that Betty was getting wherever she went, was paying big dividends, especially in West Tennessee. That activity by others allowed me to spend a disproportionate amount of time introducing myself, making friends, and putting together groups of supporters in East Tennessee. Although there were many times that I put out my hand, only to have it rejected by the other person who was obviously not of my party or was a supporter of one of my Republican opponents, I continued to be enormously encouraged by the response I was getting from people. Two exceptional new friends were Dr. Carl Duerr and his wife, Shirley, of Crossville.

I was constantly on the move. Meanwhile, my Shelby County campaign committee met regularly under the leadership of Harry

Wellford. Included on a regular basis were McGehee, Spurrier, James, Donelson, Rachels, Schroeder, Dann, and Maddox. Jim Gates and Jack Craddock became increasingly involved. The two later became co-chairmen of the campaign in Shelby County. Bettie Davis became a valued campaign headquarters director working closely with Carolyn Weins. An incredibly hardworking pair of friends were Pat James and Ann Daniels. Ann's uncle was Jim Harwood, an executive with Conwood, Incorporated, whose Learjet we had used to transport Senator Dirksen. He helped greatly with the fund-raising. As momentum grew, a pattern began to take shape. A week of hard, relentless campaigning might end on a Saturday night or a Sunday, depending on distance traveled. Monday morning would be spent at the headquarters on Getwell where I met with Harry, his committee, or others. Usually by noon I was on my way somewhere with my shadow, Rufus Powell.

I made many trips by auto to counties west of the Tennessee River in the early days. Various counties had functions to which all Republican primary candidates were invited. There were party organizational meetings, belated Lincoln Day Dinners, and various civic club meetings I attended just to be introduced as a candidate.

I was invited by the Republican county chairman to attend a meeting of Republican women in a rural West Tennessee county. His wife was president of the women's group. That opportunity was added to my schedule, and on the appointed day Rufus Powell and I drove to the meeting being held in the county agricultural center. Shortly after the program got underway, I was introduced as the West Tennessee candidate for governor in the primary. There were no other Republican gubernatorial candidates present. Then came the introduction of the featured speaker by another visitor, Mrs. Lillie Hollobough of Nashville. She was president of the Davidson County Republican women's group.

Mrs. Hollobough, whom I did not know, graciously acknowledged my presence, then proceeded to introduce the program speaker, Dorothy Ritter. It was a fine introduction, done to perfection. I had never met Mrs. Ritter, but the moment I saw her and heard her speak her first few words, I knew I was in the presence of a true professional. Mrs. Ritter acknowledged my presence and then turned to Lillie Hollobough. Smiling, eyes sparkling, and dimpled cheeks mesmerizing her audience, she thanked Lillie for the "much too generous" introduction and reminded us, one and all, that the hand that holds the bouquet always retains the fragrance! I had never heard such a gracious and memorable response! Mrs. Ritter captured my attention and admiration, never to be lost. She also totally captured her audience that day.

When I learned that the guest speaker for the women's group would be Dorothy Ritter, the wife of Tex Ritter, the famous cowboy singing superstar, I could hardly believe it. Tex had been among my favorites since, as a little fellow, I first viewed him in Westerns on Saturdays in Meridian. I had been told that Ritter, at the time a resident of Tennessee after moving from California, had expressed an interest in being a candidate for the Republican nomination for the Senate seat held by Gore. That would put him in a contested primary with Bill Brock. After hearing Mrs. Ritter address the Republican women's group, I began to think more about Mr. Ritter's potential candidacy.

I had heard a rumor to the effect that Claude Robertson and Tex Ritter were soon to announce that they would run in the primary as a team. That had not seriously registered with me when I first received the news. After meeting Mrs. Ritter and being so impressed with her, my thoughts began to focus on what added strength it might give Robertson to be tied in with the cowboy superstar who was running for the Senate nomination. I concluded early in the process that they would appear separately on the ballot, and though my opponent might benefit some from association with a popular figure, the voter would still have to cast an individual vote for Robertson, not Ritter-Robertson.

We pressed on. The groundwork that had been laid by Baker and Kuykendall in their campaigns of 1964 and 1966 became a major potential resource in seeking out politically active individuals across the entire state. It would have been physically impossible to go into ninety-five different counties and find, from scratch, people who might consider me and my cause. Senator Baker was, so far as we knew, completely neutral in the primary, taking no side. That must have been disappointing to Claude Robertson, who was his state-wide campaign manager in 1966. Dan Kuykendall had no need to be neutral, being the congressman from my district. Harry Wellford's close relationship to Baker, having existed since early in their law careers, was invaluable as we sought out and often enlisted Baker people from various counties during those intense days leading up to the primary in August. Kuykendall had maintained valuable lists of contacts, especially in the Republican-rich areas of the state. Those names were available to me. My job was to travel night and day making every effort I could to meet and gain the confidence of such people.

I found myself caught up in a swirl of activities in Shelby County and surrounding areas that seemed to develop spontaneously. Groups were forming and labeling themselves with various names that identified their common business, professional, vocational, or political pursuits coupled with the concluding phrase "for Dunn." Farmers for Dunn, Democrats for Dunn, and Home Builders for Dunn were among the organizations where I was scheduled to have my picture taken with members. I took enormous pride in a Memphis group that labeled itself Dentists for Dunn.

A number of my hometown dental colleagues, among them Drs. Franklin Miller, Sewell McKinney, Thomas Cobb, Tom Pyron, P. D. Miller, Walter Sandusky, Roy Bourgoyne, and Ed Tillman, were actively engaged in writing their fellow dentists across the state to tell them about my candidacy and to encourage their active support for me in their communities. I became the beneficiary of active Dunn for Governor centers, which were simply dental offices all across the state. One amazing fact was that so many of those good professional people were willing to support me among their families, friends, and patients without knowing me personally. Our headquarters people were under pressure to provide the campaign literature that was requested in order to be dispersed from the various dental offices.

My fellow dentists in Memphis were effective in contributing and collecting from others financial contributions to support our efforts. During those hectic days as the primary campaign took on greater dimensions, I would occasionally hear about the ladies in my dental office who were among the many volunteers at headquarters. It is fair to say that the dental professionals of Tennessee were among the foremost valuable resources that developed for me during the primary. I knew that people trusted and respected their healthcare professionals. Their willingness to embrace my political cause, regardless of party in most cases, had to be enormously influential in making me a "real" person in the minds of many, many people who might otherwise have paid little attention to candidates in the early stages of a campaign leading to a general election in the fall. I attribute that attitude on the parts of people directly to their respect for and admiration of their personal dentists. My identity as a healthcare professional was a decided advantage in the contest at hand.

I felt very comfortable with that. At the very least, many people were perplexed and some quite amused to consider a dentist to be a viable candidate for an office as significant as that of governor. The subject gave ordinary, non-politically active people something to chuckle over.

I continued to repeat my sincere belief that a candidate for governor in that particular year had to be a West Tennessean if we were to stand a chance to outnumber the Democrats. A West Tennessean running for governor, I exhorted time after time, could make the difference not only in that race but in the Senate race as well, if East Tennessee did its part. No matter which part of the state I found myself in, the audience response to those words was positive. I discovered that the stronger I projected my voice, the more sincere and confident I sounded to the listener, the better the reaction was. Experience was teaching me how to speak effectively, and I couldn't help noticing that the things I truly believed came out of my mouth more convincingly.

The West Tennessee theory had an undeniable ring of logic that couldn't be shaken by any one of my opponents. I used that argument often, and I used it hard. As I increasingly found myself before an audience or on some sort of platform with one or more of the other candidates, I discovered that it helped the audience, and it helped me, if I told them why I believed I was a better choice.

At a rally in Covington one night every Republican candidate was present except Hubert Patty. Candidates for local and county offices were also present. We were seated facing the audience as the county chairman conducted the meeting. Each candidate for governor was prepared to make remarks limited to five minutes. This was the first time the four most viable candidates had appeared together.

The decision had been made to present the candidates in reverse alphabetical order. I had met Jenkins in Nashville during the legislative session. Mr. Jarman was practically a stranger, though we had visited by phone on one occasion and in Nashville once. I had not met Claude Robertson. I had shaken hands and mingled with all of the candidates before the meeting got underway.

Robertson spoke first. Being an attorney and having been a statewide spokesman for Howard Baker in 1966, his command of language and his good presentation came as no surprise. He obviously was a sound and respectable man. Nothing in his message that night struck me as memorable, but he did a good job presenting himself. He wasn't a spellbinder.

Bill Jenkins was next at the podium. I looked forward to hearing what he had to say and how he said it. He is blessed with a naturalness that is appealing and a sense of humor that people don't forget once they get a dose of it. I think his remarks focused on his experience in state government, his leadership position as the first Republican Speaker of the Tennessee House of Representatives in history, and the fact that he would be strongly supported by Republican East Tennessee. He was not critical of his opponents, as I recall, though I do believe he stressed "Doctor" as he referred to me. His aim may have been to draw attention to the distinction between us, he being a lawyer and therefore better equipped to deal with laws than a dentist. Maybe my imagination was working overtime.

Mr. Jarman was next. A highly successful business executive with all the credentials, his remarks focused on how he would wisely manage state government and get every taxpayer his or her money's worth. I recall that he stressed his strong Republicanism, claiming to have never voted for a Democrat. I took note of that comment. I also observed that Mr. Jarman was rather dry as a speaker, taking no opportunity to inject a little humor.

As the last speaker, with the benefit of having heard the others, I tried to introduce a little humor by dredging up a story that had made me laugh once upon a time and could offend no one. It had to do with old-time politics in another era. A candidate for governor stood in the crowd as his opponent from the stump accused this candidate of having a reputation ranging from having stuffed ballot boxes in the past to being a well-known home wrecker. As his aide moved forward to protest such slander, the candidate pulled him back, saying the speaker could probably prove every word of his accusation! I assured my audience that my politics was on a higher level. After a good laugh from the audience, I launched into the same routine of words and examples I had been using for weeks, trying to get my listeners to buy into my logic regarding East and West, governorship and Senate, fresh faces in politics and government, and down with the political monopoly that kept the government away from the people. That went well enough, but I had some time left.

Without too much prior thought, I launched into my opponents. Being respectful to each man, I first mentioned Mr. Jenkins and allowed as how, in spite of his experience to date, he was nevertheless mighty young to be entrusted with the profound responsibility of leading the state government. Even more important, I stressed, he was just from the wrong end of the state. In that particular year, in that particular race, the Republican Party needed a candidate for governor from West Tennessee. It would help the Senate candidate from the East.

As for Mr. Robertson, I argued that he, too, for reasons just mentioned, was from the wrong end of the state in the year 1970. I also noted that I had heard he planned to run as a team with Mr. Tex Ritter, candidate for the Senate nomination. I surely couldn't criticize his choice of a partner, but it just seemed to me that a man ought to stand on his own two feet and not lean on anyone else when seeking an office as important as governor of our state.

With Mr. Jarman, my thoughts were that, at age sixty-five, having led a great company and been compelled to retire because of age, he was a little older than what we needed in the way of a dynamic, energetic governor. In addition, I stated that Mr. Jarman, too, was from the wrong part of the state in 1970. How, I wondered, could a Republican from historically and heavily Democrat Middle Tennesseeever expect to get enough votes in a general election to win the governor's office?

My five minutes were up, the chairman adjourned the meeting, and my opponents had to respond to my comments without the benefit of a complete audience or a microphone. I hadn't exactly planned it that way, but my supporters in the crowd were elated with the edge I seemed to get and the favorable comments from their friends. Rufus and I were soon on our way toward Memphis.

I felt good about the Covington rally and the way I seemed to be perceived. The perception part came from some feedback we received from those in attendance who were sympathetic to my cause. While not wanting to overdo the appearance of being hostile to my fellow Republican candidates, I needed to make pointed distinctions between them and me. I could do that in the presence of an opponent or on my own and not appear to be mean-spirited. I just wanted to suggest that I was a fighter of sorts. I began to believe the people of West Tennessee appreciated a little aggressiveness.

In West Tennessee I heard much talk about roads being needed, but also the crime rate being too high, too many children not getting an education, and Middle Tennessee getting most of the attention from the governor's office. In Dyer County I heard repeatedly that governors had been promising a four-lane Highway 51 North from Memphis to South Fulton for forty years and nothing had happened yet! I also heard about that old cow. It seemed they were feeding her in Memphis and West Tennessee but milking her in Nashville. I was beginning to think I might someday have to deal with that unusual cow if I could just get to Nashville officially.

At home in Memphis, my team was hard at work. It was becoming clear that our efforts were beginning to create a perception that we were running an "open campaign." There was no such thing as so-called traditional Republicans being the only ones involved. Political independents, Democrats, and many, many non-political volunteers were joining in. The Memphis Republican Party headquarters and the Dunn for Governor headquarters became increasingly busy and exciting places to be.

I was told that much of the enthusiasm and pride that was building at home had to do with the idea that a Memphian might have a real shot at becoming a strong candidate to be elected governor. Volunteers to do every sort of chore, as well as to raise money, continued to stream into headquarters. It was fascinating to me to discover that my staff people, including Bettie Davis and Carolyn Weins, as well as the campaign chairman, Harry Wellford, were in such frequent contact with people across the state I had met only briefly that they had become strong allies and friends.

Jim McGehee, Bill Rachels, Jack Craddock, and Jim Gates were working the finance side of the equation and having enough success to keep our bills paid and our offices open. As we identified and designated people in other counties to take charge of the campaign in their areas, they also had to assume the financial responsibilities. I kept hearing over and over that they were enthusiastic and busy getting a campaign going.

The work being done by Betty Dunn and her campaign committee seemed to add to the political chemistry that was brewing in Shelby County and West Tennessee. Her team of ladies planned bus tours throughout the western counties. The Dunn Dollies were often a part of such excursions, adding color and excitement. Betty was very effective with women wherever she went. At a coffee in her honor in Jackson, she was quoted as saying, "I would much rather Dr. Dunn be there to meet them [the voters] but he is having to spend a lot of his time in other parts of the state." Then, "I hope they will join with us to bring better government to Tennessee and to help elect a governor who is seriously concerned." Finally, "I started out with Julie in a stroller working for James, Baker and Kuykendall. It's quite different working for your own husband." She was pretty, she was natural, and they loved her. She made a huge difference for me.

I continued to draw strength from my conviction that the great expanse of West Tennessee territory could be my power base. The people were so open-minded and appeared one on one to be so interested in my quest. Time after time I was rewarded with an attitude from total strangers that they had no preconceived political prejudices. Their responses seemed so positive.

As the days moved swiftly along into early May, my travel schedule intensified. I was either driving down a highway, flying in a private airplane, rambling the streets of various Tennessee communities looking for just the right person we had been assured could do me a lot of good in that area, talking to one or more people about what I wanted to do for Tennessee, smiling, shaking hands, or otherwise trying with all my strength to convince listeners of my sincerity and the logic of my cause. Over and over again, my message was about new people in politics, fresh ideas, no political obligations, breaking out of the bondage of a one-party monopoly, East and West coming together for a new day in Tennessee. I never got tired of repeating it.

Rufus Powell became increasingly effective in his job. In addition to other duties, he not only took names and addresses to deliver to headquarters for follow-up, but he did a good job of confidence building with our new friends. We developed somewhat of a routine.

Late to sleep and early out of bed were the standard procedures. Always, getting back home to St. Andrews Fairway before daylight on Sunday morning was a big objective. Sunday with my family was my rest and restoration time.

Every county that made up what was referred to as East Tennessee became a specific target to produce certain numbers of votes for me in the primary election set for August 6. Dan Kuykendall made certain I understood the necessity of doing well there as the vote totals grew for all candidates on election night. The count would move from east to west because of the time zone differential. Based on his general election experience in 1964, he had a decent grasp on the number of votes each county would produce in that non-presidential election year. His guess as to what percentage of the total votes cast in each county I should work toward receiving was as good as anyone's, and better than most. I took his estimates as gospel. I knew that East Tennessee and Shelby County would make the difference.

Day after day, Rufus and I entered communities neither of us had seen before. It was a fascinating process of personal discovery in East Tennessee. I began to notice a charm I couldn't describe. I didn't know the history of the region, but it was easy to see the historical richness of landscape and structures that appeared as we drove down unfamiliar streets and through neighborhoods new to us. We were usually with someone who knew the area, and we were probably looking for some specific person or some location. The intensity of our mission didn't allow time to discuss the surroundings. Every subject that filled our thoughts or conversation resonated with heavy political overtones.

One night outside Morristown on a mission to attend a meeting with new contacts, we decided we were lost. As we drove slowly along the dark, lightly traveled asphalt road, we spied a man outside his house. Rufus stopped, rolled down his window, and told the man we were looking for Bulls Gap. The man said, "Boys, don't move an inch!" Actually, the place wasn't that small. We were very fortunate that he happened to be one of the people we were to meet.

I began to get a flavor of the general character of East Tennessee people as the days went by. Their language contained colloquialisms that suggested a special inheritance of speech patterns from many generations back. I soon learned that a piece of *tar* was probably rubber slung from an unraveling tire on an eighteen-wheeler rolling down a highway. It was distinctly different from the language of West Tennessee. When I heard the word *hard*, I soon learned that it might just be the forename of a senator named Baker. The word *far* might refer to distance but could just as likely be in reference to a blaze.

One colorful description of the average disposition of an East Tennessean was that he wouldn't do a damn thing you told him to do but that he would do almost anything you asked him to do. The people I began to meet, in ever growing numbers east, west, or middle, county by county, town by town, seemed to typify that description. I was amazed and honestly humbled by the attitudes of support, enthusiasm, and personal sacrifice that came my way. There was something about the political quest I was on that seemed to unlock and let pour forth a quality and quantity of individual commitment that I accepted with thanks and without question. Those attitudes reinforced my desire to press on. I always reported those attitudes to the people in Memphis.

With growing frequency, I was getting invitations to gatherings where one or more of my Republican opponents were present. I always offered my usual routine message about the longtime Democrat one-party monopoly, about the time having come to get rid of special interests, about the need to put the people back in charge of state government, about jobs, highways, children's education, and so forth. I also began to shift gears, focusing on my individual opponents, attempting to make a case based on who could win the general election. That was not easy because there was very little I could say to make any one of them look bad. They were good people.

As I gained greater exposure and experience, it became obvious that listening, as well as talking, was important to the process. East Tennessee people expressed their strong feelings about not being represented in the governor's office for years and years. Their need for highway development was the complaint I heard most often. A lack of highways, no new bridges, and dangerous roads that got no attention in Nashville were points made repeatedly. It was clear to me they were looking for someone they could put their trust in—someone who wasn't out to "play politics" for the sake of their votes.

A story I heard over and over again went like this. A Democrat governor in the late 1940s accepted an invitation to make a speech in Mountain City, about as far to the east as one could go and remain in Tennessee. The governor and his driver left Kingsport and headed toward Mountain City. After a long, dangerous, turning, and twisting drive on narrow roads, they arrived. Following dinner, the governor spoke to a large group assembled for the occasion. At the end of his remarks, he finished with a flourish. He wanted his audience to know he had enjoyed being in Johnson County and its county seat, Mountain City. He allowed as how the next time he came back, instead of traveling the narrow, dangerous highways, he would ride on a four-lane concrete highway with no dangerous curves or treacherous hills to climb. He would ride on a splendid route to that beautiful community. All this was greeted with thunderous applause, after which the governor took his leave. On the way back down the mountain, the driver questioned the governor's wisdom in making such a promise since building such a roadway would be an impossibility.

The governor turned to his driver and suggested he might not have been listening carefully. The governor reminded the driver he had said "the *next* time he came back." Then he said with finality, "There's not going to be a *next* time!" The story was always told with a touch of bitterness because all the governors during that time had been Democrats. We were in Republican country.

Another resentment I heard expressed over and over had to do with past promises to build a few state parks in East Tennessee. That was especially true for Upper East Tennessee. The people loved the out of doors, and they knew that the state had been building an impressive network of parks in certain parts but not in Upper East. They wanted a governor who would do right by them by supporting state parks development.

In general, the complaint was that they were paying the taxes, but they weren't getting anything for their money. Some said it was sort of like feeding the old cow in East Tennessee but milking her in Nashville! I took note of those grievances as I began to expand my talks about what a fresh, energetic governor beholden to no one or no group could do. I also began to visualize that two-headed cow that I had first heard about in West Tennessee!

Knoxville, the site of the first Tennessee General Assembly in 1796, would become well known to me. A glance at a map shows

Knoxville to be the geographical hub of a pivotal political area. Our planning and strategy compelled Harry Wellford, Dan Kuykendall, and other advisers to believe, as I did, that Knoxville and Knox County were fundamentally important to our plan. And so, that county became a central focus and point of departure for my East Tennessee efforts. That area would not only have to be an important source of primary votes—it would also be the springboard that would launch me consistently, in the days ahead, into the other pivotal and not so pivotal but important counties of the East.

Senator Fred Berry of Knoxville had provided just the right reinforcement and believability I needed by coming to Memphis to support the logic of my intentions. The senator emphasized Knoxville's importance, and I took it to heart.

In February, well before the senator had come to Memphis on my behalf, I had been invited to attend the Lincoln Day Dinner to be held at the Andrew Johnson Hotel in Knoxville. This was a major Republican function and would be attended by many active Republicans from surrounding counties. Betty agreed to go with me, and I looked forward to showing her off, as well as meeting many people for the first time.

I was anxious to experience a Republican function in Knoxville where there had been such intense party activity over many years. During the reception before the meal, we shook hands and introduced ourselves to everyone we could reach. Word of my interest in the governor's race had come ahead of me, and there were a number of comments to that effect. There was a large crowd, and the political conversations were flying fast and thick. It was clear that being a dentist and being from Shelby County kindled curiosity. The number of people in attendance that evening was larger than any Republican gathering I had seen in Tennessee.

The emcee for the dinner was the county chairman, an attorney named Warren Webster. The speakers for the evening included Senator Howard Baker, Jr., and Congressman John Duncan. Before the speeches, the chairman introduced candidates and prospective candidates. At some point I was introduced as Dr. Winfield Dunn of Memphis, a dentist and past Republican county chairman who was exploring the possibility of seeking the Republican nomination for governor. Betty was also introduced. We stood and received a healthy amount of applause.

After the dinner, Betty and I remained in the ballroom shaking hands until nearly everyone had left. As we were leaving the hotel, a person walked up and introduced himself to us. He was Dr. Jack Mobley, an anesthesiologist, of Knoxville. He had, he said, heard of me and was interested to know more about what I had on my mind politically. We talked for quite a while. He mentioned several friends who had also expressed some interest in me as a candidate. We agreed to meet again later. Jack Mobley was one more of those blessings in disguise for me.

My early exposure in Knox County began to build momentum because of Dr. David Berry. David is the youngest son of Senator Berry and I, of course, met him through his dad. David was a chiropractor just getting started in building his Knoxville practice. We hit it off, and he became a very important political resource. Besides the many friends he had locally, David had friends in outlying counties due to his interest in hunting and fishing. During the remainder of February, into March and April, he and I made numerous trips into Sevier and Union counties meeting hunting and fishing buddies that he felt could help me politically. Those were exciting drives into hill and mountain country I never dreamed I would get to see and know on such an intimate basis. It was a fascinating experience, and David was a tremendous friend.

Often, I would fly to Knox County courtesy of Alex Maddox or Ewing Carruthers, be dropped off at the airport, and be picked up by Dr. Berry. Senator Berry, a mortician by profession, owned and operated Berry's Funeral Home. It happened that young men who attended the University of Tennessee worked the dusk to dawn shift at the funeral home, serving to pick up deceased persons at all hours for funeral arrangements. David let me know that I could sleep in the pick-up team's quarters on the third floor of the funeral home any time. Because there was such a shortage of campaign funds, I spent quite a few nights there on a makeshift bunk. I was usually so tired that going to sleep under any circumstance was no problem. One exception to that rule, early in my funeral home experience, had to do with stacks of *Playboy* magazines found in the sleeping quarters. I knew about the magazine, but I had never taken time to take a look. I did lose some sleep on several occasions.

By arriving in Knoxville in the evening, I was ready to plunge into that community or to shove off early the next morning to meet a contact in another nearby county or attend some function I knew was taking place. Heading in any direction from that key location, I found unlimited opportunities to meet and talk to people who were genuinely interested in Republican politics. It seemed so easy, so natural, and so politically responsible to talk about a growing Republican Party, about a two-party state, about the end of a one-party stranglehold on the government of our state. It seemed so easy for me to make my case, and with few exceptions, I usually concluded an encounter by receiving sincere head nodding, smiles, and firm handshakes from the listeners. With growing frequency, I was also getting comments from people who asked what they could do to help me. It was very encouraging, and I made sure the folks back in Memphis knew what I was experiencing. Because, in the early stages, someone from home was often with me, the story of people's interest came from more than one source. Harry Wellford, Bill Rachels, Jack McNeil, and later, Rufus Powell were among those who might be along. It was reassuring to me that, excluding Rufus who was on the payroll, any one of these three men would give me so much of their time. I believed they could see that we were making progress.

With guidance and direction from the Berry family members and others I met along the way, I staked out a number of important people in Knox County that I wanted either to be for me or not too hard against me. Among those were lawyer and Republican County Chairman Warren Webster, Democrat Mayor Leonard Rogers, businessman Breezy Wynn, businessman and political figure Cas Walker, and radio-evangelist Reverend J. Basil Mull.

Mayor Rogers had let it be known early in the political season that he might consider running for governor in the Democrat primary. My impression was that he had a high approval rating with the citizenry. For whatever reason, he chose not to be a candidate. I had two opportunities to speak with the mayor one on one. Each time I shared with him my strong feelings about the one-party monopoly that held our state in its grasp. I stressed my interest in public schools and education in general. I had been told that he was not a part of the state faction of Democrats presently in power. Since Knoxville was basically a Republican town, I sensed the mayor had many loyalties with Republican connections. I felt he was sympathetic to my opponent, Claude Robertson, though he never expressed a preference. He understood the efforts I was making, but I didn't feel I made much progress. I took some pride in the fact that he recognized me and respected my candidacy.

Mr. Breezy Wynn was not an easy man to pin down. He was a prominent citizen and was held in high respect. Mr. Wynn had suffered a severe accident at some point in his career, leaving his face scarred, sightless in one eye, and relying on a black eye patch secured by two laces that tied at the back of his head. I sought appointments with Wynn over a period of seven or eight weeks before finally getting an appointment. We talked at great length. He let me know that, though he was a Republican, he played it close to his chest and therefore could not publicly endorse me. I knew that he was wealthy, but it did not occur to me to request a campaign donation. Becoming more familiar with Knox County as the days rushed by, a number of important people who did take up my cause carried the message of their support to Mr. Wynn. I don't know who he favored in the primary, but I felt good that he did not publicly endorse Robertson.

The most widely known of the four prominent men I was attempting to sell on my efforts was Cas Walker. This gentleman was legendary in East Tennessee. I knew if I could gain his support, it would be a big step forward. He owned a group of large grocery stores in and around Knox County. He advertised heavily in the newspapers and on the radio. His promotions in selling his goods gained him great recognition. He had a local radio talk show that was very popular. His opinion about matters of interest to the public carried a lot of weight, I was told. I had one opportunity to meet and speak with Walker. He listened to my story and wished me well, but he made no commitment to my candidacy. His support probably went to Robertson in the primary, but I never saw evidence to that effect.

Second only to Cas Walker in name identification was the last of the four Knoxvillians I attempted to sway to my cause. Reverend J. Basil Mull was a middle-aged, sightless preacher who had, over the years, built a large following in radio land. Preacher Mull, as he called himself, was assisted by his devoted wife, referred to by him as Miz Mull. As I learned by listening to his radio show and to others who admired him, Preacher Mull did very little preaching. He talked to his audience, stressed his religious beliefs in conversational terms. Miz Mull was always prepared to spin a 78 rpm recording of popular hymns at his direction. She had a soft, gentle voice that contrasted sharply with his rather harsh, raspy speech. The Mulls were a good match. They appealed to a large regional audience and were very successful.

In my first encounter with Mull, I shared my strong convictions and hopes for political success. He was a good listener and seemed sympathetic to my presentation. At some point as we neared the end of our visit, Preacher Mull said, "Dunn, I like you—but I'm a Democrat and I like that fellow Hooker." Our meeting ended on a pleasant note and I felt I had gained a friend, if not a supporter. I would hear from Brother Mull later.

In the process of getting exposure with the four prominent Knoxvillians, I also met many other people from all walks of Knoxville life. I had gone to both popular local newspapers, the *Journal* and the *News Sentinel*, to meet the editors. The *Journal* was a Republican paper, formerly owned and managed by a powerful Republican named Guy Smith. He had been, for many years, a definite force in state politics, having a strong working relationship with Shelby County Old Guard Republicans Bob Church, George W. Lee, and Millsaps Fitzhugh. Mr. Smith was deceased, and the paper was being managed by a good man named Bill Childress. The *Sentinel* was a more liberal publication and often favored Democrats. The editor was Ralph Millett, a gentleman who, like Bill Childress, immediately gained my respect.

During the weeks remaining before the primary, I had several opportunities to visit with both editors. I asked each man for his paper's endorsement, but the answer I got was no answer at all. At least that was better than a "no" answer. My three major Republican opponents were also spending time in the offices of those newspapers. I knew I had to give both editors a complete picture of what was driving me. I had spoken to each at length about issues of state importance on which I had firm opinions. I did my best to put the East-West reasoning before them on a basis that went beyond selfish partisan interest. Millett, especially, needed to know I felt a healthy, competitive, two-party state would serve everyone's best interests. My belief in that regard had grown to the point of religious fervor. I had repeated it over and over again to anyone who would stand still long enough for me to get the words out! Knoxville's two newspapers had huge influence in the region.

Each visit to the newspaper offices, both in the same building, gave me the opportunity to meet and shake hands with every person who worked there. They saw a lot of me during the months of May, June, and July. I rarely came to Knoxville without swinging by, just to touch base and let them know I was in town. The sports departments were favorite places to jawbone and swap stories. The editorial cartoonist for the *Journal* was Charlie Daniel. He and I hit it off, and I became a big fan of his.

Memphis headquarters received a call from Dr. Jack Mobley, the physician I had met in Knoxville after the Lincoln Day Dinner in February. He wanted to arrange a meeting with the candidate. A date was chosen. The time was very early in May, and the location was the Holiday Inn West in Knoxville. Along with three supporters from Memphis, I met with Dr. Mobley, a pharmacist named E. S. Bevins, and his brother, Jack Bevins, a local businessman. These men stated that they wanted to organize a Dunn campaign in Knox County and were willing to commit the time and effort necessary. This offer was just what was needed in Knox County. None of the three men were officials of the county Republican organization, but each one was a good Republican who, thankfully, was not committed to the local candidate for governor, Claude Robertson.

I immediately accepted their offer. There was no discussion regarding any selfish interest on the part of any one of the three. They just believed I had a good cause and they wanted to help. They especially believed a candidate from West Tennessee would produce the most votes statewide. Their amazing spirit demonstrated one more time the unusual appeal that political circumstances that year in Tennessee helped me generate. I was greatly encouraged. Only E. S. Bevins had been actively involved in local politics, holding a minor county position.

This group put together a large reception for me at the Andrew Johnson Hotel some days after our initial meeting. Eighty to one hundred people attended. These people were all friends of my three new supporters, and they were men and women who basically had very little political experience. They were regular citizens from a variety of walks of life. It was a good meeting, and I made my usual remarks trying to justify my reasons for being a candidate. I learned later that the impression was good but that many of those attending felt my chances were slim because of the late start and my lack of strong financial support.

According to E. S. Bevins, the county Republican Party was split up into many factions, and he felt his group could put together a "formidable" organization to help me. And so began one of the truly remarkable efforts of the campaign. E. S. at some point became the campaign chairman. A great lady named Betty Sterchi became the women's coordinator. The finance chairman was a successful chemist and businessman named Quinten Gulley, who was supported by his partner, Dick Empy. In a period of fewer than ninety days, beginning with that small core of good politicians, a major Knox County campaign supporting Dunn for governor evolved.

E. S. Bevins turned the operation of Concord Pharmacy, his drugstore business, over to his pharmacist wife, Jane. He devoted all of his efforts toward building the Dunn organization. Various groups such as lawyers were recruited. Lawyers for Dunn were led by a young attorney named Jack Draper. Bill Oldham, an insurance man, did the same among his insurance colleagues. E. S.'s mother, a widow and very prominent lady Republican, began organizing her peer group. The multitude of friends of each of these early supporters was enlisted in the cause.

A campaign headquarters was established at the Holiday Inn Central that was located next to a busy segment of interstate highway. To furnish the headquarters space, furniture was borrowed from a local school and an office supply business. There was one telephone initially, then three. Later, a WATS line was installed. The Knoxville campaign office was in touch with the Memphis office several times each day. A cyclone fence separating the Holiday Inn property from the interstate highway became an ideal place to locate a very large "Dunn for Governor" sign. It had high visibility. Betty Sterchi managed the headquarters full time at no expense to the campaign. She was joined by a terrific lady named Joanne Clark. The headquarters became a veritable beehive of activity.

The Memphis headquarters staff became well acquainted with what was happening in Knoxville. Harry Wellford was in the Knoxville

location many times, as were other Memphians. Our fledgling organization was growing, and the intensity of the effort was increasing.
I was scheduled to campaign in Knox County at least once a week.
I thought Knoxville was a gold mine of opportunity. The Bevins
boys and Jack Mobley were tremendous organizers for what we had
to do. The main campus of the University of Tennessee was a huge
economic influence in the city. Administration and faculty buildings
housed many potential votes. We did not have any campus contacts
there and chose not to visit those offices at that time.

Ward Archer, our public relations friend in Memphis, worked
with the Knoxville people on campaign literature. Knoxville had to
raise the funds to buy posters, cards, and bumper stickers. Memphis
finance, under Jim McGehee's careful control, would be responsible
for money to buy radio and television time when that became a
logical thing to do.

One benefit for me personally was that Dr. Mobley had a spare
bedroom in his home, which was always available to me. I came to
know his wonderful wife and children well. They became my family
away from home, and we became close friends. Dr. Mobley had a
dry sense of humor and a quick wit about him. Through his efforts I
was able to make many valuable contacts in the medical community
including physicians, nurses, and other hospital personnel.

E. S. scheduled me from morning until late at night. We shook
hands at factory gates; we visited firehouses, police stations, business
offices, eating establishments, the courthouse, government office
buildings, and outlying communities in Knox County. There was
no end to the handshaking and requests for the vote attached to the
hand. As each day wore on, some weariness would set in, but my
enthusiasm and eagerness never waned.

My path would occasionally lead me across that of an opponent.
Such encounters were always pleasant and in good spirits. Mr. Jarman
had a motor bus in which he traveled. We would occasionally see
the vehicle, brightly painted and prominently displaying the Jarman
name. Jenkins and Robertson we saw only rarely, usually in the
vicinity of some factory gate early in the morning. I don't recall ever
seeing Hubert Patty.

When in Knoxville, I was always driven from place to place by
E. S. I was impressed that he drove a shiny black Lincoln sedan, and

I enjoyed that luxury. He was my constant companion, along with Rufus, and I could not have been more grateful. Along with a wonderful sense of humor he had a chuckle that kept me at ease.

A memorable thing occurred in the Knox County community of Powell. I had heard references to *Pal* as a place we needed to focus on for votes. I learned that *Pal* was just an East Tennessean's way of pronouncing Powell. That was along the line of hearing *hard* for Howard and *tar* for tire. I was adapting to my changing environment, and I loved it.

I was scheduled to speak at a Republican rally at Powell where I would appear with my opponents. This occurred about the middle of May. The rally location was an old and no longer used church building. We arrived, visited with a modest crowd of forty or fifty people, then took our places on a platform where the pulpit had once existed. The candidates faced the audience. We were asked to speak in reverse alphabetical order.

The first speaker was introduced and began his remarks. Near the end of that candidate's pleas for support, I noticed a bird had found its way into the room through an open window and was soaring from one end to the other, well above the heads of the audience. Soon, everyone had noticed the bird that continued to fly in every direction within the confines of the auditorium. The next speaker was introduced, began his remarks, and attempted to ignore the little flying fellow that was obviously looking for a way out. During the next speaker's presentation, the bird continued its performance, not once stopping to rest. Each speaker had to deal with the obvious distraction. At the conclusion of the third speaker's offering, my time came. As I faced the audience and was about to make a remark about the bird, the little creature ceased to fly and came to rest somewhere in the rear of the room.

For some reason, the little fellow had settled down, and I cranked up my remarks without commenting on its presence in the room. Whether or not I was able to benefit from an audience no longer distracted by the bird I will never know. I did notice that when I concluded offering reasons for my candidacy and the concerns I thought I could successfully address as governor, my applause seemed no stronger than that for any of the other speakers. Even so, I was fascinated by my good fortune. I took the bird's performance to be a lucky omen. I never forgot it! Maybe at that time I was looking for any encouraging signs I could find!

Knoxville was looking better with each visit. The work of the Bevins brothers was relentless, and E. S. said many times that they were all working because they wanted to; no one dictated to anyone else but did the very best they could in their own ways. Quentin Gulley, according to the brothers, nearly worked himself sick, going night and day. They all agreed that it was very difficult to get money for a candidate from West Tennessee who was an unknown dentist. That was understandable. I was so appreciative. I began to feel that they all were family.

A small number of people did most of the work during the primary in Knoxville. The several phone lines were kept busy, and growth in numbers of visitors continued to climb. David Berry could not afford to take too much time away from his chiropractic practice, but he helped when possible. Senator Berry, who had willingly endorsed me in Memphis, played it close to his vest as far as my efforts in his district were concerned. That made sense. Knoxville had evolved into a major segment of my campaign.

One night as I was dropped off at the Knoxville airport by Alex Maddox, I had a chance encounter with Senator Howard Baker, Jr., inside the terminal. He, along with his pilot, Lonnie Strunk, was leaving for Washington just as I arrived. I did not know Howard well at that time. I respected his popularity, his prominence as our senator, and the fact that he was probably the most important member of the East Tennessee Republican establishment. He was fully acquainted with what I was attempting to do since I had met and spoken with him in detail the previous December during a visit to his office in Washington. I was extremely glad that he remained uncommitted in the primary as far as my race was concerned. I am quite sure he remembered the hard work Betty and I had put in for him in Shelby during his two Senate campaigns.

We chatted at length. He asked me about my campaign and how I thought I was doing. My answer was, of course, optimistic. He then asked me who my campaign chairman in his home, Scott County, was. My answer was that I did not have one as yet. To my utter surprise and delight, he turned to his pilot and said, "Lonnie, why don't you run Winfield's campaign in Scott County?" Lonnie answered that he would be glad to do so, and the deal was struck! Scott County was the senator's home, and Lonnie's as well. At the time, as in so many other East Tennessee counties, I had not developed a contact. I thanked the senator, who seemed pleased and amused with the arrangement, and another encouraging event had thus occurred. I immediately reported that good news to Memphis.

CHAPTER ELEVEN

A SERIOUS CANDIDATE

The Energy Level Rises

Knox County continued to be a major destination as the weeks passed. It remained the logical point of departure in every direction as I began to intensively develop new relationships in counties where I had a lot of ground to cover in a few short weeks. All the while, West Tennessee provided me with growing numbers of opportunities to attend Republican functions. There were many rural West Tennessee counties that, by mid-May, I needed to visit and get organized. As a part of the strategy, Middle Tennessee was certainly not ignored, but it wasn't a high priority at the time. I began to receive invitations to various functions in mid-state counties. Harry Wellford was determined, as I was, to accept as many as I could handle personally. In those cases when I could not be present, someone from Memphis stood in for me. Although Republican primary votes in the heavily Democrat central section would not be large, we all knew every vote counted. We also knew there would be Democrat votes the right Republican candidate for governor could get in the general election.

Due to the large number of candidates at all levels, Shelby County was experiencing an extraordinary dose of political activity. Bob Taylor, my Memphis Democrat counterpart, was building an active local organization. Memphis Mayor Henry Loeb was outspoken but guardedly non-biased regarding particular candidates. He had been outspoken in support of Richard Nixon in 1968, and I held out some hope for his eventual endorsement. Another popular officeholder was Sheriff Bill Morris. He was well regarded and considered likely to be interested in other political successes in the future. Bill had been strongly supported by the Memphis Jaycee organization, a group with which I had been active. We continued to send strong signals in his direction, hoping in return for a good word or outright support.

Many prominent individuals in Memphis and the county, who had business, professional, and social connections unknown to me, were helpful. As the campaign expanded, I began to hear of good comments directed toward my efforts by people who were beginning to believe there just might be a realistic possibility that Memphis could produce a serious candidate for governor. That was simply unheard of in Shelby County social and political circles. I was told by Harry and others that the "talk" was beginning to get interesting. I know my congressman, Dan Kuykendall, was stoking the fires. He was highly regarded. The "talk," I was told, was taking place in circles I could not have imagined. That only reinforced my commitment and increased my confidence that we were on the right track. No matter, I knew that I was still considered a long shot!

The "glue" that held my emotions together through all the new and amazing experiences consisted essentially of my wonderful wife and children. They, along with the relationships I enjoyed in my church, Christ United Methodist, offered me the encouragement, love, and support I needed. Chuck was away at Washington and Lee University. We kept him posted, and he was deeply interested in what seemed to be happening. Family, friends, and faith gave me the energy and confidence I needed. Each weekend at home, no matter how brief, nourished me even more than I realized at the time.

During the long hours I was on the road, my most vivid moments of each day occurred as I emerged from the place I had spent the previous night. The fresh early morning air, the darkness that usually existed because of the hour my schedule began, the differing smells in the air at various locations, the sounds of the awakening community, and the quiet, inner excitement I felt for the day that lay ahead all mingled into what I could only call a "mind-set" that pushed me forward. By the time I joined Rufus Powell, who always awakened me from a deep sleep with his phone call or sharp knock on my door, he had been in touch with some devoted person at my Memphis headquarters to get any last-minute directions or change in plans. I knew I was losing body weight because my belt was fastened at a different notch. My sleep requirements were being met adequately by sleeping where I was quartered or napping in the car while driving to the next meeting. My energy level remained high, although my diet was determined by the schedule. I was glad to consume whatever could be quickly obtained from a short order restaurant or hamburger stand. Occasionally, I was overwhelmed with whatever a host or hostess had prepared in advance of my appearing at a particular event. It was a strange mixture of nourishment, but I don't recall complaining.

The importance of both Memphis newspapers never ceased to be in the forefront of our thinking. Harry Wellford's reputation and the great respectability of so many of those who were in my corner there at home couldn't be ignored. The chief of the editorial staff at the *Commercial Appeal* was an outstanding man named Guy Northrup. Guy and his wife, Miriam, had been casual social friends of ours several years prior to my candidacy in 1970. I took some comfort from the fact that we were friends. By mid-May there had been no editorial interest in particular individuals expressed by the paper. I was an avid reader of the editorial page. I credited that page with much of my knowledge and opinions on various public issues. The political columnist was a well-respected man named Bill Street. Mr. Street had on many occasions mentioned my name and my political involvement. As a former Mississippian, Street had earlier become familiar with my father's political activity. He made reference to that in one column, and I harbored the hope that he would be reasonably sympathetic to my cause. His commentaries concerning my candidacy were always balanced and fair.

The afternoon newspaper, the *Press-Scimitar*, was managed by Ed Meeman, another well-respected publisher. The *Press-Scimitar* was considered the more liberal of the two publications. Null Adams was the popular and capable political editor. From the time my interest in the governor's race became known, as far back as late 1969, Mr. Adams had made me an occasional subject in his column. I was always treated with kindness, respect, and a degree of curiosity. Harry Wellford and I made sure both newspapers and their personnel knew we were deeply interested in what they thought. I was a frequent visitor to both establishments. Each paper was widely read throughout the Mid-South. Each had given generous coverage to the announcement of my candidacy from the capitol steps in Nashville on April 18.

The *Commercial Appeal* was the strong newspaper in rural West Tennessee. It maintained a number of contributing reporters in many communities. An excellent article about my candidacy, written by a *Commercial Appeal* reporter who also worked for the *Humboldt Courier-Journal*, was published in that paper on April 23. I had been invited to be the main speaker at the Gibson County Republican Convention. Gibson was one of only a few West Tennessee counties to hold such a meeting. It occurred a few days before I announced my candidacy in Nashville.

The article was all I could have asked for. It gave a full account of the preliminaries I had been going through for several months as I "tested the waters." It included quite a bit of background material on me personally. The article then outlined my reasoning in thinking my candidacy made sense, including the East-West synergy idea, the need to eliminate a political monopoly, and the need to have better representation in the capital for West Tennessee. It reported the title of my speech, "An Idea—An Experience—A Proposition." The idea was the logic of a West Tennessee standard bearer that particular year; the experience was what I was going through at the time to determine if I might be that standard bearer; and the proposition was that with the help of good people such as those in that audience and folks like them across the state, I would be the nominee who would give his all in the general election campaign. I was introduced by Jere Griggs of Humboldt, the outgoing GOP county chairman. The Gibson County meeting was helpful and I benefited from the publicity. That evening laid the foundation for a healthy base of support from people in the area surrounding Gibson County. Jere and his brother, Ernest Griggs, along with many others, became deeply involved in the campaign.

Earlier in the year I had met several outstanding people from Madison County, which is just south of Gibson. Harry Wellford introduced me to his Vanderbilt Law School classmate Hewitt Tomlin, a practicing attorney in the county seat of Jackson. Hewitt in turn introduced me to his senior partner, a venerable and greatly respected attorney named Roy Hall. Both of these men were longtime Republicans, well known in Jackson and in legal circles across the state. Roy Hall arranged a meeting for me with his friend Charles Womack, a local businessman and dedicated Eisenhower Republican. These three men became the core of a much larger group of people in the county who worked tirelessly as the days went by to get me good exposure to the public. Friendships were made that have lasted for years.

Jackson is the second most populous city in the western third of the state. Historically a Democrat stronghold, it nevertheless played a big role for me in the primary. One-party political domination for decades had led most of the citizens to be resigned to thinking "Democrat." Mayor Bob Conger was a strong Democrat who was popular in the city. The people who became my active supporters were those who had very little active political experience. I was discovering that previous campaigning and team building by Congressman Brock as he planned his Senate race were beneficial to my efforts. New people were becoming interested and energized politically. That was a helpful factor in many of the counties I visited.

I met solid new friends. It was encouraging to me that people became so interested and committed to a cause. The appeal of political involvement to people who had no prior interest continued to amaze me. Several well-known Jackson dentists became interested in helping me. Dr. Jim McLemore and Dr. Bob Williams became effective fund-raisers at a time when there was much skepticism regarding my prospects. Joan Williams, wife of the doctor, had been active in the Republican women's group. She became one of the most devoted supporters, and her influence with women in Madison County was a key in getting the community interested in my campaign. With Hewitt Tomlin, Roy Hall, and Charles Womack leading the way, a serious campaign began to be organized in Madison County. I was effectively scheduled to be at plant gates to shake hands, civic clubs to be introduced, and various gatherings such as coffees to get acquainted with local people.

Rufus and I, guided by Hewitt, made an early visit to the local newspaper, the *Jackson Sun*. Its orientation was firmly Democrat. The individual we met and visited with was political writer John Parish. He was well known in newspaper circles and widely read in the area. He had already included me in several columns based on my activities and the Nashville announcement. We made sure he knew how many well-respected Jackson citizens were on our team. After that visit we made our usual visit to the local radio stations. We were optimistic about chances to get good primary support in Madison County, but Dunn supporters knew they had their work cut out for them.

May 7 was a great day for me along the campaign trail. I was scheduled to ride in the annual Strawberry Festival parade in Humboldt. This event attracted large numbers of people. The area had historically been recognized for its strawberry crops, and the town called itself "The Strawberry Capital of the World." The parade would take place in the morning followed by a luncheon for political, business, farm, and professional people representing most of the counties of West Tennessee.

Betty and I drove to Humboldt early on the seventh following Jere Griggs's instructions. Although we had no Gibson County organization at that time, Jere and Ernest Griggs had agreed to head one up. Dr. Herman Stallings and his wife, Marzette, a prominent dental couple and our good friends, had agreed to be involved. Arriving at the destination, we were met by Jere and taken to our special car. What a surprise! We discovered a Buick convertible had been prepared for us, and we would ride in the parade sitting on the upper edge of the backseat where we could be seen prominently. The car was adorned with large homemade "Dunn for Governor" signs on each side with smaller signs on the front and back.

It was a beautiful day. Our vehicle was parked in line with a large number of others along a residential street near the main downtown street. We were directed to stay near our car in preparation for the start of the parade. Strawberry Festival floats, high school bands, and other groups were busy taking their assigned places.

As we waited, we politicked with passersby and occupants of other parade cars. I did not see either of my primary opponents, though I learned later that Jenkins and Robertson were there. I glanced up at the sound of a familiar voice and discovered the imposing figure of John Jay Hooker approaching us across a small park to our left. He was striding in our direction to say hello, and I feel sure he recognized the pretty blonde to be my wife. We had a pleasant visit during which he clearly attempted to charm Betty.

As we stood in the bright sunlight, I had a revelation. Hooker always dressed "to the nines," wearing finely tailored suits, usually three piece, and sporting a watch fob chain across his vest. This day he also wore a broad brim Panama hat. His tailored shirt sported French cuffs with impressive links and a pinched up collar that fit tightly under his chin. Looking at him as we talked, I saw that the upper surfaces of both collar tabs under his chin were coated with a beige- or bronze-colored substance. The outline of his chin had been transferred to the collar! I realized I was looking at pancake makeup that had soaked up from under his chin onto the collar due to perspiration!

Hooker, the startlingly handsome, bronze-faced person I had seen in the dimly lit cabin on Roan Mountain during the Ramp Festival, apparently wore pancake makeup routinely! I was not prepared mentally to absorb that fact. Makeup! Thoughts raced through my mind. *Was it really true? What would my dad say about that? What would any of that gang I grew up with in Mississippi say about that?* It didn't strike me as mannish, much less he-mannish. I decided that my earlier impression of Hooker had been an illusion. I began to reassess my ideas regarding his impregnability as an opponent. I decided then and there that, if given the chance, I would be mentally prepared to successfully take on a fellow who chose to wear pancake makeup in the out of doors. I put those thoughts aside and went on to enjoy the parade and the scattered applause Betty and I received along the route. Once again I realized how fortunate I was, in more ways than one, to have a beautiful wife, a native-born Tennessean, by my side.

At the luncheon, it was obvious, based on the public officials, candidates, and guests present, that I was still in heavy Democrat country. We were treated very respectfully. That treatment may have been influenced by the presence of the Griggs brothers, both highly successful businessmen and farmers. I was to be reminded over and over again in the early stages of the campaign that the stature and reputation of local people who let it be known they supported me made a huge difference in the reception I got from others. That's politics. Many of the counties I ventured into failed to produce support for me by more prominent citizens. Such people were cautious about political involvement, particularly involving a Republican.

Moving east out of Memphis into the counties that bordered my home state of Mississippi in the month of May, I had some lonely moments. Fayette County offered me no friendly contacts. A Republican in that county was a rarity in those days. I got some exposure by passing through Fayette on my way to Hardeman. I never failed to stop and shake hands in and around every courthouse. The political situation in Hardeman was much the same, there being few Republicans. Western State Mental Institution, a large, old facility, was a major economic factor in Bolivar, the county seat. All the employees were Democrat appointees, which told me I would waste time there. I might have had some success with the mental patients, Rufus Powell observed!

Just east of Hardeman was McNairy County. In 1964 I had worked for county Superintendent of Schools Julius Hurst, a good Republican who ran and lost a race for Congress that year in the Sixth Congressional District. I called on Julius and made my case. He was familiar with what I was doing, wished me well, but did not commit to help me. I learned later that he was working for Mr. Jarman.

May 16 was important in McNairy County because it was Adamsville Day. Adamsville lay east of Selmer, Julius Hurst's hometown, and was also the home of Democrat Congressman Ray Blanton. The occasion was the one hundredth birthday of the town and was the climax of the Adamsville Centennial Celebration. Governor Ellington had issued a proclamation officially declaring the day. A personal representative of the governor would present the proclamation.

According to newspaper accounts, between 10,000 and 15,000 people were expected to move in and out of the celebration location on that day. Local political candidates were to speak during the afternoon at City Park. Major candidates were to speak at 7:30 p.m., and a large gathering of the hopefuls was expected for speech making. Democrats scheduled to attend included Stanley Snodgrass, Ralph Waldo Emerson, and Bob Taylor. Republican candidates would include Maxey Jarman, Bill Jenkins, Claude Robertson, and me. John Hooker was the only major announced candidate for governor who would not be present. U.S. Senate candidates committed to attend included incumbent Senator Albert Gore, Bill Brock, Tex Ritter, and a relatively unknown candidate, Herman Frey. This was the largest gathering of major candidates so far in 1970, and the event was expected to be covered by news media from all over the state.

Rufus and I arrived just in time to shake hands and move toward the area where the speeches would take place. I was directed to a platform near a real stump that had been put in place in order to be the platform for each individual as he spoke. The evening wore on, and each candidate did his best to make the right points and impression. I did no less when my time came. I felt it was a good opportunity and great exposure.

For me, the surprise of the evening came when senatorial candidate and incumbent Albert Gore took the stump. My former exposure to the senator was limited. I had never heard him make a campaign speech. He was in strong form that evening. His voice was strident from the beginning, his Tennessee twang was crisp and generous, his conviction was clear that his reelection to the Senate was pivotal in terms of the economic and military security of the nation, his guardianship of the rights and benefits of the working man was irreplaceable, and his statement was emphatic that the mothers, babies, and veterans of the state of Tennessee would be in some kind of jeopardy were he not sent back to Washington. His delivery overall exposed an evangelical zeal that was unmatched by any other speaker of the evening. And at the conclusion, his shirt was soaking wet from perspiration. He impressed me as I recalled memories of Mississippi political eloquence.

With the event concluded, the senator having been the last presenter, I mused while walking toward our automobile that Congressman Bill Brock, with his low-key, somewhat understated style of speaking, would have his hands full were the two of them to face off on a platform. I also experienced a feeling of excitement and involvement I had known in other recent days. It had to be some sort of uncommon emotional high running through my mind, realizing that I was in the arena with the "big boys." It was very pleasing to me.

There in the relative darkness of the evening as the crowd dispersed and I stood by the car waiting for my assistant, a soft, feminine voice from behind me spoke the words "Doctor Dunn." I turned and, to my surprise, faced Mrs. Pauline Gore, wife of the senator. Each of us spoke and shook hands, whereupon, in the most pleasant terms, she said, "You know, Doctor Dunn, the only thing wrong with you is that you are not a Democrat!" That comment swept over me as an impression that I had just been complimented. Without recalling my exact words, I did my best to tell her that it was a real privilege to make her acquaintance. Her words lingered in my thoughts during the long drive back to Memphis, and I continued to enjoy them. Rufus agreed that she had paid me a compliment of sorts.

On another trip along that lower tier of counties we drove into Hardin County, just east of McNairy. The magnificent Tennessee

River swept northward out of Mississippi and Alabama in that area. Each state properly claimed a large part of the shoreline of Pickwick Lake. The lake was created years earlier by the TVA dam constructed on the river at a point known as Pickwick Village. Mississippi bordered on the west and Alabama on the east. Somewhere in the middle of the lake an unseen point existed where the three states conjoined. South of Selmer and Savannah were two of our state's treasury of physical wonders. One was the Shiloh National Military Park, a handsome but sober reminder of the tragedy that beset our young nation more than one hundred years earlier. Betty and I had visited there with the children. The other was Pickwick Landing State Park and Inn. It was a popular place to visit for locals and tourists. The food, lodging, and fishing gave the place a good reputation.

The major target of my visit to Savannah was state Representative Granville Hinton, a Republican serving his second two-year term. Hinton was a Jenkins man who was highly regarded by all who knew him. He was a successful insurance man with other notable business interests that included a local bank, and I knew we needed to give him our attention. Once again, that effort paid dividends. After a good visit and thorough recital of what I so deeply believed about the race I was in, he kindly put us in touch with other Savannah citizens, one of whom was a physician who carried considerable influence in the area. That gentleman was James P. Dupree, MD. We were able to have a brief visit with him, and he became a major influence for me throughout the area. Every new name we learned was passed back to Memphis for follow-up.

The other counties of West Tennessee were worked into a pattern of trips out of Memphis in such a way that we were most often able to get back home the same night. That meant a little rest for a tired body in my own bed, always a blessing. I did get weary during those days, but thankfully, the weariness always set in after the handshaking had ended and we were on our way home or to a bed somewhere. Interspersed were my longer trips to the East and an occasional visit to a Middle Tennessee county where we were beginning to generate some interest.

Going north along Highway 51 out of Shelby, we worked our way over time through Tipton, Lauderdale, Dyer, Lake, and Obion counties. The *Commercial Appeal* was widely read in that area.

Because I had received very fair coverage in the early months from both Memphis papers, we had received a number of inquiries from people who had learned of the campaign and were interested in a West Tennessee Republican candidate for governor. We followed up on every contact and scheduled visits. I had also made some friends in those counties as a result of my service as Shelby GOP chairman a few years earlier. This was heavy Democrat country, but as we had found out from other such areas, there were always a few courageous Republicans willing to speak out and stand against the local political tide. They were the kinds of people who were ready and willing to put their feelings into action. In the past, that had happened most often in county and local politics. A statewide candidate of their liking stirred their emotions. I was glad to build on those feelings. My friend Little Buck Ozment was there to help.

Tipton County was the home of state Democrat Chairman Jimmy Peeler. He wielded considerable clout across the state and was omnipotent in Covington. On my first visit there as a candidate I met a fine man named L. C. Biehrman, an optometrist. He, along with two respected businessmen, took on the task of putting an organization together in Peeler's political backyard. They went to work. That was exciting, and once more, I was encouraged.

The county seat of Lauderdale County was Ripley. There was little for me among the community's citizenry at that time. We made the usual tour of the courthouse, local weekly newspaper office, and radio station. Halls was a small town near the Dyer County border. Dr. Arden Butler became a strong supporter there. A pharmacist named Sammy Arnold took up my cause, as did a prominent family headed by Oliver Nunn. Wiley and Edna Perry, dear members of Betty's family, lived there. Edna was Betty's aunt, a wonderful woman and retired schoolteacher. Wiley was a retired businessman, having established and run a five-and-ten-cent store downtown during the Second World War. Halls had been the site of an Air Force flight training base in those years, and at the time, there was a large military presence that boosted the local economy. The Perrys and all of their friends came to my support. However, due to relatively advanced ages and totally non-political backgrounds, we did not get much organizational support from them. Some primary support did develop before the August election.

Dyer County was the ancestral home of the Prichard family, the special place where Little Buck had first added fuel to my flickering interest in the upcoming governor's race. Buck was there to help, and we laid the groundwork that would result in many Democrat votes for Dunn later on. His help in the primary would be limited because, to vote in a Tennessee primary, the voter had to declare which primary he or she wanted to vote in and it was hard for those lifelong Democrats to make that known publicly. I met a wonderful lady named Susan Davidson who ended up working for me. Looking back, I do believe President Richard Nixon's popularity in those years made it a little easier for some Democrats to declare their support for a Republican. It took courage. Betty's father had told the story of his mother's firm edict that no Prichard child could play with any children of a Republican family. Apparently, there were a few Republican residents in those early years.

Dyer County did contain a number of fine people who joined my cause—farmers, businessmen, and housewives who were willing to become involved—and they became organized for the effort. Headquarters in Memphis helped them along. The last two of the five western counties outside Shelby were Lake and Obion counties. They were a lost cause for me in the primary, and I wasted no time looking for support there. Those five counties were parts of the Eighth Congressional District. It was represented by a popular congressman named Ed Jones. The Democrats were strictly in the driver's seat in those counties.

The month of May had been amazingly busy for all of those in Memphis who had been drawn into the effort early. We had become organized, well staffed, and recognized by most media outlets to be serious and committed. The financial needs were being taken care of by Jim McGehee, Bill Rachels, and others. They had established a Finance Committee and were encouraging groups such as Dentists for Dunn and Physicians for Dunn to raise money in their own ranks. Harry Wellford coordinated scheduling and contacting major potential supporters. Headquarters was humming, and volunteers were becoming more plentiful. Ward Archer, our PR friend, was producing bumper stickers and yard signs. Pamphlets describing me and my family were beginning to be handed out in Memphis and shipped to friends across the state. There was no letup in intensity.

Steve Sharp was preparing press releases, and our friend Raymond Humphreys in Washington was sharing advice with me, Harry, and Dan. Harry had begun to seek out sources to obtain researched materials I could use in my talks on important subjects near and dear to many Tennesseans. I was reading and studying while I rode the highways, getting a little sleep in between.

Betty continued her schedule of appearances on my behalf, and we were beginning to get news clipping pictures of her surrounded by admiring and supportive ladies. She was especially effective in West Tennessee. She had not ventured east on her own, but we knew it was only a matter of time until she did so. Gayle and Julie continued to be involved through the Dunn Dollies. That group was putting together a wonderful routine that was welcomed wherever it appeared. Betty reported regularly to Chuck regarding our activities. He remained at Washington and Lee University until June.

By the end of May, I had made at least a half dozen visits to Kingsport, Johnson City, Chattanooga, and many points in between. Those visits had been productive in terms of new friends and people willing to become part of an organized political effort. Knoxville continued to be "gold to be mined" and my geographic jumping off place heading in any direction to the East.

By the first of June, an expanding political network of activity on my behalf was becoming visible in the Volunteer State. On the fourth of June, every person seeking statewide office was required by law to have filed the necessary papers and qualifying material to legitimize his intentions to be a candidate. That was the filing date. It was necessary in order to prepare the printed ballots for Election Day. My people had done the work necessary to get me qualified, including producing a required number of signatures of registered voters on a petition. A filing fee was also paid.

A number of people who had been speculated about as possible candidates began to make their intentions known. Mayor Leonard Rogers of Knoxville announced he would not run. Former state Adjutant General Joe Henry of Pulaski withdrew from consideration by making a public announcement. Former candidate for U.S. senator, then governor, Judge Andrew "Tip" Taylor of Jackson made it clear he would not run, citing a lack of financial support for the effort. I paid very little attention to these statements at the time because

I was so focused on my efforts. I had no doubts as to whom my opponents in the primary would be.

Other activities made the news. Senator Albert Gore formally kicked off his campaign for reelection from the federal courthouse in Memphis. About the same time Congressman Bill Brock announced that Dr. Nat Winston, the popular Upper East Tennessee psychiatrist, banjo player extraordinary, and former commissioner of mental health under Governor Clement, would be appointed his statewide campaign chairman.

In Shelby County, the election of a county chairman to succeed Bob James had resulted in heavy in-fighting among the New Guard leadership that had become the moving force for Republicans. Jim Harpster, the active and somewhat controversial attorney, was challenging the candidacy of Alex Dann, a great supporter of mine. The schism that had developed was a result of the support by most of the county legislative delegation for Speaker Bill Jenkins. Harpster was supported by the legislators and a number of their friends. My two legislative supporters, Curtis Person and Donnelly Hill, were steadfast for me. The county convention was held on June 8, and Dann was elected. After the contest, Dann and Harpster buried the hatchet and I was relieved. About that time, Representative Ed Williams of Shelby County openly endorsed me.

My mental preparation for running as an informed and knowledgeable candidate was a matter of concern for my strategy team in Memphis. They were using the resources of Raymond Humphreys and Associates in Washington to tap into research material available through the National Governors Association. Subject matter was made available to me for study during travel time, and I began to seriously bone up. Economic development, highway and interstate construction, adequate teacher salaries in public education, federal-state cooperation, drug abuse, and campus unrest, among others, were subjects I needed to be able to address intelligently.

Major statewide organizations and their special interests became important to me. Among those were the Tennessee Municipal League, the County Services Organization, the Tennessee Farm Bureau Federation, the Tennessee Education Association, the Tennessee Press Association, the Tennessee Valley Association, plus others. Each existed for a reason, and their specific interests would have to be addressed by me as we moved forward. The materials prepared for me to study were more than I could digest, but I spent much time absorbing what I could. A big help came from "talking papers" various people were asked to provide, based on their knowledge and background. Those items were with me constantly. I began to realize that much of the editorial comment I had read down through the years from the pages of the *Commercial Appeal* was very helpful.

CHAPTER TWELVE

THE UPPER REACHES

The People, the People

During the first five months of the year I had met many good people as I made trip after trip across the state. As the month of June rolled around, many of those contacts had turned into solid commitments, and I could sense the statewide effort taking on some muscle. I discovered a strength I was not aware I possessed. Name recall became an offensive tool as I met groups of people. My ability to go back and call an individual by his or her name without prompting following an earlier introduction seemed to impress many and amaze some. I attribute that good fortune to the flow of adrenaline and my earnest desire to please those I met.

In Kingsport, Sullivan County, I had met and attempted to cultivate a relationship with a fine young man named C. B. "Boots" Duke IV. Boots had been elected a city alderman and enjoyed a fine reputation, socially, politically, and business-wise. I met him after a visit to a Jaycee luncheon to which I had been invited. Jack McNeil and I dropped by his office for a visit. Our relationship was strong from the start. I learned that he was interested in state political activity and had been recruited by the Brock organization. My desire was to gain his support and benefit from his public endorsement. I met his wife and two fine young daughters later and knew he was a solid family man. I worked on the courtship and returned as often as possible to Kingsport, always touching base with Boots.

I learned that Boots Duke, unlike most of the local and district-wide political activists, supported but was not intimidated by Congressman Jimmy Quillen, a Kingsport citizen. More than any other Republican officeholder, that congressman appeared to be determined to control the political climate of his district. It was a situation I could not bring myself to be comfortable with. During the primary, Quillen and his people were very supportive of Bill Jenkins. That was natural enough. However, as I traveled to the various communities and counties that made up the First District, people were hesitant to take on my cause out of concern for the congressman's goodwill. The congressman demanded not only that every candidate running in the district clear all relationships with his office, he also let it be known that he wanted every dollar contributed to a candidate to clear his office first.

I presumed Jenkins had no problem with that approach. I wondered how Maxey Jarman dealt with it, or if he did. I saw little or no evidence of Claude Robertson's presence in the First District and did not dwell on what his response might be. Harry Wellford and Bill Rachels felt the weight of Quillen's preferences early on. We three agreed to basically ignore any such demands or limitations on our activities but were wise enough to attempt to avoid confrontations wherever possible.

As Boots and I became better acquainted, he made the decision to commit himself to my efforts to the exclusion of any other relationship. I couldn't believe my good fortune. He arranged for his good friend Frank Gibson, a Kingsport lawyer, to take over his obligations to the Brock campaign. Frank also became a great friend and supporter for me. Boots became my man in Sullivan County. He introduced me to another good man named Ben Brown. He also saw to it that I met a very important man in Kingsport, Mr. Harry McNeilly, president of the huge Tennessee Eastman Corporation. The Duke and Brown influences on my political fortunes would be great.

On a quick trip eastward to Johnson County and its official seat, Mountain City, I met J. D. Ashley. I was able to talk to J. D. at length about supporting me in the primary. He advised me that Quillen was insisting that the party handle all the candidates in the primary and that he didn't fit in with the organization. He was a respectable, good citizen, and I knew he could be of great help. His name, and an explanation of his problem, was passed on to Harry Wellford. Harry created a good relationship with J. D. and let him know that we were counting on whatever efforts he could make under the circumstances. He was unofficially appointed the county coordinator for Dunn.

Carter County lay south of Johnson County. All of these counties at that time were solidly Republican, and I always felt at home politically, regardless of the Quillen influence. I had received a letter from a lady named Thelma Bowman, a resident of Elizabethton, stating that she had heard of me through her brother, Carroll Shanks, in Nashville and wanted to become involved in my campaign. Our first meeting convinced me that I had hit a jackpot. This lady was young, attractive, and capable of getting anyone's attention because when she spoke, one was inclined to listen. Her husband, Dr. Hoyle Bowman, was a local physician. We wasted no time agreeing that she would be my person in her county and would get organized as best she could. I promised her help from Memphis. Thelma gave me two names in Johnson City, and I made it my business to look those people up as soon as possible. As we parted following our first visit, she also made it clear that she believed Jimmy Quillen would cause her no problem whatsoever. She also stated that Virginia and Dick Jennings, the friends in Johnson City, had similar attitudes toward the congressman. Thelma agreed to arrange for me to meet them.

I soon called on the Jenningses. They were good friends of Senator Baker's, she stated, and they were avid supporters of Bill Brock. That was good enough for me. As we got better acquainted, my impression was that Virginia was a no-nonsense lady who could get things done. She knew and liked the John Diehl family and felt they could work closely together in support of my race. Johnson City was the home of two of my dental school classmates, Drs. Herb Lawson and Bob Rowe. I talked to them. I met several other individuals who indicated a willingness to help me, including a young pharmacist named Brigham Young. The influences of Quillen and Jenkins would work against me, I knew, but I still felt encouraged. The reactions and opinions I got from a number of people I met in Washington County did not throb with enthusiasm. Some were guarded and not at all confident about my chances. Thelma and the Jenningses, however, left no doubt they believed the possibilities worth the effort, and their enthusiasm was encouraging.

I had been given the names of several people in Sevier County. We made a trip there to look for support. Among those we met were twin brothers named Ralph and Roy Maples. Their good friend

was attorney Earl Hendry. These men were part of a group outside the upper level of Republican Party activists in Sevier. The
Maples brothers owned a motel in beautiful old Gatlinburg, and I
welcomed the chance to sleep over several times in their lodgings at
no cost. I left Sevier County feeling good about these folks because
they seemed to be indifferent to the Quillen influence. There was
no hostility expressed. Rather, there seemed to be a willingness to
do what they wished politically, regardless of any influence exerted
by the congressman.

During these days in East Tennessee, I was conscious of a sense
of discovery beyond the people I came to know. The physical beauty,
the strange newness of a land I never dreamed existed as I first saw it,
added a sense of appreciation, admiration, and wonder in me regarding the state my native-born wife had led me to. I was soaking it up,
savoring the new environment, and fascinated by the beauty of that
land as springtime burst forth for everyone to drink in.

A visit to Greeneville in Greene County resulted in some excellent contacts. The county was an area framed on its northeastern
borders by the magnificent Upper Unaka Mountains. It was the
home of well-respected state Senator Tom Garland. At the time he
was a Jenkins supporter. In Greeneville I met a bright young couple
named Fran and Ray Smith. Another new acquaintance was John
Massey, a cousin of a boyhood friend of mine in Mississippi named
Bill Massey. A county schoolteacher named Harry Roberts became
a supporter. He would become an unforgettable friend for a very
special reason. I met a wonderful woman with deep East Tennessee
family roots named Iula Kilday. She took me under her wing and
promised all the support she could muster to be directed toward
primary day votes for Dunn. These people became strong supporters and began to organize their efforts. A huge Magnavox plant
located there became a prime target for early morning handshaking
at the gates where workers entered. A visit to the local newspaper
gave me the opportunity to meet John M. Jones, owner and influential publisher of the *Greeneville Sun*. Mr. Jones was an alumnus of
Washington and Lee University. I made sure he knew my son, Chuck,
was a student there.

We made a trip to remote Hancock County to visit the core
group of Republican leaders there. The drive to Sneedville, the county

seat, was over roads of poor quality. It was a small community in which we quickly found my contact. The gentleman was Tom Harrison, the head of an important and well-known Republican family. I received little or no encouragement from him. Although the county was small and economically depressed, I needed every vote I could get, and I worked hard to make my case. We soon departed, and I felt little progress had been made.

On the same trip, we visited Rogersville in Hawkins County. There we were in Bill Jenkins's hometown. Months earlier, in the dead of winter, I had made an exploratory trip to Rogersville to attend a Republican dinner held in the local school cafeteria. As I entered the building and began to introduce myself, I received a mild reception from everyone I met. It was quite different from the cordial response I usually received from strangers. Rufus and I were seated with others at a table in the rear of the cafeteria. Those in attendance, numbering approximately one hundred, finished the dinner and waited for the program to begin. The local county chairman presided, but it was soon apparent that Congressman Quillen was the featured personality of the evening. He made extended remarks, promoting himself, of course, and strongly endorsing Speaker of the House Bill Jenkins to be the next governor of Tennessee. Jenkins was seated at the congressman's table. At the conclusion of Quillen's remarks and introduction of Jenkins, we heard remarks from the local favorite son candidate.

Almost as an afterthought, the county chairman recognized a visitor from Memphis, Dr. Winfield Dunn, whom he described as also being interested in the race for governor. The applause for me was polite and light. I was not invited to make remarks. I vividly remember how far from home I felt at that moment.

The meeting soon came to an end. I stayed in the cafeteria until all had left, standing near the exit and shaking every hand I could touch. It was clearly an occasion when I felt the coolness of some and a hint of hostility by others. The fact that neither Robertson nor Jarman had chosen to be present might have suggested the naiveté that I demonstrated by being present. I have always felt that the naiveté probably demonstrated that evening was more of an advantage than otherwise. I left the building satisfied that I had done the right thing by being present. Quillen had little to say to me.

Moving on in Upper East Tennessee, a visit to Unicoi County led me to the county courthouse in Erwin. Having no good contacts there left me with nothing to do but introduce myself. I was determined to earn a little attention from the strongly Republican courthouse gang. Once again, I shook every hand I could grasp. It was strong Quillen country. I don't recall trying to locate a radio station or a newspaper office. It was a quick visit.

Cocke County was south of Greene and Unicoi counties, lying along the North Carolina line. We had attended the Ramp Festival there earlier. I had made no specific local contacts during that visit, but I had good exposure. Dan Kuykendall had provided me the names of two Newport Republicans who had been his good friends in 1964. They were Zimri Ball and Marcus Mooneyhan. We made contact and visited at length. I left feeling they would help me in the primary just because they were Dan's friends.

One of the most heavily traveled U.S. highways in East Tennessee was Highway 11 East and West. We quickly learned that 11 W was better known and often referred to as "Bloody 11 W" with good reason. We were to spend countless hours in our car on that roadway. Narrow bridges, sharp curves, and treacherous two lanes had caused many accidents. The Tennessee interstate system called for a life-saving four-lane throughway to be constructed to bear traffic into the Tri-Cities area of Kingsport, Bristol, and Johnson City. Everyone believed that state politics had relegated Interstate 81 construction to a snail's pace. A Republican governor could change that and spend much needed money on 11 E and W. That hadn't happened under the Democrats because they catered mainly to Middle and West Tennessee. I heard about those roads constantly from people I talked to. I was sympathetic to their needs and let that be known.

Hamblen County lay northeast of Jefferson. I had several names of good Republicans I should contact in the county seat, Morristown. I met a young contractor named Jimmy Helton. Jimmy, his sister, and his mother were all politically active and wanted to help. I drove many miles with Jimmy Helton calling on prospective voters and supporters from all walks of life. The owner of an Oldsmobile dealership named Lon Price had been recommended as a man who had big influence in Hamblen County. He was friendly, receptive, but hard to tie down. His buddy was Delmus Trent. Delmus's brother,

Grover Trent in Roane County, had joined my campaign a few weeks earlier. Neither Grover nor I could budge Delmus off his non-committed position, even though we tried hard. I think Lon Price and Delmus Trent were playing Mr. Jarman and me off each other, keeping both camps guessing.

Three other people in Hamblen County came into my life in a big way. "Skeet" Jones was a local auctioneer who never met a stranger. His wife, Jean, had long been active in county politics and was at that time the clerk and master of the county. Jean made sure I became well acquainted with everyone in the courthouse. Jean and Skeet were asked by a local newspaper why they supported me in the primary. Their answer was that they liked me and believed I could win. They set about to open a campaign headquarters.

They introduced me to Howard Westhaver, manager of the Berkline Furniture factory in Morristown. That factory made the popular La-Z-Boy chair. Howard became my county finance person. During the next 60 days these great people worked for me as though they had nothing else to do. The commitment was incredible. I slept a number of nights in the Jones' home. With help from headquarters in Memphis, they obtained literature and opened a small campaign office downtown. We walked every inch of the downtown business sector, shaking hands at each opportunity. Skeet was a bundle of energy. I became devoted to him and his wife.

On one occasion before I had begun to develop my supporters there, every Republican candidate for governor and senator turned up in Morristown for a civic club luncheon. I did not know anyone in attendance. I introduced myself to a gentleman who said he worked at a local funeral home and was a part-time preacher. We chatted a few minutes, after which I asked him if he would introduce me when my time came to say a few words to the audience. I told him a few facts about my personal and professional life as well as why I was a candidate. He agreed to do so. Jenkins, Jarman, Robertson, and I sat at the head table along with Bill Brock, Tex Ritter, and the club president.

After the meal, each candidate was introduced and allowed to speak for three minutes. When my time came, the undertaker-preacher stood and launched into an introduction that was a little much, even for my ego. It was almost embarrassing. He took too much time. When I stood and made my campaign plea, there were some chuckles from the audience.

Out of that somewhat humorous incident, a story developed that I heard about later and liked so much that I used it in speeches occasionally. The story was that each candidate seated at the head table had a live microphone in front of him. When the undertaker-preacher became so emotional and excessive in his lavish introduction of me, and before I could rise and speak, Tex Ritter said, in that deep, resonant voice of his, "Well, hell, if he's that good, they ought not to run him. They ought to hold him back for breeding purposes." As the story went, the audience heard every word Tex had spoken! Morristown was responsible for many happy memories during the primary.

In early June as I was working to get a foothold in the Upper East, Rufus and I drove out of Knoxville to attend a Republican County Executive Committee meeting in Dandridge at the Jefferson County courthouse. I had no contact lined up there. In the late afternoon we drove into Dandridge, our very first visit, and entered the building. A meeting was in progress. After identifying ourselves, we were invited to wait in another room while the meeting continued. I was promised some time to introduce myself to the group when the meeting was completed. No other candidate was there. I felt the same sense of excitement that often accompanied such an opportunity to make my case to new prospects.

The old building was dimly lit, and in the quiet aftermath of a work day, it seemed to have a special aroma of the people and things that brought it to life each day. It brought back memories of my experiences in other such places. Every day on the campaign trail, it seemed, was a completely new adventure for me. My Mississippi roots had not fully withered away, but I was continuously fascinated to find myself in all the interesting new places I was discovering. There were many occasions when I marveled to myself about how different the state of Tennessee was from the land of my early years! Day after day the beautiful land unfolded before me. The hills, the plateau, the mountains, and the people were fascinating. Each scene was different. The people were so genuine. There surely were discouraging moments occasionally, but the passion to tell my story seemed to dilute and wash away any momentary pain.

After a brief wait inside the courthouse, we were asked to enter the meeting room. There was not a large crowd, perhaps as many as twenty-five, but I was eager to speak to them. I did so, making a sincere and fervent plea based on the simple logic of East and West that I had become so used to repeating. I told them that I believed West Tennessee was ready to give a big vote to Republican candidates for the Senate and governorship. I also told them as much about myself as seemed proper. Somehow, I sensed a warm response from the listeners. I was right. After the meeting a number of those present gathered around, complimenting me and agreeing that I had the right strategy. The chairman, a slightly built, intense fellow named Joe Felknor, paid me the most attention. After the others had left, I continued to talk to Joe, and I know for certain that he and I bonded that night. He was to be an important person in my life from that moment on. We made plans to follow up.

Several weeks later I was advised I needed to meet Neal Scarlett, who was very influential in Jefferson City, the Jefferson County seat. Mr. Scarlett was a dairy farmer and a good man to have on my side. After contacting him, we drove to his farm to get acquainted.

I was directed to the dairy barn and found Mr. Scarlett hard at work supervising the milking of dozens of cows. He wore rubber boots that extended above his knees. His work area consisted of a concrete apron that extended the length of the barn and on which the cows stood and were feeding as they were being milked with machines. Scarlett was expecting me, and I approached to shake his hand. He held a large bucket of cotton seed meal in his left hand, and I grasped his right hand firmly. As I had walked toward him, I was careful to avoid numerous dollops of fresh cow manure, which I noticed had been and were continuing to be deposited on the concrete by various cows. I had on a light gray seersucker suit and dress shoes.

After shaking hands, we agreed to meet outside the barn to continue our conversation. I turned eagerly to exit and gingerly made my way to the end of the barn where I was about to breathe fresh air. At that moment, Mr. Scarlett called to me to come back and shake hands with his grandson. Unscathed up to that moment, I reluctantly turned and walked back to greet the young man. In the process, my good fortune failed, and I found myself being splattered by liquid patterns of falling manure. Suddenly depressed as I noticed several prominent deposits on my lower pant legs, I moved forward, met the grandson, then turned to make my exit once more. This time I succeeded in clearing the dairy barn but not without noticeable dark green splotches reminding me of where I had just been. It was a good reminder of the old saying that there's many a price to pay in politics. I was marked for the rest of the day, but Rufus and I did our best later to clean up the mess.

My visit with Neal Scarlett was a successful one. He agreed to support me and became an important resource as my new friends built a Jefferson County organization for the primary.

The contacts we were able to make during those days in Upper East Tennessee were invaluable. That region of the state was so different from the Memphis area geographically and demographically. For me there was no place like Memphis, but the differences continued to soak in and influence my conclusion that few places could be more beautiful or appealing. It reassured me that there are, for certain, good people everywhere. I also was discovering that regional history and nature's bounty affected the impressions that people were making on me. The sounds of voices with those inflections inherited from the British-influenced Eastern Seaboard and brought to those mountains and valleys by explorers and pioneers were pleasant to hear. My sense of history grew, seeing for the first time homes and buildings of eighteenth-century vintage. I recalled that Tennessee was, after all, at one time the major gateway to the West.

North of Knox was Union County. Rufus and I headed that way late one afternoon to attend a Republican county committee meeting we had heard was to take place there. We had no contact. The meeting was held in a small wood frame church on the outskirts of Maynardville. We were late finding the location, and as we were driving in to park, it appeared the meeting was breaking up. We walked into the building and found ourselves in an unlighted hallway. Several men were walking in the opposite direction. I introduced myself, and to my relief, one responded that he and his brother had been looking for me. Kyle Richardson and his brother Doyle said that they were a self-appointed committee for Dunn in Union County and they had given up on my getting there. I could not have been more surprised, more pleased, or more in the dark as to how they came to be my committee. We parted friends with the promise that my Memphis headquarters would be in touch with them. I continued to wonder at my good fortune.

Just south of Knox was Blount County, the home of a large Aluminum Company of America factory and Maryville College. My Memphis friend Lewis Donelson had given me the name of his longtime friend, attorney Bill Felknor, and it was to him that I turned. We drove in for an appointment and discovered that Bill Felknor was a gentleman who had been successful in his profession, was highly regarded, and had been active in various civic endeavors. He also had spent the early part of his life in Meridian, Mississippi, and remembered my congressman dad and lawyer uncles, Tom and Dick Dunn. Lewis Donelson had given me a great lead.

Bill Felknor agreed to help me. He explained that Jenkins and Jarman had long ago swept the county and had won the support of many local Republicans. As far as he knew, Robertson did not have a campaign chairman in the county. He told me that I was totally unknown and far behind. I would have to do a lot of hard work. I convinced him that I was willing. Bill knew how to do everything the right way. Working with the Memphis office, he soon had a Maryville headquarters up and running. He recruited a number of volunteers. He later told me they had lots of fun talking about "Winfield Who?"

We covered Maryville, including visits to the local newspaper, radio stations, and courthouse. I shook hands at the fire stations and the jail. We drove up many a county road looking for just the right person of influence, usually a farmer. I soon met Bill's law partner, Dale Young. Dale became invaluable in my effort. We worked hard in Blount County.

Loudon County was the home of two others who took on my cause as their personal crusades. I had met Roy and Barbara Cardwell early in the year at some function, and they decided they wanted to make a difference in state politics. They gave time and energy to my race that far exceeded what I asked of them. Each of them was present among the small crowd in Nashville on April 18 when I announced my candidacy. When we were running down leads and meeting new people that Roy had scheduled, he always insisted on driving. Whether in our car or his, Rufus and I sat frozen to our seats because he was a wild driver. He took curves too fast, tailgated other cars at high rates of speed, and generally scared us to death. After a few such rides together, and at the risk of hurting his feelings, I finally insisted that Rufus do the driving. From that point on I could get my mind back on winning the primary instead of being shipped back to Memphis in a box. The Cardwells played a big role in keeping my morale high in those days when we could only guess that we were making progress.

We didn't ignore Campbell and Claiborne counties, but pickings were slim. There was no one in Claiborne for me, and I couldn't afford to spend much time there. Dan Kuykendall had given me two names in Campbell, Linden Baird and Alan Carden. Linden was a hard sell, and I had no luck. He played his cards close, as they say. Alan was a good person, willing to help but unable to get himself out of Linden's shadow politically. Claiborne and Campbell counties were bordered on the north by the Appalachian Mountain chain along which the historic Cumberland Gap lay. What remarkable country!

CHAPTER THIRTEEN

Promise in the Third, Little in Middle

Looking Everywhere

The time spent in the East was somewhat balanced with time spent at home and in rural West Tennessee. Middle Tennessee was not a source of votes for me in the primary. As the month of June progressed, Memphis continued to be the center of my political universe. Harry Wellford was thoroughly in charge. The headquarters was humming. New phone lines were added. Jim McGehee and others were raising essential funds while keeping the spending in line with money available. Friends from my Mississippi days came to help. I learned that one of my old buddies, Bill Melton from Meridian, had shown up at headquarters in Memphis and volunteered. My Mississippi family stayed in close touch. Dad was writing various observations for my benefit and sent several speeches laced with humor that he thought might help.

I had spent relatively little time in our Getwell Road headquarters in May, less in June, and even less as the month of July rolled around.

The activity and interest being generated in Memphis by my campaign had a parallel in Chattanooga where the Brock influence was huge. Bill Brock had, over the years of his congressional service and in preparation for his race for the Senate, built an organization that was highly developed in terms of staff and physical setup. During several visits to Brock headquarters independent of an invitation from him, I met quite a few of his paid personnel plus many volunteers. The entire Tennessee Republican legislative delegation was solidly in his corner. These people believed in him. I had never discussed with Brock any strategy or plans I had for the primary. He was so well organized and scheduled so carefully that our paths rarely crossed. On one occasion, I happened to be in Loudon County on a day when a Brock rally was being staged. Someone in the Brock group invited me to attend. I did so and was kindly recognized as a candidate for the nomination in the governor's race as I stood in the crowd. I did not get an opportunity to speak, but I was glad to be pointed out. None of my opponents was present, and I was genuinely grateful to have the introduction.

From the earliest structured stages of putting together a strategy for the primary campaign, Chattanooga loomed large in my sights. Top priority areas were West and East Tennessee. Chattanooga, in the Southeast, was number three, and I knew we would have to make a major effort there. My first contact there was Harry Carbaugh, the gentleman I had met years earlier at a state Executive Committee meeting. Harry Wellford had enjoyed a warm relationship with Mr. Carbaugh through their earlier work on the Republican state Executive Committee and the Howard Baker campaign. Carbaugh was highly respected in Hamilton County Republican circles as well as in the community generally. For reasons unknown to me, he was not closely aligned with the Brock organization, but he certainly had the respect of everyone in his area. I feel sure the Jarman people had made a major effort to gain his support because he was a very successful businessman. He and I didn't discuss that matter. He left no doubt from the beginning that he was for me. In the days that followed, Harry Carbaugh did everything he could to support my candidacy, including making generous financial contributions.

Mr. Carbaugh was a big man, late sixties in age, slightly stooped, bespectacled, and very intelligent. He had served the party most recently as its National Committeeman. I felt the importance of his presence at all times and was never surprised by the response of others to him. He was treated with the utmost respect wherever he went in my company. To have him so completely in support of me at that stage of my efforts to gain recognition and credibility as a candidate for governor was unique and not lost on me in terms of appreciation. He was definitely a major and positive influence in his community outside the realm of politics. I was becoming increasingly aware that my efforts in other larger communities of the state outside Memphis had not produced the overt support and interest of other leaders such as bankers and business executives. Rather, I found myself successfully appealing to grassroots, ordinary citizens who had no previous political experience or who were near the fringes of local Republican activities. Harry Carbaugh's support and encouragement, along with his quiet confidence, gave me some assurance that my political instincts were valid in places other than Memphis.

I was interviewed in Chattanooga on a local radio program called *The Jaycee Question of the Week* late in April, and as reported by the *Chattanooga Times*, I expressed my opinion on a number of issues. I acknowledged being an underdog in the primary race, stated that forced busing was a detriment to public education, took a strong position against registration of private firearms, favored lowering the voting age, and was "concentrating on East and West before Middle Tennessee." I stressed my focus on primary and secondary education and named Hooker the man to beat in a general election. It was a good opportunity to get a start in that important area of the state.

During one visit, the Hamilton County Republican chairman arranged for me to meet Tom Moore, a good man whose business was stock and bond brokerage. Tom was assigned, I presume, by the chairman with input from the Brock people, to be my man in Chattanooga. He was a real pleasure to be with, well connected in all the affluent circles of Chattanooga, and with adequate time to spend with me in that county. He helped me especially in making my case before some of his wealthy friends. That resulted in financial support I desperately needed at the time. Since Mr. Carbaugh could not be expected to physically accompany me as I moved about, Tom Moore became my main man. We covered a lot of territory including factory gates, offices, and businesses. Tom took his assignment seriously, and I saw quite a bit of Chattanooga while doing my best to gain support and recognition.

Chattanooga was served by two highly competitive daily newspapers, the *Free Press* and the *Times*. The *Free Press* was led by Mr. Roy McDonald and his son-in-law, Lee Anderson. Each man reflected strong conservative political views and had given his support to Congressman Bill Brock down through the years of his political career. The publisher of the *Times* was Ruth Golden, a prominent and respected woman who had very liberal political credentials. She was a member of the Ochs family, well known for their connections with the *New York Times*. Each newspaper gave me a cordial welcome on my early visits, but I knew they viewed my chances skeptically.

Mr. Carbaugh was careful to see that I was fully aware of the Brock influence regarding every move I made in the county. He believed that Brock's people had actually selected Tom Moore to be my key man. Although he did not say so, I began to gather the impression that the Brock people fully expected Maxey Jarman to win the Republican primary. Two major players in Brock's organization were his brother Pat and another relative, Jack McDonald. I became well acquainted with these men and liked them very much. Their total focus was what was good for Bill Brock. I couldn't argue with that. I had no time or energy to be concerned about intrigues taking place among the Brock strategists. I was satisfied that they were all friendly toward me, and there were certainly no signs of hostility that I noticed.

I worked long days politicking throughout Hamilton County and made many friends. In particular, I met an oral surgeon and his wife who became hard workers on my behalf. They were John and Katie Phillips. She spent hours working for us without ever having been involved previously in such an activity. A Dunn for Governor campaign headquarters was established, and we were able to attract a number of volunteers. I do not recall crossing paths with Jenkins, Robertson, or Jarman in Chattanooga. Surely each of them must have spent time there. We did see the Jarman bus occasionally.

The counties that cradled the beautiful Tennessee River between Knox and Hamilton were Rhea, Meigs, Roane, and Blount. In the springtime, I discovered, craftspeople and a variety of curious citizens frequented fairs in various parks and other settings with water as the background. The various TVA and Corps of Engineers dams in our state resulted in fabulous playgrounds laced through those counties. I was working at my quest without letup, seeking nothing more than a firm handshake and a willing response from all those I met along the trail.

The craft fairs became natural settings for voter appeals, and I found myself being driven by Rufus from one to another. It was a fascinating experience. We started the days before sunrise on many a morning and never looked back through intense days of shaking hands, trying to think clearly on my feet, visiting on someone's front porch, eating and talking at the same time, and occasionally being practically dragged by some enthusiastic supporter from one person to another for introductions. The process, I discovered, was getting increasingly intense. At times I felt I was getting attention from everyone but the press. Rarely was a reporter present, but on more than one occasion I silently wished someone with a newspaper connection could witness the response I was getting from many of the people and groups I encountered.

I recall falling asleep exhausted in some motel room long after sunset, tired, mind-weary, and dreading the next early morning call that would come all too soon, either from the motel clerk, Rufus, or a person in Memphis campaign headquarters. I was in awe once when it suddenly dawned on me that some devoted person on our Memphis team had to be up, dressed, and at work mighty early to place a wake-up call to me. Memphis was on central time while we in the East were an hour ahead. My five o'clock wake-up call had to be made by Memphis at 4:00 a.m.! By the time I rolled out and was ready to go, Rufus had long been in conference with the Memphis scheduler, setting up, adjusting, or detailing the campaign blueprint for the day. Each day brought changes in appointments or new opportunities not otherwise expected or planned. I always appreciated those days when our schedule called for us to first appear at a gathering in a café somewhere. That meant a little bit of breakfast. Otherwise, it was just a cup of coffee to be drunk as we barreled along toward our first appointment of the day.

The Brock influence in the other nine counties that made up the Third Congressional District was usually noticeable. As we traveled into those counties, we had few contacts initially. Every Republican function we heard about we attended, if at all possible. Showing up and making a few remarks always seemed to result in finding new friends who became supporters. Monroe County was not only a garden spot of Tennessee nestled along the North Carolina Appalachian Mountain range, but it was also the home of two incredible men who volunteered to help me. Tommy Scruggs and Kenny Cagle, both businessmen and active Republicans, took me to raise, as one of them put it. We soon had a headquarters in Monroe County, and these two men and their families never let up in helping me find primary votes.

In Bradley County we discovered the national headquarters of the Church of God denomination. The Maytag appliance company operated a large factory there. We worked to get exposure at Maytag and at the Church of God headquarters. Bradley County was the home of a popular Republican state representative named Ben Longley. We gave Ben lots of attention and in return got several helpful suggestions as to people we should definitely see in Bradley. We made all the usual calls: newspapers, courthouse, fire stations, and various businesses.

McMinn County was another place where we made good early contacts. Dan Kuykendall had given me the name of a U.S. marshal stationed in Memphis who was from that county. We made plans to meet Marshal "Chief" Tallent and did just that. From him we gathered a large number of names and spent quite a bit of time on streets and roads seeking out those people. It was hit or miss, but we put in some productive time. Athens, the county seat, was famous for a shoot-out that occurred on the street and in the upper level of the courthouse shortly after the Second World War was over. Returning veterans had major concerns about those who were running the politics of the city and county. As we heard it, no one lost his life during what was proudly referred to as "The Battle of Athens." We decided they took their politics seriously in McMinn.

In Rhea County we encountered several factions of Republicans. Call after call on various personalities resulted in no commitments but plenty of exposure. I think we worked as hard in some of those lightly populated counties as we did in some of the larger ones. We didn't hear much direct talk about any of my opponents, but it was obvious each of them had had influence on those rural counties before I ever came along. Some confusion resulted among the county Republican leaders because I was pushing hard for commitments. Many of them were committed to Mr. Jarman. In Dayton, the county seat, the famous *Scopes Monkey Trial* had taken place years earlier, and we heard a lot about that.

A Republican rally and barbecue took place hosted by Rhea and Roane County people near the line connecting the two counties. White's Creek Harbor and Resort supplied the food. Jarman, Jenkins, and I showed up, and each of us had ample time to deliver a full load to those in attendance. Each time I had an opportunity to appear with one or more of my opponents, I felt good about the results. Mr. Jarman had his say without humor or eloquence, but he had a decent message. Bill Jenkins was humorous, easygoing, and always got a good reception. I usually had a decent joke, but I pressed hard with sincerity, spending little time on issues, much time on my idea of the logic of winning by putting East and West Tennessee together.

The remaining counties of the Third District produced an occasional contact, but there were no efforts to open headquarters or build organizations. I did, at one time or another, talk to each county chairman. The headquarters in Memphis was also working by telephone to find people who might help me in a number of those counties. Several county chairmen designated a person I could contact, and that was done. The pickings were slim.

In Wayne County, just east of the Tennessee River, we had several names to work with. We sought out and met a number of people who expressed interest in helping our cause. That visit resulted in several good contacts out of a county that didn't do much on the Republican side of the ledger. We were now in Middle Tennessee. While in Waynesboro, the county seat, we heard first and foremost about a "political football" known as State Highway 13. For years that miserable highway had been used as a teaser by Democrat politicians. My new friends were looking for a politician who could be counted on not just to promise, but to do something about rebuilding that tortuous stretch of highway that coursed through Waynesboro and up to Interstate 40. Rufus kept a careful record of the visit.

Several people in counties of lower Middle Tennessee provided me with help and advice. A heavy concentration of Democrat activity could always be found in this area. Murfreesboro, the seat of Rutherford County, was the home of Middle Tennessee State University. On June 16 the Tennessee Education Association (TEA) held a Leadership Conference to which it invited all qualified candidates for governor. The meeting took place on the MTSU campus with a large crowd and press representation on hand. This was an event I looked forward to and hoped would be an opportunity for some good exposure.

Most memorable about the MTSU function was the fact that all twelve of the candidates for governor showed up. This was my first opportunity to meet Hubert Patty, one of the five Republican hopefuls. His significant Republican vote in the 1962 general election for governor, running against former Governor Frank Clement, had been an early encouragement to me. He received 99,884 votes. He was a pleasant and intelligent man whose East Tennessee drawl was in fine form. When the program got underway, the candidates seated on the platform included Democrats John Jay Hooker, Nashville; Stanley Snodgrass, Nashville; Robert L. Taylor, Memphis; Mary Anderson, Nashville; Ralph Waldo Emerson, Nashville; and James Newton, Memphis; and Republicans Winfield Dunn, Memphis; Hubert Patty, Maryville; Maxey Jarman, Nashville; Claude Robertson, Knoxville; and Bill Jenkins, Rogersville. The twelfth candidate was Douglas Heinsohn, Sevierville, a member of the American Independent Party. In addition to Patty, I had never met Newton or Heinsohn. Of those present, the only one sure to be a candidate in the general election was Heinsohn since he had no primary opposition.

Each speaker addressed the large group of educators and guests. The educators listened carefully to all the comments. Each of them had a big stake in who the next governor might be. A large and influential organization, the TEA got the best that each candidate could offer, I'm sure. My adrenaline was pumping, and I gave my usual remarks about time for a change, the reasons for my candidacy, then more than my usual emphasis on public education, drugs, and mental health. Since the meeting had a long agenda, I wasted no time attempting to shake hands when it ended. I knew the TEA had a strong Democratic Party bias. We hit the road.

Because of my dental background, I was contacted by a prominent dentist in Murfreesboro named Kenneth Ezell. Dr. Ezell was a man of strong convictions, and he had wide influence. He also had a personal political agenda apart from my promise to be a good governor once elected. It didn't take me long to learn what was on his mind. I listened to him carefully. It concerned his strong sentiments regarding the president of MTSU at that time. He made no requests and I made no promises. He was a loyal Republican, and he believed I could go all the way. He committed to my campaign and became a powerful force on my behalf with Democrats and Republicans in Rutherford County and across the state. He was especially influential within our dental profession.

With quick in and out visits, I made friends in Coffee, Bedford, Giles, and Williamson counties. There were very few Republican votes in those counties for me. Mr. Jarman seemed to have done his work well, long before I showed up. One story developed while visiting those Democrat strongholds. As the story went, I approached a couple of old boys a-sittin' and a-whittlin' on a Giles County courthouse bench. I enthusiastically introduced myself and allowed as how they probably never thought they'd see a Republican candidate for governor in Giles County. To which one of them, after a pause, said, to tell you the truth, he never thought he'd see a Republican!

Nashville–Davidson County was not only a Democrat stronghold. It was a unique entity in that it had chosen several years earlier to adopt a consolidated Metropolitan government. Nashville, the state capital and the home of Andrew Jackson, would not get much of my time in the primary. I was very pleased when Hamilton "Kip" Gayden, the young attorney I had met in 1968 at the GOP Convention in Miami, contacted headquarters in Memphis volunteering to help in Nashville. We later held a small press conference and announced Kip as my campaign manager for Nashville–Davidson County. Another friend, Elizabeth Lowe, formerly of Memphis and a longtime friend, accepted the chairmanship of Women for Dunn in Nashville. Elizabeth's husband, C. Phil Lowe, had been one of my running mates when we made the symbolic legislative campaign in 1962. They had their work cut out, supporting a dentist from Memphis who was running against a business tycoon named Maxey Jarman from Nashville! They went right to work.

The capital city was heavily populated with people who either worked for the state or ate as a result of someone else who did. The word Republican at the state level, I learned, always fed fears of patronage flowing the wrong way and massive state employee firings. It was a handy political tool for any Democrat candidate. It never entered our minds that we should visit state office buildings to shake hands with employees there.

We learned that I needed to meet a Mr. Rice in Putnam County. The largest city, Cookeville, is the home of Tennessee Tech, a well-respected regional university. It was also the home of the Rice Motel, a substantial business located off Interstate 40 near downtown Cookeville. I learned that Rice had Republican sympathies but was playing the same old game I had encountered with others. He wouldn't say yes and he wouldn't say no. I had two good sessions with Mr. Rice before I decided I could make more progress somewhere else. He was influential in the area. As we did in most Middle Tennessee counties, we visited the newspapers and the radio stations but didn't spend time in the Democrat-dominated courthouses or city halls. We hoped to see Mr. Rice later, and we did, several times.

Sometime later during a visit to Cookeville, a dinner meeting was held at the Rice Motel to which the Republican candidates for governor were invited. A decent group of Putnam County Republican leaders gathered. Following the meal, all candidates present were invited to address the group. Each of us did so. Mr. Jarman's wife, Sarah Mac, was present. She was quite a fine lady. The most memorable thing about that evening was a message I got later quoting Mrs. Jarman as saying to someone that she thought I was winning the primary! I was surprised and encouraged.

CHAPTER FOURTEEN

PROGRESS

Some Substance

The Memphis headquarters was beginning to receive telephone calls, various messages, and modest press comments to the effect that I was making progress in East Tennessee. Calls were coming in from the counties where I had spent time and even some counties in which I had been unable to gain support. The campaign team at home had gained knowledge and experience in responding to new contacts and to those who were looking for information, scheduling, literature, or money. Dealing with the rising number of requests for my attendance had to be left up to Harry Wellford and members of the team. I found myself increasingly being told where to go and whom to see. Time and energy were limited. I followed the plans being laid out by my strategy people and did all I could to intensify my efforts. The ladies were making as much use of Betty as they could and worked closely with Harry. My wife continued to gather her own head of steam and was increasingly effective.

Betty attempted to devote two days a week to campaigning. Her availability for the campaign trail depended on her mother's availability to look after the children during Betty's absence. On a trip to Jackson in mid-June during which she was the guest of honor at a coffee hosted by the local Republican women's group, she was interviewed by the local newspaper's political writer. In her very special way, she charmed him apparently, as she did all whom she met. In her talk to the GOP women her concern for public education based on her personal experience as a second grade schoolteacher came through loud and clear. She also noted her concern as a mother for the excessive problems with pollution and illegal drug use. Her concluding comments were a strong endorsement of her husband as a good man concerned about good government for all the people.

"I just hope I can make people understand what a good governor he would make." I was blessed with a wonderful wife who was an effective stand-in and spokesperson.

In Memphis on June 10, Betty and I were guests at a coffee hosted by Dr. and Mrs. Kyle Creson. The crowd was large. The Cresons were popular and among the most devoted Republicans I knew. I realized I was meeting Memphians for the first time that I would never have otherwise met in the course of building a dental practice. Later that day I attended a public hearing downtown and had a chance to speak. The papers quoted me as saying, "There is a double standard on drugs. Adults have taught children that the stresses of daily life require chemical relief." I expressed concern about illegal drugs and alcohol abuse, urging greater punishment for pushers of hard drugs than for users. A change in some laws was needed. Responding to a question, I stated that a runoff law for primaries would be more desirable than the existing no runoff law on the books because the nominee would be the candidate favored by the majority in his party. Mr. Jarman had been quoted as saying the system worked pretty well the way it was. At the time, each opinion was logical for the particular candidate expressing it. I had every hope of winning the nomination, but I knew second place was a real possibility. A runoff in the primary could be valuable to me. Mr. Jarman was confident that he would lead the ticket and couldn't support the idea of a runoff.

That same day, I attended a West Tennessee campaign kickoff for Bill Walker, a Republican, in Haywood County. He was running for a seat in the state House from the Thirty-third Floterial District, made up of Crockett and Haywood counties. Maxey Jarman and Bill Brock also attended. The handshaking was hot and heavy. Bill Walker was a popular man in his home area and was the son-in-law of Everett Derryberry, respected president of Tennessee Tech University in Cookeville. All of the candidates wanted to be on Walker's favored list for obvious reasons.

During those days Steve Sharp, my communications man, was issuing press releases out of Memphis covering my positions on a variety of issues. He was getting support from Ray Humphreys in Washington, D.C. One topic was the value of more involvement in government by women. The *Cookeville Herald Tribune* quoted me as stating that "we should give women an ever increasing opportunity to serve in state government positions of responsibility." Another release stressed my feeling that rehabilitation was a major part of penal reform and was being practiced very successfully in the Shelby County Penal System run by Director Mark Luttrell. Vivid in my memory were my experiences while following my father through the Lauderdale County, Mississippi, jail. The people I saw behind those steel bars needed something they would never receive in that setting. I had firm beliefs that such people needed guidance and knowledge they knew nothing about.

An article in the *Kingsport News* stated that it would be a rich man's campaign year. Jarman, Hooker, and Brock were named. Jarman was reported to have predicted that some of the candidates would run out of money. He went on to say it wouldn't be him.

A lively reaction from the candidates occurred mid-June as a result of the Jarman campaign releasing the results of his privately funded poll showing him getting 50 percent of the Republican primary votes at the time the interviews took place. I was quoted in several weekly and daily newspapers as saying that the poll was "a mathematical assault on the intelligence of the Republican voter."

On June 16 newspaper people from across the state met at the 101st annual Tennessee Press Association gathering and predicted that Hooker would run against Jarman, and Gore would run against Brock in the general election. In telephone conversations when I was traveling, someone in Memphis always made sure that I was kept abreast of what was being written and spoken about politics around the state. The news, when it was not good, was always accompanied by comments from home base to help me rationalize the information.

Other local polls were being taken from samples of voters that were never identified. The *Lebanon Democrat* on June 24 revealed that Jarman was ahead, Robertson was second, Jenkins was third, and Dunn was in fourth place with 3.3 percent. We were not discouraged by those numbers because they came from heavy Democrat country. At that time, they may have been accurate. We had no money for polling to disprove what we heard.

I was surprised when headquarters asked us to adjust our schedule and drive to Rockwood by a certain time. A dental colleague I had known when we were students in Memphis had contacted my people in Memphis and had then opened a Dunn for Governor headquarters in Roane County. Having that happen in a significant county without a lot of digging and asking on my part was refreshing and gratifying. Dr. Paul Layne had taken charge and was getting the county organized! Paul, at the time, was serving as the mayor of Rockwood and was not a political neophyte. The unanticipated value of my dental background was demonstrated once more. Having members of my dental profession from all parts of the state observing with growing interest news stories about the primary campaign was an enormous political asset that I didn't fully appreciate at the time.

I was so completely focused on covering as much territory in West and East Tennessee as I possibly could that I had little time to follow what was happening in the other campaigns. I was shown an article in which Bill Jenkins was noted to possibly have a serious conflict of interest. The question was raised by state Senator Victor Ashe of Knoxville based on the fact that Jenkins's former law firm was paid certain fees for services provided to the state Department of Highways. Ashe, a Republican considered to be sympathetic to Claude Robertson, produced documents regarding those services and suggested that serious legal and ethical questions had to be answered. No response from Jenkins was included in the article. This charge coincided with an announcement that Republican legislators from Hamilton County were endorsing Jenkins. Nothing came of the charge.

On the Democrat side, Stanley Snodgrass charged that Hooker's business record was an issue. He declared that Hooker couldn't evade his part in the "corporate wreckage, financial shambles" surrounding the "sad debacle" of the crumbling Hooker business empire. Newspapers reported Hooker as "turning the other cheek."

Democrat candidate Robert Taylor was widely quoted in newspapers as he released his platform designed to return Tennessee "to the calm tranquility of moderation" immediately followed by a statement describing his two major primary opponents as "political Siamese twins." As I read the article, my presumption was that the two opponents referred to were Snodgrass and Hooker. There was no time for me to dwell on those kinds of accusations.

On a visit to Knoxville, I was contacted by Dana Ford Thomas, a respected political reporter for the *News Sentinel.* He indicated he would like to share with me some confidential information about a significant poll that had been commissioned by a Democrat candidate for governor from Memphis. Thomas asked to accompany me on the drive that night as we headed back to Shelby County. I quickly agreed for him to ride with us to Nashville.

Dana Ford Thomas was considered very liberal in his political attitude, and his newspaper was looked on as the liberal counter to Knoxville's more conservative *Journal*. Through the 1950s and 1960s the *Journal* had been owned and published by Guy Smith, widely known as a staunch conservative Republican, especially during the Eisenhower years. Thomas's boss was Ralph Millett, a respected publisher. I had spent considerable time attempting to persuade Millett and Bill Childress, editor of the *Journal*, to look favorably on my campaign. I had made a friend of Childress's wife, Mickey, and she was working for me along with two capable ladies named Betty Sterchi and Joanne Clark. Those three ladies, along with E. S. Bevins, Jack Bevins, and Dr. Jack Mobley, constituted the backbone of my Knox County effort. Senator Fred Berry's son Dr. David Berry continued to be an effective supporter.

With Rufus Powell driving, Thomas and I settled in the backseat for the drive to Nashville. I had looked forward to getting some rest, but the prospect of sharing the man's confidence made me forget about sleep. Although eager to hear what he had to say about the poll results, I was a bit nervous about spending so much time with a reporter I knew to be less than sympathetic to Republicans.

Avoiding any mention of his news source, Mr. Thomas first revealed that the poll, an authentic, scientifically conducted survey, contained information that would be most encouraging to me. He was not aware of any plans to make the findings public. He requested that I treat the information he was about to give me in a highly confidential manner. I agreed.

Judge Robert Taylor of Memphis had commissioned the statewide poll in mid-June. The results were that Jarman was leading in the Republican primary with 27.6 percent. Dunn was in second place with 12.9 percent. Jenkins and Robertson were tied with 12.1 percent each while 36 percent of those polled were undecided as to which Republican they would support.

Thomas said that information should be encouraging, and I

agreed. It was a huge boost to learn that I was in second place, though only slightly ahead of two of my opponents. Even more encouraging to me was the news that 36 percent of those planning to vote Republican hadn't made up their minds. That was a large part of those questioned about an election only slightly more than six weeks away. I knew I needed a lot of those undecided votes.

From the beginning of our efforts to win the primary, I realized what lay ahead for me. I was a completely unknown political person who was in a contest with four other decent candidates, each of whom had, in his own way, become identified with large segments of Tennessee's voting public. Jarman was widely known as a successful businessman whose company had plants and retail outlets across the state. His interest in politics had been given wide press coverage long before I entered the race. Jenkins was widely known in East Tennessee as a legislator and had been acclaimed for more than a year as the first Republican Speaker of the House of Representatives in the state's history. Robertson had served the statewide party as its chairman and was well known as a close personal and political friend of popular Republican Senator Howard Baker, Jr. And we were, after all, in a contest seeking Republican votes. Hubert Patty, though never seriously viewed as a possible winner, had run as a Republican in a statewide race, getting nearly 100,000 votes in the 1962 general election for governor.

The poll results Thomas shared with me made it clear that, after less than two months of campaigning as an announced candidate, I undeniably was making some progress. Mr. Jarman's lead, while more than two times greater than my number, didn't give me any room for comfort, but I was boosted by feeling that I had momentum going my way in June.

I thanked him for sharing that information and agreed it should be kept in confidence since the Taylor campaign hadn't chosen to release it to the public. I was curious about the results on the Democrat side, but I didn't press the point. Thomas was a real pro in his business, and I felt he knew what he was doing and why. The why became apparent as the evening wore on.

As we drove west through the night on partially completed Interstate Highway 40, Thomas began asking questions. He explained that he was trying to get to know all the candidates from a more personal perspective. I accepted that, although I still did not feel too comfortable with the man and, as a result, kept my guard up. I was tired, but there wasn't a chance to settle back and close my eyes.

He asked about my personal background, including family and my Mississippi childhood. How, he asked, considering that I was from a very racially segregated state, did I feel about Negroes? My response, though it was totally unrehearsed because I had not expected the question, consumed a large part of what remained of the drive to Nashville where he intended to leave us.

As honestly as I would have tried to answer any of his questions, I began to respond by having him understand that I had always had friends and playmates that included people from all walks of life. My thoughts led me to talk about one special relationship I had experienced that had remained a very happy memory for me over the years. I told him that when I was a young teenager in the eighth grade, my parents decided to move to Ft. Worth, Texas, for a two-year period while my father enrolled at the Southwest Baptist Theological Seminary in order to become an ordained minister. The move occurred after I had begun my studies, and I wanted to remain in Meridian for the rest of the school year. The decision was made for me to complete the eighth grade by living with my father's brother, Charles Dunn, and his wife, Addie. They had no children, and we were very fond of each other. It was a good arrangement.

Uncle Charles lived in Russell, a little community near Meridian but out in the country where he had a nice home, a barn for his horses, and a large pasture where livestock grazed. The barn was several hundred yards from the house, and it became my special playground as an energetic fourteen-year-old. In a small clapboard, unpainted tenant house up a slight hill behind the barn lived Dave Wilson, a part-time hired hand, his grandmother, America Wilson, and his nephew, Ezell Wilson, who was my age. They were Negroes who were good friends of my uncle.

I explained that Ezell became my constant playmate, and we spent all our spare time together. Each afternoon when I got home from school in Meridian, I'd go to Aunt Addie's breadbox and get three or four cold biscuits left over from breakfast. Routinely, I'd take each biscuit, punch a hole in its side, careful not to go all the way through, and I'd fill that hole with my favorite syrup, which was blue ribbon cane molasses. Then, with the biscuits stuffed in my pants pocket, I'd walk up to the barn where Ezell would be waiting. Without fail, I said, by the time I reached the barn, molasses would have soaked my pants pocket, and a stream of molasses would have run down my leg. The first thing we did was eat those biscuits.

From that point on, we might shoot marbles out of a circle scratched on the hard, red clay barn floor, or look for chicken eggs, or shuck and shell hard corn out of the corn crib, or play hide-and-seek among the hay bales in the loft. On mild days outside, we'd hit and shag fly softballs, run foot races, fly homemade kites, or swim in a nearby pond.

I continued with my story, hoping Thomas wasn't bored. He didn't seem to be. There were nights when, after supper, I'd walk up to Ezell's house to visit. Everyone called his grandmother "Merky," which was some sort of short for America. She was a sweet old woman who always welcomed me. If there were burning logs in the fireplace, she might put a sweet potato on the hearth and rake some red hot coals out to soften what would be a nice snack. If not a potato, she might put some dried corn kernels in a small can and cover it with bacon grease. Placed on the hearth, the hard kernels would become warm and bacon flavored. Just something for Ezell and me to munch on. He and I would usually end up on her bed where we'd read the advertisements in old newspapers pasted on the wood walls to keep the cold out. The only light came from a coal oil lamp on a table and the glow of the burning embers in the fireplace. Consistently, I'd fall asleep as Merky hummed her favorite hymns. My next conscious awareness would come when I woke up the next morning in my own bed in the Dunn household. That sort of magic occurred because Uncle Charles would come up and walk my half-limp, sleepy body down to the house.

On school days, I'd walk down the driveway and board a shiny yellow school bus for the ride to my junior high school in town. Home the same way. Ezell's school day began as he jumped off the side gallery of his house, crossed several pastures, climbed through several barbed wire fences, and continued walking to his school-house. It was an old church building consisting of one room where students representing several grades collected and studied under the guidance of a single teacher. Somehow, at the time, our different arrangements for getting an education didn't bother me or seem to me unfair to Ezell.

When summer vacation days commenced, I left Uncle Charles, Aunt Addie, and Ezell, making the move to my new temporary home in Texas. I missed Ezell, but new friends soon took his place in my thoughts.

As I spoke to Mr. Thomas during that long ride, I was trying to make the point that I had a close, personal friendship with that Negro boy, and to me, it was a very natural, unprejudiced relationship. Only later did I begin to think about the differences in our lives that made it an unusual one.

As time went by, I explained, I frequently thought about my country buddy, and I missed the fun we so innocently enjoyed. Ezell and I were about the same age. He was a couple of inches taller. I was skinny but he was skinnier. In every activity I can recall in which we competed, he was better than I was. He could jump farther and swim faster, and he could read those newspaper ads on his grandmother's wall as well as or better than I could. I wondered out loud as I spoke to the reporter, just as I had wondered many times in the years after our times together out in the country had ended, what kind of successful life Ezell might have had if he had benefited from the same good education I received at Kate Griffin Junior High School in Meridian.

I had lost track of Ezell, but I learned from Aunt Addie years later that he worked at the Staff O'Life feed mill in town, sacking livestock feed and loading it in railroad freight cars. I had worked at the same mill one summer while in high school. My objective was to earn a little money while lifting one-hundred-pound feed sacks to build up my muscles for the upcoming football season. I remembered most vividly how thick the air inside the mill was with dust from the feed bins. Breathing was difficult. Soon, our ride to Nashville was over, and I ended my story.

To be sure, Betty, Harry, and the strategy team were elated with the results of the Taylor poll. It gave all of us a huge boost at a time when we needed just that. Dana Thomas had been thorough in his interview with me, and I felt reasonably good about the time I had spent with him.

Shortly after the long night ride to Nashville, on Sunday, June

21, two significant political articles appeared in the *Knoxville News Sentinel.* On the front page, top left-hand column, under Dana Ford Thomas's by-line, the title of one article was "Poll, Reportedly Made for Taylor, Favors Hooker." Also, "GOP Picture Looks Cloudy." Thomas had broken the news of the confidential Taylor poll, and the reason why the Taylor people wanted it unpublished became clear. Hooker received 54 percent of the vote to Taylor's 9.6 percent. Thomas wrote that it appeared Hooker was in total control on the Democrat side, but the poll results suggested there was room for anything to happen on the Republican side. The preference numbers on the Republican side were as Thomas had told me. It looked good in print.

On the front page of the second section, Thomas had a feature article titled "Dunn Convinced He's Best for Governor." This was one of a series labeled "The Candidate in Profile." Mr. Thomas wrote the best article I had seen summarizing my life's history and reasons for being in the race. It was so well done, as I saw it, that I looked back with gratitude on the long ride with him headed for Nashville and the detail I went into in order to explain my deepest feelings about some matters. It was, by far, more than I expected to receive at the hands of a real pro with strong liberal leanings.

CHAPTER FIFTEEN

FROM FEELING TO FINDING

Some Encouragement

It seemed that my campaign was developing fundamentally on personality, my logical argument about East and West Tennessee's potential election clout, political reform, and basic issues of public interest. I was doing my best to out-smile and out-handshake my opponents, make a good argument for a major Republican role in the destiny of Tennessee state government and the logic of why I was the most electable Republican candidate. I didn't have the time or the resources to attack my four opponents, much less the inclination to do so. Other than occasional references to Mr. Jarman's age, political naiveté, and lack of a solid Republican voter base, Bill Jenkins's youth, and Robertson's reliance on support from a cowboy movie star running mate, I stuck to my fundamentals.

As to Mr. Jarman's political naiveté, I had picked up on a widely publicized statement he made to the effect that he took great pride in never having voted for a Democrat. He obviously and clumsily was playing to Republican audiences. That statement was made to order for a political opponent such as myself. On many occasions I quoted Mr. Jarman's statement and countered by saying that, in the South, many a general election was held in which major public offices were to be filled where there was no Republican opponent. In such cases, I stated that the only intelligent and patriotic thing to do was to vote for the best Democrat on the ticket. To waste one's vote, I maintained, was tragic, and surely Mr. Jarman should have been politically smart enough to see that!

The last days of June 1970 were pressing down on us, and it was a sobering thought to realize that July was the last month remaining between our growing campaign effort and primary election day, August 6. I spent many nights in Knoxville, with my overnight host being either Dr. Jack Mobley and family or the Berry Funeral Home interns' lounge. Later, as campaign contributions began to pick up, I was occasionally booked to stay in a motel. That was a relief because I could maximize my rest time.

At one point my schedule had me in Knoxville speaking to representatives of area-wide insurance firms. These kinds of opportunities had been rare in the early days of the campaign. I didn't fail to mention that my first job following graduation from college was with the Aetna Casualty and Surety Insurance Company. I stressed my support for tax revenue sharing between the federal and state governments and the logic of a governor appointing a commission on state and local government relations that could assist Tennessee in avoiding being "shortchanged" in the process of revenue sharing. I followed that meeting with a speech at the University of Tennessee Faculty Club sponsored by several local supporters. We then headed north to campaign in LaFollette, Lake City, and other areas of Campbell County to have lunch with supporters from Oneida and Huntsville, campaign in Jamestown in the afternoon, and finish the day at a Middle Tennessee political rally in Watertown along with other candidates for various offices.

On that same late June day, news reports had Maxey Jarman in Knoxville assuring the young people of the state that they would have a role in his administration if he was elected governor. Jarman stressed that state government was the biggest business in the state and that it should be run like a business. He believed that, run like a business, state government could save $50 to $60 million a year. Bill Jenkins was in Jonesboro emphasizing his belief that the next governor of Tennessee should possess a "good rapport" with both political parties in the state legislature. He stated that the next governor should possess "energy and vitality in greater proportions than ever before." I was quoted as saying that increased law enforcement capabilities cannot protect the nation from chaos if the youth continue to lose their respect for the foundations of order. Meanwhile, on the same day, the Tex Ritter–Claude Robertson campaign bandwagon rolled across Middle Tennessee as Robertson emphasized his understanding that people across the state wanted a state government geared to the needs of the 1970s. I was always curious to know what the opposition was saying, but I didn't dwell on it.

One respected political reporter from the *Commercial Appeal* in Memphis wrote that the 1970 statewide campaigns were becoming a "personality cult" with the candidates "talking themselves blue in the face" about specific issues, reforms, programs, and projects, but becoming aware that all too few were listening. He concluded that results would boil down to which candidates had the necessary attributes to "pull it off."

My team of political volunteers, growing in numbers day by day, were doing all we could do to "pull it off"! On June 26 in Kingsport I met with several groups, stressing concern for pollution, fiscal responsibility, better roads in East Tennessee to correct a disgusting situation, and the benefits of more tourism. My campaign manager in Sullivan County, Boots Duke, a dedicated conservationist, stated that careless people were about to bury Tennessee with bottles, beer cans, sandwich wrappers, and other litter. My Kingsport supporters were getting no cooperation from the local Republican campaign headquarters. The Quillen influence was very much in play. Since there was no separate Dunn campaign headquarters in Sullivan County, my people attempted to use the local Republican office as a destination for supplies and Dunn literature mailed from Memphis. They discovered that, more than once, what had been shipped to Kingsport for Dunn was sent by return mail back to Memphis! We did our best to work around such obstacles, and we avoided confrontations for obvious reasons.

On June 28 Rufus and I gathered with a small band of my supporters, including Skeet and Jean Jones and Howard Westhaver, to open the Dunn for Governor campaign headquarters in Morristown. They had raised the necessary funds to rent empty office space on a street that paralleled the main street downtown. Some printed material had been received from Memphis, a phone had been installed, and volunteers were being recruited from among their friends. We had a newspaper reporter and a radio person with a tape recorder present. It was a modest effort, but it was a special occasion for me.

Several days earlier, Tom Moore, Mr. Carbaugh, Katie Phillips, and other supporters opened Dunn headquarters in Chattanooga. We got coverage from several radio stations and the *Free Press*. My new friends were working, and they were never to let up in their efforts until Election Day was history. In other places across the state, similar efforts were being made. It was all a matter of faith and hope. The people were completely dedicated in their commitment to make something different happen in politics. I attended as many headquarters openings as I could get onto my schedule. It was some sign of progress that there were headquarters openings I couldn't get to.

In Memphis and around the state where we had managed to gain a toehold of one sort or another, some regular political activists and many ordinary citizens were beginning to intensify their support for me as the month of July drew near. Our Memphis office was feeling the heat of growing interest and enthusiasm. Telephone calls stressed the fact that Winfield needed to be in a particular place at such and such a time, without fail, and that the entire campaign hinged on him getting there. Each time I got such a report, I agonized that I couldn't be everywhere, but I am grateful I didn't know how heavy the pressure was on Harry Wellford. He had to deal with those requests and always scheduled me for what he thought would produce the best results. Betty was being called on more frequently to substitute for me, and she did all she could. Everywhere she appeared the results were positive. She was good at winning friends and gaining new supporters. Imagine those results from a second grade schoolteacher who had the reputation with me of freezing up at the idea of reading the Sunday school class scriptures!

As we drove from town to town, I occasionally read various political news items that had been sent from Memphis. Ralph Waldo Emerson was charging fellow Democrats with having a "plum" list that consisted of too many state employees getting a paycheck regularly for doing nothing. Snodgrass charged that Hooker supporters were "harassing and intimidating state employees," and threats and scare tactics were being used among those on the state payroll. Bill Jenkins was quoted in the *Johnson City Press-Chronicle* as urging voters to choose a candidate not on the basis of where he lived but on who was best qualified. My schedule as published in one newspaper called for me to be in Cocke, Sevier, Washington, Unicoi, and Grainger counties on Tuesday, Wednesday, and Thursday of the week of June 30. We were keeping an incredible pace trying to be in as many places as possible. All the candidates were making serious efforts to be seen and heard. I didn't cross paths with other candidates frequently as I "free-wheeled" from county to county, but I always enjoyed the events where we appeared jointly to make our cases.

Each time I returned to Memphis to touch base and get a little rest I was re-energized by my loving family. Betty later described her feelings on those occasions as being full of sympathy and concern for me as well as serious doubts about what we were trying to do. She said her optimism tended to fade during the week. Then, after I came home and filled her in on my experiences of the week or the last several days, she became reassured and enthusiastic once again. By that time I *believed*, and my optimism never waned. My feelings could be attributed, in part, to complete naiveté regarding many of the existing political circumstances in the state over which I had no control and of which I knew relatively little.

Joe Hatcher, the veteran political writer for the Nashville *Tennessean*, wrote a lengthy political overview and analysis of current events. In his comments he wrote that "Dunn is undoubtedly the most articulate and most attractive, outgoing personality among the Republican gubernatorial candidates. He is becoming a tough campaigner and a serious contender, from almost a standing start as an unknown outside Shelby County." I believe that article did as much to encourage me and the people in Memphis as anything that occurred during those days, aside from the Taylor poll. Hatcher had the reputation for being good at what he did and not given to being unnecessarily generous to Republicans. His words lingered in my thoughts and gave me new energy as we sat down in Memphis to plan the remaining days of the primary campaign.

It's difficult to put into words any description of the climate of expectancy, enthusiasm, and personal commitment that character-ized a large segment of Shelby County as the last month of the primary campaign began. Strategy sessions with important citizens of Memphis and Shelby County became almost routine as people showed their willingness to participate. Lawyers, businesspeople, physicians, dentists, socialites, church leaders, teachers, my dental patients, housewives, New Guard Republicans, and established politicians holding various elective offices throughout the county were increasingly in and out of our headquarters. I was grateful for all of that, but I was too busy and consumed with the best use of my time to show my appreciation. Even my earlier sense of amazement had given way to a feeling that we were all in the effort together because we wanted to make a difference. Nowhere did I feel the interest and intensity more than in Shelby County. It was real and it was growing.

I felt sure I was getting reasonable coverage from local radio and television news broadcasts, along with newspaper articles. I had made every effort to get before the editorial boards of both Memphis papers, as well as those all across the state, and I felt the effort was paying off to some extent.

Steve Sharp played the role of directing communications with fierce enthusiasm. In addition to a steady flow of press releases containing news of my schedule, my positions on issues, and my reception from people as I moved across the state, he contrived an effective technique for "feeding" excerpts of freshly made comments from the candidate directly to radio stations that welcomed such information. Rufus or whoever was with me on occasions when I made a speech used a small tape recorder to capture my words. When a selected statement was chosen from a tape, a telephone was used to transmit the information by unscrewing the mouthpiece of the telephone, clipping two small wires from the recorder to the mouthpiece of the phone, starting the recorder at the proper place on the tape, and sending the message to be recorded at the radio station. The process worked and was used often as we made every effort to get our message out.

In Memphis, on handshaking visits to city hall and the courthouse, I became acquainted with people I never knew existed. As an office seeker, I felt a kinship with many of those people, and it was a real thrill for me to make a swing through the buildings as interest in my race grew. The welcoming facial expressions and firm handshakes of city policemen and deputy sheriffs were spontaneous and enthusiastic. I can't deny it was a heady experience.

Henry Loeb, the mayor of Memphis, was a freewheeling, uninhibited sort of fellow who was very popular. I never missed an opportunity to ask for his support. The same was true for Sheriff Bill Morris, another popular officeholder. I shook his hand at every opportunity. Loeb labeled himself a political independent. Morris was considered a Democrat, although candidates for mayor in Shelby

County did not have to declare a party identity. These men were proven vote-getters, and I was anxious to have their support.

It became ever more obvious and logical that my physical presence in East Tennessee was essential for most of July. I intended to spend as much time as I could in the West, but I had to concentrate on counties with historically numerous Republican primary voters. Harry Wellford and his team had no doubt that was the best approach, and they planned to give me enough exposure on the west side of the Tennessee River to avoid appearing to be ignoring my home base. In most of the towns we had visited, some sort of support for me had been initiated. It was imperative that I move back into those communities and attempt to build on what some good people were doing on my behalf.

Harry Wellford, Jim McGehee, Bill Rachels, Dan Kuykendall, Jack Craddock, Jim Gates, Bob Schroeder, Bob James, Carolyn Weins, Bettie Davis, Kopie Kopald, Alex Dann, Alex Maddox, and Ann Daniels—these people and so many others were putting their hearts and their energies into the effort in ways I could not have imagined in the beginning. Financial support had picked up considerably, I was told. Occasionally, someone would slip money to me as we shook hands, but that was not a routine occurrence. Jim McGehee held a tight rein on every dollar we received.

The campaign was spending money on printed material that included yard signs, bumper stickers, and brochures. Ward Archer and Associates, the PR company, was hanging in there with us. As far as I know, Raymond Humphreys and Steve Sharp were not on a payroll as such, although some arrangements must have been made for Sharp's personal expenses. He did live in our home until Betty said, "No more!" He understood that his personal schedule was much too erratic for Betty to deal with and found other accommodations.

Betty and I paid our household and other personal expenses with whatever collections came into my dental office. My meals on the campaign trail were usually paid for by Rufus, I assume with campaign funds. When we stayed in motels, Rufus always picked up the tab. All other personal expenses, such as a haircut or a hasty dry cleaning job, I paid out of my pocket.

In our organization, the wheels were turning and the lights burned brightly in our headquarters on Getwell Road. Carolyn Weins apparently never looked at the clock. It seemed that, no matter what hour of the day or night, she was always right there.

The record shows that I was in Murfreesboro on Friday, July 3. According to our research, the Tennessee public education system did not offer statewide kindergarten classes. Several pilot classes were in place around the state, but there was no public funding provided in the state budget for general kindergarten development. That was one important example of how the state was missing a great opportunity to improve education for its children. That became a major issue. On that day in Murfreesboro I placed great emphasis on that basic need and pledged to make kindergarten education available to every Tennessee child when I became the governor. The statement was, and continued to be in the days ahead, a popular one for every audience.

The same day I attended an eight-county Republican rally in Winchester, the seat of government for Franklin County. Located in a beautiful Cumberland Plateau section of the state, these eight counties offered few Republican voters, but those who did embrace the party were strong in their political enthusiasm. A large number of GOP candidates attended. During an interview, I estimated that the Republican vote would range from 245,000 to 250,000 in the upcoming primary. In the Baker-Roberts primary of 1966, 148,660 votes had been cast. That was a non-presidential year, as was 1970. My numbers were a product of the capable calculations of Dan Kuykendall, who had taken the state county by county and come up with the figure.

The next day, Saturday, July 4, was one I had been looking forward to. All across the state, Independence Day celebrations were taking place in various communities. In Memphis, a large celebration was held annually on the grounds of St. Peter's Orphanage on Madison Avenue. Every officeholder with Memphis connections, every major statewide elected official, and most would-be officeholders or government employees made it a point to be seen there. Handshaking, politicking, and speechmaking were the order of the day.

I had attended Fourth of July celebrations at the orphanage several times while county chairman. As a candidate who had begun to be recognized in the ongoing primary, it was a totally new experience. I actually drew a crowd and found myself surrounded by well-wishers, campaign workers, and news people. Other more widely recognized politicians, such as senators and our congressman, were doing their work among the crowds. I spent the entire morning on the grounds of that wonderful institution and returned later in the day as the crowd began to thin. It was a great wrap-up to the first week in July.

On Monday we flew to Chattanooga where a rally was being held at Republican Party headquarters. Congressman Brock was present. A primary race between Jack McDonald, a businessman and cousin of Brock, and Lamar Baker, a businessman, for the Republican nomination to succeed Brock as Third District congressman was going strong. It was a good opportunity to get some exposure in Chattanooga.

Later the same day I campaigned in Ooltewah, a small community in Bradley County that obviously had a Cherokee name. I had made a few friends there, and they took me on a fast-paced handshaking tour. We then moved on to Oak Ridge. The city was well known for its excellent public education system, including kindergarten for every child eligible. The heavy presence of a highly educated segment of people who worked at the National Laboratories had resulted in a strong public education system. One enthusiastic supporter was a successful businessman who had made his fortune producing white mice that were used in the atomic energy laboratories experimentally. Another excellent backer was J. D. Johnson, DDS, a statewide leader in dentistry. These two men were invaluable to me.

I visited the local Oak Ridge newspaper and spoke to the editor and several reporters. A later news account indicated I stressed my concern for the quality of public education, kindergarten through university, more money for the University of Tennessee Medical/Dental Units, and more financial support for higher education including technical training across the state.

Betty remained upbeat over the results of the Taylor poll. She was being featured at a growing number of events and functions that were arranged by her own special group of campaign team ladies, and from all accounts she was making a strong statement wherever she appeared. A news article about Mary Anderson and Betty welcoming lady pilots of the cross-country Powder Puff Derby at Dyersburg Airport was featured around the state. Betty and Mary, both private pilots, enjoyed welcoming women fliers from all around the nation as they competed in the annual cross-country race. Betty was honored at a tea in Milan in a beautiful home. I was told the crowd was much larger than expected. Sara Jane Scott remained Betty's coordinator of events and confidante. She did so much to make events such as the tea a big success.

Betty was also working some in East Tennessee where she was honored at a Civil War–period social event to which 350 people were invited in Harriman, Roane County. She toured Roane State Community College's Child Care Center, a day-care facility run for abused and neglected children. There was a Dutch treat lunch at the college with students and President Cuyler Dunbar. She also visited the Fort Southwest Point excavation site in Kingston and the Michael Dunn Center. She was a busy lady, and I was so proud to have her working for our cause.

I worked hard in the fast-growing town of Jackson because I had strong people committed to the campaign. In mid-July I was there, and the record shows I was leaning a little hard on Jarman. I commented that the record showed Mr. Jarman made a substantial financial contribution to the presidential race of Robert Kennedy in 1968, which gave any good Republican reason to question his party loyalty. I also commented that the big spending advantage that Jarman had enjoyed early in the primary had faded because my candidacy was gaining momentum. I further criticized Mr. Jarman for remarks he had made publicly about personal habits of former Governor Frank Clement, by then deceased. I noted that there was something good that could be said about all of us and concluded that it was clear to many people that the Jarman campaign was sliding. One newspaper reporter wrote that the candidates were gearing up for the last three weeks. I just wished I had had another gear I could shift to. I was going full speed.

My campaign got a solid boost in Memphis when Mayor Henry Loeb called a press conference and announced that he was formally endorsing two individuals in the governor's race: Judge Robert Taylor, a Democrat, and Winfield Dunn, a Republican, were his choices. Loeb had a potentially difficult reelection campaign coming up in 1971, and it was obvious that he was intent on straddling the fence in the governor's race. He couldn't go wrong supporting the two

Memphians involved, and he chose the easy way out. We had been actively seeking his support from the day I formally announced my candidacy, and I feel sure the Taylor people were doing the same.

About that time, Maxey Jarman issued a statement that Congressman Dan Kuykendall was using Dunn for Governor as a stepping-stone to the Senate in 1972. Dan forcefully denied that accusation and stressed his total support for the reelection of Senator Howard Baker, Jr.

Senator Baker had been questioned about his apparent neutrality in the governor's race, even though his close friend and former statewide campaign manager had been Claude Robertson. His response was that he fully believed he, as an elected Republican officeholder, should remain neutral in all contests between Republicans. He noted with regret that in his 1966 primary race against Kenneth Roberts, his opponent had been endorsed by the current Republican National Committeewoman and National Committeeman.

Politics had certainly heated up across the state. The effect created by the energies released from four primary races for major offices could be most often noticed in the pages of daily and weekly news publications. That was an historic change. There was more to write about, and reader interest was greater. Change could be seen in other places. Personally, I knew that recent weeks had brought about a change in me. I had definitely moved from a perceived position of one who was feeling his way to that of one who was finding his way. My comfort level had grown enormously.

CHAPTER SIXTEEN

JOY AND DANGERS

A Roller Coaster

As the last two weeks of July rolled around, my pace and the efforts on my behalf seemed to intensify. The Dunn Dollies were in high gear. Joanne Fleming had done a remarkable job organizing those beautiful young girls. I appeared at a DeKalb County Young Republican rally near Smithville that cost attendees $5 per person. My message was that student unrest on college campuses was understandable but only to the degree that it was dissent, not disruption. I described myself as a "two-fisted, progressive conservative." I toured downtown Cookeville shaking hands and was quoted as saying that tourism and conservation were the two sides of a coin of prosperity for Tennessee. We opened the Dunn campaign headquarters in Kingston with Ted Wagner and Grover Trent in charge. Another news article stated that the campaign for governor was "sizzling" and quoted me as saying that state government required better communications with young people. Back in Shelby County, at a function in Frayser, I stressed the importance of law and order, noting a high crime rate and restlessness on the parts of many who opposed the conflict in Vietnam.

An article in the *Knoxville Journal* reported that their informal poll showed Robertson in first place, Jenkins second, Jarman third, and Dunn fourth with Robertson and Dunn gaining ground at the expense of the others. The *Commercial Appeal* headlined an article "Dunn Encouraged by Trip to East" in which I described the people of East Tennessee as open-minded about my candidacy. The article reported on activities of other candidates, and it was clear they were working hard. A Nashville *Banner* article dated July 14 reported on GOP "infighting" and included my comment that I was the only Republican in the race who could defeat a Democrat in November.

It included my quote that "I feel I am old enough for mature judgment and young enough to be an active governor." In the same article Jarman laughed off my earlier statement that his campaign had peaked by stating that "we've just begun to turn up the steam." Null Adams, *Press-Scimitar* political editor, wrote that some definite trends had developed in state races with a survey showing that Taylor, Dunn, and Crockett appeared to be gaining. Hudley Crockett, a former member of the Ellington staff, was challenging Albert Gore in the Democrat Senate primary race.

Out on the road on July 16, I got a phone call from Harry Wellford telling me that the *Memphis Press-Scimitar* had endorsed me in the GOP primary with a terrific editorial in the afternoon paper. Rufus and I were overjoyed at the news. We had no way of knowing if or when such an announcement might be made, but the timing seemed perfect. Excerpts from the editorial included the following comments:

> . . . *After comparisons of the records and qualifications of all these candidates, the* Press-Scimitar *is convinced that Dr. Winfield Dunn of Memphis would be the best choice among them for the people of all sections of the state. Above all the others, he stresses the need for state unity, and he has fresh ideas and the energy and enthusiasm to carry them out.*
>
> *We therefore urge all our Republican readers to vote for his nomination on Aug. 6, and we recommend him also to the GOP voters of Middle and East Tennessee.*
>
> *Up to now, Dunn has devoted his political activity to building up the Republican Party. "I believe in the two-party system, and we can't have it in Tennessee until the Republicans win on the top level," he says. But he says he believes the interest of the whole people is above any party's interest, and he hopes to move up now to a position where he can serve the general public.*
>
> . . . *Dunn has an intriguing plan of appointing a task force, representing the most talented and skilled business, professional, educational and labor leaders to research the depth of Tennessee's problems and come up with specific programs.*
>
> *That would be a good way for anyone elected governor to start his term.*
>
> *Such ideas, powered by his immense energy and enthusiasm,*

*mark Winfield Dunn as the man for Republicans to nominate
for the office of governor.*

The endorsement was somewhat overwhelming. I had talked
on the campaign trail and in conferences with editorial boards
about my desire to create a "businessman's task force" to study state
government with the idea of reforming what I believed were many
obsolete and inefficient ways of doing business. I had also begun to
promise that, on the day I took office as governor, the large, handsome highway signs that welcomed visitors to the "Three States of
Tennessee" would be replaced with a fresh message that welcomed
people to the "Great State of Tennessee." That statement had the
ring of unity that I was stressing in my remarks about bringing our
state together under fresh, new leadership. I had noticed that the
existing signs contained a large map of the state with two diagonal
lines drawn to distinguish the three grand divisions. I simply wanted
to eliminate those two diagonal lines and change the wording of the
message. Our campaign staff people in Memphis were thrilled with
the endorsement and continued to work relentlessly, communicating
with supporters all over the state.

The next day I was scheduled to appear on live television, Channel 4, in Nashville, to be interviewed by popular host Jud Collins
along with the other Republican candidates for governor. Jenkins
and Robertson did not appear, leaving the interview to me, Maxey
Jarman, and Hubert Patty. The event took place as planned and gave
me the opportunity to have my best exposure in Middle Tennessee.
I was satisfied with my performance during the one-hour program
and learned from later feedback that the impression I left was that
I would be a winner. Time and time again I heard from others that
they thought I gained much ground that evening on Channel 4.

Back in Memphis, on Saturday night, July 18, I received word
that I would receive the endorsement of the *Memphis Commercial
Appeal* in Sunday's paper. No words could describe the joy Betty and
I got from that news. We were elated. Several paragraphs from the
endorsement went as follows:

*This year for a change the governor of Tennessee is going to
be chosen in the general election rather than a party primary.*

This is due to the emergence of the Republican Party as a force in Tennessee politics, making this a real two-party state.

. . . He is a quiet, modest individual who recognizes the "limits of any one man" and the need for attracting other talent to make state government work as it should. This he pledges to do, and we suspect that if given the opportunity he will succeed.

. . . So Dr. Dunn's problem is to make himself as well known as possible in the eastern counties between now and August 6 and to hope for a big majority from the homefolks on Election Day.

He may be able to bring it off. Winfield Dunn already has built a reputation for gaining converts wherever he makes a personal appearance, and he is being supported with enthusiasm by most Shelby County Republicans.

These are good recommendations for any man.

The *Commercial Appeal* also endorsed Stanley Snodgrass in the Democrat primary, and I was not surprised since everything I had heard about the man was positive. I personally knew the editor, Frank Ahlgren, and the chief editorial writer, Guy Northrup, and I felt comfortable about their best wishes for the general election if I could keep my campaign on course. I was immensely grateful for their confidence.

That same Sunday in other papers around the state Brock was quoted predicting the biggest GOP primary turnout ever. The *Oak Ridger* newspaper endorsed Maxey Jarman; Knoxville's Basil "Preacher" Mull endorsed Hooker and said Hooker told him Dunn would be the toughest opponent to beat. Jarman predicted a 2 to 1 victory in the primary. Interest in the outcome was building.

We were encouraged by a Dana Ford Thomas article in the *News Sentinel* that stated Dunn was moving up. He noted there had been no comments by opponents that he was not qualified. He observed that Dunn had the best opportunity to unite his party.

During that week I made an appearance on Nashville's *Teddy Bart Noon Show* and had a chance to express gratitude for the endorsements of both my hometown newspapers. I campaigned in Cumberland, Morgan, Scott, and Hamilton counties. In Chattanooga we had a press conference at which I announced Mr. Harry Carbaugh, former state GOP chairman and National

Committeeman, as my county finance chairman. He gave a strong statement in support of my candidacy. In answer to a question, I called on the youth of the state to become involved in the political future of Tennessee and lauded their idealism. I was beginning to move ahead in Chattanooga, based on what we were told, and I gave Mr. Carbaugh's reputation a lot of credit for that good news.

News reports indicated that the *Clarksville Leaf-Chronicle* had endorsed John Jay Hooker for governor. Mrs. Mary Anderson was quoted in an article as saying that Tennessee needed a housewife for governor. Ralph Waldo Emerson was quoted as saying that Hooker was weak on business integrity. Hooker was quoted as saying that the economic system, not his management, was responsible for the bankruptcy of his holding company, Whale, Incorporated. Jenkins reportedly was claiming the support of a majority of GOP legislators; however, at the time, I had been endorsed by five of those gentlemen. An article reported businessman Frank Massey of Greenville announced his endorsement of my candidacy as well. Claude Robertson was quoted as claiming East Tennessee to be a stepchild of the state—104 years since Knoxville had produced a governor—50 years since East Tennessee had been represented in the governor's office.

Greene County was a beautiful place to campaign. I had become the friend of a small group of people who took my campaign to heart. In addition to Massey and Fran and Ray Smith, another was my new mountain lady friend, Iula Kilday. She accompanied me into many rural parts of the county, introducing me to relatives and friends. It was a fascinating experience, and I regret being so physically tired that I couldn't fully enjoy all that I was seeing for the first time. She told me about a special place on one of the Unaka Mountains where she had a cabin. She promised me that after the campaigning was all over, she was going to take Betty and me there and give us a piece of her property. I didn't bank on that promise, but it sounded good coming from her.

The editor of the *Greeneville Sun* newspaper was a very prominent and highly respected man. I visited Mr. John M. Jones several times and felt he was sympathetic to my cause. The paper did not endorse me. Another newspaper editor I came to know rather well was the publisher of the *Johnson City Press-Chronicle*, Carl Jones. I made several calls on Carl Jones, although I knew him to be a Democrat. My team in Johnson City, including the Diehls and Jenningses, didn't encourage me to continue working on Carl Jones. They were doing a fine job helping me build support there in Washington County, and they were certain I wouldn't get help from the *Press-Chronicle* in the primary.

My concentrated efforts in East Tennessee continued as the folks in Memphis and Shelby County worked in their neighborhoods and precincts to help my campaign maintain its momentum. Rural West Tennessee friends and supporters followed suit. The strategy team decided I needed to have Betty with me as much as possible in the East as well as in West Tennessee. She was game and ready to make the effort.

On July 20 at a Hamilton County Young Republicans Club dinner meeting for all Republican candidates, a highlight of the campaign occurred. We were gathered at the Sizzling Steak Restaurant, and following the meal, each candidate spoke. Mr. Jarman and I traded a few verbal punches, which were enjoyed by all. As Jarman spoke, he described himself as a friend of many Democrats, including former Governor Frank Clement. Just at that moment, the multimillionaire industrialist's large campaign picture poster that had been attached to the wall immediately to the rear of the speaker's seat fell off the wall and hit the floor behind him with a thud! The audience howled, and I'm sure the candidate's face got a little red. It was perfect timing and I enjoyed it. I think we all needed a laugh about that time, and I'm glad it was not at my expense.

In Blount County on July 21, I announced attorney William Felknor as my county chairman. I was quoted in the *Press-Chronicle* as pledging my cooperation with organized labor and stating that I fully supported unions in every instance where the public welfare was not threatened. In the same article I stressed my strong support for Tennessee's capital punishment laws. Maxey Jarman was quoted in a Nashville paper as saying he opposed atheists teaching in public schools. He also remarked that the GOP had lost the Negro vote while lamenting that when he joined the Republican Party, most of its members were of that race.

We campaigned in the Knox County region throughout that same day and were the overnight guests in the home of the Joe Brownlee family. Mr. Brownlee was a prominent contractor who had become a strong supporter in Knoxville. He planned to fly Betty, me, and Rufus to the Tri-Cities Airport early the next morning for various meetings in Bristol and Kingsport. These plans, unknown to us, contained the elements of a near tragedy that we would never forget.

We arrived at the airport the next morning on time only to discover that Brownlee had left the keys to his company's twin engine Piper airplane at his home. He left to retrieve the keys, and we settled in for a long wait because his home was quite a distance away. When he returned, he explained that the keys were actually to an airplane similar to his company craft because his was undergoing a maintenance checkup. We were assured he was fully capable of handling the borrowed plane, which was similar to his. We boarded and taxied out to the runway, by that time severely behind schedule. After conventional engine run ups and clearance from ground control, we headed down the runway and into the air. I sat in the co-pilot's seat up front while Betty and Rufus were in the two backseats.

There was a low ceiling, and shortly after takeoff we were in the clouds, throttles were fully open for power, and Joe was immediately flying on instruments. As we climbed out, Joe began to tap on the instrument panel. I noticed but had no concern until his tapping intensified and he began to alternately use his radio mike attempting to get in touch with the tower. In a matter of seconds, I realized that he had a problem, which was that his artificial horizon instrument was malfunctioning. The airplane was still on full throttles, we were engulfed in clouds, and I could hear desperation in Joe's voice. I could also hear the wind whistling abnormally loud at the door of the craft near my head. I knew we were in trouble, and Joe had ceased knocking on the panel and was desperately calling the tower.

I glanced over my shoulder and saw Betty and Rufus clutching each other with alarmed expressions on their faces. We all knew the pilot had lost control of the airplane. The thought rushed through my brain that my wife was going to die in another man's arms. At that moment I turned to look forward just as the plane broke through the clouds and I saw the foggy hills below. We were heading for the earth at a 60 or 70 degree angle. Without the artificial horizon we didn't know how the plane was positioned in the air. When Brownlee got his orientation, he hauled back on the controls with all his strength. With both engines still at full throttle, the little airplane shuddered severely from the forces on it. The craft leveled out. Not fully in control, the pilot continued to desperately call the tower, asking for position, which we finally obtained. He did throttle back on power. From that point it was just a matter of being directed back into a landing pattern and experiencing a safe touchdown.

Each of us was tremendously relieved and shaking from what we all believed was a fatal event about to happen. Joe Brownlee was beside himself with apologies for what did happen. As our thoughts cleared and we were outside the plane, we began to focus on where we were and where we were supposed to be. My limited skills as a licensed pilot were of no value during our difficulty. Joe had the presence of mind to make a phone call and obtain a flight for the three of us to Tri-Cities on a Kearns Bakery airplane. None of us hesitated to climb aboard, and within an hour we were being greeted in Upper East Tennessee by the party that had been advised we would arrive late.

The story of our near accident appeared the next day in the Bristol, Virginia-Tennessee newspaper. Our schedule was so tight and appointments were so pressing that we didn't have time to dwell on how close we came to dying. Betty said later that all she could think about were our three children. That figured.

Reporter Richard Boyd covered the airplane story and our time spent in the Bristol/Kingsport area. I was quoted as saying confidently that I could win the primary and that I wanted to be a governor *for* East Tennessee, not necessarily from East Tennessee. I strongly supported home rule for local governments and a crash program for building highways. I shook hands in Kingsport and then campaigned briefly in Carter County before flying back to Memphis for a rally the next day.

Reading newspapers occupied some of my time as I rode with Rufus, and he always managed to get copies of the major papers for me. With Betty as an added traveling companion, less news reading occurred, but I managed to stay current. Tex Ritter, my childhood cowboy hero, and I enjoyed several encounters as our paths crossed in campaigning. He was making a serious effort in his race, just as his partner, Claude Robertson, was doing in the governor's primary. A news article quoted him as saying that, while he hoped Robertson was the winner in his race, he, Ritter, felt he could work well with whomever was elected governor. He noted that he was particularly impressed with Dunn, a comment I really appreciated. Robert Taylor was reported to have said his opponent, Stanley Snodgrass, was in a secret coalition with Senator Albert Gore. I gathered he meant that voter support was being quietly encouraged between the two.

On Friday, July 24, a "whistle stop" auto caravan had been arranged to take our campaign through Hamblen, Jefferson, Cocke, Greene, Unicoi, Washington, Carter, and Johnson counties. We started with a rally in Morristown on the Baptist Church parking lot. The cars were decorated with various kinds of "Dunn for Governor" signs and white shoe polish messages. There was a vast amount of territory to cover, and the ample string of cars occasionally created traffic problems. At every stop a group of supporters was waiting to welcome us, and the hope was that some news people would be present. We visited Newport, Parrottsville, Greeneville, Erwin, Johnson City, Elizabethton, and Mountain City. We saw many people and tried to create news. My basic message was that my campaign was picking up speed while Jarman and Jenkins were fading. I continued to stress the importance of putting East and West Tennessee together. At every stop, Betty was a hit with the crowds, and she handled herself well. It was an exhausting trip, but there was so much excitement that the weariness was late setting in.

Later, Betty remarked that she remembered the caravan tour in Elizabethton with me for a special reason. On an earlier trip to Upper East Tennessee in late May, she had been taken by a supporter on a handshaking visit down the main street of Elizabethton. Her escorts took her from shop to shop, introducing Betty and urging support for her husband. She recalled that it was a fun and exciting thing to do and she was warmly received. However, in one store the manager interrupted to say that she had a phone call. Congressman Quillen was on the line. She answered, and the congressman told her he was in his Washington office and had been advised she was visiting in Elizabethton. He told her he was sorry he had not been advised of the visit as he would have wanted to have a member of his staff welcome her to his district. The conversation was brief, but Betty quickly let her friends with her know that she felt the congressman was determined to remind her whose territory she was in and that he expected to be advised of such trips in the future.

That incident faded in the wake of our growing campaign but remained one more example of Quillen's desire to exert total control in his area. Bill Rachels had encountered the same attitude in the early days when Quillen advised him that all campaign money collected in the First District had to be routed through his office. Rachels, of course, ignored that. Quillen was a tough character and completely different from his counterpart in the Second Congressional District, Congressman John Duncan. Quillen was also an incredibly strong political force in his district, and we were always careful not to antagonize him. Most of the voters loved their congressman. He, of course, was openly supporting Bill Jenkins.

Eleven candidates for governor presented their views at the Read House Hotel in Chattanooga. It was covered live by TV Channel 12, and the *Times* newspaper reported it well. I was quoted as continuing to question Mr. Jarman's Republican loyalty in view of his 1968 support for Bobby Kennedy. I was not alone in criticizing Jarman. Bill Jenkins, with his wry sense of humor, nudged at Mr. Jarman on occasion.

One warm night the Republican candidates were seated on a flatbed trailer that had been parked on the playing field of a high school stadium in Athens. The rally by local supporters had attracted every governor's race candidate and a sizable crowd seated in the stands. The stadium lights glared in the faces of the candidates who were chosen to speak in reverse alphabetical order. Sitting next to Mr. Jarman, I noticed that his head had moved forward during a musical presentation by the local band, and I figured he was either praying or taking a nap. His head moved up and down slightly, which gave me a chuckle. When Jenkins's turn to speak came, he thanked our hosts and the crowd, then commented that it was a warm night and he hoped "Uncle Maxey" could make it through the rest of the program! Jenkins had obviously noticed that events were taking a toll on Maxey. In his remarks, Jarman ignored the jab from Jenkins.

CHAPTER SEVENTEEN

IT ALL COMES TOGETHER

Encouraging Signs

That last full week of the campaign was an incredible time for me and my family. Each of us was moving in a different direction looking for support. The *Memphis Press-Scimitar* on Friday released results of a poll taken in Shelby County by a group of reporters who fanned out in various directions to sample public opinion. The article reported that I had garnered five times as many votes from those polled as all my opponents combined. Hooker led Snodgrass by a few votes, and Brock polled 106 to Ritter's 2. We were once again elated by that good sampling.

Near the end of July our Memphis office received word that Shelby County Sheriff Bill Morris had agreed to endorse my candidacy. That was great news. I met with the sheriff, we had our picture taken shaking hands as we toured the county jail, and good articles appeared in both Memphis newspapers. Morris stressed the fact that he remained a political independent and stated he had endorsed me because he felt that I was the candidate who could do the best job as governor of the state. That was a healthy step forward because of the sheriff's popularity as a leader in the community. It was rumored that he would oppose Loeb in the next mayor's race.

Sunday morning at home I received a call saying that the *Knoxville News Sentinel* had endorsed me in the Republican primary. It was a stroke of good fortune I had worked hard to get but didn't expect. The paper also endorsed John Hooker, although it had opposed him in the 1966 contest against Buford Ellington. The editorial for me was so positive and strong that I sensed, when I got a copy, that Dana Ford Thomas had been influential in the decision. Among the comments were the following:

> *On the Republican side the race had been even more of a personality contest. This emerging party lacked the polarization that characterizes the Democratic race, where "Browning men," "Ellington men," and "Clement men" tended to conglomerate behind one candidate or another. This lack of polarization was heightened by the decision of Republican leaders Sen. Howard H. Baker, Jr. and Representative Bill Brock, who is seeking Senator Albert Gore's seat, not to get involved in the governor's race.*
>
> *Winfield Dunn has been the real surprise—not only of the Republican Primary, but the Democratic one also. Starting as an unknown a few months ago, he has moved further in popularity than any other candidate. He is given credit in Shelby County for the revitalization of the Republican Party there. This type of enthusiasm and determination, we think, would make him a good governor, despite his lack of experience in government. He is also the only Republican that we think would stand a chance of defeating the now-apparent front running Hooker.*
>
> *Therefore in the Republican Primary we pick Dunn.*

My remarkable team of supporters in Knoxville was thrilled with the endorsement of the *News Sentinel,* as was I. Several of them, especially the Bevins brothers and Dr. Mobley, had quietly hoped that Mickey Childress, wife of the editor of the *Journal,* might persuade her husband to endorse me, but that was not to be. Earlier in the week the *Journal* had given strong endorsements to Claude Robertson and Bill Brock. I was disappointed in their decision, but I knew I had made a good friend of Bill Childress. The *Journal* wanted, above all other considerations, a governor from East Tennessee.

Monday, August 3, began with a strategy session in campaign headquarters with Wellford, Kuykendall, McGehee, Rachels, and me. My schedule was in flux because it was agreed that I would attempt to appear wherever there was greatest need. We had done everything my energy and our unseasoned political team could do to make things happen. I couldn't imagine any group of mostly volunteers doing more to cover the territory included in our long, narrow state. For me, the past eight months had provided not only time to learn what it took to be a statewide candidate for high office, but also an opportunity to discover much about my magnificent, adopted state of Tennessee. It was a rare and unique experience that I thought about every day as we covered numberless miles and met countless new friends. The decision was to attend several rallies that had been scheduled in various parts of East Tennessee, make a full-day sweep of Nashville shaking hands and seeking whatever newspaper and broadcast coverage we could find, and concentrate the last day of campaigning, Wednesday, at home in Shelby County.

Comments in various political editorial columns around the state gave us a decent picture of circumstances at that time. Someone had talked to our people in the larger cities and had learned what was in the morning papers. The Republican race for the gubernatorial nomination was described as a "Hoss Race" that was completely unpredictable, according to the pundits who were supposed to have the best insights. It was generally agreed that total votes in that primary could range between 175,000 and 300,000. In 1966 the statewide Republican primary vote was just less than 147,000 votes. Speculation was that the "Hoss Race" would generate more interest and a higher vote on August 6. The Shelby Republican vote in 1966 was just under 9,000. We had every reason to believe we would exceed that, although some estimates that we might exceed 30,000 seemed high.

A light vote in East Tennessee was considered to be bad news for Jenkins. Jarman and I were described as locked in a battle for the state's two largest urban areas. That was not accurate since my team was concentrating on getting a strong Republican vote in Shelby County where we hoped I would get a large majority. Jarman had some hopes for a decent Shelby vote, but he needed all he could get in Nashville and the rest of the Fifth District. It was not Republican country. I had little hope for a decent vote there. It was predicted that Robertson would win a large majority in Knox, the largest Republican stronghold.

Kuykendall stuck with his earlier estimates of what it would take for me to win. I needed to run second or third in the First District, we figured, a strong second in the Second District, carry or come in second in the Third, and do awfully well in West Tennessee. He had specific numbers for major counties, but they were just a blur to me.

The last organized function of the primary campaign was a homemade ice cream party at our residence on St. Andrews Fairway in the Hedgemoor subdivision on Wednesday evening. Our great friend and supporter Ann Daniels put it all together as a welcome home for me. It was a wonderful way to wind things up. Friends, neighbors, and campaign workers came together to enjoy the delicious ice cream and cookies, although some of those devoted workers were still at headquarters talking to supporters around the state. Cars were parked as far as the eye could see. The crowd that gathered was large. Our children were all present, the girls in their Dunn Dollies blouses and skirts, and Chuck just a very important fellow there for us in those moments. He had been a relentless worker during his break from college, and I was so grateful.

I'm sure I slept later than usual on Thursday morning. Betty and I were anxious to vote, and we did so mid-morning by going to our precinct balloting place in the basement of the Walker Wellford home. In past elections, we had worked at the polls there. It was quite a different feeling for us to walk in and request our ballots, which contained my name.

Betty and I had lunch with Jackie and Dan Kuykendall, just the four of us. It was a special time because he had meant so much to me during the entire process. Dan was full of enthusiasm. He was also a candidate for reelection but had no significant opposition. He remained focused on the numbers and was very optimistic. I was hopeful but restrained. Things had to go "right," as they say, and I believed they would.

That evening we drove to Bill and Betty Rachels's home where the strategy group and close friends had agreed to meet to watch and hear the returns announced as polling places closed and totals were reported to the various election commissions. The Racheleses had a beautiful pool house at their home on Cherry Road, and it accommodated a sizable crowd. The air was heavy with excitement and expectations.

From Knoxville eastward the time zone was one hour ahead of us in the central zone. We soon began to receive East Tennessee results even though our polls were still open. Metropolitan area boxes came in first, and the excitement began to build.

I tried to relax by shooting a game of pool. It was the night we had all been working toward and waiting for. News broadcasters were feeding out the numbers from various areas, and we were switching from one to another of the three Memphis TV channels, looking for the latest figures. The phone rang frequently as calls came from those in our Getwell Road headquarters. As the several hours we were together there in the Rachelses' play room advanced, we began to get a picture of results by television and radio from across the state. Of course, we were riveted to numbers from the Republican governor's race.

By 10:00 p.m., it was clearly becoming a Jarman-Dunn contest, as Jenkins and Robertson had begun to be positioned by votes in that order, slipping further behind the two front runners. The intensity, apprehension, and hope continued to find expression in the words of all those of us clustered around the television. Jarman had a lead as the vote counting moved to the west. As those numbers were reported, I began to move up, and an hour later, at 11:00 p.m., the totals showed me with a lead of slightly less than 2,000 votes over Jarman. We were reminded by the newscasters that a number of East Tennessee precincts where Jarman was doing well had not reported as yet. We were thrilled with the slight lead but still quite nervous.

By midnight, the question appeared to be no longer in doubt. My lead in numbers of votes over Maxey Jarman was approximately 10,000, and the messages from television stations were that Winfield Dunn, a hometown dentist, had won the Republican nomination as its candidate for governor in the upcoming 1970 Tennessee general election. The final and much later official tally was Dunn, 81,475; Jarman, 70,420.

Harry Wellford had been monitoring results in the Democrat primary as well. It was clear that Hooker would defeat all five of his opponents. His margin over the closest rival, Snodgrass, was substantial. That news added to our excitement and satisfaction since John Hooker had been the individual I hoped to run against in the general election.

Joyfulness and excitement reigned supreme in the Rachelses' play room. I could only imagine how the folks down at our Memphis headquarters and wonderful friends across the state felt in those moments. We drove to the Getwell Road campaign headquarters and joined that celebration. People were ecstatic, and I was falling all over myself expressing thanks to each one. Our hopes and dreams had come to pass, and we had apparently been given the approval of a plurality of state Republicans to move ahead. I am certain that a degree of numbness and pent-up exhaustion had set in on me personally. The drive home, the personal exchanges between Betty, me, and the children, and the remainder of the night in what should have been a deep sleep are only vague memories. The one sense I was most aware of was that of deep gratitude to all those who had been involved.

The next morning around ten o'clock I received a telephone call from someone asking if I was available to speak to Governor Ellington. The governor and I had a good conversation, which seemed to tie the knot on the prize package I had won the night before. He congratulated me on my win and wished me well. I had never met Buford Ellington, but his warmth and cordial tone of voice assured me he was a thoughtful and sensitive man.

The governor told me that John Jay Hooker, my opponent in the general election, had spoken with him and had requested that two state troopers be assigned to him for the duration of the general election. The governor had agreed to do so. He then said that he felt obliged to offer me that same resource and he would encourage me to accept it. Without hesitation I did so. That was my only conversation with the governor prior to the November general election. Although the Democratic Party was powerful, it was somewhat fragmented, and I was told the Ellington loyalists had supported Stanley Snodgrass. I didn't detect disappointment in his words or tone of voice.

My mind was turning from one thought to another as Betty, the children, and I savored the election results. Although it was still a long distance from us at the time, Nashville was a place I had never thought about in terms of where we might live. One night during the campaign as Rufus, another person, and I were leaving Nashville in order to be somewhere east of there the next morning, our passenger unexpectedly suggested that on the way out of town we should drive by the governor's residence. It was an exhilarating and exciting thought. We decided to do so and headed in the direction our passenger knew we needed to go to swing by the official residence. After twists and turns we angled up an inclined driveway, suddenly glimpsed the north side of the stately mansion, then headed back down the driveway and out of town.

There were no obstacles to our gaining entry to the grounds, and we felt we had sort of invaded Democrat territory. It was a light moment during a hard campaign and was my first glimpse of the governor's mansion.

Newspapers on Friday and Saturday carried the results of all the elections county by county. Hooker had won the Democrat nomination for governor by a large plurality of the nearly 600,000 primary votes cast. Hooker had 261,580, Snodgrass was second with 193,199; Senator Albert Gore had defeated Hudley Crockett 269,770 to 238,767; and Bill Brock had defeated Tex Ritter 176,703 to 54,401.

My vote was a little more than 33 percent. I received 81,475 out of a total of 244,999 votes cast in the primary. My 81,000 plus vote compared to Hooker's 261,580 was not impressive but, proportionately in the total vote cast, was reasonable. Eight hundred forty-five thousand votes were cast in the 1970 primary elections.

It was interesting to compare my results with what Dan Kuykendall had predicted I would need to win. Instead of second or third, I ran fourth in the First District. That was disappointing but perhaps not surprising. Old habits are hard to break, and sectionalism played a part. I ran a strong second in the Second District, but I was closely trailed by Jenkins. Dan was on target there and in the Third District as well. There I ran a strong second, although Mr. Jarman was an impressive winner. That figured. My results in Middle Tennessee were weak, as expected. As we hoped, I did very well in the Seventh, Eighth, and Ninth, winning each district by large margins. Shelby County gave me unbelievable support with 93.5 percent of the total primary vote. That made the difference!

CHAPTER EIGHTEEN

Sorting It Out and Getting Ready

Shifting Gears

Events played out as I had hoped, and the proper die was cast. I deeply believed I was the only Republican in the race who could defeat the one I expected would win the Democrat nomination for governor. I believed just as deeply that, from all I had learned about Hooker and his friends, he would not be good for Tennessee. And finally, every instinct in my body told me that my candidacy as a West Tennessean would do more to help Brock, and vice versa, than any other combination of candidates. We had the proper ingredients, and I believed the political climate was right.

My strategy group soon met to discuss the next steps and to review the election results county by county. The day following the primary election a steady stream of contacts began to be received by me personally, by those in our headquarters, and by every member of the strategy team. We had to put these communications in some order and sort them out for practical reasons. We were hearing from every section of the state. Not only were all sorts of messages coming from those who had supported me. It was quickly apparent that names we didn't know and names of well-known but theretofore somewhat distant persons were surfacing. People seemed to be tremendously excited.

Newspaper accounts of my winning the first hard-fought Republican primary campaign in modern Tennessee political history seemed to be magnified because of the unusual circumstances surrounding our efforts. Unknown, dentist, inexperienced, and Shelby County seemed to be the words most often used to tell the story.

Two weeks before primary Election Day, Claude Robertson had thoughtfully issued a statement calling for a unity meeting of all Republican candidates for governor after the results were known.

That made sense and became an immediate topic for discussion between Harry Wellford and other of our strategists. It was agreed that such a meeting should be held, possibly in Knoxville.

The Jarman campaign was reported to be quite upset with the results of the election. Shelby County became suspect since, in the final analysis, my victory had been a result of the historically high voter turnout in the primary and the unusually strong percentage of that vote which I received. There had been 39,860 Republican votes cast in the county, exceeding our hoped for 30,000 to 35,000 votes. Of that number, I had received 93.5 percent. Even more amazing and gratifying to me was that I received nearly 99 percent of the votes in my home precinct! My home county had made the difference in the tight race with Mr. Jarman. I was sympathetic with his disappointment, but I had no doubt the results were accurate and honest.

The outcome was directly related to the unusual interest of people in Shelby who had become involved actively in a political campaign for the first time in their lives. The image I had managed to project was that of a completely new face with no apparent ties to selfish political interests that the public often felt existed.

That appeal, certainly not carefully crafted by me or my team, was a "happening" that occurred in a heavily populated part of our state that had for years been directly affected by the powerful influence of political boss Ed Crump. Mr. Crump's death several years earlier had, in effect, created a political vacuum. Those circumstances, plus a growing awareness that for the first time in the lives of most people there was a serious possibility Memphis and Shelby County could produce a governor of the state, made a huge difference. Everyone agreed the excitement that developed over the two months leading up to primary day was unique. Realization of the hopes and dreams we had envisioned could be laid directly on the doorstep of my home county and its citizens.

The rationale that most of our campaign efforts and attention should be directed toward the western and eastern sectors of the state was legitimized by results. I ran first in votes in twenty-six of the state's ninety-five counties. Of those twenty-six, seventeen counties were in West Tennessee, eight were in the East, and only one was in Middle Tennessee. Coming in first in eight of the East Tennessee counties was deeply satisfying. Running strong, as I did, in the West Tennessee counties outside Shelby not only confirmed our judgment. It also pointed out the very honest sectional bias that existed on the parts of many who cared enough to vote.

I ran second in twenty-one counties, eleven of which were in East Tennessee. I placed second to Jarman in Hamilton County and Robertson in Knox. It was obvious that the Brock organization gave clout to Jarman in Chattanooga, and Claude Robertson was obviously and properly the hometown favorite in Knoxville. I had hoped to do better than I did in Hamilton. I was very satisfied with a strong showing in Knox. Jarman beat me by a close margin in Madison County, a result of his early organizing there. I had hoped to win that important West Tennessee county. I ran second in seven Middle Tennessee counties and three counties in the West. My results in the middle section pleased all of us in view of the fact I had given that area less of an effort.

The results had me running third in thirty counties. Among those were Greene and Sevier, where I had hoped to do better. The East Tennessee candidates, Jenkins and Robertson, were a little too strong for me. I was grateful for the votes I did get in those heavily Republican areas.

From the very beginning of a serious effort to win the nomination, finances to underwrite the effort proved to be one of our greatest challenges. Billy Rachels had proved his commitment to the cause by being one of the very first to contribute funds and other resources. Dollars were scarce for political activities. They certainly were for a completely unknown prospective candidate. I took money from my modest personal resources to pay the expenses involved in producing and mailing the critical letter that was sent to Republican voters in the very early stage of making a final decision to run. I was later reimbursed. Contributions from members of my Sunday school class, while limited, proved to be most helpful in the beginning. Those gifts were encouraging.

Many, many people were involved in the fund-raising activities. Several individuals played vital roles. Billy Rachels used his great gift for salesmanship at the outset and generated significant dollars from usually skeptical givers. Jim Harwood, uncle of Ann Daniels who was one of my most avid supporters, was well connected with the business community; Keith Spurrier, husband of Peggy, had good financial contacts; Bob Schroeder had good contacts that he leaned on; and Jim Gates and Jack Craddock used their finance skills to identify prospects. Jim McGehee shared all his skills as a money manager to keep everything financial in line with our resources.

To put early finances in perspective, a wonderful fellow named Joe Felknor of Dandridge sent Harry Wellford a check for $1,000. Joe generated the funds in small increments through his untiring efforts in Jefferson County. The check came at a critical time and sent a strong message to my Shelby County team that there was support in East Tennessee. That perhaps was the largest single contribution the primary campaign received from outside Shelby County. We were all amazed and grateful.

Other money was raised in various counties and spent locally on advertising, headquarters, and other needs. We never knew the total of those expenditures, but I do know they came from the enthusiastic, dedicated people I had met along the way who became so vital to the effort.

Another valuable contribution came from those who had private aircraft that were made available for our occasional use. The dollars those gifts represented could never be quantified, but the transportation was a blessing. Alex Maddox and Ewing Carruthers were two Memphis friends who made much of that aid available.

The amazing and unusual fact was that our primary campaign effort produced slightly less than $80,000. These funds were handled by Jim McGehee. Many gifts in kind must have been used, including very minimal charges by my valued public relations friend, Ward Archer. In relative terms, there is no doubt that a winning, major, statewide political campaign for a primary nomination had never before been conducted with so few material resources.

In the final analysis, it was the total vote that counted, not the amount of money spent. I would have been interested to know how much was spent by my opponents, especially Mr. Jarman. Both Claude Robertson and Bill Jenkins were gracious in their losses, and I anticipated their full support and cooperation in the general election. I could only hope Maxey would pitch in.

As discussed, a meeting was called for all the Republican gubernatorial candidates. We met in Knoxville shortly after the election.

Regrettably, Mr. Jarman did not attend, having left for a vacation in Europe shortly after the results were known. Jenkins, Robertson, I, along with our key people, had a thorough discussion in anticipation of the general election on November 3. Initial plans were made for waging a hard-fought campaign during the next two plus months. Afterward, all parties returned to their respective homes for much needed rest.

Betty and I turned off all outside involvement for the next few days, although I did stay in close touch with Harry Wellford and Dan Kuykendall. Harry had made a contribution to the final results of the primary election that was unparalleled by any other person. His Republican roots were deep and family based through several generations. The extent to which he had gone to do his job during that campaign would be known only to him. He put his heart into the effort, and I can think of no greater compliment he could have paid me. I could never have put a value on all he gave leading to our success. Harry had taken so much time away from his law practice to run the campaign that I knew what he would be doing while Betty and I were getting a little rest. He would just be trying to get caught up with his professional backlog and paying a little more attention to his wonderful wife, Katherine. She had played an enormous role in support of Harry and me. She had an instinctive gift for understanding the political process. Kuykendall was on the congressional payroll and was doing what came natural for an incumbent congressman. He campaigned for reelection in his district while at the same time he campaigned for me. It worked well for him. His contributions to my effort were especially significant from the start.

The flood of congratulatory messages, visits, and telephone conversations with close friends was heartwarming and encouraging. Betty and I were physically very weary. Chuck, Gayle, and Julie were thrilled with the win and the prospects of exciting days ahead. Only in the wake of our success did I learn how many things my son had done during his summer vacation to help in the effort. Our son and daughters had put their loving hearts fully into the adventure. My Mississippi family and some close friends had become caught up in the effort, and they were elated by the results.

My nomination to be the Republican candidate surely influenced every person having a serious interest in the next governor. At the time, I could not possibly have imagined its impact on many people I had never heard of. The degree of their interest, which in many instances focused on their personal concerns, would unfold in the days ahead. The people who openly supported me and many of those who simply voted for me must have begun to think of the upcoming hard-fought general election. I knew their help would be vital.

For Betty and me, and for all those who had helped me from the beginning, there was one central focus—how we could change things for the better—how we could bring fresh, new faces and ideas into state government—how we could make a positive difference for Tennessee. Total unselfishness characterized what was in our minds and hearts. There were no other agendas. We were determined to go forward and win for the right reasons. Those who supported Democrat candidates, with the exception of John Jay Hooker, must have begun rethinking their positions. The immediate priority for my family was to get some rest, and after that to begin laying the foundation for winning the big prize in November.

PART TWO

The General Election

PHOTO GALLERY

Winfield Dunn in Meridian, Mississippi

College politics

Betty Prichard, an Ole Miss Beauty

Winfield and Betty at a college prom

The wedding reception, Memphis, Tennessee
(L to R) Aubert Culberson Dunn, Dorothy Crum Dunn, Winfield, Betty,
Ruby Howell Prichard, Frank William Prichard

Phoenix Club
"Operation Flag Brag"
Memphis, 1960

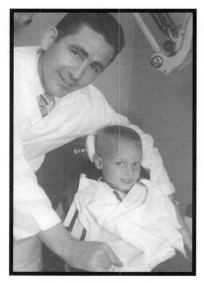

Dr. Dunn and patient

Winfield Dunn with Dwight D. Eisenhower

Son and Father
Charles Winfield Dunn and Winfield Dunn

Julie and Gayle Dunn; Dunn Dollies

The Dunn Family and Christy
preparing for a campaign

The announcement at the Capitol
(L to R) Congressman Dan Kuykendall , Winfield Dunn,
Betty Dunn, and Harry Welford

*Candidate Dunn makes his
announcement at the Capitol*

*Winfield Dunn and
Campaign Chairman Harry Wellford*

*On the campaign trail the candidate listens
to the voice of the people*

*Betty Dunn with Little Miss Petite,
Jefferson City*

Winfield Dunn with the Dunn Dollies

Betty Dunn campaigns in White Pines

A set up

A parade during the campaign in Elizabethton

The candidate thanks his Knoxville leader,
E.S. Bevins, Jr.

Winfield Dunn, John Jay Hooker
The third stop on the day of the Great Debate

Winfield Dunn and John Jay Hooker
on the campaign trail

President Nixon arrives at the Tri-Cities Airport
(L to R) Senator Howard Baker, Congressman Jim Quillen, President
Nixon, Congressman Bill Brock, Winfield Dunn

Winfield Dunn gets advice from Tex Ritter in Memphis
Lt. John White (Right)

Election Night
Major John Fields, Betty, and Governor-Elect Winfield Dunn

Inaugural platform, January 16, 1971
Governor Winfield Dunn and Governor Buford Ellington

A moment to remember
Winfield Dunn, Betty Dunn, Chief Justice Ross Dyer
(Top Left) Alfred T. Adams, Jr.

Inaugural Ball
Governor Dunn and First Lady Betty Dunn
dancing to the Tennessee Waltz

Governor Dunn with Legislative leaders
(L to R) Representative Tom Jensen and
Senator Houston Goddard

*Early Cabinet members at the swearing-in ceremony January 16, 1971;
(L to R) Russell Hippe, Finance and Administration; Claude Armour, Safety;
Eugene Fowinkle, Public Health; E. C. Stimbert, Education; Howard Kesley,
Standards and Purchases; Guilford Thornton, Agriculture; Robin Beard,
Personnel; Bill Jenkins, Conservation; Bob Smith, Highways*

Governor Dunn with Tennessee State Troopers

*First Lady Betty Dunn with Senator Howard Baker and
Governor John Connelly*

First Lady Betty Dunn with Stacy Webster and Terry Roake

*Betty Dunn with the Andrew Jackson portrait purchased
by the First Lady at auction for the State of Tennessee*

*Governor Dunn with then Governor Ronald Reagan and
Vice-President designee Gerald Ford*

Conferring with mayors
(L to R) Governor Winfield Dunn; Mayor Wyeth Chandler,
Memphis; Mayor Kyle Testerman, Knoxville

President Richard Nixon greets Governor Dunn in Washington

*Political cartoon depicting the "Keynote of Cooperation"
vision of Governor Dunn for the people of Tennessee*

*December 11, 1973; Governor Dunn signs the deed approving the transfer
of Stewart Air Force Base Property for the purpose of Vocational Rehabili-
tation's Comprehensive Rehabilitation Center. (L to R) William Harrison,
Assistant Commissioner for Vocational Rehabilitation; Governor Dunn;
Representative John Bragg, Murfreesboro; Judge Knox Ridley, Rutherford
County; Benjamin E. Carmichael, Commissioner of Education; Roy L.
Waldron, Chairman Rutherford County Board of Education.*

(L to R, front to rear)
The Cabinet

1st row: *Benjamin Carmichael, Education; Jane Hardaway, Personnel; Pat Choate, Economic and Community Development; Ben Gibbs, Labor; the Governor; Mark Luttrell, Corrections; Halbert Carter, Insurance; Eugene Fowinkle, MD, Public Health; W. Dale Young, Executive Assistant*

2nd row: *Gary Sass, Staff; George Tidwell, Revenue; Richard Treadway, MD, Mental Health; Fred Friend, Welfare; Howard Kesley, General Services; Ernest Griggs, Employment Security; Ted Welch, Finance and Administration; M. Lee Smith, Executive Assistant and Counsel; Gilford Thornton, Agriculture*

3rd row: *Chip Christianson, Staff; Granville Hinton, Conservation; Joe Hopper, Staff; Leonard Bradley, Planning; William Smith, National Guard; Bob Kabal, Staff; Ralph Marlatt, Staff; Ralph Griffith, Director of Information.*

CHAPTER NINETEEN

A DIFFERENT CAMPAIGN

Putting a Team Together, So Little Time

To the surprise of many, Bill Brock and I, with the help of countless good people, were responsible for fresh political winds that were blowing across our beautiful Volunteer State following the August primary election of 1970. It was a fascinating experience for me. I believed I had maintained enough objectivity to know that many of the new friends who were declaring their support of my candidacy were probably interested in the politics of the situation for their very own reasons and not necessarily mine. Regardless, I was anxious to have their help and grateful for it.

In county courthouses, city halls, drugstores, barber shops, beauty parlors, farm co-ops, college administration buildings, and throughout the expanse of state offices and facilities, people were talking. The idea that the long-standing Democrat establishment was about to come under serious siege by the Republican Party and its candidates for major statewide office was not going down well with many seasoned political people. Politics was the topic of conversation from the street corner to the bridge table to the golf course, grocery store, coon hunt, and places in between. I had little time to reflect on what was being discussed, but I was thrilled to be a part of the change that was taking place. And I had no reasons to discuss motives as far as new friends were concerned. I was glad to welcome each and every one.

The effect of my primary victory on those people who had been with me from the very beginning or who had joined in the effort as we became friends seemed to be almost electrifying. Their man had won! Their judgment had been vindicated. Many of them suddenly became a great deal more important in their communities because of their early and close relationship with one who just might be the next governor. Many of them had never been involved in political activity before. They had some important adjustments to make in their personal lifestyles for the next few months because their interest and involvement became so much more intense. Most of them would be involved in the general election to an extent they could hardly have imagined. Their value to me could not be measured.

The major campaigns in the Tennessee general election of 1970 would feature the race for the United States Senate seat occupied by Albert Gore, Sr., and the race to elect the governor of the state. Bill Brock, having handily defeated Tex Ritter, would square off against Gore in a contest that would draw national attention from its beginning. As for me, there was no doubt I was looking down the wrong end of a big gun barrel and the face at the other end was John Jay Hooker.

President Richard Nixon had made it clear that the defeat of Gore was a matter of great interest to him and his administration. Brock had laid the foundation for a strong challenge by developing a statewide network of support over several years. His campaign was professionally directed by a seasoned political adviser named Kenneth Reitz. It was increasingly clear to me and my supporters that Brock had a carefully developed game plan and knew exactly what he was doing. Denying the Senate seat to Albert Gore would be an enormous task for Brock since Gore was a "fixture" in the political life of Tennessee. I spent not a moment focusing on what Brock was doing. I absolutely wanted him to win, but I was completely devoted to my own objective.

Senator Gore had served in the U.S. House of Representatives for fourteen years before being elected to the Senate in 1952. After three Senate terms, he obviously was anxious for six more years to build on a notable career that had included his interest and involvement in a nuclear test ban treaty, agreements with the Soviet Union regarding outer space, and major domestic initiatives, among them medical care, tax reform, and the interstate highway system. Brock saw Gore as being too liberal and having lost touch with the people of Tennessee. That was the message he had to take to the people to be successful.

In my case, the early days of August post-primary were given over to planning and identifying various necessary steps for an organized effort to be elected governor. Having grown out of a shoestring effort by a group of sincere, well-meaning people who had never been involved in such a project, we suddenly found ourselves in the "big league" of Tennessee politics. For fifty years, Democrats had occupied the governor's chair. Each of those governors was a powerful political chief executive officer whose authority was based principally on legislative forbearance and empowerment.

The constitutional authority of a Tennessee governor was limited. However, precedent left no room for misunderstanding as to who controlled the budget, who appointed powerful constitutional officers and commissions, who selected the Speakers of the two houses, and so on. It had been, and was, the governor of the state. Perhaps that was because most every legislator imagined it was only a matter of time until he (at that time there were no women legislators) ascended to the governor's office out of a legislature that was very willing to concede great powers to the chief executive. Now, here we were, a naive group of Republicans based in Shelby County laying the groundwork to wrest decades of power from the hands of those who had long controlled the monopoly.

Harry and I spent quite a bit of time in my home or at the Wellford residence with Kuykendall, McGehee, Rachels, Donelson, Kopald, Humphreys, and others coming to grips with our opportunity. We avoided the campaign headquarters on Getwell because the place was besieged with people who wanted to wish me well, volunteers, and salesmen. The telephone lines were ablaze. Carolyn Weins, Bettie Davis, and others were constantly busy.

There was no time to be wasted. We were literally into the general election. We needed a strategy from the start that would be flexible enough for instant change when necessary. The geographic makeup of Tennessee posed a big hurdle. There were major questions to be answered. Could we mount and wage a campaign covering every one of the ninety-five counties and do it from a central headquarters located in the southwesternmost part of our long, narrow state? Could we organize and carry out the kind of fund-raising effort needed using as our base Tennessee's major city but one with little history of significant financial support for statewide political candidates? How were we to manage the continued involvement of the loyal supporters who were with me from the beginning but who, in the main, were not the recognized local Republican leaders in their counties? Would we be able to draw in the significant local leadership that supported Jarman, Jenkins, or Robertson so as to build effective countywide Republican organizations in as many counties as possible? How could we handle the human and material logistics relating to local campaign headquarters across the state from a place so far away as Memphis? How would I hold up under the added stress of the Memphis-based travel necessary to keep me in East and Upper East Tennessee with great frequency? And where were the politically committed and knowledgeable people needed to staff a full-blown campaign to come from? It was a fact that most of the people who had played pivotal roles in the primary campaign organization were Memphians who had no desire, much less the freedom, to abandon their regular jobs and responsibilities for the next sixty plus days.

These were among a large number of questions that had to be answered. When compared to Brock's preparations and progress at that point, we were already two years late. We knew that the Brock campaign had no resources that could be made available to us. In fact, we knew that we would be competing with his organization for the financial contributions needed to run a proper race. But we also knew that we could take advantage of each other's events and crowds on occasion. It would, however, not be a "Republican ticket" arrangement. Our campaigns would be managed completely independent one from the other. I continued to believe my candidacy as a West Tennessean would help Brock, and I was certain much of the good groundwork he had laid would help me.

Harry Wellford had been chairman of Howard Baker's successful Senate campaign of 1966 in Shelby County and West Tennessee. They had a good relationship. Harry and I agreed that he should make a trip to Washington and meet with our Republican senator as soon as possible. Within a week following the primary elections, my chairman was off to Washington and meetings with key Republicans. Harry's appointment as a federal district judge was still pending before the Senate. It pained me to think his approval and subsequent assumption of judicial duties would take him away from my campaign before the November election. With the fervent hope that such would not occur, Harry had agreed to continue in his vital role as campaign chairman heading up my efforts. His visit with Senator Baker could be very productive regarding timing of the judicial appointment as well as general election campaign strategy.

In Washington, Wellford met with the entire Tennessee congressional delegation. He received helpful information and advice. He told them about his candidate. The majority of his time was spent with Senator Baker because of their close friendship and the senator's in-depth statewide political knowledge. Out of those discussions came the thought that a young native of Maryville, Tennessee, Lamar Alexander, might be a good prospect to become my campaign manager. I had first met Lamar in 1969 when he came to see me in Memphis to discuss the possibility of him challenging Bill Brock for the 1970 Republican primary U.S. Senate nomination. I had not encouraged him. Lamar was very intelligent, politically motivated, and well prepared by earlier experience to take on the job of managing my campaign. He had served on Baker's Senate staff and at the time was a member of the White House staff. Senator Baker felt Alexander would be interested in the opportunity.

Further thoughts centered on two other Tennesseans who at that time were in Washington serving on the Baker staff. They were Ralph Griffith, who handled news and information, and Lee Smith, who was assigned various legislative duties. Griffith was a veteran newsman who had worked for the *Knoxville Journal* as a Capitol Hill reporter in Nashville and knew the ropes there. Smith was a young Vanderbilt-trained lawyer from Johnson City who had great interest in the Republican Party. The senator felt both individuals might be interested in returning to Tennessee to participate in the race for governor. Each man was a valuable member of the Baker team. His generosity in suggesting our consideration of them was typical of Howard. He obviously wanted us to succeed.

Back in Memphis, Harry and I met to discuss the three individuals who might be available to join our effort as the nucleus of the general election campaign staff. Instinct led me to believe we were on the right path, and common sense told me we needed politically savvy people with personal and political contacts statewide as soon as possible. We discussed the matter further with Ray Humphreys and Dan Kuykendall. All of us agreed that a meeting with Lamar Alexander was the next step. That meeting took place within a matter of days, after which I offered him the job of managing my campaign. He promptly accepted. He also assured me of his close relationships with Smith and Griffith. Lamar felt certain each would accept an offer to join us. Griffith did agree to take on the responsibility of campaign news director, and Smith agreed to work on organization, staffing, and recruiting.

A major decision regarding the location of a Dunn for Governor statewide campaign headquarters needed to be made right away. Memphis and Shelby County had "birthed" me politically, and my loyalty to the people there who had given so much in the primary was unquestioned. The logic of centering the campaign effort in Nashville, Middle Tennessee, was hard to argue against. Ray Humphreys insisted Nashville was the right place. Lamar felt the same. Harry and I could not disagree, and we set about to convince our closest Shelby County people that we were right. Understandably, there were some grumbling and perhaps unspoken feelings of apprehension that Memphis might become less important going forward. Every effort was made to reassure those associated that our Shelby County campaign effort would be critical to a successful outcome in November and that we had to keep working to organize the large, untapped voter resources in the county and in West Tennessee. Those wonderful friends never faltered, and the campaign effort in the western area was to expand and intensify.

Highly encouraging to the Shelby County workers was the fact that, immediately following the primary victory, calls began to come in from many unhappy Democrat leaders who had been strong supporters of Ellington and Clement. We were also getting inquiries from many people who had supported Hooker's unsuccessful Democrat primary opponents. These contacts, and many more that were to follow, energized the entire organization but especially our Shelby County people.

Within a few days of accepting an offer to join the campaign, Alexander was in Nashville. Griffith and Smith soon followed. Temporary offices were established in the Sheraton Hotel on Broadway. The Nashville center of activity meant that Harry Wellford and Jim McGehee would spend considerable time there. Jim's service as treasurer was indispensable, as was Bill Rachels in his role as finance chairman.

On my first visit to Nashville, two memorable events stand out amidst the whirlwind of activities that consumed my time there. First was the quiet dinner with Lamar Alexander that took place at the Sheraton. The purpose was essentially for us to get to know each other and to get our minds synchronized to deal with future events. Lamar was a young man in his mid-twenties, and I, at forty-three years of age, had no trouble relating to him even though he seemed to be smart beyond his years. As we sat down and a waiter appeared to take our order, my young, new friend asked what I'd like to drink. Before I could answer, he had ordered a martini and suggested the same for me if I didn't have another preference. I replied that I had never had a martini, to which he incredulously responded that he knew I would like it. Thus, very clearly, I remember the first martini I had ever tasted. He was right. I did enjoy it. That occasion was the first I recall on which I had something alcoholic to drink during "political" time. It occurred to me that Lamar had returned to Tennessee with some of the Washington, D.C., sophistication still attached, and I found no fault with it.

The second memorable event occurred because of an invitation I had accepted during the primary. My call on wealthy Nashville businessman Jack C. Massey soliciting funds to support my campaign had resulted in a response from him that I could not dismiss. In answering my request for funds, Mr. Massey advised me that he was supporting my opponent Maxey Jarman and therefore could not contribute to me. However, he said with a twinkle in his eye that he liked me, and if I won, I should come back to see him. I feel certain he thought he would never see me again. I made it among the first things to do following the primary victory and obtained an appointment to see Mr. Massey as soon as possible. I did so the morning after my dinner with Lamar. We had a good visit during which I was given his wholehearted support. Throughout the ensuing campaign, Jack Massey was there for me time and again. The relationship we established was to remain in place throughout his life. It became very important to me.

The dinner meeting with Alexander went well, and I was confident we could work together. Somewhat troubling were signals from many of the Memphis and other statewide people who had been with me from the beginning that the East Tennessee Republicans who suddenly emerged as power players in the campaign might "fit" into the organization and gain advantages they had not earned. I couldn't shrug that off, but there was little I could do at that moment. A certain amount of jealousy might best describe the situation. I stressed to Lamar the necessity to be as sensitive as possible to the people who had done so much up to that point, even when tough decisions had to be made. He understood.

Lee Smith arrived in Nashville in late August and went to work. His responsibilities eventually led him to be in charge of identifying and positioning the critical county political organizations we needed in order to take the campaign to the people. Campaign posters, bumper stickers, yard signs, local ads, and volunteers would be top priorities. Those were the necessary ingredients to be managed if we were to win. Emphasis was obviously placed on those key counties that could produce large voter turnouts. However, all ninety-five counties were his assignment, and he faced a big task that would require much travel and communication. He was a close friend of Alexander, and I felt sure they would work well together.

Ralph Griffith understood the newspaper business inside and out. He brought political maturity and experience in dealing with the media of Tennessee into our core group. He was frank, to the point, and well connected throughout the state's news outlets. He would give young Steve Sharp needed supervision and support as plans were developed to make certain every news publication and broadcast had the information about our campaign that we desired to make known and that they would expect.

A decision was made to bring Carolyn Weins from Memphis to Nashville. That was a sound move. She was able to take charge of details and continue to relate to those early friends we had made and whom we would need more than ever going forward. Bettie Davis would remain in her important role managing the Memphis office.

Another important addition to the group was a young employee of the Vanderbilt Alumni office who worked with Lee Smith's brother Jerry. Chip Christianson became aware of the campaign by being assigned the job of arranging a staff luncheon at the Vanderbilt University Club. He was likable and energetic. It had become clear that my devoted friend Rufus Powell should be replaced as the personal assistant and advance man. Rufus was loyal and hardworking. He was assigned other tasks at headquarters in Memphis. Lamar offered the job to Chip, who accepted. His personality and energy filled the bill. It was a good move for all concerned.

Other people came into the organization during the remaining days of August. Among them was a good man named Frank Barnett. Frank was a lawyer in Knoxville who had been active in the Baker campaigns and indicated a desire to become involved with us. He took on the assignment of campaign finance coordinator for East Tennessee. He also played a vital role in recruiting workers in the various county organizations being formed.

Another fine man recruited for the effort was W. Dale Young, a youthful associate attorney in the firm of Bill Felknor of Maryville. Dale had descended from a long line of Tennessee public servants and was very bright. Bill and Dale had been active in the primary in Blount County. As he later noted, with the primary victory came the sudden realization by many East Tennessee Republican activists that, for the first time in decades, there was a realistic possibility that they could help elect a governor of their party with the eastern part of the state playing an essential role due to the large number of Republican voters in that area. We asked Dale to assume major organizational responsibilities in East Tennessee. He accepted by first driving to Memphis to assist an exhausted and overwhelmed primary campaign staff. Attempting to respond to an avalanche of congratulatory messages, phone calls, and questions was a major burden. His presence helped and also began the process of making Memphis people somewhat comfortable with the influx into the campaign organization of people from the East. Over the course of a week or ten days, they established mutual confidence and began to discuss what would be required to translate strategy into an effort that would win.

Lee Smith was another East Tennessean who suddenly got quite a bit of Memphis exposure. For four weeks after joining the team, Lee found himself working Monday through Friday in Nashville, then driving to Memphis where he met with Harry Wellford, me, and others on Saturday and partially on Sunday. There was no time for rest or diversion at the beginning of the campaign.

David White, a young Knoxville entrepreneur with a brilliant academic background, joined our group as the principal research and issues manager. His addition became of immeasurable value as our strategy evolved and specific issues on which statements, releases, and speeches were to be based were defined, analyzed, and researched. Working in Knoxville and Nashville, David was to play an extraordinary role in the campaign, and his work product exceeded all expectations.

The Jarman campaign produced a young political activist named Robin Beard, who was identified as one who could take on the organizational duties in Middle Tennessee. He had played that role in the primary and was enthused about an opportunity to join the Dunn group. Robin was a U.S. Marine Corps veteran with the drive, stamina, and people-oriented personality that made him a natural for the role he was assigned to play. He came on board and made a significant contribution from the beginning.

Governor Buford Ellington's offer to assign two state troopers to us was accepted. In a matter of days I was advised that Trooper John White and Major John Fields would report for duty immediately. These men were selected for the assignment based on their qualifications and personal attitudes regarding my candidacy. I did not know either of them previously, but I became highly satisfied with their service and loyalty in fulfilling their responsibilities. In addition to becoming an element of security that I had not anticipated needing, each man was fully committed to becoming almost an attachment to the candidate and the campaign, doing whatever was needed to facilitate what was in progress at the time. A vital assignment was that one of these men on duty was automatically the driver of the vehicle I occupied. Most often, only one trooper was on duty at a time, but both made sure we knew they were available around the clock, regardless of location. I had no trouble adjusting to that new resource. At least one of the two men was with me constantly during the remaining days of the campaign. Each proved to be not only a valuable resource, but also a good friend.

Thus, the core of a serious organization came together. We established the main headquarters in the Parkway Towers building in Nashville. The details involved in putting all that together fell to others. My time was spent in Memphis and Nashville with several visits to Knoxville, where I met with various delegations from the eastern part of the state. Dale Young and my friend from the Ramp Festival experience during the primary, Bill Russell, set about establishing Dunn campaign headquarters in a hotel on Gay Street in Knoxville. For a considerable time, the only furniture was a desk, two chairs, and two telephones. Their assigned territory was all of East Tennessee outside Knox County.

CHAPTER TWENTY

BUILDING ON THE MOMENTUM

Unselfish Commitments

My early Knoxville friends, spearheaded by E. S. Bevins, Dr. Jack Mobley, and Betty Sterchi, continued to occupy a headquarters location they had established in a Holiday Inn near downtown. They undertook organizing Knox County. My friend Senator Fred Berry was busy with his own campaign. His son David, so important to me in the early days of the primary, continued to be very helpful. A fine young lawyer named Jack Draper, member of a prominent Knoxville law firm, pitched in. At the time, there were no funds available. My friends knew that their responsibilities included raising money. Knox County volunteers left no doubt they were anxious to get the campaign underway. Their generous contributions of time and money were awesome. E. S. Bevins continued his temporary leave from duties at his drugstore, turning the business over to his wife, Jane, who was also a pharmacist.

In the Tri-Cities area, Boots Duke and Ben Brown began to make Kingsport the focal point of steady organizational and fund-raising activity. With help from John Diehl, Thelma Bowman, and Dick and Virginia Jennings in the Johnson City area, the Kingsport team set about to build a Dunn for Governor effort that would pay big dividends. There continued to be some friction as a result of the Quillen people insisting on having input in every decision being made. That didn't happen because no one from the congressman's office was invited to be included.

My staff people in Nashville were in steady contact with our people in the East as they organized and dealt with various incidents. Things went smoothly in Congressman Duncan's Second District. We knew our efforts would not always get the desired results we wanted while working with some Republicans in the First Congressional

District. My people understood that they were not to be antagonistic with the Quillen organization. They attempted to be cooperative in every way because we all were aware of the congressman's great popularity among the people. One individual closely aligned with Quillen was businessman Ted Testerman. This gentleman owned a clothing store for men. He and I developed a healthy friendship. He insisted on outfitting me with a new suit at his expense. I was in no position to say no, and I gratefully accepted his generosity.

Dale Young recalled that he would never forget the day he traveled to the First Congressional District to quietly establish face-to-face contact with the Dunn people in Sevier County. He had made his first "call" and then traveled on to the next stop. The person he visited gave him an urgent message to call Lee Smith at the Nashville Dunn headquarters. Lee advised that Quillen's office had telephoned him within the hour, complaining that Young was "in his territory" to set up a Dunn organization and that he should not do anything to organize Dunn people in the First District until further notice. Dale said he drove back to Knoxville greatly frustrated and sorely disappointed.

Dale also knew that the loyalty and vigor of the Dunn primary people in the First District would not be discouraged by threats or intimidation. They let it be known that they wanted to actively continue their efforts in the general election campaign fully independent of Quillen. Despite the repeated protests of Quillen and his overt and covert interference at every turn, they established their own county-by-county organizations, completely independent of the congressman's organization. It was only in that way that they could be sure our interests would be protected. At some point along the way, the Quillen pressures let up. I believe it was because he knew I was making substantial progress in gaining support from the people who consistently reelected him.

Our people in the First District worked very hard to include the active Republicans we could identify, and they were successful in most cases. They had the help and gained the support of many who regularly supported Quillen. Many of these people were initially very cautious about supporting my campaign for fear they would alienate the congressman. Those problems seemed to melt away as the campaign picked up momentum. The early supporters, many of whom had never been politically active in their lives, stood their ground and will always be deeply appreciated for the courage they showed and the vote they produced.

I was told that a successful, energetic construction contractor and businessman named Robert F. Smith was a person I should meet. It was suggested that he would be an ideal Upper East Tennessee finance chairman. An appointment was made, and I met Bob Smith in late August. He was every bit the man that had been described to me. Our friendship began immediately. His home was in Limestone, not far from Johnson City. He was in his late fifties and had reduced his business activities to the management of his assets. He had raised funds for Maxey Jarman in the primary. He readily agreed to do that for me and at the same time agreed to help in every possible way to support my campaign throughout the area. This was a major stroke of good fortune.

Dale Young told of a meeting that occurred in Kingsport involving Bob Smith, Dale, and Congressman Quillen, among others. We were making every effort to be as cooperative with the Quillen organization as we could while continuing to insist that my campaign efforts in the First District would remain completely in the hands of Boots Duke, his associates, Dale Young, and Bill Russell. Dale recalled that when he stated to the group gathered for the meeting that Bob Smith was to be announced as the Dunn for Governor campaign finance chairman for East Tennessee, he clearly saw all the color drain out of the congressman's face! Bob Smith enjoyed the reputation of being a lifelong Republican who had always remained outside the orbital influence of James Quillen. He, much like Virginia Jennings and Thelma Bowman, was his own man completely and had no doubt made certain Quillen understood his position.

Congressman John Duncan and his people in the Second District continued to be cooperative in every way. Duncan had smooth sailing in his reelection bid and was fully supportive of my people in all their activities. In the Third District we experienced absolute willingness on the parts of all concerned to see that a November general election brought about a sweep in the major races. Since Bill Brock was giving up his congressional seat, that position was being sought by Chattanooga businessman Lamar Baker. He had defeated

Brock's cousin, Jack McDonald, in the primary. McDonald was a team player, fully on board and anxious to help every candidate. Hamilton County was organized as never before for a Republican effort, and I expected to do well there.

While I was in Nashville as we continued to put the pieces in place to get the campaign moving, I was asked to have a visit with James K. Stahlman, owner and publisher of the Nashville *Banner* daily newspaper. I was anxious to meet Mr. Stahlman and readily accepted the invitation. Jimmy, as he was known by friends and adversaries alike, basked in the reputation of statesman, powerful advocate, and devoted patriot. As a military veteran, staunch conservative, and influential citizen of Nashville, Stahlman commanded immediate attention by virtue of his position, and thus the position of the Nashville *Banner*, on various matters of public interest. Many issues cut across party lines. He was a strong supporter of President Nixon and had consistently supported the more politically conservative candidates in Tennessee politics. He took pride in the news and editorial competition that existed between the afternoon *Banner* and the morning *Tennessean*. In the 1966 race for governor, the *Banner* had supported Buford Ellington against John Hooker.

Mr. Stahlman and the *Banner* had strongly supported Stanley Snodgrass, a Nashville attorney, in the primary contest while the *Tennessean* had supported John Hooker. Because the *Banner* had fiercely opposed the nomination of Hooker, it was our hope that we would gain the strong backing of the *Banner*. I felt the sooner I could meet Mr. Stahlman, the better.

At the appointed time I joined a member of the *Banner* staff and was driven to Mr. Stahlman's home on Tyne Boulevard. Without a staff member from my organization present, I sensed this meeting would be an excellent opportunity for me to focus on making a new friend, make my case and, I hoped, get his total commitment to my candidacy, one on one. I was met at the door by a house servant and ushered into a room where Mr. and Mrs. Stahlman waited to greet me. Shortly thereafter, Mr. Stahlman and I moved into a bright and colorful sunroom where we sat down side by side on a couch. With a few pleasant remarks exchanged, the subject of my political campaign became the central point of our discussion. Stahlman was a man twenty plus years my senior, lean in physical makeup, and apparently easy to talk with. That was my first impression. It was quickly modified by what followed.

Jimmy Stahlman took charge. He promptly launched into a monologue that must have subconsciously caused my eyebrows to begin to rise. It was obvious that the first thing he intended to do was to give me his views on why John Jay Hooker did not need to become the governor of Tennessee. As the words flowed, the tempo accelerated and the pitch of the voice rose. There was no equivocation or softness in any phrase. Invective followed invective, character assassination, if there was character in the subject, unfolded before my eyes and ears, and language that might have been the pride of any old salty sailor flowed with a surprising degree of eloquence. The failures of Hooker from a social, business, and political perspective were presented forcefully, almost enthusiastically. Hooker's political alliances were referred to colorfully with the name Kennedy surfacing more than one time. The ritual of condemnation and denunciation, a product of experience that had obviously been long thought out and pondered over, continued to flow from Stahlman's lips. It was fascinating to witness. My only response was an occasional nod of the head, not necessarily in agreement, but in acknowledgment of what I was hearing. Finally, during a pause to take on more wind, his cadence slowed, and he stated that, for those reasons and many more, he wanted to give me his and the Nashville *Banner's* support in my race. He believed the people could not tolerate and the state could not afford John Hooker in the governor's office. With relief I thanked Mr. Stahlman and was about to offer my view of the opportunity and challenge before me when I was interrupted.

He picked up the pace again. To win your race, said Stahlman, you are going to have to be relentless, tough, and without pity. You are going to have to use every weapon at your command, he went on. You are going to have to mercilessly cut and slash your opponent at every opportunity! You can't let up! You're going to have to lay him wide open and leave him lying in the gutter! About that time, I think I quit listening and began to focus on what I needed to say to Mr. Stahlman. I had just heard the most vituperative, vehement characterization, or mischaracterization, of an individual I had ever heard from such a venerable source.

It was clear to me that the publisher knew very little about me or my background. He obviously had not expected to find me in my present position. It was also clear that I was in the presence of a highly intelligent, well-respected man who, for reasons I didn't know, had nurtured over time a deep, almost pathologic, dislike for John Jay Hooker. He must have felt desperately the need to fully educate me as to the foe I was facing and the ruthless manner by which I had to go about seeing to his defeat.

I attempted to thank Mr. Stahlman for his support and that of his paper. I sought to assure him that I was somewhat aware of Hooker's reputation and his record, all of which we were researching at that moment. I told him in no uncertain terms that I expected to win, that I had an insight into the elective process gleaned from the hustings of Mississippi politics, and that I was tough enough to bear up under whatever burden my opponents might attempt to put on my back. I needed the *Banner's* support to get the job done.

At that point I was tempted to outline the issues and my ambitions to lead the state forward. I decided that would have been a complete waste of time and might be better left to a meeting with his editorial board.

I offered my thanks and took leave. I knew the *Banner* and its support would be invaluable to me in Middle Tennessee. It would help to counteract the influence of the unfriendly *Tennessean* newspaper in a heavily Democrat section of the state, an area where I would need as many votes from members of the other party as I could possibly get. At that stage of the campaign, I had no way of knowing what position the incumbent Democrat governor might or might not assume that could potentially influence the election outcome.

I reported every detail of my visit with the publisher to Harry and Lamar. It was agreed that a healthy offset to the general Democrat vote in midstate could be gained by the close cooperation of my campaign with the Nashville *Banner* and its people. Up until my visit with Jimmy Stahlman, we knew very little about each other, obviously. That would change. A good relationship with him would become one of many important priorities. It ultimately happened. The remarkably strong support I received from the newspaper was a direct reflection of the contempt Stahlman held for Hooker. I was the beneficiary.

A critical meeting took place in Memphis as the last ten days of August rolled around. The services Ward Archer and Associates had provided in my primary campaign were invaluable. Ward believed in what I was doing and made his resources available time and time again when there was no assurance he would be adequately paid. The creative talent that went into pictures, pamphlets, bumper stickers, plaques, and broadcast time purchases was of high quality in every instance. In Nashville, our people had been contacted by a well-respected public relations firm named Noble Dury. One of the principals in the business was the son-in-law of Maxey Jarman. A request for a presentation was made in regard to working for the campaign, and a meeting was arranged. We were impressed with what we saw and heard. A major decision would need to be reached regarding public relations and our general election effort.

Shortly after the Noble Dury presentation, a meeting was held in Memphis that included campaign personnel, Ward Archer and Associates, and Noble Dury representatives. The outgrowth was a decision to contract with Noble Dury to shoulder a major, creative part of the campaign. Ward Archer and Associates would continue to play a significant role, basically focusing on specific needs while handling most of the media purchasing in West Tennessee. Lamar Alexander was left with the job of working out the details. I felt I was getting the best of both PR worlds, but I also was disturbed that Ward Archer might have felt he was not being treated as fairly as he deserved to be treated. It was a tough decision for me to make, but I felt some comfort in having the support of Wellford and Alexander.

The scheduling of my activities and allocation of my time became a process in which I found myself having less input than had been the case during the primary. Lamar, with Harry's input, was quickly taking charge. An early priority was to begin to videotape various political messages and to make decisions regarding the content. It was time consuming but necessary. Events around the state where I could get good exposure began to be scheduled. Professional, business, and trade association organizations made it clear they would be willing to give the candidate or candidates for governor time to appear before their various meetings. Requests from community and political groups began to be received. Members of the staff were assigned the job of detailing future meetings of such organizations as the Farm Bureau Federation, the Council of Mayors, the County Services Associations, Judicial Councils, Insurers of Tennessee, the

Tennessee Municipal League, the Tennessee Education Association, the Road Builders Association, the Tennessee Association of Realtors, the Tennessee Bankers Association, the State Bar Association, and the Tennessee Medical Association. The Tennessee Dental Association would be a special consideration. It had become apparent in the primary that fellow dentists across the state would continue to be valuable resources.

Early on, my dental colleagues throughout Tennessee let it be known that I would have their unreserved support in the effort to be elected governor. Requests, and later demands, for campaign literature that would be placed in dental waiting rooms came rolling in. A group of colleagues in Memphis had formed an organization called Dentists for Dunn, and they undertook, on their own, an effort to recruit as many other dentists as possible to raise funds and to line up support for me. I was gratified.

Through the efforts of my staff and many volunteers, other groups were encouraged to form or were assisted in their voluntary efforts. Farmers for Dunn, Doctors for Dunn, Law Enforcement for Dunn, and Teachers for Dunn were among the various supportive groups that appeared. These groups did not emerge at the same time but over the course of the next four to six weeks, with encouragement from our team. A young Memphis businessman named Tommy King came forward with a plan to build a Democrats for Dunn organization in West Tennessee, and he did a tremendous job of putting together that group.

The professionalism of Noble Dury provided me with the challenge of being as forceful, convincing, and sincere before a video camera as I felt I had become before live audiences of all sizes. I recognized my good fortune in being an effective communicator one on one. It was a strength I was grateful to have. I found myself being transported to various sites for the purpose of filming my ideas on one or more subjects. We spent much time at Nashville's Parthenon using the building with its stately columns as background. I walked in wooded areas and through fields of soybeans and tobacco, talking for the camera and audio instruments, all the while attempting to get my prompts from assistants holding roughly printed cards with messages in my line of sight. I was taped riding in an automobile and on a bridge over Interstate 40 east of Nashville. One memorable taping session involved Chuck and me in the studios of WSM Channel 5. The assignment was to produce a father-to-son conversation that focused on the importance of leadership, responsibility, and family. Chuck did a good job holding up his part of the conversation while I found myself uneasy attempting to be sincere while spontaneously finding the words that fit the occasion. I don't recall any script for the session, and I remember that we worked very hard trying to produce something worthwhile. We failed to produce anything worth using, but I did enjoy that unusual time with my son.

One evening as we drove back to Nashville from a series of meetings in Middle Tennessee, I was told that we were to drive to a studio on Music Row to record "my" song. That was news to me. I hadn't heard about that project but learned that Noble Dury had created a campaign jingle and it was being recorded that evening. Arriving at the studio, we entered, and I discovered a large group of people consisting of campaign staff members, some volunteer workers, and others I didn't know. I was introduced to a young man named Jackson Brown, who had written the song. Then I met Jack Barlow, who was introduced to me as a country music singer and songwriter. He was the voice on well-known Jolly Green Giant radio and TV commercials that were broadcast throughout the nation. I recalled hearing that deep voice and how it resonated "Ho, ho, ho" at the end of the commercial. What a thrill that moment was for me.

Jack Barlow was a tall, lanky fellow who was easy to know and seemed to be very enthusiastic about what was to take place. I was told that the group of folks present were to be the backup singers and that they had been rehearsing. Since I liked to sing, I was encouraged to join the chorus as they worked to get a feel for the jingle. I joined in. What followed was a little bit of magic for me. The jingle was a terrific piece of work, and I found it easy to sing along with the other voices. In no time at all, with an introduction of just a few musical notes on the bass strings of a guitar that had a solid country music sound, Barlow sang the song with a fresh, catchy tune that was sure to be well received. In no time, the recording was completed, played back several times, and then pronounced a "wrap." The title of the finished product was simply "The Dunn Campaign Jingle," later called the "Dunn Jingle." Bill Brown of Noble Dury had done a masterful job, and the jingle would eventually win several awards within its industry. The words were as follows:

> *From the Smoky Mountains to the Cumberland River through the rolling hills of Music City, 'cross the cotton fields that reach the river,*
> *From Mountain City to the Memphis Delta, from the northern boundary to Hamilton County, Winfield Dunn's the man for you and me.*

The arrangement included Barlow saying, at the end of the second verse, "Sing it with me now," at which point the chorus joined in for a repeat of the verses. At the end of the jingle, Barlow's final words were "For all Tennessee it has to be Dunn. Winfield Dunn for governor!"

The little song did have a magical quality about it. It was eventually made available to every campaign manager in the counties that became organized. Usually, each county organization raised funds to buy radio time for local advertising spots that were carefully selected. It became our Nashville headquarters' responsibility to see that the song got as much exposure as we could afford. The jingle became a "hit" of the campaign, a little song that children loved to sing, I was told. Jackson Brown, along with his associate Harold Goodrum, was a big part of some remarkable creativity I was fortunate to have on my side.

CHAPTER TWENTY-ONE

GETTING IT ALL IN PERSPECTIVE

Plowing Ahead

As the general election process evolved, the city of Nashville became a place quite different from my earlier impressions. My exposure during the primary was very limited. The early friends I had made remained an important part of the Nashville–Davidson County effort. Maclin Davis, who had appeared on the capitol steps the day of my primary announcement, was a solid friend. Alfred Adams, a former Democrat legislator and a fine man, joined such people as Elizabeth Lowe, Kip Gayden, and Roy Elam, DMD, a fellow dentist, along with my dental classmate Allen Harrison of nearby Hendersonville, as the Nashville nucleus that was with me from the start.

What amazed me was the treasure trove of new friends ready to assist us. Suddenly, it seemed, I was on a virtually endless circuit of meeting influential members of the community who made it clear they wanted to be part of making my election happen. I was introduced to a highly respected businessman named Dortch Oldham. He was chief executive officer of the Southwestern Company, a publishing and sales company that recruited college-aged young people to become salesmen nationwide for its many products. The principal product was the Bible, and the company had been very successful. Dortch was an energetic and magnetic executive who agreed to become finance chairman for me in Davidson County. That was a huge stroke of good fortune, and Dortch Oldham became not only a great friend but an enormously successful raiser of funds for the campaign.

I found myself on a first-name basis with important business and professional people, some of whom I knew by reputation, but few of whom I knew personally. Men such as J. C. Bradford, Sr., whose company bore his name; William Weaver, head of National Life and Accident Insurance; former Ambassador Guilford Dudley of Life and Casualty Insurance Company; Alvin Beaman; Dan Brooks; Thomas L. Cummings, Jr.; John Sloan, Sr., of Cain-Sloan Department Stores; and David K. "Pat" Wilson, among many others, made their personal commitments to help me. Nearly all of these individuals, along with my new friend Jack Massey, ultimately became very important in the general election for two reasons.

First, they were solid gentlemen who could be depended on regarding any commitments they made. They had been loyal to their friend and fellow Nashvillian Maxey Jarman. They stayed with him throughout the primary. Loyalty was important, and their example influenced others on my behalf. Second, these individuals, for reasons of their own, didn't want John Jay Hooker, Jr., to become the governor of the state. They were determined. From the beginning of my journey in statewide political life, I had sensed that there would be a decided advantage coming my way if Hooker became the Democrat nominee. After all, he had made one run for the office, and he was a known political commodity. However, there was no way I could have expected the unusually strong feelings of opposition that I was beginning to discover among important people of Hooker's hometown who knew him best. The fact that my opponent failed to carry his own precinct in the primary, to say nothing of his county, was a good example that explained the attitudes I was encountering. Once again, I was grateful.

By the end of August an enormous amount of organizational groundwork had been accomplished. The statewide headquarters had begun to function in line with a basic strategy that was still evolving. Harry Wellford and Lamar Alexander had shown great leadership. The Memphis headquarters continued to work effectively. Betty and our girls were in high gear with Betty's personal campaign taking shape, thanks to Sara Jane Scott, Isabel Strong, and others. The Dunn Dollies had taken on a life of its own, thanks to Joanne Fleming and Barbara Somers. We all agreed that Chuck should return to Washington and Lee University for his sophomore year beginning in September. Spirits were high, and each person involved seemed to have made a personal determination to leave no stone unturned along the trail. With little more than two months to go each of us knew there was much to be done. The people who had taken on the job of financing our task were pretty much on their own. In spite of the new interest in me by the media, I knew that my sudden emergence as a statewide political person was a matter of little or no concern to thousands of people whose votes I would need to be successful. My job was to reach out to as many of them as possible and gain their confidence.

At that time, I knew only superficial things about my opponent. That he was handsome, charismatic, and blessed with a deep, rich voice was apparent. Another strength was that his wife, Tish Fort Hooker, was a beautiful woman born to a prominent Nashville family. He practiced law and had served as staff lawyer to U.S. Attorney General Robert Kennedy during the *Baker v. Carr* litigation that was eventually decided by the U.S. Supreme Court. I knew that he had served as legal counsel to the Nashville *Tennessean*. He had been quoted as saying that he desired to establish a reputation in business as a further qualification to hold high public office.

When he became a candidate for governor for the second time, a fast-food company he had formed called "Minnie Pearl Fried Chicken," initially a stock market rocket that had begun to fall on hard times, was in the throes of failure. Although some friends and associates had made money by investing in the fried chicken company and selling out at the right time, most people who had invested lost money. Mismanagement characterized many of their opinions of Hooker. Detractors were beginning to refer to him as the "chicken man." He and his brother, Henry, had created a holding company named "Whale" that had consumed a number of corporate acquisitions, drained most of them of their assets, and was at that time on the road to failure. His overwhelming ambition remained that of being elected governor of his state. It was rumored that a higher ambition was to seek the presidency of the United States. He enjoyed a close relationship with the John F. Kennedy family and apparently felt he had qualities similar to JFK that could lead him to the White House.

An abiding comfort to me was my deep feeling that Hooker, as primary winner, would be the most vulnerable in a general election among all the serious Democrat contenders. His nomination fit perfectly what I hoped could happen. In his 1966 race with Ellington, where nomination was tantamount to election in November because Democrats completely controlled state politics, the party exhibited a serious schism. The Kefauver faction had long opposed the Clement/Ellington group of hard-line party loyalists. Ellington's victory over Hooker, following a rancorous campaign in which ugly rumors played a heavy role, left the divide even wider and deeper. I felt I could capitalize on that situation by gaining the support of many Democrats who were quick to say, when they could be persuaded to say anything, that they just couldn't take Hooker. I hoped they would either vote for me or stay home on Election Day. I knew that I had to try to get my message to them, in any event.

From the beginnings of my Tennessee political experience, one ever present thought dwelled on the absence of two-party competition. My adopted state had become over the course of many years a one-party political monopoly. Of course there were factions within the Democratic Party, but it was all under one banner. Early in the campaign I had met the finest sort of people who despised that monopoly and wanted a change. One-party domination in politics is a way of assuring greed, self-serving, and disregard for the people. That wasn't the way it was in so many other states. I felt deeply that Tennessee could benefit from a strong, competitive two-party system where nomination in August was just one step along the way in giving the voter a chance to come to terms with what the elected public servant represented. Howard Baker had taken us far down the road to constructive change through his election to the U.S. Senate. However, the state capitol was the seedbed from which leadership that touched the people most directly had to originate. Their free choice between candidates in November was the surest guarantee of good government. In Tennessee it was up to the Republican Party to make that happen. Two viable, competing parties offered the American way to choose good political leadership. To me, it was a thrilling prospect knowing that such a thing could become a reality through the election of 1970.

Although television had become a resource for news and entertainment that was commonplace in nearly every household, newspapers occupied a special place in the minds of most Tennesseans as far as the realm of politics was concerned. Throughout the history of our country, the freshly printed word had been a major influence in the selection of public servants. That was certainly the case in Tennessee where highly respected daily papers displayed editorial opinion usually set apart from their duty to report the news, honestly and fairly. I had to focus on each of those newspapers, seeking to persuade those I felt were fair game and trying not to anger those who were hostile to my cause.

The Nashville *Tennessean* was owned and published by Amon Carter Evans, who had inherited the business from his family. Mr. Evans was a strong Democrat who employed as the editor of the paper John Seigenthaler. Mr. Seigenthaler had served for a time in the administration of John F. Kennedy, was highly respected for his work, and was a close friend of John Hooker. The newspaper was dedicated to Democratic Party aspirations, and I knew it would editorialize firmly on the side of my opponent.

The *Chattanooga Times* was closely related to the *New York Times* through family ties. Martin Ochs, the publisher, was a descendant of Adolph Ochs, owner of the Chattanooga newspaper who borrowed funds to purchase the *New York Times* and moved to New York to run what became a world-renowned publication. Ruth Golden, another Ochs relative, was the editor. I could look for nothing but opposition from the *Chattanooga Times*. Apparently, more important to those two newspapers than changing the political destiny of our state was the continued strangulation of Tennessee's political process. At least, that was how I saw it. I took little comfort from the realization that Brock would get the same treatment in his Senate race.

Having received the endorsements of both Memphis newspapers and the *Knoxville News Sentinel* in the primary, I felt I could get their endorsements in the general. I had to pay attention to the *News-Free Press* in Chattanooga, the *Journal* in Knoxville, and the Nashville *Banner*. I also had to keep in mind the importance of the remaining major urban papers' support plus as many other daily and weekly newspapers throughout the state as I could possibly get. Those endorsements wouldn't assure my election, of course, but they could play a vital part in a winning effort.

As the Republican nominee for governor, I quickly learned that there was no lack of attention from the news media. On August 18 Betty and I, along with Bill Brock, Howard Baker, Dan Kuykendall, and Lamar Baker and his wife, Sue, visited President Richard Nixon in his offices at the White House. The visit went well with much of the time spent discussing important issues bearing on Tennessee. The president was complimentary and encouraging. The advice we received from the president was that of a successful politician who had demonstrated he was a "fighter" and never let up. He urged us to return home, wage our individual political battles, and win the elections.

After our meeting with the president we were confronted with news people who wanted to know why the two main candidates described their plans to run "coordinated" campaigns rather than "integrated" efforts. Brock and I did our best to give the impression that we would work closely together but that we would be running two distinctly different races with different issues. We attempted to emphasize the point by excusing ourselves to go to a strategy meeting. Actually, we went to a luncheon hosted by Senator Baker, after which each of us made plans to return to Tennessee.

A good, hard look at the primary election results left no doubt about the task ahead. The total vote in Shelby County, which had more than 300,000 voters registered, was slightly more than 139,000. Officials had hoped for at least 200,000. Nearly 42,000 votes were cast in the Republican primary. I received more than 39,000 of them. My opponent John Hooker received over 40,000 votes in his Shelby County primary race. His opponents received the balance of approximately 56,000 Democrat votes. My goal had to be to carry Shelby County in November.

I was very much aware that I did not get a majority of the state-wide Republican primary vote that nominated me. I received about a third with the balance going to my four opponents. With no runoff required, I won the nomination with a plurality. In the general election, I would have to have, in effect, a majority. Although it would be a three-man race, since Douglas Heinsohn was on the ballot as a member of the American Party, he was not expected to get more than a handful of votes.

The 1966 primary vote for governor totaled over 900,000, a record at the time. The primary vote in 1970 was 100,000 less. It was encouraging to note that the 1966 Republican primary vote was 147,000 while in 1970 it was 245,000. A large part of that difference came from Shelby County, and the balance was due to the fact that we had the first seriously contested Republican primary in recent history. This was a non-presidential year, of course, but comparatively, we obviously didn't create as much interest overall as was created in 1966. It would take a great effort. We needed to get as many of the 1.8 million Tennessee registered voters as we could possibly influence to vote in November. Less than one million had voted in the general election of 1966.

Hooker had carried eight out of nine congressional districts in the 1970 Democrat primary. He lost his home district, the Fifth. He also lost the vote in his home county, Davidson. It was won by Stanley Snodgrass. In winning, I had carried only three of the nine districts, the Seventh, Eighth, and Ninth, all in West Tennessee. Still, running second or third in the other six districts gave me the overall strength to wrap up the victory with Shelby's remarkable vote.

The facts and figures produced by the primary plus information from previous elections came into clear focus as we turned to the task of traveling into every county to get votes. The numbers were always at the forefront of our thoughts. Dan Kuykendall continually stressed the vote potential of every one of the ninety-five counties, and he seemed to have all that information near the tip of his tongue. He made sure that everyone in the organization remained conscious of what we had to do vote wise. Of course, he had his own race for Congress to run, but he seemed just as interested in the governor's race. For that I was grateful.

The organization was in place; the game plan was there to be adjusted as necessary. The subject of campaign financing was one item that I felt unqualified to deal with. Dr. Bill Rachels became the driving force behind our efforts to find funds, and he was uncompromising. He never let up looking for dollars. He recalls that the only area of the state that was problematic was Upper East Tennessee, due entirely to the concerns of Congressman Quillen. On a trip to Kingsport at the congressman's request they fell into a discussion of how Dunn for Governor campaign funds collected in the First Congressional District were to be handled. Quillen insisted that all such funds had to be routed through his office. Dr. Rachels declared, "Well, Congressman, that dog won't hunt! We'll just have to make other arrangements." And we did. Other arrangements included several clandestine nighttime meetings with supporters who understood the problem but didn't want to gain the wrath of the congressman. Rachels was always ready to go, anywhere at any time. Bob Smith's acceptance of the finance role in Upper East Tennessee smoothed out many obstacles.

I can't imagine that Quillen would have made similar demands on Brock, who was also running a statewide campaign. After all, the two had served together in the House of Representatives. I was left to assume that Quillen simply felt that our team was so new to the game of politics that we would be inclined to concede to his demands. I am glad we didn't. No other area of the state offered problems as far as fund-raising was concerned. Congressman Duncan could not have been more helpful. Frank Barnett of Knoxville did a yeoman's job in the eastern region coordinating fund-raising, and we were thankful for the dollars that we collected.

CHAPTER TWENTY-TWO

INTO HIGH GEAR

Friends Old and New

As the month of September came around, the relentless process of covering as much territory and shaking as many hands as possible set in. As in the primary, I insisted on spending a portion of Saturday night and Sunday at my home in Memphis. Commercial air transportation was used frequently, but I was fortunate to have Alex Maddox, Ewing Carruthers, a new friend named Joe M. Rodgers, and a number of other friends around the state offer the use of their private aircraft. I soon lost track of which friend did what to get me to the next destination, but my staff in Nashville and Memphis kept everything somewhat coordinated and organized.

In the early days of September my schedule called for much time to be spent in West and Middle Tennessee. I spent very little time in our Nashville campaign headquarters. I do recall meeting one beautiful young lady named Marsha Echols. I noticed she was very pregnant sitting at a typewriter as we were introduced. She was a devoted volunteer and the wife of a fine young man named Robert Echols. Echols, an attorney in Nashville and a great volunteer in my campaign, escorted me through the Davidson County courthouse on Tuesday, September 3. Then and there I got a taste of cool cordiality from the consistently Democrat officeholders and employees. Their jobs depended on their politics. For me, it was exhilarating to shake hands, smile, and sincerely ask for support from folks whose faces couldn't hide the disbelief they obviously felt. To them, it was just unnatural that a Republican candidate for governor could be campaigning through their courthouse asking for their votes.

The remainder of the day typified the effort we were to make for the next sixty-plus days. We left that historically Democrat courthouse after shaking countless hands of people who opened their office doors and moved to the center of the building driven by curiosity to see "Winfield Who?" in person. I shook hands on Nashville's streets, moving along briskly, campaigning, and asking everyone I could reach for their support.

At 10:00 a.m. I met with a group of Middle Tennessee advisers for the purpose of getting better acquainted and seeking advice on goals and objectives in the one part of the state I needed to know better as soon as possible. We departed the meeting and headed for Murfreesboro where I spoke to the Rotary Club. Then back to Nashville where I shook hands at the Ford Glass Plant during a shift change. My next appointment was at 5:00 p.m. with prominent attorney and former Democrat state legislator, Bob Taylor, whom I had never met. Mr. Taylor had let it be known that he was interested in supporting me. My visit to his office went well, and I gained his support and influence. At 6:00 p.m. I joined my staff for a private dinner at the City Club. Following a meal and good fellowship, I was driven to Kenneth Roberts's home where the next several hours were spent discussing campaign issues and reviewing the growing number of position papers that were being produced by David White. Later in the evening I arrived at the Sheraton hotel for an overnight stay. The following day, a Wednesday, we were up and out early to follow the schedule that had been carefully prepared.

Throughout the two months leading up to November 3, Election Day, the pace was intense, jammed full of events and opportunities to meet people, shake hands, speak to groups, record and broadcast messages, and otherwise make myself known to the people of Tennessee. I found much needed relief in getting back home to spend Sundays with my family and touch base with my Memphis team on Monday mornings. My adrenaline continued to run at a high level. One great advantage was that I could remember the names of people I met. I constantly made it a point to look back and repeat as many of the names of those in my presence as I could recall. I received feedback time and again that people were amazed that I remembered their names. We pushed on without letup. Travel remained principally by automobile, but I was increasingly using air transportation to conserve time.

On September 8 after a full day of campaigning I participated in the Memphis kickoff of the Bill Brock campaign for the Senate.

The event took place in a large space formerly occupied by an automobile dealership on Poplar Avenue. It had been converted by Shelby County Republicans into a joint headquarters for Brock and Dunn. There was a large and enthusiastic crowd present. Following entertainment by a local musical group, Dan Kuykendall took the microphone and did his usual good job arousing the combative instincts of all the supporters present. He then introduced me, and I took time to add to the encouragement Dan had offered. Then, with what I hope was an adequate job, I introduced to my hometown friends the "next United States senator from Tennessee, Bill Brock!" The candidate took it from there and formally got his campaign off to a good start in West Tennessee.

Several days later I was in Chattanooga. I made a brief speech to the local firefighters association and then drove to the office of Lee Anderson, editor of the *News-Free Press*. While there I had the privilege of meeting Mr. Roy McDonald, publisher and highly respected member of his profession and the community. There was no doubt as to the conservative philosophies of the newspaper and the two gentlemen. We had a good discussion of state issues. The next day I attended the official campaign kickoff for Lamar Baker, who was the Republican nominee to replace Brock in the U.S. House. My "man" in Chattanooga, Tom Moore, was with me during my entire time in the city. In addition to either John White or John Fields, I was always accompanied by Chip Christianson.

On September 14 my schedule called for a series of meetings with newspaper editors and publishers. I met with John M. Jones of the *Greeneville Sun*. The paper had not supported me in the primary, but I felt good about the prospects for support in the general election. In Johnson City, I met and spoke at length with Carl Jones of the *Press-Chronicle*. Later, at the *Kingsport Times News* we were hosted by political reporter Ellis Binkley. That visit was followed by meetings at the *Bristol Herald Courier* and the *Bristol Tennessean*. During each of these opportunities, I had to answer questions with knowledge regarding problems and concerns facing all the people of the state. More specifically, these Upper East Tennessee news people made it clear that they wanted to hear about roads and highways. They were also interested in state parks. That area had been bypassed in the development of a series of state parks in recent years. They wanted to hear that the next governor would change the pattern and help that section of the state catch up. Good material from our staff people had made it possible for me to speak honestly in response to their questions.

With all due respect to West Tennessee and its needs, it was clear to me that the people of the upper reaches of East Tennessee had also been neglected over the years by past administrations. This was basically due to the strong Republican leanings of that area. I made certain those interested knew that I would do everything in my power as governor to alter that imbalance. I was careful not to make specific promises regarding individual items, but I stressed the fact that we were one state, not the three states of Tennessee, as the welcoming signs along our highways suggested.

Our plans were to have a Dunn for Governor statewide campaign kickoff function by mid-September. After much conversation, it was agreed that we would hold that event in Knoxville because of East Tennessee's Republican strength. I was comfortable with that plan since we also scheduled a kickoff rally in Memphis to follow Knoxville a few days later.

September 15 was the day of the formal campaign kickoff. For me it began at 7:00 a.m. with an appearance on the *Big Jim Shaw Show* on WTVK-TV, included a press conference at the Farragut Hotel, a TV taping at the hotel, a meeting with Chubb Smith, publisher, and Bill Childress, editor, of the *Knoxville Journal,* a meeting with Dr. Andy Holt, Ed Boling, and Joe Johnson of the University of Tennessee, a TV filming on the UT campus, more TV filming at TVA offices, and a meeting with my local advisory council. After dinner with my family, we headed for the Municipal Auditorium. Chuck had driven over from Lexington, Virginia, and we were glad to see him.

In the auditorium the program got underway at 7:00 p.m. Archie Campbell, the radio and TV personality so popular in country music and the Grand Ole Opry, was the master of ceremonies. The National Anthem was followed by an invocation, and the program was underway. Tex Ritter and his band entertained for some time, after which all the elected public officials seated on the stage were introduced.

On our arrival, we were escorted to a holding room. There seemed to be a large crowd in attendance, and the excitement was obvious. We could hear the Doyle High School marching band warming up the audience. At eight o'clock. Betty, Chuck, Gayle,

Julie, and I were led to the east side of the auditorium. We were then directed down the aisle of the packed room toward the stage where all invited public officials and guests were seated. The band played a rousing tune, the people were cheering and applauding, balloons and confetti fell from overhead, and we were caught up in the intense excitement. Our people had done a remarkable job of planning the event. The news media present could not mistake the determination that was reflected by that crowd.

It was an electric moment for me and my family. We welcomed the cheering and applause. It came to us as a kind of energy. What we were engaged in was almost unbelievable to me. I accepted without question the devotion that seemed to be flowing toward us at that moment, but a sense of humility and gratitude nearly overwhelmed me.

Archie Campbell introduced Congressmen Quillen and Kuykendall followed by candidate Lamar Baker. Senator Howard Baker then stepped forward and introduced Bill Brock, who received a strong ovation. Archie Campbell introduced Congressman John Duncan, who in turn took his good time and introduced me. Once again, the band struck up a tune, more confetti and balloons fell, and I made my remarks.

As I looked out over the audience, I could recognize new friends from all across the eastern part of the state. The spirit and the excitement were sensations that couldn't be denied, and it was a strong formal beginning of our quest to win the governorship. I restricted my words to the basic theme that had taken me so far up to that point. Two-party politics was politics at its best—competition rather than monopoly by the "old crowd" that had been in control too long—bring the state together to focus on what was good for all the people and not just a special few. I didn't miss any one of the many arguments I had made throughout the primary as to how important it was to have fresh, new faces and minds at work on all the problems Tennessee faced. My comments did not make reference to my opponent directly, but there were in the audience and on the stage quite a few plucked rubber chickens. Those grotesque items gave more than a slight hint that John Hooker, the "chicken man" as he was frequently being called, was the target in our sights that night.

The Knoxville kickoff rally came to an end on a high note. I left the auditorium thrilled by what I had witnessed and determined to leave no stone unturned in my efforts. Betty and the girls headed for Memphis, Chuck drove back to Lexington, and I turned in at the Rice Motel in Cookeville. I was scheduled the next day to cover a large segment of Middle Tennessee, shaking hands, meeting key people including Democrats, and making several brief speeches. The next two days would take me to West Tennessee, covering the lower tier of border counties, arriving in Jackson to speak to the Kiwanis at noon. That afternoon I met with leaders of Tennesseans for Dunn, held a press conference, and attended a public reception in my honor in Humboldt. We then flew on to Dyersburg where sleep was the next order of business. The next morning we attempted to cover Dyer County in depth. We then drove south, arriving in Memphis for a speech to the Retail Merchants Association and the formal campaign kickoff at Blues Baseball Stadium that evening, September 18.

The tireless, committed friends who had helped us get to Blues Stadium that September evening by virtue of their support and hard work from the beginning of my campaign were as excited as I was. Joanne Fleming had the Dunn Dollies out in force, and they were ready to brighten up the stadium. At 5:00 p.m. the entire complex was ablaze with lights, the American flag was flowing in the breeze from the tallest flagpole, and a crowd was gathering. Charlotte Ruppelt, a devoted Republican worker, with her team of volunteers had made every effort to knock a political "home run" in Blues Stadium.

At 5:30 the program got underway with Berl Olswanger's Dixie Land Band making great music. At 5:45 a drum roll announced the Dunn Dollies, who marched onto the playing field in front of the bandstand. They were young, beautiful, enthusiastic—and quite a sight to see in their red, white, and blue cheerleader uniforms. I saw Gayle and Julie among them. They came to a halt and stood at attention as master of ceremonies Congressman Dan Kuykendall called for the invocation. He then invited the audience to accompany the Dunn Dollies in singing the National Anthem and join in the Pledge of Allegiance to our flag.

Among those participating were Tom King, chairman of the Shelby County Tennesseans for Dunn (representing independents and Democrats), Mayor Henry Loeb, and City Commissioner Jimmy Moore. Each of these men was important in his own right.

King was a very successful businessman who had friends all across the state. Having him so enthusiastically on my side was a strong signal to many people who had never supported the Republican cause. We had talked, and he knew I was in the race to ultimately serve every Tennessee citizen to the best of my ability. Loeb was a very popular mayor near the end of his term. He was not popular with black citizens, primarily because he had, in the past, been bluntly outspoken on his racial views and because he was the obstacle that Memphis's organized sanitation workers couldn't get past. The tragic death of Dr. Martin Luther King was a result of the confrontation between the city and the Sanitation Workers Union. Jimmy Moore was a former professional baseball player turned businessman. He had been elected to the three-person Memphis City Commission by large majorities. He was not a part of the Democrat establishment of Shelby County but could be called a nominal Democrat.

Kuykendall recognized these people for various purposes, including Jimmy Moore to introduce me. We had music from a group called the Westernettes, remarks from Mayor Loeb, and then an entry onto the platform by Betty and me. After a bouquet of flowers was handed to Betty, I was introduced, and the audience gave me a wonderful welcome for several minutes. Right there, in my hometown, the recent thrill of winning the primary was experienced again.

My comments were honestly chosen to remind the people present that without them and the support of my home county, none of what was happening could have happened. I urged the crowd to continue their support. I made reference to the huge challenge we faced and how important it was in my view that our state have fresh, non-obligated leadership as we entered the decade of the seventies. At the end of my remarks, no one present could have doubted that I knew I needed their help to make victory a reality. Commissioner Moore shook my hand, and I went down into the crowd to shake every hand I could reach. It had been a wonderful event, carefully planned down to the final detail. When the last announcement had been made, it was time to turn to the unrelenting job of hard campaigning. All the elements of a carefully organized effort seemed to be in place.

The next major event was scheduled two days later when I flew to Louisville, Kentucky, to meet Vice President Spiro Agnew. Mr. Agnew was to appear in Memphis to participate in a public ground-breaking ceremony in the afternoon followed by an appearance at a Republican rally, fund-raiser, and dinner later that evening. I met the vice president and flew on his official airplane back to Memphis where we were greeted by a large crowd at the airport. At that time Agnew enjoyed a high level of popularity.

Bill Brock joined the motorcade for the drive to the ground-breaking. Several days prior to the Agnew appearance in Memphis, a message from Senator Albert Gore was delivered to someone responsible for the public function. Gore shrewdly announced that he intended to participate, along with other state, city, and county officials, in extending the sort of welcome to the vice president of the United States as befitted the second highest office in the land! He asked for the necessary pass or permit to gain access to the premises and point of arrival. This was a shrewd move on Gore's part to neutralize his opponent Bill Brock's obvious advantage in being seen with his Republican vice president. Senator Gore did appear and seemed to take great satisfaction in letting the vice president and Brock know he wouldn't meekly accept less than major status, particularly in Shelby County where he had always had a large Democrat following.

That evening Agnew appeared before a partisan Republican audience of several thousand people. He received round after round of applause, reflecting the popularity of the Nixon administration. We received excellent coverage in the news media. And although no date had been set, it was believed that President Richard Nixon would make an appearance in the state on behalf of Republican candidates. His determination to see Albert Gore defeated was well known.

The single aspect of the general election effort most difficult to deal with was that of finance. We had been given estimates by Noble Dury and Ward Archer of what would be required financially to get my message out. Unlike the primary campaign that was conducted on less than $80,000, it was generally agreed that my campaign would require approximately $800,000. That amount represented a goal I could not logically deal with. I didn't have any idea how to approach it. I was reminded that a steady stream of small contributions was coming in to both the Memphis and the Nashville offices.

Bill Rachels and Jim McGehee didn't have any pat answers to the question of where the money would be found. We all agreed that no major debt would be incurred.

On September 25 a meeting of the finance team concluded that $760,000 would be required to meet our needs in rent, payroll, printed material, radio, and television plus incidental expenses. As of that date, receipts for the general election totaled more than $136,539. We had spent $125,670 plus up to that point. The campaign had borrowed $23,000 and owed $13,000 on that debt. Bills payable totaled more than $3,000. Clearly, we had a deficit of some $16,000.

Our plans called for campaign funds to come from contributors in six areas, each represented by the major city in the area. Memphis was budgeted to produce $200,000; Nashville, $175,000; Knoxville, $125,000; Chattanooga, $110,000; Kingsport, $100,000; and Jackson, $50,000. Those goals totaled $760,000 and appeared to me to be an enormous hurdle. I knew I wanted to do as little as possible in generating the funds, but as the candidate, I had learned that contributors often wanted to give their money directly to the prospective governor or to someone else in the candidate's presence. Having collected only $136,500 as of September 25, everyone involved knew there was a lot of work to do.

In addition to the funds needed at the upper level of the campaign, every person who was assuming a county chairmanship knew that he or she was responsible to raise local funds for area radio and print media. It was up to them to generate the funds to meet their needs. Our headquarters offered to be responsible for providing each county chairman with posters and bumper stickers, plus cassette tapes of the "Dunn Jingle." All in all, the financial concerns of the campaign were out of my league.

Occasionally, I was requested to meet in person with someone who was interested in making a substantial donation. These folks insisted on putting their checks in the hands of the candidate. Such meetings became fairly frequent as the campaign progressed. I was always grateful for such a meeting. Not once, as I recall, was I asked for any special favor or consideration of any specific thing. Consistently, the contributor merely wanted to be remembered as being a supporter. Such were the ways of the political process in Tennessee as I was experiencing them.

CHAPTER TWENTY-THREE

THE POLITICAL GAME

No Time Out

As the pace of the campaign intensified, it was very encouraging to learn that numerous politically prominent individuals were beginning to take sides. One great weakness my opponent would be contending with was the number of local and county officeholders who were defecting from the Democratic Party ranks in the case of the governor's race. We had counted on the fact that there was bad blood throughout the ruling party based on the 1966 race between Hooker and Ellington. That condition had been built into my thinking from the start of the effort, but there was no way to quantify it. As the end of September rolled around, name after name began to flow from our offices through press releases. Not only were elected personalities declaring their support. Several Democrat leaders who had supported Stan Snodgrass in the primary announced they were for me. A well-known former judge in Cumberland County, a strong Frank Clement Democrat, joined our efforts. We were getting endorsements from individuals prominent in party politics in their home areas. Some were party officials, some had worked for Ellington in 1966, and others were prominent business and professional people who had been active in political circles. My schedulers attempted to coordinate many such announcements with my presence in the area. That allowed for pictures and joint statements. Time after time such endorsements included language emphasizing that the endorser was not abandoning his party. That suggested Bill Brock would not necessarily reap the benefits of those willing to vote for a Republican for governor.

My Nashville headquarters office was contacted by a representative of Claude A. Armour, a member of the Ellington administration, seeking to arrange a meeting between Armour and me. My heart must have skipped a few beats when I was told that the purpose of the meeting was to discuss Mr. Armour's endorsement of me. Arrangements were immediately made. This was very significant. Claude Armour was a giant among those in law enforcement in Tennessee. A decorated veteran of World War II, he returned to Memphis and the career in local law enforcement he had left in 1941 to join the military. He had come up through the ranks in Memphis, had been appointed, then elected as commissioner of fire and police, assuming the title of vice mayor in the process. His service in Memphis for more than twenty years included special FBI training and had resulted in national recognition for Memphis year after year in fire and law enforcement circles. He had long been considered a Democrat, but his involvement in the process of politics was minimal.

Following the tragedy surrounding Martin Luther King's assassination, the rioting, looting, burning, and general anarchy in Memphis, Nashville, and across the nation, all elements of law enforcement were up for examination, reassessment, and major change. Arising out of completely new attitudes regarding race relations and maintaining peace in our communities, Governor Buford Ellington requested Claude Armour to bring his knowledge and skills to Nashville to serve in a cabinet-level position as chief state security officer. Armour accepted and had served the state and governor since late 1968. I had known him only casually in Memphis, but I had always admired him and what he represented.

A meeting was arranged, and I met with Claude Armour. We had a lengthy discussion concerning his interests. He questioned me in depth regarding my commitment to law enforcement at all levels, my feelings about student unrest on college campuses, juvenile problems, and so forth. I was curious as to his motive. He assured me he was interested in one thing, and that was my election as governor. He told me he had approached Governor Ellington and had stated his desire to endorse my candidacy. He offered to resign from the cabinet in order to do so. I was thrilled to hear him say that the governor told him he did not have to resign his position in the administration and that he should get on with his intentions. That position on the part of the governor told us that he had no intention of endorsing my opponent, his fellow Democrat, John

Hooker. I accepted Armour's support, and we immediately made plans to announce the good news.

On September 28, the day that happened to be Chuck's nineteenth birthday, Claude Armour and I held a joint press conference in a Nashville hotel at which time he stated his intention to endorse my candidacy. His action was motivated by his great interest in the future of law enforcement in Tennessee and his conviction that I was the best candidate to address those needs. He referenced his Democrat background, stated that party had no bearing on his decision, and encouraged all people involved in law enforcement across the state to follow his lead and vote for Dunn.

That announcement was a high point in the campaign and gave me great encouragement. I took much comfort from the signals that came, by way of the announcement, from the Ellington administration. The governor had a loyal following throughout the state. About the same time, rumor had it that the governor's beautiful daughter, Miss Ann Ellington, had a Dunn bumper sticker on her car!

The month of October signaled the approaching end of an amazing experience for me and my family. Just a year earlier, we could not have dreamed up the series of events that were taking place. Betty was with me more frequently at various functions, but she was also keeping up a hectic pace on her own. Mrs. Prichard continued her priceless work of looking after our daughters, who were busy in their schools. We received support and cooperation on every front. The dental practice had long since faded from my mind, but I subconsciously took comfort knowing my staff and Dr. Dan Morgan were taking care of my patients.

I was getting valuable support from those producing written materials on the many subjects I had to address and be prepared to discuss. Through many discussions with David White, Lamar, and others, I had made my feelings, my intentions, and sometimes my lack of knowledge on certain subjects known. The result was a series of position papers and speeches prepared and ready for my approval. Finding time to review so much material was a challenge for me. A steady stream of information "From Dunn" flowed out of our headquarters into all the news channels of the state. The environment, crime, drug abuse, education at all levels, highway development, economic growth and rural development, healthcare, planning, strip mining, coal supplies for TVA, agriculture, and gun control were among the subjects of various position papers.

My campaign speeches were consistently delivered without prepared texts, and the various platforms I used ranged from a grassy pad under a tree in a state park to some elegant rostrum in a large hotel dining room. Occasionally, stacked bales of hay were resting places for notes I used in attempting to remember what county or community I was in at the time and who I should recognize and thank on that occasion. I spoke from flatbeds of trailers parked near town squares and from hastily constructed stands in baseball or football stadiums. It was not unusual to make my pleas in an incredibly crowded small town campaign head-quarters, a reception room in a nursing home, a street outside the gated fence of a large factory, or the shady dirt surface of the ground under a courthouse yard tree. It was quite interesting, at the end of the day, to reflect on some of the places I had just visited. How strange, I thought, to stand before a retirement home audience pouring my heart out about the future of Tennessee and its exciting opportunities, to a group of people, many of whom sat there with glazed eyes, thoughtless expressions, completely unaware of where they were, who was speaking, or what was being said. I could only hope the staff personnel of the facility were listening. Such experi-ences were counterbalanced by back-slapping, applauding crowds who whooped and hollered over every phrase that was critical of Democrats in general or my opponent. A good joke or two delivered under those circumstances usually firmed up the general approval of partisan crowds. Somewhere in between were the courteous, curi-ous small groups I sought to speak to in the banks, business offices, and merchant establishments visited while accompanied by my local supporters. It was an amazing experience.

Certain catch phrases became standard and automatic in my remarks. "Creating a climate of confidence in state government," "more jobs for the underemployed," "opening the lines of commu-nication between the statehouse and every county," "the 'three states of Tennessee' unified at last," and "kindergarten for every Tennessee child" were among those most frequently used.

It was a fact that our state lagged others by not offering every youngster a critical kindergarten experience at five years of age. Data verified that more than 30 percent of entering high school students would drop out before graduating. Taking a strong stand in favor of remedying such a situation, attracting more jobs to the state, cracking down on crime, arresting drug dealers, and opening the doors of the governor's office to the ordinary citizen came very easily, and I meant every word I said. It was very important to talk about specific problems that were being experienced in certain localities if I expected to get the best audience, newspaper, and voter reaction.

As I periodically met with Wellford, Alexander, and other close advisers to assess our progress or to identify problems, it became increasingly obvious that nearly all of the issues and challenges facing the new governor were recognized by both me and my major opponent, John Hooker. The campaign between Hooker and me was in danger of becoming a personality contest rather than a hard-fought battle based on differences in philosophy. Of course, there was a third candidate named Douglas Heinsohn, and he could not be ignored. His name would appear on the November ballot in every precinct because he had run unopposed in the primary as a member of the American Party.

Heinsohn was a longtime member of the John Birch Society and called Sevier County home. He had appeared at several of the primary functions but was low-keyed because he had no opponent. However, in the general election he made every effort to be present at any function to which the major statewide candidates had been invited to appear. He had adopted as a campaign symbol a double-bladed ax, and he personally carried the ax wherever he appeared. Mr. Heinsohn mixed national policy concerns with legitimate state problems in his remarks. His exposure to the public was more limited than mine or Hooker's. He got comparatively little press. Even so, he was a factor not to be totally ignored for many reasons.

I was later told that, on one occasion, Betty and our friend Barbara Harrington were in Chattanooga to fill in for me at a public function, and according to Betty, the two ladies found themselves in an elevator with Mr. Heinsohn and his ax. She recalled that they feigned some concern about the ax. Heinsohn assured them they need not worry. Pointing to each of the two blades, he noted that the name Dunn was on one and Hooker was on the other. She said he offered no further explanation. She wondered what he had in mind.

Betty made a guest appearance on my behalf at the Chattanooga Kiwanis Club weekly meeting that resulted in a windfall of good press and public relations for me. I was told she hit a home run! When invited to say a few words about the campaign and her husband, she spontaneously came up with the thought of telling the large audience that, actually, Winfield wasn't the only candidate for governor in the Dunn family. She noted that my uncle, Tom Dunn of Meridian, had been a candidate for the Kiwanis governorship in his district. *And,* she followed up, he was elected! That brought a huge round of applause from the audience and resulted in an excellent article with pictures in the *News-Free Press* newspaper. What a girl!

Several interesting strategies surfaced in the Hooker camp. I received a call from my father in Meridian advising me that representatives of two Tennessee newspapers were there in my hometown attempting to do research on my life as a young Mississippian. The *Chattanooga Times* publisher, Martin Ochs, and John Seigenthaler of the Nashville *Tennessean* were responsible for that tactic. Dad, being well connected in legal and political circles in the small town, had no difficulty tracing their efforts to uncover any fact about my personal life that might be useful political fodder. The "strangers" visited the *Meridian Star* newspaper morgue in search of information. They visited the local high school from which I had graduated. They searched courthouse records and attempted to interview several of my childhood friends. According to Dad, the fruits of their research consisted of one local word-of-mouth story about a watermelon that disappeared from a display in front of the Triangle drive-in, a downtown sandwich and soda shop where I, along with my buddies, often hung out. Perhaps I had been, at one time, a suspect in the case. I could not recall the incident. The presence of the reporters in Meridian was made known to my key people. There was nothing we could do to counter that apparently harmless effort to dig up some dirt on their opponent.

Another tactic that had surfaced in the second week of September was an attempt to associate me with statements purportedly made suggesting my support of a state income tax for Tennessee. The Hooker camp went so far as to announce that a series of anti-income tax rallies would be held across the state. The purpose of such rallies would be to assure the public that, though Winfield Dunn might very well look with favor on such a tax, John Jay Hooker was totally opposed to the idea. My people took rumors of such an effort very seriously, in part due to the fact that a widely respected Nashville attorney, Jack Norman, would be the moderator of each rally. Mr. Norman was a high-profile Democrat whom I had never met. He obviously was a strong Hooker ally.

Lamar Alexander set about to counter the rallies and whatever bad effect for me they might represent. I had never made a statement in support of such a tax, and we were confident none could be produced. He issued press statements containing his letter to the state chairman of the Democratic Party, Jimmy Peeler, who had announced the rallies. He requested a schedule for the rallies in order that we might attend, support the anti-income tax idea and, if necessary, defend my position. Lamar received no response. Apparently few functions were held. Newspapers quickly identified the rally concept for what it was, a ploy without substance. Only the *Tennessean* gave the issue coverage.

About the same time the anti-income tax rallies were being announced, the Nashville *Banner* published a story reprinting a 1966 *Banner* article. In the article, Hooker was quoted as saying that a state income levy and a four cent sales tax should be studied with other sources of revenue to finance programs of state government. He was also quoted as saying that there needed to be a revision of "the archaic tax structures which exist in the state." Although I made no statement in response to the article, I knew that he was correct. I made no attempt in my talks to tie Hooker to an income tax. It appeared to my advisers that his campaign strategy was to link me with sympathy for an income tax as some sort of counter to the Nashville article quoting Mr. Hooker on the tax question. The subject of new tax revenues was never a serious topic for either candidate during the campaign. Hooker did take a position in the 1966 campaign that I used at every opportunity in 1970. He advocated repeal of the Tennessee right to work law, a statute that organized labor strongly opposed. My conservative position was that no worker should be required to join a labor union in order to obtain or keep a job. I supported the state's right to work law.

As the campaign progressed, it became increasingly clear that my opponent would have strong support in the black voter community and solid backing from organized labor. I attempted to appeal to all segments of voters, but I did not court either of the two groups with specific proposals directed to their particular interests. We agreed it would be a waste of time and money to do so. Hooker would find that he not only had my candidacy to deal with. He had to contend with two other factors. One was the Nashville *Banner*. Mr. Stahlman continued to attack the Democrat with such volumes of adverse publicity that it obviously exceeded the norms of partisan newspaper support. The other was the cluster of prominent Democrats across the state who refused to accept his candidacy for a variety of reasons. Most of them could be identified as Clement/Ellington Democrats. Some of that opposition to Hooker was predictable, and it had been built into our strategy. However, the intensity of feelings adverse to my opponent was an enormous asset to me, and it was more than we had expected.

Rumors fed the conversations taking place among those interested in the politics of the day. We heard that Mr. Hooker was showing signs of nervousness. We got word that he was exhausted and unable to put in a full day campaigning. None of the rumors was substantiated as far as I knew, but they added a bit of intrigue to our outlook. My adrenaline was flowing at such a rate that I needed no other stimulation. Each evening, when my head hit my pillow, sleep came immediately, and I always had to be awakened the following morning. I was physically very tired. My brief visits home to check in with the family, to compare notes with Betty, and to enjoy the familiarity of my own bed were all too brief, but they helped. There was never a minute when something exciting was not on the agenda to keep the "juices" flowing. I was getting incredible personal support from Chip Christianson, Trooper John White, and Major John Fields, plus many others. My chairman, Harry Wellford, was always available. I was blessed with great support.

CHAPTER TWENTY-FOUR

ONE ON ONE

Debate?

A communication from the opposing camp posed a challenge to me to meet Mr. Hooker for a series of debates. The venues suggested were various television studios around the state. He was quoted as saying the people were entitled to hear the two candidates for governor sitting quietly before the cameras discussing the issues of importance to Tennessee. I had never thought in terms of such a means of getting my message out to the people. Obviously, the Hooker people were very serious.

A discussion with my advisers about the challenge confirmed what I felt. We agreed that it would be nothing less than foolish for me, an unpolished though sincere speaker, to find myself set up for a debate with my opponent in some television studio. He was a handsome man, he had a resonant voice, his profession as a lawyer had included training in persuasive articulation, and he was very familiar with the use of such resources as facial makeup. My group concluded that I should not be "suckered" into such a situation. Rather, because of the rumors we had heard regarding his general exhaustion and dependence on chemical stimulants, we decided on a logical tactic. Our excuse for not accepting his proposal would be based on the fast-paced and previously scheduled series of campaign appearances that I could not afford to cancel in order to appear in such settings across the state.

The strategy we settled on was outlined in a telegram to J. J. Hooker, Jr., sent by personal delivery on Friday, 9 October 1970, at 12:45 p.m., which read as follows:

> *Dear Mr. Hooker:*
> *Let me suggest that you pick a day so that we may campaign together and debate from every stump and platform we can*

find. We'll publicize these head-to-head confrontations and if the media want to cover them, they are more than welcome.

The voters need to know how both candidates stand on the issues. The people of Tennessee are entitled to look at the candidates as they really are. I am willing. A day of campaigning together will give us an opportunity to take our cases directly to the people. I am for that, because that is what I have been doing all along. I should warn you, however, that my days run from 16 to 18 hours.

I look forward to hearing from you about a convenient day and to meeting you on the campaign trail.

Winfield Dunn

Both Mr. Hooker's message to me regarding television studio debates and my telegram to him had been made available to the news media. For that reason, some sort of confrontation had to be forthcoming. On several occasions both Hooker and I had been invited to attend functions at which we would appear jointly. They included a taping of *The Jaycee Question of the Week* in Chattanooga and meetings of the Junior Chamber of Commerce of Nashville, the Knox County Education Association, the West Tennessee Mayors' Conference in Newbern, and the West Tennessee Newspaper Publishers' Association in Jackson. I attended each of these functions, but Hooker did not show up for any of them. I was quoted as saying that I believed John Jay didn't want to debate. Rather, what he wanted to do every day was to say that Dunn didn't want to meet him "eyeball to eyeball."

At some point, a discussion between Lamar and Gilbert Merritt, representing Hooker, led to an agreement that he and I would meet on a specific day and conduct a series of three debates. The locations for the debates would be Nashville, Springfield, and Jackson. The first two were proposed by Merritt while Lamar pushed hard for Jackson. In each case the debate would take place in an outdoor setting, somewhat "stumplike," and there would be no holds barred. Once the details as to locations were determined, I put those thoughts aside, continued to concentrate on matters at hand, and felt comfortable my staff would handle the arrangements properly. I soon learned that October 23 had been agreed upon.

Everyone in my campaign was totally engaged in the effort. Betty seemed to be in demand almost to the extent that I was. She was advised that an invitation had been extended her to appear before a luncheon meeting of the Auxiliary of the Nashville Bar Association. She was requested to speak on behalf of her husband. The wife of my opponent, Tish Hooker, had been invited to represent her husband at the occasion. Word of Mrs. Hooker's beauty and chic wardrobe, plus her affluence in the community, had been known to Betty for some time. The joint appearance, to be made at the Woodmont Country Club in Nashville, seemed formidable to my wife, perhaps even a bit intimidating.

Betty recalled how she had had to "grow" into the role of spokesman. Speaking before groups had never been an activity in which she felt comfortable. I remembered one occasion years earlier when I had asked her to read the scripture on which a Sunday school lesson I was teaching was based. She did as asked but told me later that she trembled miserably as she read before the group. As my campaign for governor got underway, she agreed to fill in for me before a rather large group of people that I had been invited to address. As she later told the story, she began her remarks about her husband and soon found herself rambling off course, talking more about her wonderful children than her husband. She described herself at that moment as helpless. Suddenly, she was aware that Chuck was standing at her side. He said, "Mom, your baby boy to the rescue!" and then proceeded to let her be seated while he finished off a few words about his dad. I always appreciated that story and the quick thinking of my son.

At the luncheon for the Auxiliary, Betty later described herself as highly nervous and apprehensive. Following the meal during which she met the dazzling Mrs. Hooker for the first time, Tish was selected to make her remarks first. Then, to Betty's surprise, she left the meeting before my wife spoke. Betty had no prepared statement. Several days earlier I had been endorsed as the next governor in a generous editorial by the *Chattanooga News-Free Press* newspaper. She explained her source to the audience of Nashville ladies, then proceeded to read excerpts from the endorsement. That seemed to please the audience, and the speaker was very relieved. She definitely made a hit with those in attendance. She never failed to live up to the moment. That event, about which Betty was so very nervous, was another big plus for me.

Another important date was rapidly approaching. President Richard M. Nixon had agreed to appear in Upper East Tennessee in support of the Republicans seeking election in little more than a week. The date the president would arrive on Air Force One was October 20.

I spent Monday, October 19, in Memphis. Accompanied by Jim Gates, I spoke to the Insurers of Tennessee at the Sheraton-Peabody Hotel at 9:00 a.m. For the next two hours, I toured and shook hands in state and county office buildings. At noon, I spoke to the Life Underwriters Managers Group at the University Club. At 1:30 I met with Dr. R. Paul Caudill, a prominent and influential minister. I then toured the South Central Bell Telephone Company building, shaking hands at every opportunity. At 3:00 p.m. I did a television taping. At 3:30 p.m. I met with Professors for Dunn at Memphis State University. At 4:30 p.m. I did a TV interview at WKNO, a Memphis State station.

Rest time was next. At 7:30 p.m. I made a speech to the Shelby County Social Workers Association at the Sheraton-Peabody Hotel. At 8:30 p.m. I met with black community leaders at the Chisca Plaza Hotel, accompanied by Harry Wellford. Bedtime was next. The advantage of campaigning in a large city such as Memphis lay in the fact that only a small amount of travel was necessary. This day was typical for the campaign in terms of intensity and number of appointments.

The next morning we left Memphis on the Conwood Learjet for Tri-Cities Airport in Upper East Tennessee. President Richard M. Nixon was scheduled to land at twelve noon. Right on time, a group consisting of Senator Howard Baker, Bill Brock, me, Congressman Quillen, Congressman John Duncan, and congressional candidate Lamar Baker met the president as he came down the steps from Air Force One. Cars, including two limousines from the White House, were lined up to transport the group to the campus at East Tennessee State University in Johnson City. The president was ushered to his special car, and Bill Brock was right at his side. The two of them entered the vehicle. I was directed to the next car in line, the second presidential limousine. I turned to the president and requested that I be admitted to his car. He readily agreed.

As a result, during the drive into Johnson City, the three of us—Brock, Nixon, and I—stood, our upper bodies rising through the section of the car's roof designed for such occasions, and waved to the many people who lined the route from the airport into town. The president could not have been more courteous to me. I wondered what Brock was thinking, in view of the obvious fact that he had arranged to be featured alone with the president during the drive.

We were greeted on the campus by thousands of students and supporters. It had rained intermittently that day, but there was no rain while we were on the steps of the college administration building.

At 12:35 p.m. Bill Jenkins, still the Republican Speaker of the state House of Representatives, made brief remarks, then introduced Senator Baker to the excited, cheering crowd. I was excited as well. It was a momentous time in the campaign. Senator Baker introduced me, and I spoke for approximately two minutes. Baker then introduced Brock, who spoke for two minutes. Baker then introduced Quillen, who spoke. Baker then introduced the president of the United States, who spoke for approximately fifteen minutes. He was generous in his comments of support for Brock and me, as well as in appreciation for the support he had received from the people of Tennessee in his own election. After enjoying a warm welcome from the large crowd, we were back in the presidential limousine headed for the airport. We enjoyed the return trip sitting down in the closed vehicle. Both Brock and I had good conversations with the president. He wished us well. He made it clear he wanted to see Albert Gore replaced, and he was nice enough to give me strong encouragement. I spent the night in Senator Baker's home and continued my campaign in East Tennessee the next morning.

The pace did not slacken. On Friday, October 23, the much-discussed day of the "great debate" featuring Hooker and Dunn was at hand. I was awakened at 5:00 a.m. and soon joined my team in the Sheraton Motor Inn in Nashville. Lamar and Ralph Griffith were ready to go, as were Chip, John White, and John Fields. At 5:45 we drove to Rolling Mill Hill near downtown and on the west bank of the Cumberland River. We were aboard a nice motor home obtained from a friend and supporter named Ralph Holt. This vehicle would be used for travel to the first two of the debate venues.

Rolling Mill Hill was a place I had never seen. Located high on the downtown hillside, it was the headquarters of the garbage and sanitation workers for Davidson County. Garage buildings and large trucks were aligned on a vast asphalt apron illuminated by many lights. There was a large crowd of sanitation workers already present. These people were employed by a city government totally controlled by local Democrat leaders. Their regular work day started before dawn. My two security men advised me that they would stay very close to me in that environment, and I didn't object. I had been warned that the only welcome I would receive would probably be catcalls and boos.

As I stepped out of the motor home, I could hear voices, whistles, and jeers coming from the crowd. That loud noise seemed to set the tone for that event. I could see a platform that had especially been put in place for the debate. I glanced up to see that a large motor coach had just pulled up. The door had opened, television cameras and lights were directed toward it, and I noticed well-dressed men and women stepping down onto the asphalt. Some of the women had fur coats or stoles that glistened in the glare of the lights. What a contrast! These people were my supporters who had gone to much trouble in order to be present. Most of them were from the West End part of town. Many were from Belle Meade, my opponent's neighborhood. I was struck by the contrast—handsomely attired middle-class and wealthier Nash-villians who had the courage to venture into an uncertain setting to champion their candidate where the major elements present were hostile blue-collar workers who supported his opponent.

I can only recall the event as one that was completely out of order. Hooker and his aides were already mingling in the unruly crowd. I mounted the platform and sat facing the glare of the television camera lights. It was still dark. I don't recall who had been appointed moderator, but I didn't know him. I was introduced as the first speaker. There were no rules of debate, apparently. I stepped up to the microphone amidst a roar of catcalls, booing, heckling, and general disrespect from the overwhelmingly partisan Hooker supporters. It was clear to me that they were following orders.

My first sentence was drowned out by hostile noise. Every word

I attempted to speak from that point on was lost in the roar of several hundred garbage workers. There was no doubt in my mind that the folks had been worked up to a fever pitch by local Democrat activists. They did a good job. The noise never let up. I must have spoken for twelve or fifteen minutes, trying to justify my candidacy, attempting to outline the issues I wanted to address as governor, and otherwise stating my reasons for believing I was the better choice to be the governor. I concluded my statement and sat down to a further round of boos and catcalls. My team and the crowd of supporters who had come out on my behalf stood by helplessly as I had attempted to speak. My voice was totally drowned out.

John Hooker then stood and addressed the crowd. He received cheers, whistles, handclaps, and other signs of support from the people. My little group did their best to answer in kind the reception I had endured, but they were too few, less than seventy, to have much effect. The speaker plunged into his standard platform pitch, seeking to justify his candidacy. Somewhere along the way, he repeated a line he had used on more than one occasion. It seemed to him that the people of Tennessee didn't need another governor who was born in Mississippi. Rather, they had the option to vote for a native-born Tennessean who more clearly understood the needs and ambitions of the people. When I first heard the criticism leveled at me because I was not native born, I answered with the following comment.

It seemed to me that the most valuable resource a governor could bring to the job would be that of common sense. I allowed that, even as a newborn infant, I had enough common sense to know I needed to be near my mother when I was born, and bless her heart, she just happened to be in Mississippi. I went further to say that, with all due respect to my native state, I did come to Tennessee as soon as I heard about it! That early morning on Rolling Mill Hill I didn't have an opportunity to rebut Mr. Hooker's statement, for a lot of obvious reasons.

As he neared the end of his remarks, Mr. Hooker turned again to me and bellowed out his feeling that the people of Tennessee didn't know enough about me. He challenged me to level with them. "Tell it all, Winfield, tell it all. The people have a right to know!" He repeated the "tell it all" demand several more times, and then he was through. The crowd roared its approval, we descended the platform, and the next thing I recall was my team attempting to tell me I had done a great job as we boarded the motor home. They must have known that I would feel very ineffective as a result of such a poor reception. They were right. Even though we all knew the deck was stacked against us in such heavily Democrat-controlled territory, such treatment was hard to accept.

In the motor home again, I felt suddenly exhausted and decided to lie down on one of the vehicle's beds. It was a blessing since it seemed all my energy had left me. Headed for breakfast and some new energy, Lamar and I discussed the result of the encounter. Unable to draw any conclusion other than that I was overwhelmed by the noise, disorder, and partisanship of the crowd, we dwelled for a moment on Hooker's challenge to me to "tell it all." It was an unexpected twist that neither of us understood. Since the next confrontation was in Springfield in two hours, we agreed the only thing to do was to put out feelers in the crowd at the Robertson County courthouse.

I continued to rest as we finished breakfast and headed for Springfield. As we drove in and approached the town square, I heard oohs and aahs coming from our driver, Ralph, and some of the other occupants. I heard comments such as "there she is," "can you believe it?" "damn their time," "it's against the law," and so forth. As the courthouse came into my sight I understood what the comments were all about. In addition to a large crowd, automobiles parked everywhere, and a small platform situated in what was considered the front of the building, the courthouse building itself was draped with large banners that stretched across and above the entrance. Banners and posters had been placed on or attached to this very large and imposing public building on every side. Two banners stand out in my memory. One read "John Jay Hooker for Governor" while another claimed "This Is Democrat Country." Other posters and pictures featured Hooker's picture or name in some fashion. There wasn't a Dunn poster or picture to be seen. I was amazed!

Springfield and Robertson County obviously had a long and steady Democrat history. The word Republican, which we didn't dwell on in West and Middle Tennessee during the campaign, just wasn't mentioned in acceptable circles there. Even so, it was outrageous to me that this public building could be adorned in such a partisan fashion. I felt there had to be a law against such, but I didn't have time to worry about it at the moment. As the vehicle was parked, my team and I rolled out for round number two in a memorable contest. My energy level had returned to normal, and I was ready to get on with it.

Hooker spoke first. The crowd was largely his, but I was encouraged by the fair number of my supporters who were present. This time the people were more orderly, there were no glaring lights from television equipment, and the sun was shining. It was 10:00 a.m. on a beautiful autumn day. Hooker's people gave him a rousing welcome, and he wasted no time making a statement regarding the benefits that would come from his term of service as governor. As he neared the end of his remarks, he launched into a challenge to me to "tell it all." "Tell it all, Winfield, tell it all," he once again bellowed. His only complaint was that I wasn't being honest with the voters of Tennessee. Once more, he didn't elaborate.

My turn came, and I made my case to the crowd and the news media as best I could. The rhetoric was hot and heavy on both sides, but there was little time to get into issues. Neither of us did. I cannot recall making any critical comments about my opponent other than that he had a poor business record. I don't recall responding to his challenge to "tell it all." At the conclusion, Hooker and I stepped down from the platform, and each of us shook hands with our loyal supporters. Surely, few if any minds had been changed by that "debate." Eventually, back in the motor home, we shared opinions about the event and concluded that Hooker clearly had the advantage in terms of crowd reaction. I felt good about the outcome, however, and looked forward to the next meeting later that day in West Tennessee.

During the drive to the Avco plant where I was scheduled to shake hands with employees at the mid-day shift change, I learned that rumors had been circulated by my opponent's people that they would issue a news release later in the day unfavorable to me. Talking to news people in the crowd at Springfield, my staff learned that information had been uncovered that would reflect badly on my character. The Hooker people felt obligated to share that information with the people of Tennessee!

The gist of the rumor, we learned, was that in Memphis several years earlier, I had been arrested for assault and had posted bond, then I had forfeited the bond rather than make a court appearance to defend myself against the charges. In addition, it was learned that I would be accused of changing my name years ago for some mysterious reason. Lamar, Ralph Griffith, and others were in the dark as to the facts of the matter and listened intently to me as I explained the circumstances of my past that allowed such rumors to be floated.

My explanation was interrupted by the stop at the Avco gates, but afterward I recounted every detail of the events in question. I had not thought of such things for several years and never dreamed they would surface as issues in my campaign. After shaking hands with employees heading to work, I continued my explanation in the following way.

One evening in the late 1960s Betty and I were invited to play bridge by our neighbors next door, Bonnie and Mildred McCarley. During the evening we met a couple, the Eubanks, whom we did not know. Tom Eubanks, we were told, owned and operated a building supply and lumber business on Summer Avenue in Memphis.

On a Saturday several months later as I drove home from my half day of work in my dental office, I stopped at Eubanks's store to purchase hardware and several small pieces of lumber to repair a swinging door that permitted our dog, Christy, to gain entrance to our house. In the store, I re-introduced myself to Tom Eubanks, purchased a small package of hinges and screws, then placed my order for the lumber I needed. I paid for my purchases and went out into the lumber yard where an employee was about to cut the wood to the proper dimensions.

As I stood by while the black employee picked out the material and prepared to use his electric saw to cut it, we heard an angry voice behind us demanding that the employee get his job done right away. It was Tom Eubanks standing in a doorway that looked out over his lumber yard. It was quitting time, and he was ready to close for the day. He was not only belligerent; he was also profane. His cuss words directed toward the black man were offensive.

I turned, looked up at him, and calmly stated that I thought that was a lousy way to build business. Eubanks came down the steps and walked up to me. For a moment he just scowled, and then he suddenly reached out and snatched from my hand the sack of hardware I had paid for. Automatically, I reached out and grabbed the sack from his hand. As I did so, he, facing me, kicked me in the left hip with his right foot. His shoe or boot was heavy, and it struck a small metal tape measure that was in my left pants pocket. The blow drove the metal tape container against my hip bone, creating a sudden shock of pain. As it turned out, the kick had ruptured a blood vessel lying over my hip bone. Reacting to the pain, I swung my right fist and hit the man flush on his jaw. I must have hit him hard because he went down to the ground on his back. I glanced around and saw the black man standing there with his mouth agape, shocked at what he was witnessing. I was shocked as well at what had happened so suddenly. Eubanks lay there on the ground. He was a big man, taller than I and much heavier. I expected him to get up and come at me. Instead, lying there, he growled that he was going inside to call the police. I responded I thought he should do just that.

Eubanks re-entered his store, and I followed close behind him. He told a salesclerk to call the police and have them send someone to his business. As I stood there, Eubanks walked over to his desk drawer, opened it, and grasped a U.S. Army .45 caliber pistol that he pointed at me. He was breathing hard and scowling. As we stood facing each other, the thought that flashed through my mind was, *This man is just about to make a widow out of my wife.* The next thought was whether I should try to take the gun away from him. We were eight or ten feet apart, and it didn't make sense as he was aiming the weapon directly at me. I said, "Tom, that isn't going to solve anything." Seconds passed, and he suddenly lowered the gun, walked over, and replaced it in the drawer.

I felt a sense of relief, standing there, but it quickly vanished as he walked to a corner of the room and lifted a shotgun that had been leaning against the wall. Then he broke down the weapon and removed two shells from its chambers. Once again I felt relief, but I didn't know what to expect next.

Within several minutes a uniformed policeman entered the building and asked what was going on. Eubanks babbled his side of the events that had occurred. I then explained the situation from my side, making sure the policeman knew that I was shocked by what had happened, including my effort to defend myself. I described the incident involving the weapons. After hearing explanations, the policeman suggested that since no one had been seriously injured and because it appeared to be a misunderstanding, we should go our separate ways and forget the matter. We agreed to do that. I could hardly believe what had happened.

I was in a mild state of shock driving home. My mother was visiting from Mississippi. She and Betty were sitting in the breakfast room as I walked in and sat down. I told them what had happened and who was involved. Betty remembered Eubanks but was totally surprised at his conduct. Mother was sympathetic. We all agreed that I should try to forget the incident. Still very uptight and restless, I changed into old clothes and went out to mow the front lawn.

Midway through the lawn-cutting process, I glanced up and was surprised to see a City of Memphis police cruiser come to a halt in my driveway. I stopped my machine as two officers emerged from their car, walked up, and introduced themselves to me. Almost apologetically, one explained that a warrant had been sworn out for my arrest! They were obliged to take me to a precinct station to be booked, and I would have to post a $50 appearance bond. Once again, I was shocked! One of the officers knew me by reputation because I had been chairman of the county Republican Party. He also noted that I was Dr. Dunn, a professional person. Those facts accounted for his apparent respect for me, even under the circumstances.

I went next door and borrowed $50 cash from my neighbor, Richard Austin, who was surprised at the events that I quickly explained to him. He agreed to follow me to the booking station and bring me home. I had never had such an experience. The new precinct station was named the Claude A. Armour Substation. I learned that Tom Eubanks had filed the warrant and that a time would be set at which we would appear before a city judge for a hearing. Personnel at the station couldn't have been more considerate. I was fingerprinted, but I don't recall being photographed. I posted my bond money and was free to leave. Richard drove me home. My sense of shock was giving way to a growing feeling of resentment and anger, but there was little I could do at the moment.

That evening I discovered that the broken blood vessel caused by the kick to my left hip had become a very large area of discoloration. I had Betty take a color photo of a badly bruised left hip. The next day I called my friend and attorney, Alex Dann. The story was related to him, and he agreed to accompany me to court when a date was set.

Weeks later, having been notified of the time for my appearance in court, I appeared in the city hall chambers of City Judge Bernie Weinman. I was accompanied by attorney Alex Dann. For the first time since the incident, I saw Tom Eubanks. He had an attorney with him. The warrant was read, both sides stated their positions, and the judge acted promptly. He dismissed the charge with the observation that our dispute created no basis that merited damages from the complainant. Alex Dann commented that I could have expected no more. I remained upset with what had happened but saw no logic in pursuing the matter further. I am sure I would have enjoyed taking one more swing at my opponent.

Sometime later I received a letter of apology from Tom Eubanks. I was glad to have his acknowledgment that he had done wrong, but there wasn't enough regret expressed to warrant my responding to him. Shortly after the run-in with Eubanks, Betty pointed out to me that his business advertisement in the telephone book yellow pages read "Tom Eubanks—The Crazy Lumberman." The ad featured a cartoon character with facial features drawn to give a helter-skelter appearance. I also learned from my neighbor Bonnie McCarley, who had originally been responsible for me meeting Eubanks, that he had some information on the man. It seems that Tom Eubanks was a combat veteran of the Second World War who, after discharge, had been a patient in three separate veterans' hospitals. It all added up.

The final stage of the incident took place when Eubanks, several years later and in spite of his letter of apology to me, decided to confide to the Hooker campaign what had happened at his lumber yard. Several years later I was to learn that the court record of the warrant and hearing before Judge Weinman had been mysteriously altered to indicate that I failed to show up at the appointed time and had forfeited my bond. I can only assume that the Hooker people turned to some Democrat person in the Memphis city hall and had him or her alter the official record. The idea, obviously, was to make me look as bad as possible. I was disturbed that such a thing could happen in our court system. Of course, in those days, the city hall was totally controlled by the same old crowd that had been in charge for years. That would eventually change.

The Hooker people also let the rumor float that I had, for some mysterious reason, changed my name when I became a Memphis resident. There was no mystery. I explained to Lamar and Ralph that I simply changed my telephone listings to emphasize Winfield as my first name, rather than being listed by my full name, Bryant Winfield Culberson Dunn. That change was made in the early days of my dental practice to make it easier for friends and patients to identify the fellow they knew as Winfield, not Bryant, Dunn. Very little mystery was involved in that decision. Neither my opponent nor his people could make much out of it.

After hearing the story, my people went to work. We looked for a strategy to counter the effect of the news release we were expecting at Jackson. It turned out to be no problem at all. We produced a statement prepared for release if necessary, which said that a man wasn't worth his salt if he would not defend himself. Dunn proved his manliness by doing just that, defending himself. Tennessee needed a man as governor who was capable of doing that. Tennessee needed Winfield Dunn. No other comments were included in the prepared release, although I would be prepared to respond in more detail to anyone, particularly the media, who inquired.

Our group left the motor home at the airport and flew to Jackson for the final confrontation with Mr. Hooker. Arriving there, we drove to a Holiday Inn for an hour of rest. Nearing the hour of 4:00 p.m., we drove into town and approached the Madison County courthouse. A fairly large crowd had gathered, and I quickly saw familiar faces that gave me some comfort. As I walked up the steps to the courthouse entrance, I was relieved to hear a loud cheer from the crowd. Finally, I was in friendlier territory. There were many supporters from West Tennessee counties, and they all looked good to me. Many Memphis friends had driven to Jackson for the debate.

I recall that there was no platform. Hooker and I were seated in chairs on the landing outside the building. A speaker's stand covered with microphones had been made ready. The weather was mild and clear. The crowd was possibly as large as five hundred people, all of whom were standing. I was the first speaker.

At last, on what had been a miserable day for me up to this time, I felt I could make my case with my opponent present. A real opportunity to address the issues existed, and I lost no time talking about jobs, crime, Tennessee's young people, our highways, our state parks, and the need for new faces and new ideas in our state capital. I made sure they knew that I believed I was the only candidate who could give our state a fresh start. I didn't fail to make reference to my opponent who was seated behind me. I stated that he was a part and parcel of the old politics of Tennessee that needed to be changed. He was a frustrated former candidate for governor who lost his first race and decided to become a businessman to get some experience that he was lacking the first time around. And now his new business career had reached the point that he and many of his friends had more trouble than they bargained for because bad judgment had put the business into a mess of trouble. I said that my opponent had spent the entire day attacking me instead of offering new ideas for Tennessee and telling the people why he should be their governor. I said that his business and his campaign were failing. The crowd cheered and treated me well.

Hooker arose to speak and proceeded to do what he had attempted to do throughout the day. He attacked me, offered no new facts, programs, or promises. From the reaction of the crowd, he had to know he was outside the comfortable boundaries of Middle Tennessee. Hooker once again accused me of not leveling with the people of the state and urged me to "tell it all." I learned later that his people were handing out his release accusing me of assault, forfeiting bond, and changing my name for some mysterious reason. I didn't learn if my supporters had tried to counter that with their press release. My opponent had his say, but very little, if anything, came of the accusations he did his best to get across.

Finally, the last of the three "debates" was over, and I was tremendously relieved to have the day behind me. After stepping out into the crowd and shaking every hand I could reach, we headed for the airport. We flew to Dickson, where I made a speech at the local high school, then headed for Nashville and a night's rest. I needed that rest. It had been a long, hard, grueling day. I didn't feel that I had overwhelmed my adversary, but I felt I had held my ground. Hooker's people had probably hoped the debates would be a turning point in what they had to believe was a campaign that was not building momentum.

CHAPTER TWENTY-FIVE

THE FINAL PUSH

Coming Together

My schedule was jammed with activity as we prepared to enter the last full week of the general election campaign. Chuck had come from college to spend the last two weeks of the campaign with me. I think he was also happy to spend some time with those pretty Dunn Dollies. I spent Saturday, October 24, in Davidson and Maury counties. That night I flew to Memphis. I was exhausted but elated because I felt that we had momentum and were gaining every day. We had done no professional polling to sample public opinion, and I could not gauge my feelings by anything other than what I was hearing and what I was reading. At that stage of the campaign, newspapers across the state had begun making their editorial comments in candidate endorsements. I was getting some good news.

On October 20 I had received the endorsement of the *Johnson City Press-Chronicle*. One paragraph read, "After careful consideration of the candidates, the *Johnson City Press-Chronicle* gives its endorsement to Dr. Winfield Dunn."

Two days later the *Memphis Press-Scimitar* endorsed me. About that time I received the first ever endorsement in a Tennessee governor's race from the *Loudon County Herald*. They strongly approved of my position that Tennessee was one great state, not three.

The Nashville *Banner* gave me its strong approval in an editorial on October 22. While remaining proud of the outstanding Democrat governors it supported in the past, the *Banner* said it was equally proud to endorse me as a Republican candidate. It ended by saying it looked forward to a new era of progress in our state.

Support came from the Bristol, Kingsport, and Elizabethton papers. The *LaFollette Press* endorsed Dunn and Brock, the *Elk Valley Times* and *Observer of Fayetteville* announced its endorsement, as did the *Morristown Citizen Tribune*. My opponent received endorsements from the Nashville *Tennessean* and *Chattanooga Times,* as expected. He also received endorsements from many smaller Middle Tennessee publications and some in West Tennessee. I could not have been more grateful or pleased to have such strong support from my two hometown newspapers plus almost solid backing from publications in East Tennessee.

I frequently spoke to someone on our campaign headquarters team in Memphis. I was concerned about these people who had been with me from the beginning, and I felt the need to personally encourage them regarding my progress. I knew they were getting regular reports from Harry Wellford and others who had traveled to various parts of the state. I felt they needed to hear directly from me, and they did on those Monday mornings as we got ready for a new week of campaigning. I appreciated the fact that they often expressed concern for my physical welfare. I had lost weight, and it showed. I recall telling them of the intense excitement that seemed to be building among the various audiences I spoke to. They never slackened their drive. They never let up for a moment, and those who were full-time workers made the most of every volunteer who offered to help.

All the hard work and careful attention to the media appeared to be paying off. I was getting good press. With only a week left in our effort, I gave a statewide radio broadcast on the subject of retiring with dignity. This was an appeal to senior citizens for their votes. I pledged to provide the support of the state government to any federal action to ease the tax burden on those who had retired from full-time jobs. It was a clear burden to people who had reached the age of sixty-five, had become eligible for Social Security benefits, and were having to stretch their dollars, to be penalized because they continued to work and earn wages. Although the state's nursing homes had to be ready and able to serve those in need, those people healthy enough to continue to work needed the support of their governments, not interference and over-regulation. Pride, dignity, and self-sufficiency were the watchwords. Some of these statements were getting good coverage in daily and weekly newspapers.

I sent a letter addressed to every state employee in which I made two promises. First, I assured them that I would offer no one an opportunity to come to work for the state in return for his or her support. Second, I promised that during my term of service as governor, I would never ask or require a state employee to make a financial contribution for any political purpose. The Democratic Party, through its elected leaders, had become notorious for putting pressure on state employees to contribute to political candidates. I had learned state employees were so poorly paid that it seemed inhuman to me to do such a thing. I hoped every employee would have an opportunity to read my promises.

Plans for the last week of campaigning attempted to stretch my physical presence to nearly every part of the state, beginning in Memphis. Those beautiful little Dunn Dollies had boarded a Greyhound bus on October 23 and, accompanied by quite a few chaperones driving their cars, headed for Clarksville and a grand reception at the Republican headquarters there. Each Dolly was hosted for the night by a Clarksville family. Then they drove to Nashville the next day, touring the capitol, entertaining various groups, and campaigning in the Green Hills shopping center. They then joined the Nashville Dunn Dollies and campaigned in four more shopping centers. After a box supper at Centennial Park, they campaigned across the street from people arriving for a college football game at Vanderbilt University. Later, the Memphis group boarded its bus and returned to Memphis for a well-deserved rest. The Dollies, my beautiful and effective wife, along with my great children, all had a large and positive impact on our progress in the campaign.

In the middle of October I had joined Congressman Quillen and Bill Brock for an intensive three-day bus tour of Upper East Tennessee. I was so glad to have my son along. We started with a breakfast in Sevierville and finished up with a rally at Mountain City High School in Johnson County. We visited every county in the First Congressional District and several bordering counties in the Second District. The big bus was crowded with the three candidates, staff people, and those local supporters who rode along in shifts. It was an exciting time as we moved from stop to stop, and I had the thrill of seeing my new friends who were so enthusiastic and hardworking. I was physically very tired, but adrenaline rushed in at every rally.

Of course, we were in "Quillen country," which gave the congressman automatic credentials to be in charge. Time after time, stop after stop, the three of us would stand shoulder to shoulder before the crowd. Quillen always stood in the center. We wore hard-brimmed straw hats. My hat had a Dunn bumper sticker, Brock's had a Brock sticker, and Quillen had a Quillen sticker on his hat. He always welcomed the crowd, recognized his local leaders, and told a few humorous stories. At that point he'd say, "Now, my friends, on my left is the next senator, Bill Brock. On my right is Winfield Dunn, the next governor. And everybody wants to know 'Where's Jimmy?'" Then with a flourish, his hand would sweep up and remove his hat. "Why, Jimmy's under the hat!" he declared, after which he and the crowd would roar with laughter. I would laugh as well, but after a while the sheer monotony made laughing a little difficult. At that point I was able to force a laugh when necessary because the only thing I was looking for was results! Quillen was very popular with the people. By that time any unease or distrust that may have existed between us was washed away in the tide of political optimism that engulfed all of us.

The last three days of campaigning prior to Monday, November 2, the day before the election, were spent in the Third Congressional District, touring with Brock, the Second Congressional District with John Duncan, and back in the First District with Quillen. We felt it was essential to have a heavy East Tennessee presence near the end in order to stoke the fires of Election Day interest and to make very clear to one and all how much I was depending on those good Republicans in that area.

In the Third District we visited a large fire hall for photo ops with the personnel there, worked our way through the large Jubilee Center shopping complex, toured Benton, Etowah, Athens, and Cleveland where we visited the Church of God worldwide headquarters. Back in Chattanooga, I got a short rest break, then joined Bill Brock at a rally at Engles Stadium sponsored by the League of Women Voters and the Chamber of Commerce on behalf of all candidates. Finally, we drove to the airport and departed for Oak Ridge, where I was met by Dr. Jim Kile, my friend who had made a fortune raising white rats for use at Oak Ridge Laboratories. The Holiday Inn was home that night.

The next morning I held an enthusiastic meeting with volunteer precinct workers, attended a conference with a group of coal mine owners, shook hands at an East Tennessee Teachers Association meeting, then politicked with citizens out on a mall. Lunch with the Civitan Club was followed by a rally at Chapman Highway and Highland View Road. We drove to Maryville and attended a meeting in Bill Felknor's office before going next to a Blount County rally at the Maryville Junior High Gym. There we enjoyed a free chicken dinner served to a large crowd. Out to the airport, a flight to Tri-Cities Airport was the last movement of the day. The Holiday Inn in Johnson City was our resting place for the evening.

Early the following morning we drove to Elizabethton for breakfast with supporters. From there we drove to Bristol, visited TV and newspaper offices, then drove to Kingsport to do the same thing. Out of Kingsport and on to Johnson City, we visited the *Press-Chronicle* newspaper offices, then went to a rally on Fountain Square where we were all entertained by the Blackwood Brothers quartet. I felt so fortunate to have such well-known artists perform to benefit my candidacy and Quillen's. One night earlier in the campaign, we had driven into Cookeville for a rally and only then learned that Roy Acuff and his Smoky Mountain Boys were warming up the crowd. It was a bit of a shock. I had never met Roy, although I knew he was a Republican and one-time candidate for governor. He was a giant in country music. He was the "King"! What a thrill for me! We finished up in Morristown and flew to Memphis for our last Sunday before the election.

Sunday was a day of rest at home. At four in the afternoon we headed for the airport and a flight to Tri-Cities. Mr. Jarman had arranged for the Genesco jet airplane to be at our disposal the entire next day. The plan was to begin the final day of my campaign with an airport news conference and to swing completely around the state getting as much media attention as my people could generate from Nashville and Memphis headquarters by telephone and wire services. Everyone in my party was physically worn out, but psychologically each one was pumped up for the last day.

After an early breakfast, the news conference at the airport took place. My sense of being ahead in the race was never so strong, and I hope I showed it. We flew to Knoxville, drove to the Farragut Hotel, and held a news conference on the sidewalk. I campaigned in and out of stores and businesses until it was time to leave for Chattanooga. I campaigned in Chattanooga, held a news conference, solicited votes at the Jubilee Center shopping complex in Brainerd, then departed for Nashville.

At the airport in Nashville, I was met by a group of supporters. We drove downtown in a small caravan. Riding with me was a very prominent Democrat, close friend, and former campaign manager for Governor Frank Clement named Noble Caudill. Having such a significant member of the other party publicly on my side had to be a big help in Middle Tennessee. I campaigned in downtown Nashville near the capitol. The chief photographer for the Nashville *Banner* had made arrangements with my staff for me to be positioned in a crowd of supporters, including Nashville Dunn Dollies, so that he could get my photo with the beautiful state capitol building in the background. The next day, which was Election Day, that photo appeared across the front page in full color. It was a great effort by the *Banner*. We soon departed for Memphis.

Arriving in mid-afternoon, I held a press conference at the airport, then joined Harry Wellford for handshaking at several factory gates. After a brief rest and dinner, I attended a reception for Memphis precinct workers. I then drove home to my family and a decent night's rest. My emotions were mixed, and my body was drained. I had lost eight or ten pounds during the final sixty days, and my clothes fit my body loosely. I don't recall being with anyone but family that evening, although I knew John White and John Fields were not far away—probably in the driveway. They were incredibly devoted to the cause, and I'm sure they must have made some interesting arrangements in order to get a little sleep while continuously providing me with security. The intensity of crowds in the last ten days of the campaign helped me understand the role those two big, muscular fellows were playing.

CHAPTER TWENTY-SIX

A NEW DAY FOR TENNESSEE

It Happened!

Election Day, November 3, 1970! Betty and I were up early, and by 8:15 a.m. we had voted at our precinct polling place. This was the same polling place she and I had worked during the years when we were trying to build the Republican Party. What a thrill to walk into the Walker Wellford basement, our official voting place, see attractive Dunn poll workers with signs of support keeping the proper distance from the balloting, greet old friends who still worked at the polls, and cast our votes. As in the primary, I voted for myself. I don't know who was more excited, Betty or me. Through the remainder of the morning, Harry and I toured various precincts, shaking hands and thanking workers.

In the afternoon I rested at home with my family. After an early dinner, along with Betty, Chuck, Gayle, and Julie, we headed for the airport and a flight to Nashville. A twin engine Martin 404 commercial airplane capable of carrying a large number of people had been chartered. At the airport, I was thrilled to be among all the familiar faces of those who had been a part of our effort from the start. I can't begin to recall who was there, but I have never seen a more excited crowd. It was almost surreal. A large group boarded the aircraft, filled every seat, and flew away to Nashville.

At Nashville's Berry Field the plane taxied to a designated spot where cars were waiting to load the passengers for a drive to the Vanderbilt Holiday Inn on West End Avenue. There was heavy pedestrian and automobile traffic in the vicinity of the inn as we arrived. I recall being concerned for Julie as she had a knack for slipping away on her own. Such conduct was forbidden that night. We were led around to the rear of the inn and entered the building near a loading dock. Soon we were in a nice suite of rooms.

All of my family and other key people were gathered in the suite. Several friends from Nashville were present. I remember Jack Massey and his lovely friend Alyne Armistead in particular. There were several television sets in operation, and the crowd was cheering or groaning, depending on what was being shown at the moment. For the most part, I was riveted watching the TV consoles. Each channel was switching between the several locations where major candidates had chosen to await the election results: Hooker in one location, Gore in another, and me at the Vanderbilt Holiday Inn. Reporters were interviewing various personalities at each location and reporting on the latest tabulations as they were reported in to the state Election Commission headquarters. East Tennessee returns were the first reported because of the time differential. I was ahead early in my race because of the heavy Republican vote from that region. Middle Tennessee returns brought Hooker back into contention. West Tennessee was the final area to report in, and by the time those votes were tabulated, it seemed as though I would win my race. I can't describe my feelings at that moment, but I was "full up." Cheers accompanied every new report of vote totals.

Soon the hotel suite was in a state of pandemonium. Betty and the children came into view and then were lost in the crowd as people moved about. Sometime after 9:30 Lee Smith or Lamar came to me and said Hooker was on the phone, calling for the purpose of advising me that he was about to make a concession statement and offering congratulations. I vividly remember that his voice was very heavy, incredibly emotional as he said over and again, "You won, you won, you're a horse, you're a horse. Congratulations." There were other words spoken, including mine expressing thanks for the call and hoping that he didn't feel the hurt I knew was unavoidable. He wished me good luck as our conversation ended.

I remembered vividly at that moment the attitude I had expressed on primary election night in August. At that time I didn't feel the confidence that I felt toward the end of the general election campaign. During the primary I had said to Betty many times, and to others who were close, that I really was prepared to lose. I described myself as being like a drunk falling down the stairs, so relaxed that he wouldn't get hurt. I felt that I could pick myself up, brush it off, and get on with life. A little later, as we prepared for the general election,

I realized that my feelings about being like the drunk, totally relaxed, weren't accurate. I realized that, had I lost to Mr. Jarman or either of the others, I would have taken it hard. How lucky I was not to have had such an experience. There was no doubt that circumstances over the last two months did not prepare me to be a good loser—to be magnanimous. I would have been crushed if I had lost. I truly felt for Hooker at that moment.

I left the quiet room and went in to tell the crowd that I had just talked to my opponent. They were looking at John Jay Hooker on television as he conceded the race. Everyone in the room seemed ecstatic. I looked for and embraced Betty and the children. I left the suite and headed downstairs to make my acceptance remarks, to comment about how I felt and what the future held as I saw it.

Stepping off the elevator at the lobby, I was engulfed by a throng of friends. For the first time in my life I felt the threat of being seriously injured by the crush of people. John Fields was on one side of me; John White was on the other. Chip Christianson joined them in doing their best to relieve some of the pressure from the crowd. I saw faces from all across the state. Boys from Union County and from Upper East Tennessee came into view. They had driven down to Nashville as the polls in their counties closed. It was an amazing scene. I headed for the microphones and cameras, all the while looking for Betty and the children. They were there.

I cannot recall what was said, but I am sure my remarks were respectful of my opponent. The words, whatever they might have been, had to be framed in expressions of gratitude to all those who had done so much to help us win. My family was by my side, and that was what I needed at the moment. I feel sure I said Tennessee had voted for a new day in its political life. We would be, I promised, an administration for all the people of the state. I stepped down after waving to the crowd and hugging everyone around me. There was another crush of well-wishers. People seemed to be everywhere. We worked our way slowly through the huge crowd. It was an emotional time for many people, including me.

The hour had grown late. My group finally headed for the airport and the flight to Memphis. We were told a large crowd of supporters was waiting for us at the headquarters. It was after midnight when we arrived and joined some loyal friends who had been patiently waiting at the airport. My friend Bill Rachels had arranged for four black funeral limousines from the Memphis Funeral Home to take me and my family, plus staff, to our headquarters at 2500 Poplar Avenue. What a friend! He was always there for us.

We walked in and were greeted by the same enthusiasm we had received in Nashville, although the crowd was smaller. They had been waiting for hours, and it was nearly 1:30 a.m. I climbed a platform along with Betty, and we spoke to the group. I kept looking for Harry Wellford but couldn't find him in the crowd. The joy seemed to be boundless. We celebrated thoroughly until exhaustion set in. Then we all went home to get some rest. It was 4:00 a.m.

The next day, Wednesday, was unscheduled. I was told that the doorbell rang continuously beginning early that morning. All visitors were intercepted by a state trooper who was stationed outside my front door. I was up at 11:00 a.m. and shortly afterward received a telephone call from Governor Ellington. He extended his congratulations and suggested a meeting as soon as convenient. Following a brief conversation, we agreed to meet the next day, Thursday, in his office at the state capitol. He said that a state airplane would be at my disposal. The chief pilot, Colonel William Pickron, had been given his orders. I continued to sense the magnitude of change that was continuing to take place in my life.

Several times that morning as I moved about the house I heard someone use the expression "the governor." It dawned on me that someone, probably a trooper, was referring to me! The wonder of it all! I had little time to dwell on such things as having a new title. I had adjusted to being called "the candidate," and now I would happily be required to adjust to a new title, "the governor."

The remainder of the day is a blur in my memory, but I do recall that my first meeting was with my remarkable friend and chairman, Harry Wellford. We agreed that the remainder of the present day should be given over to the flood of phone calls and messages I was receiving. We took time to meet with a number of news people who were waiting out front. There were many questions but few concrete answers at the moment. The time for rhetoric and pronouncements had come and temporarily gone. In the immediate future there were contacts and decisions to be made. It was sobering to realize that in slightly more than two months, I would be sworn in as the governor of the great state of Tennessee.

Harry and I agreed that several fundamental things had to begin happening. There would be a large number of cabinet and sub-cabinet positions to be filled. Attention would need to be immediately paid to the budgetary concerns that had been alluded to over recent months. Word had gone forth from various sources that there was likely to be a revenue shortfall before the fiscal year was over on June 30, 1971. My longtime Republican ally Lewis Donelson would be asked to take a preliminary look at those numbers. Harry and I would pay attention to people who might be available to serve in state government at a high level. I had said a great deal during the campaign about fresh new faces and ideas being needed to guide our state forward. My opportunity to deliver was assured.

After our meeting, I used what was left of the day to be with my family and close friends. I spent quite a bit of time on the telephone speaking with friends all over the state and my Mississippi family members who called in to express their feelings. It was quite a day.

The next morning we flew to Nashville, landed, and taxied into the State Aeronautic Commission's special hangar. From there we drove to the capitol where, at 10:30 a.m., I met Governor Ellington. He was a tall, friendly man, plain spoken and very easy to be with. It was a time to get acquainted and to begin learning from the governor some of what I could expect regarding my new job. There was no doubt that he wanted our relationship to be positive and productive. He had an opportunity at that time to meet Lamar and Harry. We, in turn, met several of his key staff people. Relationships began to be established, which would lead to many visits between specific individuals representing the governor and me as a transition and transfer of authority were planned.

Following that meeting, I shook hands with various individuals on the second floor of the capitol building. People came out of their offices and met me in the hall. Since all of these individuals were either hard-core Democrats or owed their positions to such, I felt I was an object of real curiosity. To the person, they were all warm and welcoming. It was a reassuring experience. The governor, with his very pleasant demeanor and warmth, made it easy for me.

After a quick lunch, we headed for the airport and flew to Knoxville. My dear friends E. S. Bevins, Betty Sterchi, Frank Barnett,

Jack Mobley, Senator Fred Berry, David Berry, and many others had put together on short notice a reception at the Farragut Hotel. There was a huge crowd present, and I got to say thanks once again. The Knoxville group, aside from my Memphis friends, had been the most giving, the most supportive and productive among all the wonderful people I had come to know in less than a year. I was still at a high level of excitement and appreciation for all they had done. I savored every moment being with people who had become as close to me as family. At some point, I found myself alone with E. S. for just a moment. We literally put our arms around each other for a big hug, and when we separated, I noticed a tear streaming down his face. The bond was set, if not before then, between me and that good man.

Arriving back in Nashville where I was to spend the night, I met Lamar for dinner at the Vanderbilt University Club. He had done a solid job managing the general election, and I made sure he knew how much I appreciated his skills. He also knew I would expect him to help me move forward in preparation for all that lay ahead. We did not discuss his possible interest in becoming a part of my administration, but there were many other subjects we needed to address. I knew the time would come when we could discuss the role he might play during the next four years.

On the third day following the election, I met with Lewis Donelson, with my campaign staff, and with my statewide advisory group. Later, I returned to Memphis, headed home to freshen up, then accompanied Betty to a dinner hosted by Harry and Katherine Wellford.

I was advised that I had been invited to the White House for Sunday morning church services with the Nixons. I immediately accepted. I had also been invited by Republican Governor Linwood Holton of Virginia to Richmond to get acquainted and be briefed on matters relating to the governing process. That, too, was accepted. The chain of events continued to build.

An invitation was received from my new friend Jack Massey. He proposed that Betty and I invite a couple close to us on a personal basis and join him and several of his friends for a few days of rest and relaxation at his home on Cat Cay Island in the Grand Bahamas. The plan, if we agreed, would be to invite our friends to join us and fly down on Mr. Massey's private aircraft. After discussing the matter with Betty and Harry Wellford, I gratefully accepted the invitation. We chose to invite Joanne and Bob Fleming. Apparently, Joanne and Betty had been discussing a brief rest period of some sort. This was a perfect opportunity. They quickly accepted. We began to carve out a time for the getaway. It couldn't come quickly enough for us.

The trip to Washington and the White House was an interesting experience. Chuck drove up from Lexington, Virginia, and accompanied us on our visit with President and Mrs. Nixon. The president expressed his pleasure at my success and pledged cooperation with my administration. On Sunday morning we attended church services in the East Room of the White House. Later in the day we flew to Richmond. There we were met by members of Governor Linwood Holton's staff and driven to the governor's residence. That meeting provided Betty and me the opportunity to get acquainted with Governor Holton and his wife, Jinx. Their hospitality and advice were pleasing and very helpful to us.

Linwood was the first Republican to serve as governor of the Commonwealth of Virginia in many years. His wife had shared the task of putting together inaugural and pre-inaugural activities in Richmond. She gave many suggestions and much information to Betty.

Eventually back home in Memphis, we made preparations for some time off and within several days were on our way to the Bahamas with Mr. Massey, the Flemings, and others. I was ready for a brief period of rest and relaxation.

Before leaving Memphis, Harry Wellford and I plunged into important discussions. My plate was full, and he did all he could to help me deal with what I faced. A detailed list of initiatives was put together so that no time would be wasted in getting a series of important projects underway. Permanent administration staffing, selection of capable people to be involved in the activities leading up to an inauguration in less than two months, decisions as to how we would finance the social activities involved, contacts with the Democrat leadership of the legislature, serious preliminary discussions regarding state finances in the ongoing fiscal year, and many other subjects were discussed. I felt comfortable getting away for a few days and leaving those subjects, plus many other items, in Harry's capable hands. Lamar Alexander, Lee Smith, Lewis Donelson, and several other close advisers would be on hand to help.

We enjoyed a restful change of pace on our visit to Cat Cay Island, compliments of Mr. Massey. We returned to Memphis refreshed and eager to continue preparations for assuming the office to which I had been elected. A date for the inauguration of the new governor was yet to be chosen. That process would be the responsibility of the legislature's elected leaders. It would be a mutually agreed on decision, but I learned we had been reminded that the Democrats were in charge. That came as no surprise. However, my staff and I felt confident that goodwill and cooperation would be the order of the day, and they were.

I immediately commenced meetings with my staff. At that stage the staff was basically an informal group. Several individuals who had played significant roles in the general election remained on the payroll. Valued friends such as Wellford and Donelson, among others, simply served the cause voluntarily. Names were being accumulated for prospective cabinet members. Decisions were made regarding permanent staff members. One major item on the agenda was to designate leaders to take over the planning and implementation of inaugural activities. No one, I discovered, had more firm ideas about the first Republican inaugural function in fifty years than Betty Dunn.

Never, during the campaign, had Betty and I discussed any matter having to do with festivities that would take place on the inaugural weekend. I didn't pause to consider on what day of the week the formal ceremony would take place. While the date was yet to be set, I was told that it would take place on a Saturday, for many logical reasons. Perhaps we didn't broach the subject because we were feeling our way in a new environment and didn't want to be presumptuous! I had not spoken with any legislative leader on the Democrat side. I was aware Senate and House caucuses would be held at an appointed time to choose the leaders of the new General Assembly. Those individuals would have the authority to designate the date of the inauguration.

It was never in doubt that Betty would play a major role in planning events leading up to the official swearing in ceremonies.

Nothing pleased me more. My agenda was as full as it could be on matters relating to personnel, policy, planning, and learning. After considerable discussions, a group was officially designated the Inaugural Gala Committee. Those persons consisted of Dortch Oldham, Lucius W. Carroll, Jr., Mrs. Marshall (Ruth) Trammell, and Mrs. Henry (Roberta) Lochte. All were Nashvillians, a clear necessity because of the demands that would be made on their personal schedules. The committee immediately identified Memphians who would have major input on all plans. Robin Beard was appointed executive director of the Inaugural Committee.

My input on the pre- and post-inaugural activities was limited by choice. I did engage in a discussion as to whether the Gala invitations would require formal attire. I was concerned that many of the good and honorable people who helped to elect me may never have seen a tuxedo and black tie. I couldn't recall being so dressed up since I wore a tuxedo at my wedding. We were told that the usual attire for past inaugural social activities was a business suit for the men and cocktail dresses for the ladies. I was quickly advised that our Gala would be different. The invitations, I was told, would stipulate formal wear. That came directly from Betty. When Alexander heard of Betty's insistence, he called her to suggest that perhaps business suits would fit the occasion. He decided that resistance would be futile! With that major decision out of the way, I left other such concerns with Betty and the committee. I had no idea what a demanding task lay before those devoted people responsible to plan and carry out our part of an inaugural weekend.

It was necessary for me to be in Nashville for the heavy schedule of meetings and appointments that were building up. Arrangements were made for a two-bedroom apartment in a downtown motel with enough space to accommodate both Harry Wellford and me, plus adequate space to have small conferences and meetings. From the middle of November up until December 20, I used that space plus space in a state office building to conduct the myriad of meetings and discussions that filled every waking moment. Provision of the state office facilities was the thoughtful work of the governor.

Buford Ellington offered every convenience he felt was necessary to assure that an orderly and detailed transition process be set in motion. For the first time in fifty years, the authority of the governor's office would be placed in Republican hands. The governor had advised his entire staff that the election of 1970 would take place between two candidates, neither of whom had had previous experience in state government. He stressed the importance of a thorough and complete transfer of every detail of the state's ongoing service to its people. He made no distinction between the two candidates. It was understood by all concerned that an historic shift in opportunity and responsibility would take place. The governor had designated an excellent representative from his administration to lead the transition. His name was S. H. "Bo" Roberts, who served the governor as executive administrator. He was an outstanding associate and aide to Ellington.

Several days prior to the November 3 election, Roberts had communicated with each campaign advising of the governor's directive that assistance to the newly elected candidate would become available immediately. Information, he advised, would be provided regarding pressing issues facing the incoming administration. Department by department breakdowns on existing programs and alternatives to be considered going forward would be addressed. Briefings were being prepared concerning basic procedures such as appointments, expenses, hiring, and other routine information. Through a series of task force meetings involving various state employees, a number of presentations were being prepared and designed to fulfill the governor's intention that this would be the most successful transition in the state's history. The information was directed to my campaign manager, Lamar Alexander.

Roberts turned to the Office of Urban and Federal Affairs for the talent required to achieve the governor's goal. The head of this important agency was Leonard K. Bradley, Jr. Bradley was formally educated at the University of Tennessee with a major in political science. He had served in the Office of Urban and Federal Affairs since its creation in 1968 and had been appointed to head the agency in 1970. To complete the governor's transition team, he selected four division heads from the office. Those individuals were Patrick A. Colley, James A. Payne, Richard D. Sivley, and John L. Wellborn. The five men were talented in their respective areas and collectively composed as capable a group as could have been desired by any incoming administration. Each person was to eventually play a major role in the newly elected government.

The logical choice to head up my transition team was Lamar. He was designated chief of staff for the transition. Those asked to serve in support were Harry Wellford, James McGehee, Lewis Donelson, M. Lee Smith, Frank Barnett, Howard Kesley, David White, Robin Beard, Roger Kesley, and Robert Echols. Although no one of these individuals had experience in state government activity, both Alexander and Smith had gained extensive exposure to the governing process at the senatorial level in Washington, D.C.

In mid-November a two-day session with all participants present was held at Montgomery Bell State Park. Although I chose not to be present, it was most encouraging to me to receive reports of substantial progress and goodwill attendant to the gathering. Additional meetings were held with various elements of the original group gathered at the state park. Specific issues were addressed, each selected based on timing and priority. As Harry Wellford and I focused intently on identifying and selecting various individuals to be invited to serve in the new cabinet, I took much comfort in being assured the transition process was proceeding in a productive fashion. It was essential that all the significant services being provided to the people of the state under the direction of the governor be permitted to continue without disruption.

A very important aide to the governor, Colonel Bill Pickron, the state's chief pilot, was always available and completely dependable. He was a veteran of the United States Air Force and a decorated combat pilot in the Second World War. Governor Ellington had confided that he didn't like to fly and that I should make full use of the colonel. He and I became great friends. The principal state aircraft, a King Air twin motor plane capable of carrying seven and a crew of two, became an invaluable shuttle between Memphis and Nashville. I spent four or more days each week in Nashville, but I always managed to get home for some fragment of each weekend.

I had been notified by the Council of State Governments, an arm of the National Governors Conference, that as a governor-elect, I was invited to a seminar for newly elected governors to be held at Southern Pines resort in North Carolina. Shortly thereafter, I received an invitation to attend the annual meeting of the Republican Governors Association to be held in Sun Valley, Idaho, in mid-December. A decision was made to attend both functions. I was the only Republican to be elected governor of a southern state in 1970. The total number of Republican governors as of 1971 was a modest thirteen. My election gained more notice at the national level as a result of those meager numbers than perhaps it might have received if the figures had been greater. I was delighted with the attention.

Although golf was an option, the late November two-day Council of State Governments seminar was an all-business affair as far as I was concerned. The attendees were wined and dined in superb fashion, but my focus was on learning. The flow of information was intense, and I absorbed as much information as I could with the expectation that everything I could learn about governing would be very helpful in the days ahead. I had an opportunity to meet a number of governors-elect representing both parties.

Several weeks later, with my entire family along, we flew to Frankfort, Kentucky, where we were welcomed and entertained by Governor and Mrs. Louie Nunn. As a Republican governor who was entering the third year of his administration, the governor was an immediate source of good advice and support. Beulah Nunn, the first lady, took Betty in hand and proceeded to share many insights and much information about her role, not only as the governor's wife but also as the decorator who refurbished the aged executive residence of Kentucky. Betty was very impressed with Mrs. Nunn.

The next day we were picked up and flown to Sun Valley, Idaho, by a large corporate aircraft that had been made available to Governor Nunn. Our hostess for the flight was an impressive woman who was identified as the well-known chief state government lobbyist for the company providing transportation. I was advised that the company did extensive business in the state of Kentucky but not in Tennessee. I made a mental note of that fact.

Sun Valley was a pleasant mix of work and play. I had the pleasure of watching each of our three children become acquainted with snow skiing. Betty and I enjoyed watching the youngsters have their thrills and take their falls. The second evening at that special resort all those in attendance were treated to a moonlight sleigh ride along snowy trails. The moon shone brilliantly, illuminating snow-covered mountain peaks and giving the occasion a magical quality. It would remain a very pleasant memory.

I attended two days of meetings with a distinguished group of governors and their aides. Among the most notable of those present were Nelson A. Rockefeller, governor of New York, and his brother, Winthrop Rockefeller, governor of Arkansas. The first day of meetings consisted of committee reports and presentations on a variety of subjects concerning state government. I was recognized as the governor-elect of Tennessee and given a warm welcome.

The second day, only a morning session occurred, and it was memorable. Vice President Spiro Agnew was a guest representing President Nixon. Following a series of reports concerning the status of the Republican Governors Association, the vice president brought greetings from the president and offered additional remarks. At the conclusion of his remarks, Governor Tom McCall of Oregon requested the floor. What followed made me wide-eyed. McCall addressed the vice president directly and began to dress him down as representative of a president who had done much too little in the election just passed to assist in electing more governors. McCall was a large man, a former newspaper publisher, who apparently pulled no punches in expressing himself. Standing immediately adjacent to Agnew, McCall admonished the president severely for what he described as inexcusable indifference to the plight and dwindling numbers of Republican governors. I was amazed at what I was witnessing. I would not have been surprised if the two had engaged physically. The vice president was a large man, at least as tall as McCall, and it was very obvious that he was bristling and doing his best to control his emotions.

None too soon the chairman of the association intervened and brought about a degree of calm. The show of temper and the feeling of resentment toward the Nixon administration for its apparent lack of support of the governors were a complete surprise to me and a naked indoctrination to what might occur within the circles of power I had happily joined. For this newcomer, it was an unforgettable experience. We were all grateful that, since it had been an executive session of the governors, no news people had been in attendance. It would have been a story with dark headlines.

Once again at home after an interesting meeting, my attention was riveted on pressing matters. Concerning the many questions to be answered and decisions to be made relative to the makeup of my cabinet members, Harry and I had agreed that fresh faces and experience were to be a hallmark of that group. We also agreed that, while Republicans would be sought for all positions, party affiliation would not be an overriding consideration. We needed the best people we could find. I was surprised to learn that two very prominent and highly respected members of the Ellington cabinet had let it be known that they were available to continue to serve. That information was noted, but for various and sound reasons, I felt confident my judgment in not accepting either individual would be the proper decision. I discovered that making the decision was easier than letting each individual know my position.

I had gladly accepted temporary space in a state office building near the capitol several weeks before the date of the inauguration. I learned that an appointment with the governor-elect had been requested by Commissioner of Education J. Howard Warf, one of the two cabinet members interested in continuing to serve. Warf was physically a small man, but his stature and credentials as an educator plus his reputation as a highly partisan Democrat were substantial. I had been made aware of his strong support for my opponent, John Hooker. At the appointed time we met, and our visit lasted approximately twenty minutes. After appropriate cordiality, the gentleman came straight to his point. He had served the state as its education commissioner under two distinguished governors. He had been responsible for the development of a strong momentum in public education, with an emphasis on higher education in community colleges. He felt his continued efforts were necessary to sustain that momentum. He felt it essential that he be appointed to continue that important work. He requested my strongest consideration of his availability.

I thanked the commissioner for his contributions to public education and his willingness to join my administration, but I advised him that his services would not be needed. He shook his head in disbelief on hearing my decision. I had clearly stated my position, and with few parting words, he took his leave. I was comfortable that I had done the right thing, in part because I knew his loyalty to me would be questionable, and in part because I knew he had done everything in his power to see to my defeat. His membership in my cabinet would have sent shock waves through the ranks of many good educators and notable Republicans who supported me fully. I could not disappoint such people.

The other commissioner interested in joining my administration was Frank Luton, MD, a highly respected psychiatrist who was the commissioner of mental health. Dr. Luton was an elderly gentleman who had served the state and its people very well. I had been advised that the Department of Mental Health posed serious challenges to any leader because state funding had in recent years been totally inadequate to meet many obvious needs. I wanted a fresh face with high energy and a commitment to make major changes. Although I had not at that time identified a candidate for the position, I had requested an in-depth search to find such an individual.

During our first and only visit, Dr. Luton expressed his desire to remain in service. I advised him of my belief that, in spite of his good service, it was time to bring new talent to a demanding opportunity. He graciously accepted my position, and we parted on friendly terms. He was, indeed, a gentleman.

While one of the two men, a highly partisan Democrat, could hardly believe I would not accept his availability, the other could not have responded more appropriately. These two encounters were among the many opportunities and challenges those pre-inaugural days presented me.

One day while in Memphis I sat down in my dental office with Dr. Dan Morgan, my dental associate. He had expressed an interest in acquiring my business. I felt he was capable of taking on that responsibility, and it seemed only fair that he should be the man in charge of seeing to the dental needs of my patients as well as his own. I could not predict my future, but I had no doubt that the next four years for me would be totally focused on matters beyond the scope of my profession. We made arrangements for him to assume the office lease and purchase my dental equipment. Although my patient clientele had been nurtured and developed over fourteen years, I was fully aware that I had inherited many of the patients I cared for following the death of Dr. Frank Prichard. As to the value of the business, I limited the purchase price to an expert's estimate of the office furniture, fixtures, equipment, and supplies. Although it was conventional to do so, I chose not to attempt to place a value on the future business my clientele represented. Dan and I quickly came to terms. That was that.

Over and done with! The transaction was completed with a firm handshake but not without emotion on my part. A strong bond of friendship existed between me and my dental assistant, Glenda Smith, and my dental hygienist, Patricia Murphy. My office manager and receptionist was Mrs. T. L. Hill, known and loved by all of us as Annie. This fine lady was a widow who had family in Clarksville. I offered this dear friend a position on my soon-to-be office staff in the capitol. She happily accepted. I had the quiet pleasure of hearing Annie make the transition from calling me Dr. Dunn to referring to the "governuh." Having her go with me to such a great new adventure was a wise decision. She was a wonderful lady and a very special source of comfort and advice going forward.

Governor and Mrs. Ellington, each of them gracious and thoughtful, suggested that Betty and I should plan on moving our belongings to the Executive Residence well in advance of my assuming office. They were to move into their new home in the Oak Hill area not far removed from the Residence. We were quick to accept their kind offer and made plans to move shortly after January 1.

Following a hectic but very special Christmas at home on St. Andrews Fairway in beloved Memphis, the entire family turned to the task of making the move to Nashville. Once again, my wife displayed her strength and ability. She saw to nearly every detail while I remained free to continue preparations for assuming office. Chuck, Gayle, and Julie certainly did their shares in terms of making the move. They were real troupers. Even Christy, the family pup, seemed to take the move in stride. Betty recalls that several members of her Memphis bridge club came over and helped pack all her kitchen wares. She was a skilled cook and possessed many special items that she knew would be needed in order to continue to prepare the meals that we had become spoiled with over the years. We moved our entire household furnishings to Nashville seven days before I was sworn in to office. The governor's mansion, which we were later to designate more properly "the Executive Residence," contained a great amount of attic space.

My schedule on the Friday before inauguration included an appointment with Harry Roberts from the Glenwood community of Greene County. What followed was memorable. Harry and his family had become early supporters in my campaign. He presented me with a large package that I was asked to open immediately. The contents revealed a magnificent handmade quilt. He explained that the gift was from his mother, his immediate family, and the people of the Twenty-fifth District of Greene County. I was in awe of the beautiful object and all that it represented. The dominant color of the cloth was gold. It was bordered on both sides with handsome freehand designs.

One side consisted of more than thirty quilted squares, each one representing an object that had been used during the campaign to draw attention to my candidacy, or a number that represented some significant news concerning my progress. Each was unique and completely original. In one square was written, in indelible ink, the following:

Western Union Telegram.

To the Hon. Winfield Dunn

Praise God from Whom All Blessings Flow. What had to be Dunn, was. The greatest moment in Tennessee history of our time. Be as great in the Chair as you were on the trail. With you all the way into "The Spirit of the Seventies."

> *Mrs. T. H. Roberts and Family*

November 3, 1970
Glenwood
Greene County

On another square was recorded as follows:

The 25th District of Greene Co.
Republican Primary Dunn 58
         Jarman 33
         Jenkins 32
Glenwood.
The only one to go for Dunn

On the reverse side of the quilt was written in script the following message:

The Dunn Quilt

We were so gratified and relieved at the announcement that "Dunn had been elected" that we set about writing the telegram. It was then that we realized that mere words could not express our real feelings. The "Dunn Quilt" is the result of our search for an adequate expression of our gratification and concern for you, your administration and the Volunteer State.

In addition to the campaign paraphernalia we have filled in with some mementos of special significance to us. (The "Dunn Buggy," the results of the Primary in our home precinct, Glenwood, etc.) The tag attached to the balloon was written on the back side of one of your picture posters. The "Dunn" hat was purchased at the booth of the Knoxville Fair. Brent's proudest moment was shaking your hand and wearing his Dunn hat at the Fair. The unfamiliar banners were made at the Dunn-Brock headquarters at the local high school where I teach. We took five busloads of students to rally at ETSU with banners like these. The other squares represent our admiration for you and family, and our expectations for the best administration in Tennessee history.

With unlimited optimism and sincere best wishes, we are with you all the way as we enter a new era for all Tennesseans.

Sincerely, and with great expectations.

Louise and Harry Roberts and Family

This border was pieced by my mother, Mrs. T. H. Roberts, 82. She plans to attend your inauguration. The quilting was done with the assistance of neighbors of the Glenwood Community. H. R.

The gift of the quilt was among the most touching I had experienced. Today, it occupies a position of prominence in my home. It represents, better than any words of mine, the heartfelt interest demonstrated by so many citizens across the state in trying to make a difference for the public good.

It was a pressure-packed time in our lives. January 16 was designated by the legislature as the official day for the changing of the guard. That day would be a Saturday. The Inaugural Committee immediately prepared and ordered printing of 10,000 invitations to the inauguration activities. The preceding night, Friday the fifteenth, became the Gala evening. Of that large number of inaugural invitations, we made sure a minimum of 20 percent went to Memphis and Shelby County friends.

As part of the festivities, we planned to have a brunch at the Residence on Sunday morning following the inauguration in honor of members of Betty's family and mine. Also invited were close friends of family members. Included were my father, my two sisters and their families, cousins, uncles, an aunt, and many close friends. Betty's family included her mother, brothers, aunts, and one uncle. The one person missing was my beloved mother, Dorothy Crum Dunn. She remained in Mississippi, unable to be present because of her illness. Her absence was the only painful part of what was taking place as far as I was concerned. I deeply regretted that her frail health would not permit her to be with us. She was surely with us in spirit. By the time the large group of relatives and friends gathered, my family had become reasonably settled in the beautiful residence occupied by the governor and his family. It was formerly the home of the prominent Wills family and had been named "Far Hills." There was a great air of excitement. Each family and a number of close friends from out of town had been assigned a dress-uniformed member of the Tennessee National Guard as their escorts. Undoubtedly, each person was thrilled with the attention received from those fine military people during that brief period.

On that special Friday evening Betty and I, along with our children and their friends, left the Residence to attend the grand Gala to be held at Nashville's Municipal Auditorium. It was a brilliant event, planned to perfection. In attendance were 1,400 friends and supporters who had paid $100 per person for that privilege. That was a considerable sum of money then, but it satisfied the expenses of the occasion. Betty and the Inaugural Committee had done a wonderful job. Everyone looked splendid in black tie and evening gown. I saw political acquaintances from remote parts of Upper East Tennessee and elsewhere, decked out in tuxedos, that I would never have expected to show up in such dress. My wife's judgment was vindicated. She was absolutely beautiful in her evening gown, as were my girls in theirs. Chuck, our college sophomore, looked his handsome self in his tuxedo.

As the large gathering settled in to enjoy the evening, the sensation I had was that a massive family reunion was taking place. Individuals moved in and out among the tables, putting faces with names and reliving exciting moments that occurred during their recent political experiences. It was an incredibly happy time for everyone. The delicious meal was followed by a unique group of professionals who entertained us. Marguerite Piazza, our dear friend and Metropolitan Opera star from Memphis, was a hit with everyone. Boots Randolph and his "Yakety Sax," Floyd Cramer and his piano, and Chet Atkins, "Mr. Guitar," enthralled everyone. These nationally popular musicians were spellbinders, and I am confident everyone in attendance felt they got their money's worth.

Bone weary but exhilarated, we were driven home to rest before an early wake-up call to begin the day of the inauguration. That day, Saturday, January 16, 1971, would be filled with pomp and ceremony, plus celebration, far beyond my expectations. It would begin at 7:00 a.m. with a light breakfast and prayer services at historic McKendree Methodist Church on Church Street in downtown Nashville. Our minister in Memphis, Dr. Harold Beaty, pastor of Christ United Methodist Church, would deliver a message that he had titled "What One Man Can Do."

The next morning as our party entered McKendree Church, I was directed by a security officer to the basement level of the church where a large crowd had already gathered. Breakfast was being served. At that point, I recognized my friend the newspaper reporter from the Knoxville News Sentinel, Dana Ford Thomas. Standing beside him was a slight black man who smiled shyly. To my utter amazement and pleasure, I realized that the man was my boyhood best buddy, Ezell Wilson, from Meridian, Mississippi. It was an emotional reunion for me, and I took it all in as best I could under the circumstances. Mr. Thomas had, unbeknown to me, traveled to Meridian, located Ezell, and made arrangements to bring him to

Nashville for the inauguration. There were no words to describe my emotions at that moment or my gratitude to Mr. Thomas. There was very little time to visit, but it was a deeply satisfying experience for me. I hope the occasion meant something to Ezell. That was the last time I saw him. Years later I learned that he had died in Meridian. Surely, his death was premature, and I surmised that he might have developed a lung condition working in the constant dust of the feed mill where he was employed. Engulfed as I was in my new responsibilities, I simply didn't think further of that long-ago friend who had meant much to me.

The prayer service led by Dr. Beaty was moving and meaningful. That fine man of God spoke eloquently and generously about the opportunities that lay ahead. I was grateful for his presence, his prayers, and the large number of friends and relatives who made that occasion so memorable for each of us.

From the church services we moved on to other events of the morning taking us up to the time when we would mount the inaugural platform and I would assume my official responsibilities.

At last the time came for my official party to gather in Governor Ellington's office preparatory to moving en masse out to the inaugural platform. Governor Ellington took Betty, our youngsters, and me aside for a few final words of advice. He told us we would be amazed at how rapidly the four years just ahead would pass. Having served a total of eight years as governor, he advised us, as he had advised his own family years earlier, that we should avoid changing when we enter the role as the state's first family so that we wouldn't have to change when we were finished. In other words, don't change when you come in so you won't have to change when you go out! It was sincere and valuable advice from a good man.

The governor then handed me, on a most confidential basis, an envelope he had removed from his coat's inner pocket. It was, he said, a message from Judge Preston Battle of Memphis bearing on the fate of five men on death row in Shelby County. It was addressed to "The Governor." Ellington said that the message should be read by me at an appropriate time and retained. He stated that, during my term in office, if certain circumstances developed, I should act on the basis of my best judgment in the matter. Without knowing the contents of the letter, it was then that the hard evidence of the awesome responsibilities that would rest on my shoulders began to become apparent. The fates of five human beings living in the state's maximum security prison on death row were quite unexpectedly being placed in my hands. I placed the envelope in my coat pocket with thanks to the governor.

Buford Ellington offered me an additional suggestion. He felt I would be well served to employ his personal secretary, Mrs. Mary Smith, as an addition to my staff. Her intelligence, knowledge, and ability would serve me well, he advised. I thanked him and said I would give that thought serious consideration. I did so and finally concluded that, while I would see that Mrs. Smith remained an employee of the state, I would not bring her into my small circle of assistants. I lived to regret that decision. Mrs. Smith would have been a valuable resource. She has remained my dear friend down through the years.

The moments were fleeting. We were just minutes and a few nervous steps away from what would be a significant high point in the lives of my family. Another high point, second only to the swearing in ceremony that was about to take place, occurred the next evening but bears telling now.

At the Inaugural Ball, a golden moment for Betty and me occurred when, before the orchestra began playing and quite unexpectedly, someone with authority tapped me on the shoulder and suggested it was time for the governor and the first lady to have the first dance of the evening.

I was not briefed on what was expected of us, but I quickly reacted and asked my wife to join me on the dance floor. The orchestra began to play "The Tennessee Waltz." She and I embraced and began to dance. We realized we were the only couple on the dance floor, floodlights were shining on us, and the audience was applauding. What an incredible moment for the two of us! We completed the waltz, a dance style not familiar to me, and were soon joined by other dancers.

Some days later, Congressman Dan Kuykendall commented that he enjoyed a newspaper picture of Betty and me as we danced our "Tennessee Waltz" that evening at the Inaugural Ball. "Oh, Betty," he said. "It was a romantic moment! The governor was looking down at you as you danced. You were looking up at him! I just wonder what in the world you were saying to him?" Betty replied, "I was saying to Winfield, one, two, three, one, two, three!" That was exactly what she was saying. I will never forget it!

I am now satisfied that this part of my story has been adequately told. There are names, occasions, experiences, and emotions that have not been revealed for lack of recall. Each one remains priceless to me. Events that were to follow our pre-inaugural moments in the capitol immediately and for the next four years will be parts of another story that I will tell. For the moment, certain facts were clear, and I have recorded them as best I can. I have waited nearly too long to write this chronicle, but time has not dimmed my memory completely. It's now time to begin recalling many significant details of the next four years in which I had the privilege of serving my state as its governor. For the present, this much has now been told by the one who dreamed the dream.

The race was over! It was history! Our hopes to have an opportunity to make a difference in the destiny of our state had become reality. From little more than a standing start we had successfully run an uncharted course. Such a brief period of time, relatively speaking, had passed since the drive home from Dyersburg with the words of Little Buck Ozment ringing in my ears. "Winfield, you ought to think about running for governor." The very idea that I could presume to be the governor of my state! The very idea that a Republican could be elected governor of Tennessee! The very idea that I could summon the courage to ask my dear wife to let me try or that she would agree! The very idea that I could interest a man like Harry Wellford or other friends in the task! And yet, in less than twelve months from the date of my walk around the square in Dyersburg, shaking a few hands and being introduced by Little Buck as a possible candidate for governor, the dream had become a reality.

The prize was won! The hopes, the dreams that had coalesced around a common and worthwhile goal were about to become a challenging opportunity!

It all boiled down to this—the political events that occurred in so brief a period in Tennessee had happened because the timing was right, the Republican candidate for governor was from the right part of the state, the Democratic Party was divided, and honorable people with sound political instincts were there to help one who was willing to make the effort. The system worked. A sea change event in

Tennessee political history had occurred, and now its story has been preserved from a very personal point of view.

One more memorable fact about Inauguration Day was that it was bitterly cold. That, however, did not dim our enthusiasm. After all, time and again we Republicans had heard from the Democrats that, as far as the governor's office was concerned, it would be a cold day . . . !

PART THREE

The Winfield Dunn Administration

State of Tennessee, 1971-75

INTRODUCTION

For the first time in fifty years, the executive branch and the legislative bodies of Tennessee government were to be represented by different political parties. The historic shift from business as usual would occur on Saturday, January 16, 1971. This was a major departure from the recent political history of our state. Election of a Republican governor had stirred waves of apprehension and speculation that flowed through the capitol building, into state office buildings, state highway garages, the public school systems, courthouses, and in countless conversations following the general election of November 3, 1970.

It is among my fondest hopes that those who may have felt a lack of personal security arising out of that election learned quickly their concerns were unfounded. I must qualify that statement by noting, for the record, that there were several exceptions. There were a small number of individuals who, because of their overt partisanship during the recent campaign, should not have expected future job security with the state government. That would be the case, and my action in those instances was fully justified. For those whose reasonable expectations and hopes were raised, I trust their optimism was satisfied. As the newly installed governor, the first Republican to take office since Alfred Taylor took the oath of office in 1921, I was totally committed to being the governor of all the people.

The unusual political events leading up to that moment when I raised my right hand and took the oath of office in Nashville on January 16, 1971, have been recorded. My purpose now is to draw from recollections, documents, and a not unbiased point of view in reflecting on my stewardship as the governor of our great state for one four-year term.

The years following my service in state government have taken a certain melancholy toll. Many good people who were intimately involved in my election and the business of state government during my years of responsibility are no longer living. Yet many devoted citizens remain from whom the faint glimmer of a smile might be detected if reminded of some role he or she played in support or opposition during those days when fresh faces and new ideas took charge on Capitol Hill in Nashville. It was an exciting time for those of us with vast responsibilities and a curious time for those who were deeply interested in the business of state government as it had been managed in the past or who looked forward to its future. For others including the thousands who cast their ballots for or against a candidate, I believed there was an extraordinary interest in what was to follow in terms of new leadership at that level. As to those who failed to vote, it was merely business as usual in Tennessee, a very good place to be.

And Tennessee was a good place to be. The magnificent landscape from border to border was then, as now, a thing of beauty. Miles and miles of navigable rivers, forests, fertile fields, lakes, streams, playgrounds, and scenic vistas enthralled the visitors and the thoughtful residents who paused occasionally to appreciate their good fortune to be citizens of the Volunteer State offered opportunity and potential for growth throughout our system of public education. Eager minds could acquire knowledge and skills designed to enhance ability and ambition. Ribbons of concrete and asphalt roadways existed to connect the metropolitan areas with rural society, assuring dependable access to personal and commercial pursuits. Business, industry, higher education, and agriculture offered an attractive balance of economic possibilities for those interested in improving their material well-being. The spiritual needs of its citizens were fulfilled by the easy availability of churches and temples in its communities. And the state enjoyed an unprecedented balance of political opportunity because a healthy, two-party political environment was taking root in which competition based on ideas, goodwill, and determination could produce good leadership at every level of government.

Those advantages we must continue to use to improve the chronic existing deficiencies in the state that impede progress toward a quality of life future generations have every right to anticipate. Today, at the beginning of a new century, Tennessee is ranked poorly by national statistics in terms of population health status. Obesity has become a major health and economic threat to our citizens. The education establishment is challenged by data revealing that less than 20 percent of our people have a bachelor's degree. The national average is close to 25 percent. High school dropout rates are unacceptably severe. And underemployment continues to deprive hardworking Tennesseans of more fruits from their labor. Solid progress has been made over the years through cooperative efforts between the public and private sectors. An enlightened electorate can see to the acceleration of those efforts.

On a more personal note, I am occasionally reminded of memories that reside in the thoughts of some citizens reflecting on my days of service as governor. Several incidents come to mind that have occurred in the years since I left office.

While I am seated at a large dinner party in progress, a hand touches my shoulder. I look up to see the pleasant, smiling black face of a waiter. "Hello, Governor. You signed my papers and let me out." Followed by a broader smile, I see and then hear, "Thank you. I'm doing fine!"

Seated in a busy restaurant, I'm greeted by a diner making his way to an exit after finishing his meal. "Hello, Governor. I meant to call you and say thanks. You saved my life! I am that state revenue agent who was taken hostage in the dry cleaner's store in Memphis. Thanks for coming down there!"

Standing in a Wal-Mart, I'm hailed by a fellow who asks, "Aren't you the governor?" My positive response is met with a handshake and a grin. "You fired me! I was a guard at Brushy Mountain. It didn't matter. I just came down to Nashville and went to work at the big prison. I'm glad to see you."

Such incidents and many others remind me of those four intense years of learning and making the most of opportunities that came with the office I sought and won. Down through the years of its existence, the state of Tennessee has been served by capable, sincere, and dedicated individuals in the office of the governor and in the legislative bodies. We take pride in being the sixteenth state to become part of our great Union. Many chief executives of the state preceded me. History records that Tennessee's journey has been steadily onward and upward. The end of that journey is nowhere in sight nor should it be. So much remains to be done to make our state an even greater place to share one's life with others. I count it among the very highest privileges of my life to be included in the company of those governors who have served our Volunteer State.

CHAPTER TWENTY-SEVEN

A NEW ERA GETS UNDERWAY

The Transition

One of many examples demonstrating the wisdom and states-manship of Governor Buford Ellington can be singled out by reviewing the transition between administrations that occurred as I assumed the governor's office. My point of reference is a thesis submitted by Leonard K. Bradley, Jr., to the Graduate Council of the University of Tennessee in March 1971. Titled "Gubernatorial Transition in Tennessee: The 1970–1971 Experience," the thesis outlines in detail the diligent preparations that took place following the August primary and extending through the general election date. Immediately following my election, the incumbent governor's transition staff was prepared to begin meetings with a team I designated to participate in this vital exercise to assure a smooth transfer of authority from one governor to another.

Mr. Bradley was assigned by Ellington's executive administrative assistant, S. H. "Bo" Roberts, to direct a staff task force chosen from the state Office of Urban and Federal Affairs. His agenda was to develop the necessary materials for a successful transition experience. At the time, Leonard was director of urban and federal affairs. He selected four of his associates to compose the transition team. They were Patrick A. Colley, James A. Payne, Richard D. Sivley, and John L. Wellborn. These young men were steeped in knowledge of state government affairs and well acquainted with the growing relationships that were occurring between federal, state, and local governments. They were talented young men, and each man was destined to become an integral part of my administration at significantly higher levels of responsibility.

For eighteen years, Tennessee had been served by only two gov-ernors, Frank Clement and Buford Ellington. Both men were very popular. Ellington became a leader among the nation's governors during his second term. He served as chairman of the National Governors Conference. He also served as a member of the Advisory Commission on Intergovernmental Relations. Out of those experiences he saw the logic of creating the state Office of Urban and Federal Affairs to prepare for increasing state involvement with federal social initiatives. During its three years in existence, the office had recruited a group of bright, young professionals. It was from these capable people that the transition team was selected.

My campaign staff was advised in October of Governor Ellington's intention to prepare the necessary materials for a series of meetings during which a new administration could be fully briefed. Pertinent information regarding existing state programs, critical issues to be dealt with, and pressing problems facing the executive branch of the government were appropriate subjects. During his second term, the growing complexity of governing and the independent nature of the legislative branch were apparent to Ellington. He had become acutely aware that at the completion of his term any successor would face severe challenges. In Tennessee political history, the primary selection of a Democrat candidate was tantamount to his election as governor. A five-month period, from August to January, allowed ample time to prepare the new leader to govern. In 1970 the November general election would leave scant time for the winner to become adequately prepared to govern from the outset. Governor Ellington's own political experiences in earlier years gave him clear insights into the desirability of a smooth transition of leadership. Neither John Hooker nor I had previous experience in state government. Without partisan consideration, Buford Ellington was determined to serve the best interests of the state by assuring that, whatever candidate was elected, he would experience a successful transition. He knew firsthand the difficulties involved in appointing a cabinet, preparing a budget, developing a legislative agenda, and literally managing government on a day-to-day basis.

A significant amount of time was spent gathering appropriate information. The documents produced from every administrative agency of the state represented thousands of hours devoted to assuring that all aspects of the business of the state were clearly presented. It was a large task to reduce such a volume of information to a

250-page briefing manual. The citizens of the state were beneficiaries of this undertaking.

A meeting took place the day following the general election. Involved were the five Ellington team members and my representatives including Lamar Alexander, state Senator Tom Garland, who had participated as a member of my campaign staff, and David White, my research and policy analyst and speechwriter during the campaign. It was agreed at that time that a series of meetings would be held at Montgomery Bell State Park within a matter of days.

Formal briefings were held in mid-November, as planned. My team consisted of Lamar Alexander as chief of staff for the group. Included were individuals who had been keys to the campaign or who would play important roles in the administration. Among them were Harry Wellford, James McGhee, Lewis Donelson, Representative Leonard Dunavant, Lee Smith, Frank Barnett, Howard Kesley, David White, Robin Beard, Roger Kesley, Robert Echols, and two representatives of Warren King, a consultant who would play a major role for me. A total of fifteen hours of briefings took place, and white papers on seven issues deemed to be important to the new administration were presented for study.

Nothing as significant as this transition had ever been attempted in Tennessee state government. My staff and early appointees were given full access to every department of the executive branch and each commissioner. Chief among the sobering facts facing the state was the question of sufficient revenues to meet continuing obligations and limited new initiatives. Every aspect of state responsibility and many insights into new opportunities were topics for discussion. The outgoing administration offered total cooperation and support. It will remain an historical fact that the Ellington initiative was responsible for a transition of power that was considered positive and beneficial to all concerned. As noted by Leonard Bradley, the exercise was a success. In the process certain shortcomings were identified that would ensure more effective transitions in the future.

Inauguration

The day was overcast and people were bundled in their warmest clothing as they gathered on the legislative plaza at noon before a platform and scaffolding erected to serve for a brief period on January 16, 1971. The large crowd of spectators faced the stately columns of the War Memorial Building. To the spectator's right, the south side of Tennessee's historic capitol building, one of the oldest in active service, offered a majestic view. The inaugural party faced toward the east where the General Assembly sat in outdoor session, surrounded by the crowd. The hearts and minds of those present were filled with emotions that ran a broad gamut of pride, knowledge, imagination, disappointment, and curiosity, the centerpiece of which was an almost palpable affection for state and nation.

The inaugural platform was occupied by Betty and our three children; Governor and Mrs. Ellington; Senator Howard Baker, Jr.; newly installed U.S. Senator Bill Brock; members of the U.S. House of Representatives' Tennessee delegation, including my congressman, Dan H. Kuykendall; John Mitchell, U.S. attorney general representing President Richard Nixon; Speaker of the Senate John Wilder; Speaker of the House James McKinney; Governor Linwood Holton of Virginia; Governor Louis Nunn of Kentucky; Governor Edgar Whitcomb of Indiana; Governor Jack Williams of Arizona; actor Robert Stack representing Governor Ronald Reagan of California; other public figures; designees of my staff and cabinet; members of my immediate family; and individuals who had played prominent roles in my campaign and pre-inaugural preparations, including Harry Wellford and his wife, Katherine, among many others. My father, former Congressman Aubert Dunn, was present. Missing from that intimate group was my mother, Dorothy Crum Dunn, who remained in Mississippi because her health was severely compromised. Her beautiful spirit, her love, and her constant faith in her only son filled me and added to the meaning of that special day.

Seated at the front of the large crowd of enthusiastic citizens who braved the cold weather was the entire membership of the 87th General Assembly of Tennessee convened in joint session. The event was official state business, declared to be so by the Convention president, Lieutenant Governor John Wilder, as he gaveled the meeting to order. At that time I was essentially a stranger to most members of the legislature. I had spent time briefly with the newly elected Speakers of both houses during a trip to New Orleans to attend the 1971 Sugar Bowl football game between Tennessee and the Air

Force Academy. I had a strong bond of friendship with the Republican members of the legislature from Shelby County. Senator Fred Berry of Knoxville was my friend. I was beginning to develop a firm friendship with the elected leadership of the Republican caucuses, Senator Tom Garland of Greeneville and Representative Tom Jensen of Knoxville. I wanted to be understood, from my first official words, as one who was anxious to build a spirit of cooperation and mutual understanding with those who represented the various Senate and House districts that encompassed the state.

An invocation was given by Dr. Charles W. Grant. That good and gentle man was the founding minister of Christ United Methodist Church of Memphis. The prayer was followed by a rendition of "The Star-Spangled Banner" by Mrs. Curtis Person, wife of my friend the senator. Governor Buford Ellington was introduced. He then moved to the podium and offered a brief and most appropriate speech in which he thanked the people for their trust and confidence in him over many years of public service. His words were focused on the future and expressed his great faith in the people of the state. He wished the new administration well and concluded his remarks on a note of optimism. He was a true gentleman and statesman.

The moment had arrived for me to take the oath of office. With Betty standing by my side and my children close at hand, I faced the distinguished Chief Justice of the Tennessee Supreme Court, Ross W. Dyer. The Bible on which I placed my left hand had been a gift from the members of the Kingswood Class at Christ United Methodist Church of Memphis. Betty, who, at that time, had been my wonderful wife for more than twenty years, held the bible. As I completed the last sentence with "so help me God," a nineteen-gun salute provided by units of the Tennessee Army National Guard boomed forth the fact that a new governor was now at the helm of the government. Each cannon boom seemed as two because the sound reverberated against the many buildings surrounding the inaugural location. The crowd roared and warm handshakes were exchanged. I turned to my address.

My first words to the people of Tennessee as their governor had been carefully chosen to focus on a spirit of bipartisanship, new opportunity, and greater citizen participation in the process of governing. It was designed to be brief and without reference to specific issues.

Inaugural Address of Governor Winfield Dunn

January 16, 1971

Mr. Convention President Wilder, Mr. Speaker McKinney, distinguished ladies and gentlemen of the 87th General Assembly, Governor Ellington, Mr. Attorney General Mitchell, Mr. Chief Justice Dyer, Senator Baker, Senator Brock, distinguished members of Tennessee's congressional delegation, Governor Holton, Governor Nunn, Governor Whitcomb, Governor Williams, my fellow Tennesseans.

Our presence here today is substantial proof of the very solid foundation on which our form of government was built.

This inauguration ceremony is a product of political action by those who cared enough about our heritage to want to protect, preserve, and extend it to others.

The people have exercised their freedom through the elective process, a new governor has been chosen, and the foundation of our state government, the democratic process, remains unshaken, as it has since 1796.

History may take little note of this particular occasion . . . perhaps it might seem a commonplace occurrence that one more in a succession of devoted citizens today pledged his faith and loyalty to the sovereign state of Tennessee as its governor.

But to me, this is a solemn and momentous occasion. . . . For this man who stands before you now, a personal history will record that this was a day of sober reflection . . . of dedication . . . of total commitment to a great opportunity for service and leadership.

As a point of personal reference, let me remind you here today that I have for nearly all my adult life been a reasonably normal, and I hope, productive member of the private world in which most Tennesseans live.

I have never known the pleasure, or perhaps the pain, of elected office. I have lived in the private world of the private citizen . . . as the taxpayer . . . the parent . . . the Sunday school teacher . . . the boss . . . the breadwinner . . . the citizen politician.

I have lived and worked in my community—often concerned about the quality of education available to my children . . . the safety of the streets and sidewalks . . . the cleanliness of the air and water we used. I cared about and participated in my community and church affairs. I actively supported good people for positions of public trust. I did what I could to be a positive rather than a negative force. I tried, as an individual, to make a difference.

Today I stand before you in very different circumstances, elected by a majority of my fellow citizens to be the governor of Tennessee. I find myself humbled . . . challenged . . . and deeply impressed with a sense of gratitude to my fellow Tennesseans for the confidence they have placed in me. I will shortly become the newest member of the public family of our state.

To the members of the 87th General Assembly I extend my sincere best wishes and fondest hopes for full cooperation in the interest of our beloved Tennessee and her citizens. I compliment and congratulate each of you on your successful efforts to be afforded the opportunity to serve your fellow men. You have been selected, as have I, to be servants of the public. I share with you the sense of honor and pride which you must feel.

I pledge to you this day my wholehearted desire to work with you in total unselfishness for the good of all the people of Tennessee. We share essentially the same goals. We know that we are here to do the people's work. We are aware of the magnitude of government. We have much work to do . . . our business is at hand, and we must soon turn to its demands.

In Tennessee, it has been more than half a century since the governor came from one political party and the majority of both houses from another. This unusual situation might cause concern if I did not know that the dedicated men and women of this general assembly are equally as determined as I to govern this state for the benefit of the people who elected all of us. We recognize the same problems . . . we will be working to find the best solutions.

I am confident that the relationship of the governor and the general assembly will be one of partnership, not partisanship. We can . . . and we will . . . work together toward common ob-

jectives . . . not as members of a political party, but as concerned, responsible Tennesseans.

No better example of understanding, co-operation, and common purpose could be described than that of our present governor and his cooperation with me following my election as governor. Governor Ellington has made this transition . . . this exchange of responsibility . . . a meaningful and pleasant experience. Such thoughtfulness and statesmanship is the hallmark of this great Tennessean, and I am most grateful.

My friends . . . I recognize and accept my responsibilities to provide the leadership that will chart a successful and progressive course for our ship of state. On this inauguration day, I pledge to you an active administration. My presence as your governor will be felt, not only on Capitol Hill, but in the courthouses . . . in the schools . . . the prisons . . . and other institutions of this state where I may be privileged to go in order to listen . . . to learn . . . and to communicate with my fellow Tennesseans. I will take this government of the people to the people.

I will provide positive and creative leadership to promote that climate of confidence in government which will encourage every citizen to fully pursue his individual goals and dreams. I pledge my devotion to the concept that unity is the bedrock of our strength . . . and I will constantly encourage the attitude that we are truly the one great state—not the three states—of Tennessee.

Faced with the cold, hard fact that we as a state have the not uncommon problem of a financial crisis in the conduct of our state responsibilities, I pledge to you an administration which will use the soundest . . . the most practical, common-sense business principles which can be employed to keep the cost of government as low as possible.

In the area of state finance, what we do here, or fail to do here, will touch the life of every citizen in this sovereign state. I pledge to do all within the authority of my office to provide a modern, common-sense administration which will stay close to the source of its strength . . . you, the people. Therefore, I hope to inaugurate with this ceremony today, not a simple exchange of power from one man to another or from one political party to another, but a new era of citizen participation in the affairs of government in Tennessee.

If this process of involvement is begun, then we will create a new day for government in our state. We have an arsenal with which to attack our problems . . . new, fresh talent . . . minds free of chains of habit and custom . . . minds which are eager to deal directly with problems, minds which will not be willing to leave them for someone else or for some other time.

I will labor to make certain the conscientious citizen knows his energies and abilities are needed by his government . . . that his ideas are valued . . . that his opinion is worthy of consideration . . . that his involvement in public service—at any level—can truly make a difference. I pledge my continued efforts to make my official family—my cabinet—a group of whom you will be proud.

I take great pride in those devoted friends who have offered their remarkable talents and ability in service to this state and as additional appointments are made, that quality of character and integrity will be maintained at all costs.

I have addressed you today in general terms and with broad reference. The programs, the facts and figures, the specifics which relate to the legislative and executive responsibilities of state government are not far behind. For weeks, we have been preparing for the enormous task of directing a government . . . of charting a course. These are challenging days for industrious people.

There will be no shortage of energy in this administration as we move out into our four years of opportunity. There will be understanding . . . compassion . . . interest . . . and enthusiasm for all people, from every walk of life. I challenge the youth of Tennessee to continue their outstanding interest and willingness to be part of making our state a greater place.

It is my intention to request or propose, legislation which will—after proper testing in our courts—give them the right to vote in state elections when they become 18 years of age. I have great faith in our youth.

I challenge our older citizens to continue their constructive, productive efforts to improve the quality of life in Tennessee. We have done well, but there is much more we can do. I challenge every Tennessean: let us pull together—proper and effective partners working toward a worthy goal. . . .

Let us strike a spark of enthusiasm which will rekindle the volunteer spirit of Tennessee through citizens' participation in government. Today, I dedicate all my energies and abilities to you and to our state. At the same time, I urge you to take an active part in our government. Support me when you can . . . oppose me if you must . . . but above all, participate. I know that some of the things that should be done cannot be done. I know that some of the things I have pledged to do will not be done at once. . . . And I know that in four years many tasks will remain to be done by future administrations.

Therefore, I ask that you grant me patience. I need your help, your confidence. And as the next four years go by, you will know—I give you my solemn promise that you can know— Winfield Dunn is doing his best. Thank you.

At the conclusion of my remarks an Air National Guard flyover took place by aircraft from the refueling group based at Knoxville. It was a thrilling spectacle.

We then turned to view the inaugural parade. The magnificent marching band of the University of Tennessee stepped out, leading the way and playing "The Tennessee Waltz." During the next hour, marching bands from high schools and universities representing every region of the state stepped smartly past the viewing stand. Military units of the state National Guard, Shrine groups, chambers of commerce, and various cities displayed their colors, their local pride, and their endurance. Elaborate floats representing organizations and communities as well as various vehicles colorfully decorated added to the festivity on that cold afternoon.

At the conclusion of the parade, the official party retired to the capitol building where arrangements had been made for visitors to be received by the governor, the first lady, and members of his cabinet who had been formally sworn in earlier in the day. Excellent work by building personnel and military staff made it possible for several thousands of people to wind their ways through the executive office of the building. Enthusiastic greetings were exchanged and best wishes extended for several hours before leaving the capitol to prepare for the evening's inaugural events.

Back at the Residence, the entire family welcomed an opportunity to rest briefly before dressing for the evening's activities. Members of my large group of family and friends had been assigned personal escorts composed of members of the Tennessee National Guard in their dress uniforms. Each of those happy people was thrilled by such attention, and they expressed their gratitude many times.

The Inaugural Committee had shown vision and consideration in their preparations for the official locations of the dances to be held in celebration. Our first stop of the evening was at the Inaugural Ball held at Nashville's Municipal Auditorium, the location of the Gala that was enjoyed the previous evening. There was a large crowd present at the site, and only hard work and careful planning by our Department of Safety security personnel allowed my family to enter the building unscathed. People were pushing, shoving, and reaching out to clutch a hand in excitement and joy.

The pride I felt as I took my wife in my arms and danced to the strains of "The Tennessee Waltz" while the large crowd looked on was a bit overwhelming. Those were moments neither she nor I would ever forget. And we never forgot how many wonderful, generous people made it possible for us to have that memorable experience.

The evening events had been carefully planned to accommodate a large gathering of citizens from across the state. There was such a demand for tickets that a second site was chosen to accommodate happy individuals anxious to dance the evening away. The National Guard Armory was the second site. In order to accommodate the wishes of the young people, a Young Tennesseans Inaugural Ball was scheduled at the downtown Sheraton Motor Inn.

Each Inaugural Ball site was sparkling with happy faces, beautiful evening gowns, and black ties. Betty and I attended each ball. Her inaugural gown had been carefully selected, and she made a beautiful impression wherever she went. At the beginning we were accompanied by our three children and many close relatives. Somewhere along the way the youngsters eased off to more comfortable settings where the action suited their dispositions at the time. I was in the company of what I knew for certain was the world's loveliest first lady, and I made the most of our special time together. The whirlwind tour across town led us to the National Guard Armory where an overflow crowd enthusiastically welcomed us. Our last stop was the ball for the young people. There at the Sheraton we danced "The Tennessee Waltz" a final time before the evening was complete. At some late hour of a memorable evening we were driven home for needed rest and preparation for a busy new day.

Sunday morning was reserved for a gathering in the Residence of many close relatives and friends who had journeyed from out of town. Every member of my immediate family was present with the exception of my mother. It was a happy time for that large group to be together, remembering those not present, eating good food, and recalling old times. The Mississippi influence was dominant, but Betty's family from Memphis and Dyersburg didn't take a backseat. It was interesting to me to observe the two groups become somewhat acquainted in a brief period. There were several professional photographers who captured the moments very well. I was pleased with that special time. The visitors were impressed with our new, but temporary, home.

Shortly after noon on that Sunday, a large group of visitors began to gather at the entrance to the Residence. An announcement had appeared in the local papers stating that the new governor and first family would receive out-of-town visitors for a personal welcome and tour of the Executive Residence as part of the inaugural celebration. The article invited Nashville citizens to a similar open house the following Sunday. Guests were directed to several church parking lots in the vicinity of the Residence from which they were transported by bus to the driveway entrance of our new home on Curtiswood Lane.

Department of Safety personnel were out in large numbers to offer directions and assistance to those who gathered. Inside, Tennessee National Guard officers in dress uniform attended Betty and me, helping to move the receiving line along. Captain Talmadge Gilley stood to my right side and introduced each visitor. After greetings were exchanged and a hand was shaken, I turned that person over to Betty for her greeting. After those initial greetings, the guests were grouped together and directed through the Residence on a tour of the first and second floors.

The reception was the first such formal occasion of its kind. People seemed thrilled to see firsthand where the first family of the state resided. We were proud to show it off. The success of that venture encouraged Betty to suggest permanent arrangements for the public to visit the Executive Residence on a regularly scheduled basis. That afternoon, Sunday, January 17, 1971, in excess of five thousand excited, caring Tennesseans trekked the length of the long driveway, stood single file in severely cold weather, and entered the Residence to be welcomed first with a warm cup of punch and then our personal greetings. At the end of the exciting afternoon, when the last hands were clasped, Betty and I, along with our youngsters, retired to the living quarters upstairs, exhausted but very satisfied that we had done the right thing. The following Sunday, Nashvillians were welcomed to our new home. That day was not so cold and the crowd not quite as large as the previous Sunday, but it was a very successful event. We felt we had been generously welcomed to Nashville by many of its finest citizens.

The unfolding of a memorable weekend in our lives came to a close. What had occurred in the capital city set a new standard in Tennessee for gubernatorial inaugurations. The intense energy and planning that had been brought to bear by so many volunteers and professionals made a huge statement. Press coverage of those three days, January 15, 16, and 17, was generous and thorough. The people of the state seemed to appreciate the fact that our state was moving forward with new faces, new talents, and much enthusiasm.

Monday morning, January 18, would be my first day on the job as a new governor. The legislature, having convened to organize and install the chief executive of the state, had adjourned until February 23. The thirty-six days that lay immediately ahead would be among the busiest of my life in preparation for the reconvening of the House and Senate.

The Cabinet and Staff

My first thoughts regarding those who would compose membership in the critically important positions of a governor's cabinet occurred the day Claude Armour and I sat down at a press conference in early October. My political campaign was developing momentum. I was about to enjoy the privilege of announcing that Armour, a cabinet-level member of the Ellington administration, wished to endorse my candidacy. He told me he had advised the governor of his desire and offered to resign his post. The governor told him his resignation was not necessary. Armour's commitment and Governor Ellington's approval sent a strong signal to the media, the public, and the opposition that we were building a winning effort. Knowing firsthand of Armour's outstanding record as commissioner of fire and police in Memphis and his service as special assistant to the governor on law and order for Ellington, I felt confident he would be an outstanding commissioner of safety for the state. The subject was not discussed and no commitments were made. I knew Armour could be a strong member of my executive team if he were to accept an appointment. I left that press conference feeling very optimistic about the upcoming election.

Immediately after the election, names began to surface identifying a large number of persons interested in serving with the new administration. When Harry Wellford and I temporarily settled in Nashville with private quarters at our disposal for conferences, we began a series of meetings, interviews, and planning sessions. A substantial list of applicants had accumulated, each application supported by documents verifying facts about that person's background. It was mid-November, and time leading up to inauguration was passing swiftly. We worked intensively, taking time to get back to Memphis on Sundays. Harry was soon to be sworn as a federal district judge. His assistance to me was invaluable and remarkable, under the circumstances.

Although work had gone on without letup since my election, it was obvious that I would be unable to identify all those I was required by statute to appoint to the twenty cabinet-level positions making up the top tier of my administration. On the day of my inauguration only ten of the twenty cabinet positions were confirmed. Five top staff people had been selected. Each of these good men was anxious to serve and had demonstrated an ability to excel during the general election.

In the capitol building immediately after the inauguration and parade, those ten members of the cabinet plus my five staff members were sworn in by newly installed Federal District Judge Harry Wellford of Memphis. It was another proud moment for me. The new commissioners were Claude Armour, Safety; Bob Smith, Highways; Bill Jenkins, Conservation; Mark Luttrell, Corrections; E. C. Stimbert, Education; Robin Beard, Personnel; Eugene Fowinkle,

Public Health; Guilford Thornton, Agriculture; Ernest Griggs, Employment Security; and Russell Hippe, Finance and Administration. Staff members, whose authority placed each one at a cabinet-level position, were W. Dale Young, executive administrative assistant; Joe Neal Hopper, administrative assistant; Frank Barnett, administrative assistant; Ralph E. Griffith, director of information and administrative assistant; and M. Lee Smith, counsel to the governor.

I had been correct in believing Claude Armour would serve as commissioner of the Department of Safety. He gladly accepted my invitation. His outstanding record of public service and expertise in law enforcement gave me assurance the state would be well served. He had the able assistance of Colonel Charles W. Danner of the Highway Patrol.

My mind was firmly focused on certain ideas that had developed over the course of the campaign. Repeatedly, I had heard from the eastern part of the state that people were expecting specific things from their new Republican governor. Chief among their expectations was a major state commitment to build much needed highways, repair faulty roads, and replace outmoded bridges. Second only to roads was a great interest in new state parks and natural resources conservation. It was obvious that I should focus on cabinet members who understood the sentiments I had heard expressed so often. People had emphasized their beliefs that East Tennessee, and especially Upper East Tennessee, had been neglected by previous governors. Now, they felt, their time was about to come.

Bob Smith, my highly capable fund-raising friend from Limestone, in Washington County, emerged as the right person to serve as commissioner of highways. He was a successful contractor and businessman. He had no previous service in government, but he was well acquainted with how the state did business. He was from Upper East Tennessee, he knew the people intimately, he was a thoughtful student of human nature, and he had strong character to go along with his business experience. After several long meetings and in-depth discussions, Bob Smith agreed to serve. I was confident he would provide the right leadership to serve the legitimate needs of the entire state.

I was aware that the state had made a strong commitment to improve its state park system. Substantial progress had been made under Governors Ellington and Clement. Unfortunately, limited resources meant certain sections of the state would be underserved. Republican Upper East Tennessee had been singled out to receive less, over the years, and there was strong demand for attention to its needs. I was determined to fulfill the expectations of those good people who had supported my candidacy and without whose strong vote I would not have won my race. I decided to offer the commissioner of conservation position to my former primary opponent Bill Jenkins. He was popular, had served as the first Republican Speaker of the state House of Representatives in modern times, was from the right part of the state, was a dedicated outdoorsman, and had the ability to lead. The Department of Conservation's responsibilities ranged far beyond state park management and development, particularly with the growing environmental pressures being felt by government. I was certain Bill Jenkins, a resident of Hawkins County in the upper east, would be a popular and effective choice as the commissioner. After lengthy discussions Bill accepted the opportunity to serve.

I had been made increasingly aware of general unrest and inadequate funding for the state Department of Corrections. The previous administration had taken positive steps toward resolving the shortage of prison beds by building new facilities. A great deal more needed to be done. A growing crime rate and increasing numbers of felons being sentenced kept the pressure on the system at a disturbing level. Compensation throughout the department was inadequate, and a serious movement was underway to attempt to unionize its employees. The state of Tennessee provided no authority for the recognition of unions in collective bargaining. I needed the best talent to be found in my appointment of a commissioner of corrections. I knew just where to go, and I was not disappointed in my effort.

Mark Luttrell was a West Tennessee graduate of the University of Tennessee. His experience in agricultural education and business gave him an excellent background for managing a large county penal system. Since 1962 he had served as superintendent of the Shelby County Penal Farm. He became active in the American Corrective Association, the Tennessee Correctional Association, and the Law Enforcement Planning Commission. I approached Mark and told him there was a great challenge ahead at the state level if he would accept it, and he did so. He had long been associated with the

Democrat leadership of Shelby County. I welcomed him into my administration with no concern whatsoever regarding political party loyalty. He fully understood my commitment to serve one and all. He had a tough job to do, but he was a seasoned professional. I was satisfied I had chosen the right man to do it.

The Tennessee Department of Education was the largest tax-supported agency of state government, consuming nearly one-half of all state revenue. I had become acutely aware of chronic under-funding, particularly at the level of higher education. My commitment to the creation of a publicly supported kindergarten program across the state had been spelled out clearly. It was essential that the incoming commissioner of education be a strong person, not only professionally, but also in terms of his willingness to respond to the leadership of the governor. The commissioner chaired the state Board of Education. That board had great responsibilities, and I wanted a commissioner who could firmly lead a group of twelve members, none of whom, at that time, were my appointees. I had declined to consider the incumbent commissioner, J. Howard Warf, for obvious reasons, primarily political in nature. It was necessary that I find the ideal candidate, and I was fully confident I had the right person in mind.

E. C. Stimbert had served the Memphis City School System since 1946, coming to the city from Nebraska, where he had received his education in school administration. There he had worked as superintendent of rural school systems. Mr. Stimbert had compiled a distinguished record in Memphis, assuming the role of superintendent of the Memphis City School System in 1957. He was very popular with the public generally and received strong support from the two major newspapers of the city. I went after this distinguished educator with enthusiasm and was successful in persuading him to move to the state's highest level of service in public education. My selection of Stimbert drew strong support in the city of Memphis. I was pleased to place a Memphian in that vital area of responsibility. I had no doubts that he was aware of my priorities for state public education.

Robin Beard was a young businessman who had become active in the Republican primary working as a field man for Maxey Jarman. He joined my campaign in the general election and did an outstanding job organizing county groups working for my election. He was a graduate of Vanderbilt University and a former officer in the United States Marine Corps. Following his military service, he joined the Alumni Development of Vanderbilt University. He had leadership skills and a devotion to the future of the Republican Party. I offered him the commissioner's position in the Department of Personnel. He accepted, and I felt the department would have the energetic leadership of a compassionate and devoted Tennessean.

My choice to serve the state through the Department of Public Health was logical. I had worked with Eugene Fowinkle, MD, when he served as director of the Department of Public Health for Memphis and Shelby County. His entire medical background, including a degree from the University of Tennessee College of Medicine and post-doctoral work at the University of Michigan School of Public Health, demonstrated a love for public health concerns. He had joined the Ellington administration in 1969, and I was determined to have him continue his work for the state. He agreed to do so. I felt very fortunate to be able to include him in my cabinet.

The selection of a commissioner of agriculture would be carefully measured by a large segment of Tennessee's citizens. The role of agriculture in our growth and development as a state remained a high priority concern for any governor. The department had been ably served by Buford Ellington during the first Clement administration and later by Commissioner Red Moss. My challenge was to maintain that level and caliber of leadership in the department throughout my Republican administration. I chose Guilford F. Thornton for the position. Gil had been influential in the agricultural community on my behalf during the election. A native of Haywood County and a graduate of the University of Tennessee majoring in agriculture, he had been active in county government service and successfully engaged in several businesses related to his field of expertise. He was gifted with human relations skills and a high degree of character. He was an excellent choice.

Based on our close relationship that developed during my campaign, I chose Ernest Griggs for a position in my administration. A University of Tennessee graduate majoring in agriculture, he was a farmer, successful businessman, and prominent citizen of Humboldt. He had been elected mayor of his city in 1966. The Department of Employment Security was a service facility for the entire state, having been responsible for concerns of the unemployed since the Depression days of the 1930s. As the economic base of the state changed with the movement toward industrialization, helping citizens adjust to new and uncertain work opportunities became a legitimate concern for government. The department needed strong leadership, and I knew Ernest Griggs could serve well.

The Department of Finance and Administration coordinates all the finance and general administrative responsibilities of state government. In a real sense, it is at the heart of any Tennessee governor's administration. The commissioner serves as the chief staff officer to the governor, and a close and confidential relationship is necessary for state government to proceed rationally. I was aware that, since its creation in 1959, the commissioner's position had been filled by outstanding individuals. My duty was to maintain that level of skill. I was also aware that the department included a significant number of professionals whose ongoing presence and service would be essential to a new commissioner. I appointed Russell H. Hippe, Jr., as my commissioner of finance and administration. At the time a member of a prominent Nashville law firm, Russell was a graduate of Vanderbilt with a major in economics. He was a graduate of law school. He applied his knowledge and skills in the area of finance and corporate law in his practice. As a new commissioner, he faced enormous responsibilities. I was grateful that he would have the advice and counsel of Lewis Donelson of Memphis and Representative Leonard Dunavant of Millington in preparing the first budget my administration would propose for the next fiscal year. Each of these men had much talent to offer regarding state finance.

Those who made up my immediate staff were people who had worked closely with me during the campaign. There were no longtime friends or associates available to move to Nashville. Those who had been closest to me from the beginning of my efforts, all Memphians, had their own responsibilities at home and remained available to me on an advisory basis. Lamar Alexander was offered a position but chose to join a Nashville law firm. He was interested in establishing himself in the private sector. It was clearly a disadvantage to have no one on the staff with previous experience in state government. We were all committed to getting the best advice available from various sources, then moving ahead as good judgment and common sense directed. No doubt, in the minds of seasoned observers of state government, mistakes would be made as we moved forward, but there was no absence of enthusiasm and desire to do the right thing.

Dale Young became my executive administrative assistant. He was a bright young attorney with a good legal foundation based on his relationship with an outstanding Maryville attorney, Bill Felknor. He had been an assistant attorney general for the Fourth Judicial District of Tennessee before joining the Felknor firm. At my invitation he assumed the role of day-to-day management of the governor's office and schedule. Among his major responsibilities would be direct contact with commissioners and appointees to various major positions on boards and commissions. He had an excellent temperament and unbounded energy.

Joe Neal Hopper accepted my offer to assume a major role as administrative assistant to the governor. As a corporate attorney and before that an assistant attorney general in the Memphis District, he had strong credentials. Born in Sardis, Henderson County, a strong Republican pocket in the mainly Democrat western part of the state, Joe was endowed with a love for the Republican Party and an understanding of what it took to get along with all factions of the political process. He would be invaluable assisting me in dealing with the demands of those who put a political slant on every consideration, every need, or every desire. He had to be strong. He had to be able to absorb the often pent-up ambition, wrath, or other emotions that would propel many people toward the governor's office for one reason or another. He was a good man.

Frank Barnett was a University of Tennessee–trained lawyer with sound and positive political instincts. Long a friend of Senator Howard Baker, Jr., he had been active in statewide campaigns for the senator and became a dependable resource for me during my race. I asked Frank to accept appointment as administrative assistant to the governor for legislative matters. I was pleased with his acceptance of a key role in assuring that the administration nurtured a healthy relationship with the Republican legislative minority leadership. As an East Tennessee Republican, this fine man would represent my determination to lead with a balanced representation, East and West, of those who had labored so effectively on my behalf.

Ralph Griffith was the closest thing to a Capitol Hill insider that my administration could boast. He was a veteran of more than twenty years as a newspaper reporter, primarily for the *Knoxville Journal*. He had spent much of that time at the capitol. For fifteen of those years he was political editor of the *Journal*. He had been publicity director for the first Eisenhower campaign in Tennessee. That was the first time in modern political history a Republican had won the state presidential vote. At the time he joined my campaign he was news director on the Senator Baker staff in Washington. He had spent much time in the state during my campaign. There was no doubt in my mind that Ralph was the right choice for director of information and assistant to the governor in my administration. I knew that my fortunes dealing with the press and the public would be greatly enhanced with him at my side. I was gratified when he accepted my offer. He was happy to return to Tennessee.

The youngest of those I selected to be among my closest advisers was M. Lee Smith, a native of Maryville and an honors graduate of the Vanderbilt University School of Law. He had clerked for Federal Judge William Miller one year before joining the staff of Senator Howard Baker, Jr., as legislative assistant. A close friend of Lamar Alexander, Lee accepted the position of field director for my campaign and worked closely with Lamar. He did an outstanding job in that role. The responsibility of the governor to set policy and offer program content across the broad spectrum of state government administrative activity was a major consideration. Increasingly, federal-state government relations were expanding. I felt it was an excellent opportunity for me and Lee Smith to combine our strengths on behalf of the state. He accepted the position of counsel to the governor, and it was a good day's work for me when he signed on.

My administration began its work on the Monday morning following the inauguration. It was a time during which people new on the job, including me, were best served by getting acquainted with those for whom life in state government service was a full-time commitment. Throughout the capitol building and in owned and leased office space across the state, individuals new to state government were getting to know the veterans. For many of the approximately thirty thousand individuals employed by the state there were feelings of uncertainty based on concerns for the politics of the newcomers. It was clearly understood by those representing the new administration that the only requirement for continued employment was that there had to be a job to do. In certain instances numbering fewer than the fingers on two hands, certain state employees had made the mistake of being so overtly involved in the recent election for governor that they had in effect burned their bridges back to normalcy. Those individuals did not retain their positions.

It was a fact that many state employees routinely expected to be asked to contribute to certain political races. Many were relieved to learn that mandatory financial contributions for political purposes would no longer be a requirement for employment. For the average state employee it would be business as usual. But there were inevitably some reservations by many veteran employees as to just what the future would hold for them with new leadership now in charge.

My inability to complete selection of all cabinet members by the time I assumed office was a matter of not having adequate time. A widespread search was being conducted to identify the best candidates we could find. It was a time-consuming process, and we were limited as to funds and personnel. There was no shortage of good people anxious to be a part of the new administration. Applications continued to flow in. Key individuals were assigned the tasks of trying to identify exceptional prospective commissioners. Every post yet to be filled was important. Several of those were exceptionally important as I considered specific challenges that I intended to meet head-on.

For example, the Department of Mental Health was critically in need of fresh, top-level leadership. Due primarily to inadequate funding for seven of the eight major hospitals and institutions for mentally disabled people in our system, Tennessee found itself near the bottom of any list designed to quantify progress in the field. Five additional months were necessary to locate and recruit an outstanding physician specializing in psychiatry. The man was Charles Richard Treadway, MD, a Vanderbilt-trained physician who had distinguished himself at the National Institute of Mental Health, as well as in other major positions. He was young, brilliant, and devoted to the idea of public service. He agreed to serve as commissioner, and it was to be a fortunate selection for the state. The position was not filled until June of 1971. I was grateful that the former commissioner, Dr. Frank Luton, was willing to remain in his position while the search went on.

I was convinced that adequate revenues to fund the ongoing business of the government and to launch many desperately needed new initiatives would be a challenge not only for me and the legislature, but specifically for the individual assigned the duty of collecting and managing those revenues. An outstanding individual who had spent his career with the federal Department of Internal Revenue was identified. His name was George M. Tidwell. Through cooperation with federal officials, we were able to persuade Tidwell to become state commissioner of revenue. He lost no federal benefits and was able to adapt state service to the time required to fully qualify for retirement at the federal level. He was an outstanding choice to lead his department.

The Tennessee Department of Standards and Purchasing plays a major role in managing the business side of state government. Millions of taxpayers' dollars are spent with a variety of businesses and professionals whose goods and services are essential in meeting the responsibilities of the state to do business effectively and efficiently. Years of one-party rule had allowed certain interests to access and maintain firm control of where the dollars were spent. I needed a strong, highly ethical businessperson to manage that vital department and spread the state's business around. I requested only that he make absolutely certain that the soundest business principles be employed and that every legitimate vendor be given full opportunity to do business with the state. Computers had become a new resource. The technology was changing rapidly. Up-to-date management, purchasing, and production procedures existed in the private sector, and these needed to become part of routine business procedures used by the state. It was essential that new practices be employed by a government responsible for millions of dollars in commercial transactions each year.

I identified an energetic, experienced businessman with a desire to make a difference. He was Howard Kesley, a UT graduate, World War II Air Force pilot highly decorated, and a founder of a large steel fabricating company in Knoxville. Following his early retirement from business, he became politically active in Knoxville, serving four years as vice mayor and additional time as city finance director. Howard accepted the commissioner's job, and the state was the beneficiary.

The Tennessee Department of Insurance had diverse responsibilities focusing on six major divisions. Fortunately, this department had a reputation for recruiting and utilizing outstanding personnel. Supervising the insurance industry, which collected premiums in excess of $1.3 billion, was a major duty. Its role as a collector of taxes and fees was second only to that of the Department of Revenue. A number of creditable applicants for this position made their interests known. After thorough study of the need for strong leadership, I selected Halbert L. Carter of New Tazewell. He was a seasoned insurance executive, a former member of the 85th and 86th General Assemblies, a good Republican, and a loyal Tennessean. This was an excellent appointment.

Further into my term it became apparent that a separate department dealing with financial institutions was needed. At my request the legislature approved creation of the Tennessee Department of Banking. Granting of new bank charters, supervising savings and loan interests, and examining and supervising hundreds of state banks were the responsibilities of this department. I offered the commissioner's position to a good man. Upon his retirement from First National Bank of Memphis, Hugh F. Sinclair joined the administration. This distinguished gentleman was a popular choice within the banking industry. Educated in the law, a veteran of four years in the U.S. Navy, and an experienced banker, Sinclair was a strong addition to the team.

An impressive group of friends from Chattanooga introduced me to Ben O. Gibbs. This seasoned businessman had excelled in management and industrial relations over an extensive career that concluded with his retirement from Combustion Engineering Corporation. He had an outstanding record of community and public service in Chattanooga and was an excellent choice to be my commissioner of labor. In addition to being responsible for enforcing existing laws across a broad spectrum of commercial and industrial activity the commissioner was required to be ready to assist in the adjustment of labor disputes. Since Tennessee was proudly a "right to work" state, the commissioner needed to demonstrate a balanced attitude toward the interests of management and labor. I was proud to appoint Ben Gibbs commissioner of labor.

The Department of Public Welfare is an agency dedicated to serving human need across a number of categories. From financial assistance to specialized help for those medically needy but not qualified for Medicaid to a growing food stamp program to social service and assistance to the blind, leadership at this level required not only experienced business management skills but a special touch of compassion and sensitivity. Fred Friend, a devoted Republican ally, graduate of Duke University, insurance executive, and part-time Church of Christ minister, offered the skill set I was seeking to lead a department frequently targeted by the news media seeking human interest information. I asked Fred to leave Chattanooga and join my administration. He agreed to do so. It was a plus for my administration.

The Military Department, responsible for all state armed forces as provided in our Constitution, presented a special challenge. Consisting of various military units widely dispersed across the state, this vital agency of the government had, over many years, become politicized. The overwhelming sentiments of those in command had, quite naturally, been slanted toward the Democratic Party. My objective became not only to support and strengthen the department, but to modify where possible, the political influence of those who had come up in the ranks while showing no disrespect for their professionalism and commitment to the public safety. I appointed a high-ranking leader of the Air National Guard, a Memphian, Major General William C. Smith. General Smith had an outstanding record of military service and a personal reputation that was exemplary. At the time of his appointment to be adjutant general, he was base detachment commander at Memphis. He was the first Air Force officer to assume the adjutant general's post. He was somewhat set apart from the Army group, and I believed he would offer a change of pace through strong leadership from the perspective of the Air Guard.

The Division of Veterans Affairs existed to serve the needs and interests of veterans of the armed services across the state through ten regional offices. A successful businessman and native of Memphis, John C. Mask, agreed to head up the division. "Jack" Mask was a capable, sensitive person, long devoted to Republican causes, and particularly close to Senator Bill Brock. It was my opinion that some tip of the hat toward the Brock element of Republican Party strength was a practical move for my administration to take. I did so fully confident that Mask would do a good job as director.

An additional position directly responsible to the governor was the staff Office of Industrial Development. During the campaign, I had become committed to reorganization and revitalization of this important role state government played on behalf of the people. Eventually, the name Pat Choate would become well known relative to economic and community development. A complete revamping was in order, to be preceded by an in-depth study of needs. Legislation would be required. In the meantime, the office would be staffed by a person already within the system.

Members of the cabinet and staff immediately began to experience the endless variety of initiatives and influences that were directed toward the new and untested administrative team. Each commissioner moved into the circle of activities central to that division of government responsibility, getting to know his associates and beginning to build an understanding of the new administration's priorities. Every commissioner was well acquainted with the major goals and objectives on which I had based my campaign for governor. It would be up to me and my immediate staff, working closely with legislative leaders, to create a flow of information that would allow each commissioner to function in harmony with administration policy. During the first formal meeting of the cabinet, attended by my entire staff as well, I laid down one general rule of conduct I expected to be followed without exception. It was simply that every individual was responsible to make no statement or take no action that he would not be comfortable seeing reported on the front page of the Nashville *Tennessean* newspaper.

It was understood that I expected three specific goals to be pursued. First, each commissioner was expected to manage well. Second, the commissioner was to work closely with my staff on initiatives relating to his department's responsibilities. Third, his support in assuring cooperation from individual legislators would be essential where appropriate.

Getting Started

From the first moments of our work as a team in the capitol, staff members encountered challenges and stressful moments that soon became the norm. The first session of the 87th General Assembly, having met to organize in early January, was to reconvene and take up its legislative duties on February 23. Preparing a new budget, drafting legislative documents, considering revenue needs, holding meetings to develop policies and programs, touring state facilities, meeting with interest groups, writing speeches, juggling my personal schedule in a sincere effort not to offend loyal supporters anxious to bend my ear, working with Betty on matters having to do with her new responsibilities, responding to immediate requests to attend to administrative duties that had accumulated over time—all these matters and others made for an intense and demanding orientation to the job.

It would not be possible for me to adequately recapture those early moments and events that were experienced in learning to fulfill my duties as governor. I was aware that certain patterns of conduct and procedures had been created over the past eighteen years by the two men who served before me. I had decided to adapt those practices that seemed useful to me but to set my own pace as common sense suggested. My office hours began at 7:00 a.m. Buford Ellington began his work day at the same time, and I was told that, if the legislature was not in session, he had a habit of heading for Henry Horton State Park's golf course when the noon hour arrived. Our problem was that there was not enough time. My administrative assistants, Dale Young and Frank Barnett, were hard pressed keeping the appointments flowing and my time properly utilized. The demand for personal appointments never ceased. My presence was insisted upon by associates across the state. I found myself on the ground in Nashville throughout most days and on the road or in the air after dark, heading to one community or another to make an appearance and to offer remarks appropriate to the occasion. My personal security people, John White and John Fields, were totally dependable in their support over long, weary hours. Colonel Bill Pickron, Ken Dudney, and Walt Harris were state airplane pilots who never failed to be available when needed.

CHAPTER TWENTY-EIGHT

MOVING AHEAD

The Legislature

Initiatives were taken to prepare legislation to be presented to the first session of the 87th General Assembly. The talented people in the Office of Urban and Federal Affairs, all of whom I had encouraged to continue their work in my administration, were indispensable in getting my staff people up to speed on various matters. The business of government clearly overlapped successive administrations. Various proposals being considered and researched by the previous administration merited uninterrupted consideration by the newcomers. Goodwill was evident among those of us who were new to the jobs and those who had been parts of the previous administration. The smooth transition process, without rancor or bitterness based on partisanship, prepared a way for maximum benefits from human energy expended during those days. We were grateful for the tone of responsible governing we inherited from the Ellington team. A number of legislative proposals that had begun to take shape during the previous administration became items for my consideration and promotion, if desired. Additionally, immediate attention was focused on matters related to campaign commitments I had made.

The Republican legislative caucus in each house had chosen those individuals who would take leadership roles working with the administration. Representative Tom Jensen of Knoxville, a businessman and three-term veteran of the House, was designated the point man for all legislative proposals originating there. Senator Houston Goddard of Maryville, an attorney beginning his third Senate term, took on the challenge of working closely with me and my staff as we moved forward. Both men were competent, trustworthy, and devoted to the highest standards of service to the state. Each had become my good friend during the campaign. These two, along with Senator

Tom Garland of Greeneville, Senator Fred Berry of Knoxville, and my close Republican allies representing Shelby County, composed a core of legislators in whom I put great trust. I would develop positive relationships with many others as the days went by.

Democrat legislative leadership presented an interesting contrast in personalities. Prior to entering office, as the governor-elect I had, at Governor Ellington's suggestion, invited Senate Speaker-elect John Wilder of Mason and House Speaker-elect James O. McKinney of Madison, along with wives, to fly with Betty and me on the state airplane to New Orleans for the 1971 Sugar Bowl game. Both parties accepted and joined us for the flight down and back. Our time together consisted of that spent on the airplane and little more, since every party went its separate way while in New Orleans. I made a serious effort to get to know each Speaker. We were virtually unacquainted but obviously about to become active coworkers on behalf of the people. The results of those efforts varied.

John Wilder was in every way a gentleman who was seasoned by maturity, background, and experience. He was an attorney and a man of the soil. His personal history suggested he was very accomplished in a variety of special relationships. He had been elected Speaker, and therefore lieutenant governor of the state, in 1971 as he began his third term of service. Senator Wilder and his wife, Marcelle, were pleasant companions on the Sugar Bowl trip. He gave every indication that he would be a willing and cooperative associate in the days ahead. There was no doubting his Democrat credentials and his partisan loyalty. He showed great respect for the office of the governor, and I was reasonably at ease with him.

James McKinney was an entirely different type of individual. He had been elected Speaker after having served one term in the House of Representatives. He was an attorney and active member of civic groups in his community. From the outset of our relationship he was cool, somewhat disinterested, lacking in personal warmth, and clearly unwilling to unbend, relax, and be natural in my presence. I could feel a certain hostility in our relationship that I was unable to get beyond. There was never an expression of disrespect between us, but it soon became apparent that Speaker McKinney would be a difficult person with whom I was compelled to work during the first two years of my term in office. He would be highly partisan. I was not encouraged by his attitude during our trip to New Orleans.

I remained anxious to create a climate in which work with all participants of the two legislative bodies could find some degree of comfort. The utter reality of a sitting Republican governor was still very much an influence on the attitudes of many Democrat members. Some were still in shock. There were no precedents in terms of degrees of cooperation by the various individual legislators toward the administration. It was my nature to encourage the greatest amount of goodwill toward each elected person. I was plowing new ground in terms of understanding the various attitudes, goals, and ambitions of individual members, both Democrat and Republican. I was completely new to the processes of legislating and governing. I didn't forget that fact. Every member of both houses harbored his or her own goals, ambitions, and relationships, each of which would influence his or her attitude toward me and what I hoped to accomplish. I recognized my own naiveté and saw it as somewhat of a handicap. Much later I was to realize how valuable a human trait naiveté was to be for me in terms of what was ultimately achieved. I engaged in deep consultations with my legislative allies as actions were undertaken to build relationships with members of both parties. My Republican legislative colleagues were indispensable.

As a result of the general election of 1970, Tennessee state Senate Democrats would hold 18 seats, Republicans would hold 14 seats, and a seat would be occupied by Senator Bill Jim Davis, a member of the American Party. Republicans were in the minority in the House with 43 members, while the Democrats numbered 56. With Democrats in control of the legislature, my challenge was to appeal to the best instincts of all members without exception. I counted heavily on Republican support, but I was to learn that none of them could be taken for granted. An era of legislative independence was well underway, having taken root during Ellington's second term.

For a majority of the years in which Clement and Ellington occupied the governor's office, it was clearly the governor who dominated the capitol and those who served therein. The General Assembly, based on long-standing precedent, played a comparatively docile role in moving the ship of state ahead. The governor was the captain, and he had a reasonably loyal crew, the legislature. Up until 1968 the legislature convened in regular session once every two years, subject to call for special sessions. The move to annual sessions was enacted into law in 1967 at the same time a Fiscal Review Committee, reporting directly to the legislature, was established. These two significant legislative initiatives brought into full play the democratic principle so dear to all Americans known as the separation of powers. This assertion of independence sent a clear message to the sitting governor, Buford Ellington, that henceforth things would be different on Capitol Hill. During the remaining two years of his last term, things began to change rapidly. No longer would the governor designate the speakers, name the constitutional officers, and control the budget. Responsibilities shared between the executive and legislative bodies became the order of the day. To add to Ellington's need to adjust to change, in 1968 the Republican Party gained a one-vote majority in the House of Representatives, thereby choosing for the first time in history a Republican Speaker of the House of Representatives. Regrettably, that slim one-vote majority was lost by the Republicans as a result of the general elections of 1970.

It must have been obvious to any seasoned observer that new ground was being plowed not only on the executive side, but on the legislative side as well. I was undertaking to do things without prior experience to guide me. The legislature was well into employing authority that had long been its province but that had by custom and long-standing precedent been conceded to the governor. My personal view of the situation was somewhat limited because I was so totally immersed in the process. I would have been well served had I taken the initiative to pull back and view the entire scene more circumspectly, but there was no such time.

An important step involved making plans to entertain all General Assembly members at the Executive Residence with a seated dinner. This was a large undertaking, first of all requiring the support and assistance of the first lady. Betty, of course, was willing to do all she could to move us forward. The staff Betty inherited from the Ellingtons included two maids who were responsible for housekeeping on the second floor of the Residence. These were fine women who valued their jobs with the state and were anxious to please the new occupants. Two other individuals were assigned to the Residence in different capacities. The manager of the Residence was Mrs. Elmer

Wood. Her duties included directing the people and activities associated with the Residence and meeting the needs of the governor and his family. The other individual was responsible for physical maintenance inside and out. The landscaping, household utilities, and general condition of the physical facility were his responsibilities. Each of these individuals was extremely cooperative and made members of my family feel at home.

In preparing for the two seated dinners that were required to accommodate every member of the legislature and a companion, an extraordinary effort was necessary from the staff as well as Betty. There were skeptical comments that such an undertaking had never been attempted. We were told that the legislature was routinely entertained at the Residence with a standup barbecue meal. The same treatment was expected from us, we learned. That would never do as far as my wife was concerned. A seated, semi-formal dinner or nothing would be the order of the day for our first efforts to become acquainted with members of the legislature, and vice versa.

To Betty's great credit, the two separate gatherings, including dining, remarks from the governor and first lady, and entertainment, were very successful. The dinners contributed to a growing reputation that would prove Betty to be an outstanding first lady. A number of the legislators and their guests arrived quite early on each occasion and found themselves having to sit and mark time. Obviously, they had not read their invitations and had relied on memories of previously held barbecue dinners as to the time of the event. Several legislators while dining, we were told later, had mistakenly assumed the contents of small containers found on each table, called salts and containing salt, were sugar. They had to choose between drinking salty coffee or correcting their mistake by taking a fresh cup.

These two events were significant because they offered the first opportunities for many of our elected state officials to meet me, my cabinet, staff, and family. I was anxious to meet each legislator. Every effort was made to personalize the encounter. It quickly became clear that I would experience a wide variety of attitudes in the days ahead. There were varying degrees of partisanship apparent from the outset as we began to know many of the Democrat members. For some, it was quite obvious that they had not completely moved beyond the attitudes of hostility they had felt for the name Dunn during the general election campaign. Many of the more seasoned legislators handled themselves quite diplomatically regardless of their innermost feelings toward a new, and Republican, governor. Quite a few of the newly elected members, representing both parties, were innocently quite excited to meet the governor and first lady. We appreciated that and felt it reflected somewhat our own newness to the jobs and our relative innocence.

From the start of the 87th General Assembly my schedule was often filled with appointments given to various legislators. Often such visits were initiated by the visitor. I also scheduled meetings with key members to discuss issues important to my goals. Special local projects and campaign promises were frequently the subjects discussed. It was often my objective to learn the position of the legislator on a key matter. I worked hard to understand and to cooperate with each individual wherever possible. My desire was to make a friend and to be sure I stressed certain matters in which I would need that person's support. It was a matter of give-and-take, always being careful not to promise more than I could deliver.

My office door was always open to members. A favorite memory is that of glancing up to see Senator William D. Baird of Lebanon striding into my office. I noticed that he wore bright red suspenders and bright red socks. Each item of apparel was within easy view. His hair was completely white, and he was well groomed. I stood and offered him my hand in welcome. Completely to the point and somewhat physically at attention, he greeted me and expressed his respect. Then, almost abruptly, he turned and made his exit. It was an unusual meeting and, I was to learn over time, one that would be repeated each of the remaining years in my term of office. It occurred on the first day of the legislative session. On those special visits, he always wore his red suspenders and socks. Senator Baird was a true gentleman and a serious public servant. We never discussed the suspenders or socks. I believe he enjoyed a deep-seated sense of humor for which he felt no explanation was necessary. He fully respected the office of the governor, and he became my good friend as we worked through our mutual responsibilities. A Democrat representing the Fifteenth Senatorial District of Tennessee, he earned the respect of all who knew him. I looked forward to working with Bill Baird.

Pulls and Tugs

From the early days of the administration, and especially in the first three or four months, I became aware that quite a few of the people who had been so instrumental in helping me get elected would become sources of concerns and frustrations. The list of people seeking appointments seemed endless and included many of those early friends. I was determined that I would never intentionally fail to spend time with good friends and supporters when that time was requested. The daily calendar of scheduled events pressed in relentlessly, it seemed. Briefings by staff members on legislative proposals and executive responsibilities were of major importance. That consumed much valuable time. We struggled mightily to find time for friends who needed a word or two. They came from all parts of the state. One pressure point was the receptionist's desk in the lobby of the governor's office on the second floor of the capitol building. Emily Chapman Floyd, the beautiful and gifted lady who served in that position, was called on to deal with a wide variety of visitors in various stages of temperament. She handled most visitors with skill and ease. There were occasional exceptions in which she was grateful that two uniformed state Highway Patrolmen were present in the area. Those men were routinely assigned that duty. Telephone calls were routed by Emily in several directions. When a loyal friend and supporter was identified, that person was routinely handed off to my secretary, Lucretia McDonald. This young lady was also a gifted diplomat and did her best on all occasions to satisfy the caller. I found myself using breakfast and lunch times to visit with friends on political matters. Most often, in the evening, I was on the state aircraft flying out to fill some commitment.

I discovered, as time passed, that the greatest drain on my physical energy and emotional reserves came through relationships with some of my friends. Any early impression I might have gained that everyone was kind and generous to me simply because I was such a nice fellow and good candidate was soon to fade away. Requests for favors, appointments, appearances, or benevolence flowed in a steady stream. Had it not been for the able assistance of Joe Hopper, Bill Russell, Frank Barnett, and other staff aides, all of whom at times found themselves nearly overwhelmed by requests or demands for various considerations, my situation would have been hope-lessly uncomfortable. We all simply did our best to deal with those unusual circumstances.

One memorable event occurred when Lucretia advised me that one of my closest Memphis friends, a valuable campaign fund-rais-er and adviser who had appeared in my outer office without prior notice, literally stormed out of the building infuriated because he was told that it would not be possible to see me for several hours. The incident got the attention of everyone in the office. It took some time to restore the friendship. The problem was that my staff didn't know the individual. That was a learning experience. I advised Lucretia that, in the future, whenever an easily identified close friend insisted on seeing me, I should, in nearly every circumstance, be notified. I would make a decision as to whether it made sense for me to stop whatever I was doing and shake the friend's hand and explain the situation. There was no way I could forget from whence I had come and who had made it possible. The desires of my friends had to be given every consideration. They were of utmost importance to me. Among my deepest regrets were those times when I had to disappoint the interests of good people who had helped me along my way toward the statehouse. One example remains clear in my memory.

Knoxville and Knox County had been pivotal in my primary campaign and in the general election. One of my most stalwart sup-porters was a new friend who had worked tirelessly to build a strong political organization in Knox County on my behalf. He was a suc-cessful businessman. He, along with others, did a heroic job helping me build a base of support in the area. He made certain I understood he was interested only in good government and building the Repub-lican Party. Approximately two months after I became governor, the new and valued friend made an appointment to see me. Once seated in my office, he advised me that he wanted to become involved in the whiskey business in Knox County and asked me to help him fulfill his ambition. He stated that he knew the governor appointed members to the state Alcoholic Beverage Commission, and he knew I could see that he gained control over wholesale alcohol distribution in the county. In his enthusiasm to state his case, he made sure I understood that such action on my part could be good for "everybody." I was surprised by his request but lost no time in letting him know that the three incumbent members of the ABC were appointees of the previous administration. I also let him know that I would not be dealing with appointments at that level for quite a while. I do not believe my friend felt he was asking me to do anything that wasn't completely aboveboard. He saw the opportunity to be one of those situations where the old adage "to the victor belong the spoils" was appropriate. I advised him that I couldn't give him what he wanted. I had nothing else to offer him. He didn't like my response, and from that moment on, I was without his friendship. It was never easy to say no to a friend.

I was very fortunate in the choices of office personnel that were made. They were attractive young women who were bright, energetic, and devoted to their jobs. Anchoring the group were two wonderful women, older and more seasoned, who kept steady hands on the entire office force. These women were Mrs. Annie Hill, my longtime dental office assistant and friend from Memphis, and Mrs. Mary Jane Creel of Nashville. I felt a sense of loyalty and commitment from these ladies that reinforced my energy level on a daily basis. Their help was invaluable. Another key player was a fine young man who served as Dale Young's assistant. He was Chip Christianson, a Vanderbilt graduate who had been a great aide for me during the general election.

The Republican Party

It was never a secret among Tennessee Republicans that electing a governor also created the titular head of the state party. I assumed that role with pride and enthusiasm. Serious discussions were held with party leaders across the state seeking to determine the right course to take in leading the vital political movement that had been instrumental in my successful campaign. Tennessee had always been considered by those interested in its politics to be a Democrat state. That did not change with my election, but it further eroded the Democratic Party reputation of being totally in charge. Our unspoken mandate was to continue to build by eroding the reputation of the Democratic Party as the better choice. The real beginnings of two viable political parties began to occur with the 1962 election of Bill Brock in Chattanooga. It gained momentum with the election of Dan Kuykendall and Howard Baker in 1966. The election of a governor in 1970 sent a clear signal that the Republican Party had arrived to stay. My role as titular head of the party was to provide leadership and work closely with the official governing body, the Republican State Executive Committee, to build our base.

As a result of the successful inaugural activities in January, substantial private dollars were raised that were put to work to establish a permanent party office and develop a serious budget. The office would logically be in Nashville. I had met a fine young man named Ron Rietdorf during the campaign. A citizen of Oak Ridge, Ron was a devoted Republican enthusiast who was pleased to accept a position as state director of the party. Although a job description for the position did not exist, it was understood that the director would travel the state extensively. Our party success in the general election had stirred the minds and hearts of Republicans in all ninety-five counties. Organizing and fund-raising would consume most of the director's time. He would gain valuable information and guidance from the Republican Governors Association in Washington, D.C.

It was necessary then to focus serious attention on the position of state chairman of the party. In the recent past there had been a succession of good men serving as chairman of the Republican State Executive Committee. With the election of a governor, an unheard of new momentum was at our disposal. We had to make the most of it. The idea grew stronger in my mind that the new chairman should possess two important qualifications. First, I wanted the new party leader to be a person of impeccable personal credentials, totally above reproach and popular with all active workers. Second, that leader should be a citizen of Shelby County, if possible. Shelby had made its mark in the August primary, and because it was number one in terms of population, it offered the most fertile field for growth and development of the party. One individual stood out in my mind as an ideal choice for chairman. He was S. L. "Kopie" Kopald of Memphis, a great friend who from the start of my political venture had made his support well known. I approached Kopie with the thought and my ideas of what we could accomplish through his leadership of the party. He was a senior executive with the Humko Corporation of Memphis. He agreed to approach his associates with the idea. It was a great relief to me to learn that he had been given encouragement by his fellow executives to undertake the chairmanship. Kopie received his appointment through the Republican State Executive Committee and proceeded to become one of the finest state chairmen we have known. He and Rietdorf made an effective team.

Good Government Committees

I was determined to resist the harsh demands of some Republican leaders in various counties who had for years worked honorably and occasionally not so honorably to gain even meager political influence and patronage in their communities. Battles had been fought that were related to local election commission positions, Highway Patrol assignments, state highway jobs, and a wide variety of other positions. I was frequently bombarded with such war stories. Many of the people involved on a local basis harbored long-standing grudges. With a Republican victory at the statehouse level, they were determined to exact their versions of political revenge. Frequently, we dealt with loyal Republicans who were descendants of previous partisan generations. Family ties and party loyalties often fueled the intense emotions. Time and time again I found it necessary to deflect verbal broadsides to members of my staff because I simply did not have the time necessary to deal with those issues. Much valuable energy and time were consumed by such matters.

Sheer necessity resulted in a political solution of sorts. A plan was developed to create a committee in each county to deal with local political problems that might eventually be solved by the governor's office. Every committee would consist of a local person representing one of the three major Republican officeholders, those being Baker, Brock, and Dunn. In counties represented by a Republican congressman, that person would have a representative on the Good Government Committee. In addition, should the county be represented by one or more Republican state legislators, those individuals would be represented on the committee. These committees became the responsibilities of our state party director, Ron Rietdorf.

Over a period of time, such groups were created in each county desiring to be represented. An earnest effort was made to give consideration to the interests of every Republican officeholder. Because it was known that I was unwilling to terminate veteran state employees in order to give a hungry Republican a job, an unimagined series of circumstances eventually forced their way out of the local scene and onto the broader stage of state government. We were feeling our way, trying to placate where possible or create some understanding of the rules I had made, and it was not easy. Sadly, matters on which we were called to give attention did not always constitute legitimate state government business. Most often it involved the granting of ordinary state jobs of one description or another. It was understood that, when a position needed to be filled and no statutory guidelines existed, we would always hire qualified Republicans if possible. Unfortunately, loyal, devoted supporters were often disappointed and our friendships strained to the breaking point when requests or demands could not be met. Minor factionalism arising out of personal jealousies or favoritism for one Republican officeholder or another added to the mix of emotion. I was anxious to keep the peace on every question, but there was no way to fully realize that goal. Official demands on my time made it impossible for me to be involved. My staff, including Ron Rietdorf, absorbed all the harsh words uttered by advocates from every corner of the state. I was fast learning the realities associated with the fruits of political victory. They were not easy lessons, and they continued to manifest themselves as we moved forward with a serious agenda for governing. People in politics can get their feelings hurt in a hurry. Others have skins as tough as rawhide. Our goal was to create goodwill wherever possible and pave the way toward building the party when an opportunity presented itself.

The Good Government Committee was a noble effort to include all the proper interests. I was aware that many people had helped me achieve my political success. It was my nature to want to respond in kind when I could. I had quickly learned that congressmen and senators of our party were being approached to use their substantial influence with the governor's office. Having these officeholders represented on the Good Government Committees often softened the intensity of efforts by congressional staff people. Rarely was I approached directly by a congressman or senator on a matter of patronage. The single exception to that was manifested through the actions of Congressman Jimmy Quillen.

In retrospect it is fair to say the idea for those committees was reasonable. I recalled having been advised on many occasions that in the past there were special people in nearly every county who bore the title "Ellington's man to see" or "Clement's man to see." The need for a network of people willing to play the political game was obvious. It was a practice used down through the years when one political party dominated the landscape. Our plan, attempting to represent all the major officeholders of my party, was obviously different. Regrettably, on a cost-benefit basis, I am certain valuable time was wasted.

Low License Tags

During the Clement/Ellington years a very popular way to recognize citizens close to the seat of power in the governor's office was to issue automobile license tags with numbers that ranged from 1 to 2,000. When such a number was sighted on an automobile, it was safe to assume the driver was well connected with the governor. Many times during the 1970 campaign someone would mention that the new governor might enjoy granting favorite numbers to his friends. It was a topic of conversation that occasionally occupied time on long trips across the state. I'm quite sure that I looked with favor on having the privilege of dispensing low tag numbers.

In fact, one evening in Memphis when Betty, the Wellfords, and I were driving across town, Katherine brought up the subject of the special tags. Surely, on occasion she must have identified some holders of such favors, all of whom were prominent Democrats. She lightheartedly made the statement that when I was elected, she wanted only one favor from me. She, for some reason that was not explained, said she wanted low license number 99. I recall telling her that she could rest assured it would be hers.

As time went by I became so engrossed in the campaign that I completely forgot her request and my promise. However, once my election became a reality and I entered the governor's office, the subject of low automobile license tag numbers became a major consideration. I was shocked by the level of interest that existed among people anxious to obtain a low number. Large quantities of staff time had to be devoted to that one topic. In retrospect I realize I would have been wise to discontinue the practice by executive order at the outset of my administration. License tags were issued each year.

Many people were looking to the new administration to meet their requests for the distinction they were convinced came with a low numbered plate. Some of these good people were anxious to flaunt their new numerical low license plate before those on the losing side who had enjoyed such distinction in the past. Local political jealousies and envy were common ingredients in many local cultures, and I understood that completely. Congressman Quillen was personally on the telephone frequently, asking, among other things, for low tag numbers for close supporters. Often the people he wished to favor by allowing them to retain a particular numbered tag were prominent Democrats in his district. These people were supporters of the congressman, but they were recognized members of the other party. My loyal Republican supporters in the area did not like the idea of their political enemies receiving favors from a governor they did not support. The problem became chronic and demanded staff attention that needed to be focused elsewhere. Staff personnel actually came to dread an incoming call from Quillen because he was very difficult to deal with and he was relentless in his insistence regarding certain matters.

Shortly after I became governor, a request for an appointment with me was received from a very prominent Middle Tennessee Democrat who had publicly supported me against my opponent. This gentleman was a wealthy, influential businessman whose endorsement and support were very likely valuable to me. He was given an appointment, and on the date set he appeared at the capitol and entered my office. At the time I occupied a small space that had been used by the former governor. I had decided to move the governor's office to a larger conference room, but that had not taken place. The visitor had a substantial number of people in his party, and we met in the conference room. Among the visitors were his lawyer, his insurance agent and close friend, his son, and his son-in-law. I was impressed but not surprised to see such a strong support group.

After being seated and exchanging pleasantries briefly, my guest got right down to business. He told me that after years of loyal support for the Democratic Party and, in particular, his close relationships to the two most recent governors, although he did not know me personally, he became convinced that I should have his support in the recent governor's race. It was not an easy decision for him, I was told, but it was one he was highly satisfied he had made. He stressed that he had no use for my Democrat opponent, John Hooker. He emphasized that, of course, there had been no strings attached to his support of my candidacy. He deeply loved his state and wanted for it only the best. I listened intently, nodding my approval and occasionally muttering an appreciative comment. He only wanted what was good for Tennessee. I noticed by the nodding heads of those in his party that they were in complete harmony with his remarks. I merely listened.

He continued by stating that he had always valued his relationship with past governors. He was proud that his close friendships with such powerful political leaders had been good for his community. What he had been able to do for his county was a special point of pride for him and his family. Almost as an aside, he said one of his most prized possessions was the special low number of his personal automobile license tag. His car was easily recognized across the county by his special tag. He had been extended that courtesy from the governor's office for years, and his tag number had become symbolic of his identity and status. He continued. In fact, each member of his immediate family displayed the same number, adjusted only by an A, B, C, or D, depending on which family member's car was involved. His wife, of course, had tag number 99A on her automobile, and the three children displayed the other three letters of the alphabet, the oldest taking the B and so forth. The purpose of his visit, he declared, was only to request that he be granted the privilege of continuing to enjoy the ownership of low license tag number 99!

At that moment I thought of Katherine Wellford and her request to have license tag number 99. I vividly recalled our lighthearted moment when I promised her that if we won the election, tag number 99 would be hers! She and her wonderful husband, Harry, had been at the heart of our effort from the beginning. Obviously, this situation involved no heavy gubernatorial decision making. There was no doubt about what my response to this important Middle Tennessee visitor would be. However, in view of the importance he attached to his mission, I was not comfortable with the task before me. I had no time to dwell on my discomfort.

I wasted no time letting him know that, although it was disappointing to me to say so, that particular tag number had been promised to another person, a close friend. I proceeded, as carefully as I could, to tell the visitor of my commitment to the wife of the man who had been chairman of my campaign. I let my visitor know how grateful I was for his support and that my desire and commitment to him were that he be granted as low a number as was still available but not number 99. As I talked, to my dismay I saw large teardrops make their ways down his substantial cheeks. Obviously, the gentleman couldn't completely control his emotions at the moment. My discomfort in giving him news he didn't want to hear was probably apparent. The meeting soon ended. My visitor and his party left the room with my promise hopefully ringing in his ears. He was a disappointed man. I could tell he was crushed. I could only hope his good friends and family would give him comfort. Later, when I recounted that story for Katherine Wellford, she found it highly amusing. Little sympathy from that strong Republican lady would be spent on my esteemed Democrat supporter, it seemed! I was amazed at the importance my visitor attached to that special number.

Another incident involving the low license tag is ingrained in my memory. One day I was scheduled to meet briefly with an important citizen who wanted to "simply" express his appreciation to me. Obviously, my scheduler thought it was worth my time. At the appointed hour he entered my office, took a seat, and began to make a statement. He said it was a great sacrifice for me to have interrupted my professional career to seek the governorship. It was obviously a financial sacrifice for me and my family to devote the next four years to serving our great state. At that point he reached inside his suit coat and produced a white envelope. He wanted me to accept the small financial gift his envelope contained. He leaned forward and placed it on my desk.

I thanked him and stated that I could not accept his gift. I went further and said that such a thing was unnecessary and unneeded. We were completely comfortable, I said. His response was to insist that I take his modest offering and use it for my children. Use it in any manner I chose. He then stressed that there was nothing he wished in return. It was merely a gift he wanted us to have. Once again, I declined and pushed a button to signal to my secretary that I wanted her presence. The gentleman rose from his chair as Lucretia came in the door. He couldn't understand my unwillingness to accept his gift. As he moved toward the threshold, he returned the envelope to his pocket, looked at me, and said there was one thing he was interested in. He would very much appreciate a low license tag number if one could be granted him! Relieved that he was leaving, I told Lucretia that I would be pleased to see that he got a low number. He expressed his thanks. His final remark in my presence was, "I really don't understand why you won't take my gift. The others did." With that he was gone.

I didn't dwell on that experience. I didn't have the time. And yet, I didn't forget it. The gentleman probably felt there was nothing wrong with what he offered. It was clear that what he wanted was a low license tag number. I had accepted contributions in cash while on the campaign trail several times. I always turned them over to Chip or whoever was with me. My judgment just told me to refuse his offer. It was an awkward moment, and I was glad I could do something for him. That low license tag number was one I was glad to grant and be done with.

A Questionable Opportunity

A few weeks after the offer of a cash contribution was made in my office, something occurred that was of a more serious nature. An opportunity was presented to me, and it needed an immediate response. In this instance, I have never doubted that I made the right decision in response to the offer.

I took a personal telephone call from a prominent Nashville businessman. He said that a well-known local highway contractor and land developer would like to have a quiet visit with me, preferably in his home. I had become well acquainted with both men and felt comfortable giving the contractor an appointment. He and I met the next evening at his residence.

The sum and substance of the meeting was that the gentleman wanted to do something for me that would at some time in the future be very rewarding financially. His company held options on valuable farm land in Alabama that had been designated as a part of future interstate expressway property. He assured me the information that led him to put the land under contract was completely reliable. Therefore, he had identified a section of the future expressway that he was in a position to sell to me personally and confidentially, as he put it. There would be a cash consideration on my part amounting to approximately $30,000. A significant interchange was to be built on the property.

There was never any suggestion that what I was offered was not completely aboveboard. It was stressed that the transaction obviously needed to be confidential because newspapers would find some way to suggest that it was, if not unlawful for me to be involved, an unethical thing to do. My friend assured me that it was not and that I deserved an opportunity to "make some real money" as compensation for my time in service to the state. He urged me to seriously consider it.

It would have been a mindless thing for me to do. The governor, as chief executive officer of state government, had the authority to personally make major changes in the Highway Department's proposed activities. Although the planning process had been carried out under the past administration and all details as to the land acquisition in question were a matter of public record, I could just imagine the media reaction if I had become involved as a landholder. The proposal to me did not appear dishonest in the sense that state law would have been violated. But I was quite surprised that my supposedly intelligent and successful contractor friend would make such an offer.

Like the fellow with the white envelope containing cash, my contractor friend seemed to feel he was doing me a major favor. Sitting there in his living room, I suddenly felt very uncomfortable. Several thoughts crossed my mind, not the least of which was the fact that I had enough on my plate to deal with. There were major legislative proposals to be developed, big decisions of a strategic nature to be made, a budget shortfall looming, demands from friends, criticisms from those not so friendly, individual legislators to deal with, and thousands of voters who were counting on me, among many other things. There was no need to give what I was offered any further consideration.

I thanked my potential benefactor and told him I had no interest in what he had described. He was an important man who was highly respected, and I didn't want to offend him by being abrupt. But my words were chosen to leave no doubt that I wasn't interested in pursuing the offer. After a handshake, I called the trooper who had driven me to the meeting, and we returned to the Residence. As I walked through the entrance and headed upstairs to find my wife, I felt a sense of relief that such an unusual visit was over and that I had made the right decision. I told her about it. I also chuckled, saying that if the offer had been appealing, I would have had a hard time coming up with the $30,000 consideration!

Throughout the four years of my administration, the white envelope incident and the interstate property offer were the only two occasions I experienced that could have been described as unethical, illegal, or bordering on the illegal. Rumors and tales of questionable transactions at high levels of political office have long been a part of the political scene. Based on my real-life experiences, I could accept the fact that character and integrity in government were frequently tested in many ways. And I knew that a fifty-year period of time during which one political party was in charge of doing all the state's business allowed some bad habits to develop. One of my major goals in being politically active was to see that a check-and-balance situation could exist where two political parties were in competition to keep each other honest. Often there is a gray line separating what is legal and what is careless. With the advent of a two-party system, I was satisfied that such a situation finally existed in Tennessee. Perhaps the gray line would become more distinct.

Keeping Promises

The campaign promise has long been a subject for humor and ridicule on the American political scene. Those reactions have frequently been fully justified. During the fall campaign of 1970, we attempted to avoid making commitments the public would be completely justified in expecting to be fulfilled. Many statements were made reflecting the hopes and aspirations of an eager and often exhausted candidate. I wanted to build a climate of confidence. I wanted to give the government back to the people. I wanted real political competition to replace one-party domination in state politics. Those words flowed freely and frequently in my prepared and extemporaneous messages.

Actual promises were few and far between. My lighthearted promise to Katherine Wellford was easily fulfilled by license plate number 99. A more serious promise to the public was that I would see that the language on large, attractive highway signs welcoming visitors to Tennessee would be changed. I took great heart in receiving reports from the Highway Department and through newspaper stories that on the day of my inauguration, temporary language welcoming visitors to "The Great State of Tennessee" covered words welcoming visitors to "The Three States of Tennessee." Permanent changes in the wording would soon be made.

A major campaign promise I made was to conduct an in-depth study of how the state government did business and an in-depth look at the various agencies through which that action took place. A former governor whose record of service I had come to admire was Austin Peay of Clarksville. This able, reform-minded leader who was elected in 1922 took an initiative I felt was appropriate for that time. He turned to talents and resources outside state government for a study, analysis, and professional summary of the conditions that existed in the business of government at the time he assumed office. He employed a business consulting firm from New York City. During my campaign I pledged to create by executive authority a study team to examine every detail of the manner in which Tennessee state government conducted its business. I further pledged to have this study done at no expense to the government.

The Governor's Study on Cost Control
A Survey Report and Recommendations

During the campaign a contact had been made by a group named Warren King and Associates, Incorporated, of Chicago. The key man, Warren King, made my staff people aware of the successful work his organization had done for several states studying the structure and organization of their governments. Emphasis was on organization and cost control. References were given and a comfort level established with King. The information created a desire on my part to explore the possibilities that might exist in Tennessee for such a study. I mentioned the subject on the campaign trail as something I intended to pursue.

Shortly after my election, a meeting was held in Nashville with King and his associates. The result of that meeting was a written proposal received days later. After study and discussion, including inquiries of other states regarding their experiences in such an undertaking, a decision was made to proceed. A volunteer group of Tennessee businesspeople would be recruited to review state government and determine what might be done to improve the way it conducted its business and thus serve the people in better ways.

I thought carefully about the leadership for such an undertaking. It was encouraging to me that the public generally, and the business and professional communities specifically, were highly enthusiastic regarding the new administration and its potential to bring about change in state government. Economically, politically, and socially the climate for cooperation and change was healthy and promising. After lengthy discussions with key advisers, I offered the opportunity to lead this unique study on cost control to my former adversary in the Republican primary, Maxey Jarman. Mr. Jarman was a Nashville resident, highly visible over the years in the business community, and a man who had a reputation across the nation as one of its premier entrepreneurs and business executives.

Fortunately, this opportunity to lead an in-depth, wide-reaching examination of administration and management procedures with the full authority of the governor's office was appealing to Jarman. After becoming satisfied as to his credentials for the study and gaining confidence in the reputation of Warren King and Associates, he signed on with enthusiasm. This opportunity came at a time when Mr. Jarman was still nursing his deep disappointment over being deprived of the opportunity to seek the governorship and was likely looking for something to fill the void created when early retirement from Genesco Corporation set him free of those responsibilities. I was delighted to have him accept the challenge of putting together an organization to man the non-profit, non-partisan corporation that had been created to conduct the study.

A carefully chosen group of approximately 60 executives was recruited from across the state. Included were individuals and businesses that were willing to donate their time and some financial support. A total of 320 sponsors contributed manpower, financial aid, or both to the effort. The Cost Control Study, as it came to be commonly known, required the full-time involvement of those executives for twelve weeks. Seven teams were organized. An Executive Committee of respected, high-profile citizens served as oversight participants who processed reports of various team members as they were submitted. Mr. Jarman had a select group of six assistants who worked closely on a daily basis with him. In addition, another group of special assistants worked closely with the seven teams to examine various aspects of the state's administrative activities.

Nothing of this nature had ever been attempted on such a scale and with a total commitment from the chief executive of the state. It was an exercise long overdue and clearly necessary to move the state government into a more competitive posture relative to its sister states. As teams representing the study moved into the heart of state business activity, the very best private sector management techniques were employed. These visitors from the outside were welcomed by state personnel. Every finding was carefully reviewed, revised as necessary, and considered in weekly meetings. Input was sought from various departments of other state governments.

I was totally consumed with the job of approving legislative proposals, meeting with various representatives of the two houses, and seeing to duties and obligations that came with my job as governor. There was little time for me to get involved in the study on a daily basis, but reports I received from staff indicated the process was moving ahead at a good pace. Several weeks were consumed recruiting the right participants, assuring adequate financing, and getting all concerned in position to make the twelve-week timeframe allocated to conduct the study as productive as possible.

Some time after the effort was launched, I was advised by a staff member to read a news article quoting Mr. Jarman. As chairman, he had called a press conference to make several announcements regarding the study. In a question-and-answer session, he volunteered information regarding multiplied millions of dollars he anticipated the state would save by implementing changes the completed study would recommend. At that time, I was doing everything in my power to persuade the Democrat-controlled legislature to implement a major tax increase I had proposed. Such statements by the chairman of the study could only make my struggle to gather enough votes extremely difficult, if not impossible. I took immediate steps to discuss the matter with Jarman. The meeting did not resolve my concerns.

The Jarman statement was troublesome for me based on my growing awareness of the nature of the legislature. Republican members of both House and Senate were completely cooperative as

I presented my proposals for progress. I had experienced a certain amount of partisan harassment from Democrats both before taking office and after being sworn in as governor. After several months in office, I had identified at least three distinct groups of legislators, all members of the other party.

There was a small but vocal group of legislators whose hostility exceeded decent behavior, in my opinion. These people needed no excuse to launch biting criticisms and various demeaning comments merely because the governor was a Republican and therefore worthy of no consideration regarding any matter, with or without merit. They were dedicated to the proposition that my administration should be demeaned or derailed at every opportunity. I concluded they were beyond my reach. I could expect to make no headway with these people individually or otherwise. My impression was that they thought if they kept their vindictiveness up long enough, I might just go away and let the state return to the position of "normalcy" they had enjoyed for the last fifty years. I was grateful it was a small, misguided group of people who could not adjust to the presence of a Republican in the governor's office.

Another group of Democrats consisted of those who were reasonable in their responses to my initiatives and with whom I could discuss appropriate issues. Many among this group sought appointments in order to request my support for various matters of interest to their constituents. I welcomed the opportunity of give-and-take in dealing with those individuals. Partisanship, however, was not lost on this group. At the slightest hint of weakness in a proposal or misjudgment on my part or some member of the executive office, these people were more than willing to criticize, ridicule, or embarrass the administration. Often such action was fair enough, but on many occasions circumstances did not warrant the extent to which their hostility was exercised. The members making up this group were by far the great majority of legislative Democrats. I did receive significant cooperation on legislative matters from them, however.

The final group was relatively small in number and consisted of mature, seasoned individuals who clearly understood the game we were all involved in and the rules of fairness by which it should be played. Although loyal partisanship was displayed at the appropriate times in votes that should have fallen along party lines, there was never a display of disrespect or vindictiveness from these statesmen toward the governor. These people respected the high office and me as a person. Individually, they were very courteous and considerate regarding my wife, the state's first lady. It was a genuine pleasure to work with them. Their leadership was highly significant in the passage of sound legislation and in the process of carrying on responsible government.

On the subject of partisanship, another small but vocal group should be mentioned. Two major daily newspapers were notable for their often unreasonable attitudes toward a Republican governor and perhaps toward me personally. These were the Nashville *Tennessean* and the *Jackson Sun*. Each was a widely circulated publication. I was never concerned with legitimate editorial criticism. What were biting and occasionally discomfiting to me were irresponsible articles and editorials containing half-truths or complete misrepresentations. I appreciated my staff making available to me a balanced collection of newsprint on a daily basis that permitted me to gauge public sentiment to some degree. To an overwhelming degree, the state's various media outlets were very fair and highly professional.

Maxey Jarman and I met on numerous occasions in the process of getting the study underway. Once things were moving smoothly, such meetings were a rarity. I met with him in my office shortly after reading his quote regarding the significant savings he hoped the state would experience once implementation of recommendations was underway. The difficulty such a statement posed for me was obvious, and I spelled out in no uncertain terms how much I regretted his words. He expressed his regrets but felt my reaction was an over-reaction. I felt his enthusiasm for the project clouded his judgment in the matter, and I made certain he knew such statements in the future should be avoided. As events unfolded during the remainder of that first legislative session, it became clear that my concerns were well founded. Biting comments by various Democrat legislators were published, thus having some effect on public opinion. Speculation from one in Jarman's position was fuel for the fire from those opposed to an always unpopular tax increase. My distress regarding the obstacles created by such a statement was equaled by my regret that such potential problems were not addressed prior to launching the study.

Along with a letter of transmittal dated September 1, 1971, the first copy of the Governor's Study on Cost Control was presented to me by Chairman Maxey Jarman. Despite the fact that my proposed increases and adjustments in our tax program had been substantially reduced by the legislature, thus seriously altering the pace at which I had hoped to proceed with implementation of a statewide kindergarten program, among other initiatives, the finished document was received with great appreciation on my part. The entire exercise had been a major success.

A total of 575 recommendations for improving the means by which state business was conducted was submitted. It was suggested that more than three-quarters of the proposals could be implemented by executive order. The remainder would require legislative action. A large number of suggested changes and initiatives had begun to be implemented as the study process went forward. This reflected the positive attitudes of state employees who were anxious to take action. The report suggested that full implementation could result in a total potential net annual savings of nearly $178 million. Such savings would only be fully realized incrementally over future years. A number of simple but significant organizational changes were proposed for the top level of state government. Improved budgeting and accounting systems were proposed. There were no fiscal savings notes attached to these proposals.

Appropriate fanfare accompanied the presentation, and there was no shortage of appreciation expressed by me and others in leadership positions. The next step for me was to designate an individual to supervise the implementation of the proposed changes going forward. It was on this important subject that Mr. Jarman and I found ourselves in complete disagreement.

Chairman Jarman and I had not discussed who would be asked to take the leadership in implementing changes proposed by the study. At a meeting following the presentation ceremony, Mr. Jarman directly asked me to appoint him to head up that effort. Without hesitation I told him that I could not meet his request. I noted that his contribution to the exercise had been immeasurably valuable and that I was indebted to him. There was no doubt he would energetically approach the job if I would ask him to do so. However, I knew that such an appointment would have the potential to create a feast for the bloodthirsty elements in the unfriendly body politic of the state. I frankly told him that I could not afford to run the risk of a perception that two governors were at work on behalf of the state. Mr. Jarman, no slacker when it came to stating where he stood, heatedly disagreed with me. In response I reminded him of a single occasion at a press conference where his reference to future savings resulting from the study created a political situation that I believed contributed to my failure to get approval of the complete tax package I had submitted to the legislature. I was prepared to give him a list of logical reasons that his continuing presence at that level of authority and visibility would be a hindrance to my goals and objectives, to say nothing of the distractions that would occur. It wasn't necessary. We parted company in complete disagreement, and our relationship suffered a fatal blow, regrettably. The evidence of that fact is a letter in my private files received from Jarman shortly after our final visit.

I did appoint a seasoned state administrative official to take on the responsibility of implementing the study. His role would be to work with the bureaucrats under whose authority and responsibility the various initiatives proposed would be pursued. It was the right move. My single regret associated with the entire enterprise was the bitterness with which Mr. Jarman departed my company. I could not understand why he failed to see the logic of my position. I had no doubt that I made the right decision.

The Governor's Study for Economic Development

During the campaign I became aware of what several southeastern states were doing to enhance their abilities to promote economic growth and development. Three states in particular were North Carolina, Virginia, and Georgia. The accomplishments of Governor Luther Hodges of North Carolina were often brought to my attention. He had become well known as an innovator and aggressive leader in bringing the many resources of his state into clear focus. As a result those resources were uniquely employed. The state of North Carolina had become a textbook example of how to improve the civic and commercial growth that could result from careful, organized analysis and planning to advance its economic interests. The people were the obvious beneficiaries.

In August 1971, I asked my close friend Dr. W. H. "Bill" Rachels of Memphis to lead a study to examine the present level of economic development in Tennessee. I wanted a thorough analysis of the functions and services being performed by state government with a view toward recommending a possible reorganization of the existing efforts. I knew that what I had heard referred to as "chasing smokestacks" was no longer in order as a way for the state to do business. True to form, Bill Rachels eagerly accepted the task. An outstanding group of business and civic leaders was chosen and appointed to compose a committee. Advice and input were sought from heads of various state government offices already in place supporting economic development. Lieutenant Governor John S. Wilder and the federal co-chairman of the Appalachian Regional Commission were among a large number of outstanding leaders serving various constituencies whose guidance was invaluable. A Technical Advisory Board was designated and invited to carefully review findings as the study progressed.

The result of this major effort was a report of the Governor's Study Committee for Economic Development that was placed in my hands by Chairman Rachels on January 31, 1972. The report identified four principal areas in which new and revised efforts should be concentrated to begin to achieve my objectives. Those were planning, human resource development, financial resource development, and economic and community development. The committee and its support groups did a brilliant job of coming to grips with the needs of a Tennessee state government that was determined to be competitive in a rapidly changing society.

A copy of the report was distributed to members of the legislature and media representatives, among others, in preparation for a major legislative effort to enact into law certain recommendations of the report that could not otherwise be implemented. That initiative became one of the cornerstones of my administration's legacy. I had previously pointed out in various speeches and statements that, while Tennessee's unemployment rate was lower than the national average, underemployment severely limited the individual earnings potential. Our average annual personal income was only three-fourths that of other Americans. Such numbers were unacceptable. An aggressive program of planning, offering incentives, and supporting manpower training was an initiative the state should undertake. The state could be a catalyst that would mobilize Tennessee's leadership to create the widest range of opportunities for our citizens. Our challenge was to build on a strong foundation put in place by leaders of state government in previous years. My desire was to foster a program so competent that, by its very nature, it would transcend future partisan politics.

That was a large order. It became a legislative and political struggle to some extent because of partisan resistance. I was assisted by two prominent Nashville businessmen who had been active in a variety of business and industrial matters affecting the state. Those men were E. Bronson Ingram, CEO of the Ingram Barge Company, and Victor Johnson, CEO of Aladdin Industries. The General Assembly did pass my bills to create and fund a cabinet office for economic development and a separate and centralized state planning agency reporting directly to the governor. Included in the legislation was authority to appoint an Industrial and Agricultural Development Commission. Due to partisan resistance, however, we worked the remaining three years of my administration to put in place all the critical elements necessary to get a competitive economic and community development program in motion. We failed to fully encompass local government planning within the new department, regrettably. I look back on our struggles to bring order, vision, and expertise to bear on economic and community development as one of my administration's greatest accomplishments.

CHAPTER TWENTY-NINE

FIRST SESSION, 87TH GENERAL ASSEMBLY

The Process

For years I have toyed with the idea of writing memoirs as governor of Tennessee in which I would emphasize the personal impressions and experiences that came flooding into the lives of Betty and Winfield Dunn. Such a recounting would explore the political and social intrigues of suddenly being transformed from a respected member of the dental profession and a lovely mother and housewife into political powers that neither of us fully recognized at the outset. Such a recounting would be at the expense of major policy decisions and struggles with the legislative process. That story is currently being told. The only title that seemed to fit such memoirs was one obviously too clumsy to be appealing. *What It Was Like to Be the First Republican Governor and First Lady of Tennessee in Fifty Years* would exhaust a prospective reader before a page could be turned. I repeatedly put the idea aside. It remains an intriguing thought.

My personal transition from citizen politician to governor of the state was an experience that defies ease of expression. The move from owning and operating a private dental practice grossing approximately $100,000 annually to assuming the state's chief executive authority in the middle of a fiscal year in which approximately $1 billion had been earmarked to be spent was more than mildly daunting. It was a somewhat traumatic transition, not only for me, but for my family as well. As a governor with no prior experience in government, I stepped forward to assume immediate responsibility for meeting the constitutional requirement that Tennessee maintain a balanced budget. Having had no influence on the amount of taxpayer revenues appropriated for the ongoing year, it was nonetheless my solemn duty to assure that at the end of the fiscal year occurring on June 30 following my inauguration on January 16, the finances of the state would reflect absolute fiscal soundness.

The responsible manner in which the state had been managed during the prior administration made my challenge feasible. Information from the Department of Finance and Administration made it clear that, with five months remaining in the fiscal year, prudence and caution on the part of the new administration were called for. I issued executive orders curtailing excessive and not absolutely necessary traveling throughout the executive branch. Another directive put a cap on new hires. Those actions plus other executive decisions across the board by new commissioners seeking to get a firm grip on their department's financial obligations gave me comfort that we could meet the budgetary limits established at the beginning of the current fiscal year.

The first session of the 87th General Assembly unfolded relentlessly in terms of the ongoing duties of government. Earlier organized and ready for business, members convened in February with individual agendas that were of paramount importance to each representative or senator. The constitutional offices, secretary of state, treasurer, and comptroller, were occupied by veteran functionaries who knew their business and were hard at work on a continuing basis. Each constitutional officer was a product of the Democrat political establishment. Both houses of the legislature being in the majority Democrat left no question in the minds of the newly arrived Republican executive branch personalities that our work was cut out for us. I was determined that we would and could work constructively on matters relating to the common good. In strictest terms, the duty of the governor is to execute the will of the legislature. Down through the years, precedent had broadened that duty to a point where, through assumption of various powers delegated and presumed, the governor's reach and influence were much broader.

From the day of my inauguration, I had been relentlessly under the pressure of a shortage of time in assembling proposals that covered a wide range of public duties and responsibilities. The administrative proposals that were submitted to the clerks of the respective houses were a work product reflecting my priorities as expressed on the campaign trail. Chief among them were initiatives relating to public education, acceleration of interstate highway development, public health and mental health needs, environmental enhancement, and emphasis on drug abuse and rehabilitation. Of major importance was the need to find additional tax revenues to adequately fund these major proposals and to support ongoing programs vital to the health of the state.

I had inherited a state budget for fiscal year 1970–71, which, including general state tax revenues, federal funds, and department reserves and revenues, slightly exceeded $1 billion. There was a general attitude that no thought should be given to a "standstill" posture on the part of state government. The demands of modernization, growth, new technology, and federal matching fund programs could not be denied, nor, indeed, were there meaningful opinions to the contrary. The leadership in both houses of the legislature was aware that the pressing need for reasonable tax increases was justified. Democrats made it clear they were somewhat relieved that a Republican governor would bear the initial brunt of any adverse public opinion in reaction to proposed new taxes.

Public attitudes in 1971 strongly reflected what was perceived to be a new climate of thinking and sense of purpose in the state capitol. There was no reservation on my part concerning any adverse voter opinion as I made my request for new tax revenues to the legislature. I identified as an additional source of revenue an increase from 5 to 6 percent in the corporate excise that would produce $14 million. I proposed a change in the filing date for inheritance tax returns that would produce a one-time amount of $4 million. Next, my recommendation was to add one cent to the state sales tax and to extend the base of the sales tax to include a variety of commercial transactions not previously covered. This one cent increase would be expected to yield an estimated $77 million. These changes represented a total of $95 million in new revenue that we estimated would be needed to make the new fiscal year the success it could be.

In reaching a decision on these added revenue requests, I had worked long and hard looking for the fairest possible means by which to ask the people of Tennessee for additional tax dollars. My staff and I talked to literally hundreds of people in government, in the private sector, and in our universities seeking input and advice. I took some comfort knowing that our citizens paid less per capita in state taxes than did the people of Mississippi, Alabama, and Arkansas. The absence of a payroll or tax on income in Tennessee allowed us to make that claim. I frequently made the telling point that if per capita taxes in Tennessee were equal to those of North Carolina, our state tax collections would be increased $230 million. That was a powerful statement in support of my request to the legislature. The state tax burden borne by our citizens was reasonable.

It was vital that I build as many tactical bridges with key legislators as I was capable of putting together. The seated meals at the Residence honoring the Assembly members had never before been attempted. It was a huge job beautifully done by Betty and her staff. It paid off in terms of promoting good relationships between me and many members. As the first session got underway, I scheduled regular meetings at the beginning of each week with the Speaker of the House, the Speaker of the Senate, and my Republican legislative leaders. These meetings were often productive and always informative. It was essential that everyone in a leadership position understand the needs and opportunities that lay before us.

During the last two years of the Ellington administration, the legislature adopted an annual state budget to replace a long-standing practice in which the governor presented a single budget document for a two-year period. Preparation of the document is the governor's duty, and the commissioner of finance and administration directs the budget preparation. For many of the veteran employees of the department, this new procedure required major adjustments. The new commissioner relied heavily on these loyal Tennesseans. Our first budget would be a big challenge.

Prior to submitting my administration's priority legislation, in fact, during those pressure-packed days in which the various proposals were being created and drafted, two time-honored and significant messages from the governor were required by precedent to be delivered to separate and highly significant audiences.

State of the State, 1971

On January 22, 1971, only six days after assuming the office of governor, I addressed the annual meeting of the Tennessee Press Association (TPA) in Nashville. My purpose was to present the annual "State of the State" address to a large assemblage of newspaper representatives from across the state. In the intervening days between my election and my presentation to the TPA I had learned a great deal about the status and condition of our state government. I had been briefed by department heads, military representatives, members of a multitude of state boards and commissions, and spokesmen of the three constitutional offices. I had met with members of the U.S. Congress and White House staff. Personnel from the National Governors Association and Republican Governors Association had counseled with me and my staff. No doubt I had been exposed to intimate details regarding government that would be helpful as we moved ahead. The challenge of informing news leaders of all grades and persuasions as to the state of the state these same people had been covering for years, even decades, was formidable. I was determined to use this occasion to begin officially setting the course for four ensuing years. I was equally determined to present my case as one earnestly in need of their guidance and support.

In the early part of my address to these publishers, editors, and writers I made a point of acknowledging many of the exceptional public servants, past and present, whose love for our state went beyond party and above partisanship. The stress was on a common goal of working together for a greater Tennessee. I then proceeded to reference each major area of administrative responsibility across the broad spectrum of the executive branch. Specifics regarding past accomplishments and future needs were detailed in each area. Emphasis was placed on particular subjects including public education, industrial growth, mental health, revenue, and purchasing. I reminded the audience of Tennessee's potential to further develop tourism as a productive business. Noted was the state's rich endowment of natural resources that had only been modestly tapped and remained a major promise to enhance our society. I concluded by assuring those molders of public opinion representing major and minor publications throughout the state that I had no illusions regarding my leadership. I needed support wherever I could find it. Success for the next four years would be a product of whatever we the people had the wit, will, and courage to make it.

I was not prepared to do what would have been quite normal in speaking to such an important group under other circumstances. It would have been politically helpful had I spelled out several of the crippling shortcomings we had been made aware of or had earlier identified as in need of immediate attention. Certainly, there would have been no lack of a positive response to my message. The absence of a tax-supported kindergarten experience for five-year-old children in our public schools across the state spelled future disaster in educating and retaining our young people. Horrific conditions existed in a number of our major mental health institutions. The spread of drug addiction in our schools and in society generally begged for strong initiatives to stop it. Rural healthcare was non-existent in many areas of the state. Prison overcrowding and growing recidivism were problematic. Inadequate rural roads, state feeder highways, defective bridges, and a straggling rate of interstate highway development made reasonable and safe transportation difficult for public and commercial driving. A deficient and ineffective state-supported program of regional economic planning and development limited the state's ability to compete for new industry and more, better-paying jobs. There was much to talk about in terms of seizing the initiative and getting the job done. I reserved those comments for the legislature.

Governor Ellington had advised me that my four-year term would end all too quickly. No doubt he was correct. The TPA address was not the proper forum to address those challenges, however. My first budget message was scheduled to be delivered to a joint session of the General Assembly on March 1. It would be there that I could propose formally a program of progress and change, all across the board, to get the Volunteer State moving in the right direction at the right rate of speed. I did not deny that many sound and productive moves forward had occurred in other years. Regardless, as I considered the multiple opportunities to build on foundations already in place, it was obvious that other foundations had to be laid by new minds and energies. In those days I often imagined those of us elected to serve at the state level as stepping out onto fields of newly fallen snow where our footprints of progress could be easily measured. I felt very privileged.

With the first of my "State of the State" addresses behind me, I continued to adjust each day's routine to meet the immediate demands before me. Two particular responsibilities became especially burdensome. One had to do with placing the signature of the governor on official documents of state business. What seemed to me a mountain of folders was placed on my desk containing papers to be signed. Each item had been approved by the commissioner of finance and administration and did not require study on my part. These folders, by the hundreds, had accumulated over a substantial period of time. They reflected business transacted during many previous months. I assumed Governor Ellington, perhaps for reasons of personal health, deferred action on such mundane business in order to address more pressing issues. I remember vividly the large number of documents to be signed and the excessive amounts of my time required to get it done. I decided to seek relief from a necessary duty that required the official signature of the chief executive. Without a doubt my time during the next four years could be more productively spent in other ways. I asked my staff to inquire of other state governments how this matter was handled. We learned of a rather complex and expensive signature machine that would be recognized as an "official" signature of the governor. Such a machine was eventually acquired and, properly adapted to my personal signature, became a valuable resource.

The other pressing responsibility was that of examining recommendations of the state's pardons and parole committee, making a final decision in agreement or otherwise with what the committee proposed. These recommendations had accumulated over a substantial period, not unlike other documents requiring the governor's signature that I was dealing with at the same time. A major difference was that state business documents came to me with the approval of the commissioner of finance and administration. In that case I needed only to affix my signature to each document.

Folders from the Department of Corrections contained the entire records of individual state prison felons seeking their freedom. These people had earned the opportunity to appear before the committee that reviewed each record and heard each request. The state prison population was at an historic high, space was limited, and several programs were in place attempting to move prisoners back into society and make room for newly convicted offenders. The result of those hearings was a large volume of appeals that came to me through recommendations of the Board of Pardons and Paroles. Only the governor had the power, granted by the state Constitution, to make a final decision in these matters. I was shocked at the volume of requests awaiting my attention. They had been accumulating for many months prior to my taking office. In order to maintain some normalcy in my life, I requested these folders be delivered to my office at the Residence.

I took on the task very seriously. Each folder represented not only a human being behind bars agonizing over a decision to be made by some unknown power called the governor. The prisoner likely did not understand why so much time had elapsed since he or she had been heard by the board. It also often represented family members who had been crushed under the legitimate weight of our judicial system and who needed to know something. I found it necessary to carefully study the recommendations of the board. Occasionally, I had to make telephone calls to various people such as a warden or a board member. The recommendations fell into two categories. One was a recommendation by the board that the prison sentence being served should be concluded and the prisoner processed back into society. It was called a commutation and amounted to a reduction in the length of the original sentence. The other category was called a recommendation for a pardon. These recommendations were very rare. A pardon granted by the governor required that the entire judicial and prison record of the person involved be expunged with government retaining no record of that person's encounter with the law. Only under the rarest of circumstances could such action by the governor be justified.

Nothing more clearly defined the awesome power granted the governor than matters pertaining to our penal system. I sat at my desk in the Residence countless nights reading, analyzing, praying, and often making phone calls regarding individual cases. The state trooper on duty at the Residence during those frequently late hours had little time to relax. Because the residential telephone number of the governor was listed in the local telephone directory, the phone rang constantly, always answered initially by a trooper on duty. Quite often in the late hours of the night, intoxicated individuals would call for the governor. It was interesting but always a waste of the trooper's time. I frequently kept the same trooper busy attempting to contact some individual who could shed light on a particular case from the board. Occasionally, although the board might vote to recommend clemency, a note would be attached to the record detailing the opinion of the trial judge or a victim's family that opposed the action suggested. That always made my task of being the ultimate decision maker more difficult. I acknowledge that my usual attitude was one of taking a firm line in deciding the fate of each human being. Capital murder convicts received little sympathy from me. There were, of course, exceptions. Other offenders received my closest attention, and more often than not, I agreed with the board's recommendation. It was a tough and demanding process. It required several months of intense attention to the accumulated folders to reach a point where the board's recommendations became a more routine part of my workload.

An interesting situation occurred. Frequently, as I exited my office at the capitol building, I used a small corridor to reach the outside of the building. I was always accompanied by my security man, either John White or John Fields. More often than not during regular work hours, there was a slightly built, elderly man standing near the exit. Occasionally, he had a broom or some other cleaning instrument at hand. As my trooper opened the door for me to exit, the man always said, "Hello, Governor," and I always spoke to him. These incidents occurred over a period of at least two years. Without giving the matter much thought, both the trooper and I probably assumed the man was one of the several prison trustees who did janitorial work in the capitol.

One day, my security man told me that the fellow we often saw standing near the exit to the capitol was a state prison inmate, originally convicted of murder, who had earned trustee status. His request for a commutation of sentence had been refused by me in the early months of my term. Obviously, that detail had not been made known to personnel at the Central Prison facility who assigned work details for trustees. My trooper added that when the information was made known, the trustee had been promptly moved to another section of the building to do his work. I felt a little strange. That was as close as I had come to a personal encounter with one whose fate was in my hands, much less one who must have been disappointed, if not embittered, by my decision. I commented that if he had been a vindictive person, he might have shown me some hostility. Later, I reviewed his record and was satisfied that I had made the right decision. Perhaps a future governor would be inclined to favor him with a time cut.

The First Budget Message: Fiscal Year 1972

On March 1, 1971, I stood outside closed doors leading into the magnificent chamber of the state House of Representatives. I anticipated a welcome inside from a convening of the two houses of the General Assembly. The mission was delivery of my first budget proposal to those who would authorize appropriations of the necessary dollars to move our state forward in a new fiscal year beginning the following July 1. It was a moment of great excitement for me; my family and the devoted staff and friends who had helped me structure what I believed to be a sound plan of progress for Tennessee were already seated inside the chamber.

I heard the sergeant at arms announce to the Speakers that the governor of the great state of Tennessee was present, and he spoke my name. The doors swung open, and I, along with legislative leaders in escort, moved toward the rostrum to reassuring applause and cheers. As I greeted the Speakers and turned to face the imposing body of public servants gathered in joint session, the applause continued. Gaveling the audience to silence, Speaker John Wilder then introduced me and permitted another round of applause to burst forth. It was a satisfying time for me. My family and my cabinet, along with members of the Supreme Court, were seated in the front. I enjoyed every moment. Soon the noise subsided, and it was time for me to speak.

My core message contained four essential references around which I hoped to build a strong and productive relationship with the legislative branch during the next four years. First, I chose words that would leave no doubt that my new administration had taken charge and that I would demonstrate clear vision supporting a brighter future for our state. I listed steps already taken to ensure maximum value from every tax dollar.

Next, I laid before the assembled audience the sobering fact that all was not well with our state's ongoing efforts to serve the people. I referred to our state's judicial system being served by judges who were the most poorly compensated in the nation. I noted the deplorable conditions known to exist and others recently revealed at several of the mental institutions serving our people. I then referred to our comparatively low ranking in financial support of public education, the unmet challenges of environmental pollution, severe inadequacies in our corrections system, and the growing menace of illegal drug use. I stressed the fact that there were other challenges too numerous to mention.

The third element was my commitment to own up to major responsibilities where Tennessee government had fallen behind. The point made was that we had options either to remain idle or to accelerate and move our state forward. Included was a reference to the high priority I placed on creating a state-funded kindergarten experience for every child, making serious salary increases for public school teachers and state employees, enhancing our commitment to highway development, establishing environmental initiatives, and undertaking other major administrative improvements. These subjects and more would require funding at new and historic levels.

The fourth major emphasis dealt with the adequate revenues to meet our needs and opportunities. I was not acquainted with past efforts by governors to persuade legislatures to raise additional revenues. There was no concern about a comparison of what I was requesting with any action by a former chief executive. My willingness to endure the certain partisan criticism that would follow a proposed tax increase was a given. It was a matter of necessity, and it came due on my watch. I requested changes in our revenue program that would produce the $95 million we had carefully estimated as required to effect a new day in Tennessee state government. I offered in detail my recommendations for the steps that would produce additional funds. I challenged my listeners by asking if we could be satisfied with glaring inadequacies when we knew they could be addressed and overcome.

The budget message was designed to get our state moving ahead, and it was undoubtedly filled with hard choices. I concluded my address with the remark that we were chosen by people who trusted that we were competent to meet their expectations for a greater Tennessee. It was simply up to us to act.

My budget proposal was received as might have been expected. Generally, the public response was favorable as measured by state news media. Republican support was strong. I expected no kind words from the Speaker of the House, James McKinney, and I was not disappointed. A number of Democrats took their shots. The sheer logic of the budget message made it difficult for valid criticism of my proposals to stand. The majority of Democrat members demonstrated by their support that they wanted to move forward.

This fact became well known by the time the first session of the 87th General Assembly adjourned several months later.

Results: First Session, 87th General Assembly

The entire Republican leadership team did its job very well. Minority Leaders Tom Jensen in the House and Houston Goddard in the Senate did everything that was asked of them by the administration. They received solid support from other Republican members in various leadership roles. The staff of the Office of Urban and Federal Affairs worked to the point of exhaustion day after day representing every new initiative that merited consideration. It was reassuring to me to have a number of Democrat members of the legislature step forward to offer guidance and leadership in the legislative process. For those of us who were untested up to that time, a wealth of experience was earned by each one.

Based on legislation passed and signed into law, I considered the first session to have been positive and productive. Many important proposals were assigned a pending status awaiting consideration during the following year's session. The opportunities to begin making my mark were ample and diverse across the broad slate of state government responsibility. I was highly motivated by the prospect of public kindergarten for children from all parts of our society. We were developing promising ideas for enhanced economic and industrial growth. We were discovering the vast potential for more efficient government. Better ways to do business and substantial savings could result directly from the Governor's Study on Cost Control then underway. It seemed to me the opportunities to improve government service were vast. It was a good time to be involved in the business of government. However, unlike Mr. Crump who ran things in my beloved Memphis, I didn't always get my way.

I was disappointed that both houses of the legislature refused to approve my request for a one cent increase in the state sales tax. My recommendation was reduced to one-half of one cent. Additionally, partisan politics stepped in, and the Democrat-controlled legislature chose to make the increase temporary. That meant it would be necessary to ask for the same tax increase each succeeding year if my programs were to be adequately funded. I had requested $4.5 million for kindergarten operations and $13 million to meet capital outlay needs. My expectations were suddenly reduced. We were able to increase kindergarten opportunities from 3,300 to 9,400 students. That was not my goal, but I was resigned to settle for what I could get. We would be compelled to approach the kindergarten program piecemeal rather than implement the valuable educational experience for our five-year-olds immediately.

Fortunately, a number of other positive revenue measures were proposed and approved. New funds would be available for other important steps forward. Unfortunately, many Tennessee children continued to languish at home, compelled to wait until age six and the first grade public school experience. Valuable kindergarten learning time would be lost.

In spite of restrictions, the 1972 fiscal year would see a record number of dollars put to work for a brighter future. Supplemental funding for existing programs was approved by the legislature. Teachers' salary increases, state employees' salary raises, additional funding to support the UT Medical School in Memphis, funds to deal with narrow, deficient bridges in the highway system, and a major new emphasis on pressing needs in mental health were among the strong steps forward. I was grateful for the attitude of the General Assembly. They were dedicated to moving ahead beyond old boundaries. Our state enjoyed vast potential for renewal, growth, and competitiveness with sister states. Bold action was a necessary ingredient.

Sound legislation was passed dealing with environmental degradation caused by air and water pollution. Existing standards were widely known to be inadequate. A water quality control act was passed, setting in motion administrative mechanisms that would prove to be of great value in the future.

Legislation was introduced and passed designed to increase penalties for illegal drug dealing and to offer rehabilitation measures. The drug problem was growing in size and complexity.

A non-administration measure was introduced and passed that changed the manner by which state appellate court judges were chosen. The Modified Missouri Plan was a concept designed to improve the caliber and qualifications of future members of the judiciary, according to its sponsors. A nominating commission appointed by the governor and Speakers of both houses would select three nominees for any appellate court vacancy and refer them to the governor. From the three nominated, the governor chose his appointee. If none of the three proposed suited the governor, he could ask for three additional nominees. I approved this new approach, although its opponents believed it would enhance the power of the Democrat-controlled legislature. The attractive feature to me was that the new process removed appellate court judges from the statewide political arena. No longer would candidates for either the Supreme Court or Courts of Appeals be required to run statewide campaigns, soliciting necessary financial contributions and incurring obligations. Rather, at the end of his eight-year term, the judge would appear on the ballot for a yes or no, up or down vote. This process was later to be a controversial issue for me as I attempted to fill a vacancy on the state Supreme Court. There were some who, with justification, questioned the constitutionality of the new law.

Legislatively, the first session of the 87th General Assembly was a success by any measure. My administration, in addition to proposing a positive, constructive agenda, was deeply engaged in preparing major proposals that would necessarily have to wait for the second session, one year away. Seven priority administration bills were proposed and became law the first year. Of the legislative proposals we offered, a total of 79 in all, 47 were passed. The balance was left pending serious attention in the second session.

The new dollars appropriated for education were pivotal. We obtained a $400 average increase in annual teachers' salaries. Substantial funds were dedicated to strengthening higher education, with special emphasis on the needs at the UT Memphis Medical Center, which had been long-suffering and bordering on the loss of official accreditation. Highways, mental health, environmental protection, corrections, and state employees benefited substantially from a state budget with total expenditures amounting to approximately $1,229,000,000 of taxpayers' dollars. I felt we were off to a healthy start, in many instances merely attempting to catch up to reasonable levels, and in some areas taking bold new steps.

The Veto

The governor's veto was a Tennessee executive power rarely used prior to my administration. In the past, with one party fully in charge of the executive and legislative branches, rarely did a bill reach the governor's desk that had not been fully agreed on by all interested parties in both branches of government. As a Republican governor, I found it necessary to put the veto to work, and I did so.

Our Tennessee Constitution requires only a simple majority vote in each house to override a veto. The federal Constitution requires a two-thirds vote of both houses to override. My record of vetoes sustained by Democrat majorities in both houses was mixed.

In May I vetoed a House bill that called for a runoff election in primary races for governor or U.S. senator or representative where there was no clear majority winner. My reasoning was based on the fact that Tennessee had become a two-party state that offered voters a clear-cut choice in general elections. Primary runoffs were no longer necessary. In addition, the expenses of the necessary election process could be avoided. It was a significant veto, and to my surprise, the veto was not overridden. My own experience in the Republican primary election the previous year, in which I won nomination by a plurality, not a majority, of the votes quite likely reinforced my decision to veto.

A Good Idea

The annual Presidential Prayer Breakfast I attended in Washington, D.C., earlier in the year was a good experience and sent a message far beyond its setting in the White House. I asked a staff person to look into my idea that a prayer breakfast sponsored by the governor be held in Nashville during the first session of the legislature. There was no modern precedent, I learned. I directed that plans be made in March for such a breakfast with members of the legislature and other active laypersons to be included in the invitations. Plans went forward. I invited my new friend Jack Williams, the governor of Arizona and a respected Christian layman and news professional, to be our first speaker. He readily accepted.

The first annual Tennessee Governor's Prayer Breakfast took place in mid-March and was attended by people from across the state. A similar breakfast was held in each of the next three years of my administration, and the event has occurred each year since. I valued the fact that legislators, members of my administration, and guests could enjoy time together completely free of political considerations.

A Summit Meeting

While the legislature was still in session it became necessary to deal with a growing problem. The source was Congressman Quillen from the First Congressional District. Jimmy Quillen was causing several members of my staff much distress. He was unhappy with what he considered to be total disregard of his wishes as far as projects and state jobs in his congressional district were concerned. He insisted that a meeting be held somewhere in his district so that he could air his grievances. They were primarily with the Department of Safety and the Highway Department. He requested that I, my immediate staff, and two particular commissioners travel to the First District for a showdown on several major issues as soon as possible. I decided that I had little choice but to give Quillen the opportunity to confront those giving him trouble and to vent his frustrations. A mountain cottage near Gatlinburg was selected as the meeting place, and a time was fixed. It was highly disconcerting to me to have this important congressman so agitated. He was the major political power in his district, and he had been helpful to me in the general election.

The meeting could not have occurred at a more inconvenient time for me. We had major legislative proposals before the General Assembly. I was learning as I went forward, and every moment was stressful. I needed the complete attention of my staff, particularly Smith, Griffith, Young, and Hopper, in dealing with the necessary and the unexpected events of each day. Complicating the entire process was Congressman Quillen with his phone calls from Washington. At the appointed time we traveled to Gatlinburg to meet with this highly vexed congressman.

Joe Hopper told me later that as he arrived for the meeting, parked his car, and headed for the cottage, Quillen drove up and began walking in the same direction. Joe recalled that he said, "Hello, Congressman, glad to see you." Quillen's response was, "Don't lie to me, Hopper!" He was more than a little agitated.

The meeting got underway immediately. The congressman stated that he was completely frustrated in dealing with Joe Hopper, Bill

Russell, and Dale Young, members of my staff. He was also constantly at odds with Commissioner of Safety Claude Armour and Commissioner of Highways Bob Smith. The main subjects involved low license plate awards, state highway jobs, transfers in the Highway Patrol, and failure on our parts to seek his approval of personnel changes in his district. He cited specific examples, and he demanded explanations from the appropriate person for each one of them. Efforts were made to appease the man, and our people were quick to admit their work was not perfect. Claude Armour and Bob Smith, each of whom was a highly capable administrator, were quick to stand their ground and tell the congressman in no uncertain terms that they stood by their decisions and had no apologies to make. It was a tense meeting, perhaps a good example of how difficult it was to get things done the right way and at the same time understand the vested political interests of others. The meeting lasted several hours. As we parted, I was confident little had been accomplished. Quillen was unique among the entire Tennessee congressional delegation. Unfortunately, our relationship would not improve going forward.

Adjournment

The first session of the 87th General Assembly adjourned early in the month of May. I was somewhat surprised at the sense of relief I experienced in realizing that I could freely turn my attention to matters other than dealing directly with legislators. The tension-filled days that seemed the norm while the legislature was in session were in stark contrast to the more reasonable times I began to enjoy as I adjusted to an entirely different daily schedule. The 7:00 a.m. breakfast meetings I routinely held in the smaller dining area just off the Residence kitchen were replaced with quiet and peaceful meals, usually alone and quite early in the morning. The cooks who staffed the kitchen were individuals from the main prison who were transported before daybreak to the Residence. They were good people, for the most part, who chose working directly for the governor rather than spending their days at the prison facility.

Those first few months of my term in office were not without pleasant intervals and interesting experiences. The people of Tennessee continued to treat Betty and me with kindest expressions of affection and good wishes. Our daughters were making a normal transition into a different world. Our son continued his education at Washington and Lee University. He was a good student and a solid young fellow. We paid his tuition, and he earned extra money cooking for his fraternity. We were so proud of him. Betty and I had become good friends with our next-door neighbors, Sarah and Henry Cannon. Sarah was the famous Grand Ole Opry star Minnie Pearl, and we always called her Minnie. They were to become devoted friends as the years went by. We received invitations to social engagements in Nashville, many of which we were able to accept. I continued to make frequent trips by aircraft to various parts of the state, visiting schools or projects, making speeches, and frequently supporting legislative proposals.

Newspapers across the state were, for the most part, fair in reporting the news from the capital. However, the *Jackson Sun* and Nashville *Tennessean* were my most active critics. On two occasions the *Tennessean*, apparently not restrained by the tradition of reporting news objectively, wrote critical articles that were grossly inaccurate and designed to demean me. In one instance I received a very apologetic telephone call from the editor, John Seigenthaler. He was, in my opinion, embarrassed. In the other instance, I received a personal visit from the same gentleman in my office, once again very apologetic and embarrassed over the inaccuracies reported. I must admit I enjoyed each conversation.

A Close Call

Early in January I had received an invitation to address a joint session of the Mississippi state legislature in Jackson, Mississippi. This was an honor and an opportunity I had never considered. What a courteous gesture from my home state! I was overjoyed with the opportunity.

The invitation was accepted with full consideration of my obligations while our Tennessee legislature was in session. On February 21 Betty and I boarded the state's King Air plane with Colonel Bill Pickron at the controls. We were accompanied by Lieutenant John White who headed the governor's security detail. It was a cloudy winter day as we departed the airport and were soon flying toward

Mississippi's capital city. The plane reached cruising altitude, and everything seemed to be in order. I was reading a newspaper, Betty was reading, and Lieutenant White, sitting beside us, was his usually alert self. At some point over Alabama, a memorable, totally unexpected event occurred.

An incredibly loud explosion sounded and seemed to come from the area of the cockpit. The airplane shuddered severely and just as quickly stabilized. I looked at Betty and John White, both of whom were wide-eyed. I glanced toward Colonel Pickron, who in turn was looking back at us. He said we had been hit by lightning and then advised us that we had lost all radio contact. He began to look for the best location to land the aircraft. Coincidentally, we were near my hometown of Meridian, Mississippi, and it was there we landed. An examination of the King Air showed a large bite-sized part of the left wing trailing edge had been burned away, all the external radio antennae on the plane's underbody had been blown away, and many of the wing rivets had been melted into the metal they were securing.

Our pilot ordered another airplane to take us on to Jackson while John White reported in to his immediate boss, Commissioner Armour, regarding the event and our safety. Betty commented that she wouldn't mind riding a bus back home, and our sturdy trooper volunteered to provide security on her trip. We summoned some courage and continued on. We realized that we had suffered a close call and were grateful to have landed safely. John White said later that he was amazed that I calmly continued to read my newspaper after recovering from the initial shock of the lightning jolt. I replied that I was probably frozen into that position and the newspaper was my crutch. The King Air was later flown to a Beechcraft service center for a total examination and safety check.

We flew on to Jackson where I had the privilege of being met by Governor Bill Waller and the two legislative Speakers. It was a high point of my life to address the joint session of my native state's General Assembly. We were warmly received and made welcome. As in many of life's rich experiences, standing in the state capitol building before elected representatives and senators from across the state, I felt the moments came and went all too swiftly. I savored the time as best I could. Later in the day, we returned to Nashville tired and thankful for our safety on such an eventful day during which we were close to a tragedy that passed us by.

A National Governors Association Winter Meeting

The first of four National Governors Association's Winter Conferences offered a pleasant diversion prior to legislative adjournment. Betty and I, along with members of my staff, made arrangements to attend the conference in Washington, D.C. It was a grand event designed to showcase the nation's governors conferring about significant issues and opportunities that cut across state lines.

Among the major issues was that of federal revenue sharing with the states. Senator Howard Baker was a strong proponent of this idea. For too long, I had begun to learn, the federal government was guilty of enacting unfunded legislative mandates that states found it impractical or impossible to fund from state tax revenues. Such programs frequently failed to measure up in terms of priority but were often attractive. Tennessee was a good example of a state that simply did not have excess revenue to spend. I strongly supported some degree of federal funding in order to participate in constructive activities most often devoted to social and economic welfare.

The conference convened at a large downtown hotel. Two plenary sessions were devoted to the business of the organization and to major issues. At the first session a report of a Nominating Committee was offered proposing new leaders for the ensuing year. To my surprise and delight, I received a phone call earlier in the day stating that I had been selected to be among the nominees to the Executive Committee. This group would work with the new chairman on appropriate conference business. Following the report of the Nominating Committee, a vote was called, and the election was unanimous. I was certainly pleased to be more involved.

The highlight of the conference was a state dinner hosted by President and Mrs. Nixon at the White House on Saturday evening. We, of course, had never attended such a function. At the appointed time, Betty and I were driven onto the White House grounds where we were greeted by handsomely attired military personnel. We were escorted into a reception room in which the governors and their wives were gathering. It was a thrill to be inside the nation's first residence where everything in sight, from furnishings to artwork to floral arrangements, was, to be sure, not only authentic but assuredly the very best in every instance. The White House was, and remains, a remarkable symbol of our great nation.

In due time, the governors and their ladies were requested to line up in order of statehood admission into the Union. We were to proceed to an entryway just outside one of the large rooms. Everyone was quite naturally excited. As Betty and I stood in the sixteenth position, I was very proud of the beautiful woman at my side clothed in a glittering gown that made her stand out among all the others. I wore a tuxedo. Soon we moved forward when signaled by an attendant for whom this affair was simply one of many that took place at the White House.

As we approached the dining area, I saw that each preceding governor and his first lady presented themselves to an elegantly attired Marine Corps officer standing near the president, who waited to receive his guests. A military orchestra in the background played delightful music. It was an enchanting time. When our turn came, I introduced us to the aide as Governor and Mrs. Dunn of Tennessee. He turned and announced our names to the president. Mr. Nixon offered his hand warmly. I trust he remembered that we had met on several prior occasions. We shook hands, and as that occurred, the president of the United States said, "Ah, Governor Dunn," opening his mouth quite widely and pointing with his left index finger at his upper molar teeth. He chuckled as he did so, obviously quite proud that he remembered I was by professional training a dentist. Quite surprised by his greeting, I turned and presented Betty. He was most gracious in his welcome to her. We moved along, next shaking hands with our nation's first lady, Pat Nixon. She was a warm and welcoming person.

As we moved down the reception line composed mainly of members of the president's cabinet, we were directed toward our table. I remained slightly puzzled by the president's greeting. I was somewhat disappointed, thinking that it would have been more appropriate and certainly more reassuring to me if he had made some favorable comment about Tennessee or asked an interesting question about the affairs of my state. After all, he must surely have been aware that Tennessee had carried the day for him in the election of 1968. Instead, he pointed to his teeth! *Oh, well,* I thought, *at least he remembered something personal about me.*

The evening was memorable for more than one reason. The meal was beautifully served and quite delicious. Following dinner there were remarks by the president and a response from the chairman of the National Governors Association. It was an impressive occasion. The next morning we returned to Nashville. I valued meeting governors from across our land. It was a good experience. One, in particular, became a favorite of mine. He was Calvin Rampton, governor of Utah, a Democrat and very intelligent man. He and I would later serve on several committees, giving us an opportunity to become better acquainted.

Life at the Governor's Residence

We returned to Tennessee with good memories of our first NGA conference. Many demands of my office awaited me. About that time my wife had become convinced that attention needed to be given to the décor at the governor's Residence. With the assistance of an experienced and talented friend named Rupen Gulbenk, she proceeded to initiate the creation of a private foundation to receive gifts of money and furnishings reflecting the heritage of our state. The Tennessee Executive Residence Foundation became a reality. This activity captured the attention and interest of many Tennesseans who realized the lasting value, as well as the practical utility, of upgrading the Residence's appearance. The impressions Betty received when we visited the governor's Residence in Frankfort, Kentucky, inspired my wife. Mrs. Beulah Nunn, wife of the governor, had made a variety of positive changes in that state's official Residence. Our new foundation, once established, flourished, and it has served the state well.

Mr. Gulbenk brought to Betty's attention the fact that a rare and valuable portrait from life of Andrew Jackson by Samuel L. Waldo done in 1817 was to be auctioned in Washington, D.C. A flurry of activity resulted in the directors of the Potter Foundation of Nashville committing to providing my wife an opportunity to attend the auction and bid for the portrait. Mr. and Mrs. David K. Wilson and Mr. and Mrs. Albert Menefee were generous benefactors who represented the Potter Foundation. They were as anxious as Rupen and Betty to obtain that historic work of art.

Arriving in Washington, Betty and her party were soon at the auction site. I am told they were most anxious and apprehensive. Eventually, bidding commenced on the Jackson portrait. It was an exciting time for my wife. She found herself in a bidding contest with one gentleman. As the dollar amount of the bidding grew to serious proportions, she later stated that she became very nervous. With encouragement from Gulbenk and Mr. Menefee, who said he would nudge Betty when she should bid, she countered each bid until finally the other bidder withdrew, and *sold* was the magic word. Betty stood, and the gallery broke into applause. The magnificent portrait of President Jackson became a prized possession of the citizens of Tennessee. The gentleman who had been bidding against Betty introduced himself. He was Clem Conger, curator for the White House. Mr. Conger stated that, although he very much wanted the portrait for the White House, he was pleased that Andrew Jackson was going home to Tennessee. The portrait of Jackson now hangs in our state Residence.

Another positive contribution by Tennessee's first lady was her initiative to open the governor's Residence to visitors on selected days of the week. A group of eager Nashville ladies was organized by our good friend Jan Scantlebury to act as docents on visitation days. It was an exciting and well-organized effort to personalize objects of curiosity for the visitors—namely, the first family of the state and its official Residence. Tours of the first floor and the attractively land-scaped grounds became a popular happening for Nashville residents and visitors to the city. It was even more exciting for visitors on those occasions when my wife found time to personally welcome them. Our volunteer docents became skilled at knowing the historical significance of many items of furniture and décor. They enjoyed sharing that information with guests. I was very proud of Betty's contributions. Her responsibilities were demanding across a wide variety of activities. She did a beautiful job.

There was never a dull moment. One Sunday morning as we drove toward the Residence following church services, we were notified by radio from the Residence that we were to avoid approaching its front entrance. Rather, we were to exit our car and enter through the kitchen. The reason given for this unusual procedure was that an agitated visitor was being detained in the reception area. We were asked by security personnel to proceed to our normal living quarters on the second floor. The downstairs area had become "locked down." The trooper in charge gave me a briefing. I was told that my wife's hairdresser had been admitted through the secured gate off the street as scheduled. Immediately behind her another car had cleared the gate, unknown to our security people. The hairdresser was admitted to the Residence, as was one man walking close behind her. He identified himself as one who had been seeking state employment without success and had reached a point of frustration that led him to want to see the governor personally. That was his reason for the visit. As he was pacing the floor, prior to our arrival from church, he had blurted out to a trooper that he might as well give up what he had in his briefcase. He then opened the bag he was carrying and produced a loaded pistol that he immediately surrendered. There was never any actual danger, but the event made it clear that security measures were inadequate. Later, surveillance cameras were installed and were monitored from within the Residence. No information about the incident was released to the news media. My wife was not satisfied until the security desk manned by a uniformed trooper was removed from the front entrance area to another less conspicuous location in the building. That move was made possible by the installation of security cameras. For the first time since the Residence became the official dwelling place of the governor, an unsightly desk and uniformed trooper no longer greeted every visitor. It was a pleasant change and the result of Betty's insistence and my support for the changes that occurred.

A Call to Memphis

Later in the year a call from Memphis law enforcement agents to my office captured my immediate attention. I was advised that state revenue agents seeking to collect back taxes from the proprietor of a dry cleaning establishment were being held hostage at gunpoint by the owner inside the dry cleaning business. The hostage taker was threatening the agents and demanding to see the governor personally. This standoff had been in progress for several hours, we were told, and the situation was considered dangerous.

Hearing those facts, I decided to go to Memphis immediately. Using the state airplane, we arrived in the vicinity of the dry cleaning shop within two hours. Meeting the local police and state troopers who had been called to the scene, we received a complete briefing. Telephone contact with the suspect was ongoing. I used the phone to talk directly to the shop owner holding the revenue agent. After an extended conversation in which I refused to meet him personally until he surrendered his weapon and released his hostage, he agreed to that. Within minutes he emerged from his business and surrendered to police. His hostage was free to go. A short while later I entered a local motel nearby where the suspect had been taken. I met the man, shook his hand, and satdown to talk about his problems. He told me he had a troubled business, had become delinquent in paying his taxes and, upon being confronted by the two revenue agents, had become frantic. He pulled his weapon from a drawer, threatened both men, then forced one of the two agents to undress and leave the building completely unclothed. Shortly, police arrived at the scene, and the encounter continued.

After a full discussion during which I listened carefully to the desperate man and promised the prisoner he would be given every consideration as he owned up to whatever punishment for his acts was appropriate, I left. Members of my staff were not happy with my decision to go to Memphis, but when the event was over, everyone agreed that it was a satisfactory outcome. Later reports were that the fellow was treated fairly in every respect, though I never learned to what degree he was punished by law.

Puerto Rico

The annual midyear meeting of the National Governors Conference in 1971 was to be held in San Juan, Puerto Rico. Plans were made by my staff to attend, and I requested that the arrangements include my wife and daughters on the trip to such a unique location. I was made aware that an Air National Guard aircraft assigned to the Operation Airlift Center had been modified by Governor Frank Clement with an interior that would accommodate a substantial number of passengers. We decided to invite members of my staff and representatives of the state press desiring to attend the conference to travel aboard the airplane. A substantial group of approximately thirty persons signed up for the trip. The group met on the appointed day, and we were soon on our way to the Caribbean.

We were an excited group, but no one was more enthused than our nine-year-old daughter, Julie. She was lively and entertaining. Members of the news media were fascinated by the young lady. Her presence and antics very likely made the long flight seem not quite so tedious. One member of the press corps, a fun-loving woman named Drue Smith, seemed especially enthralled with Julie. They became fast friends.

As our craft landed and taxied to a stop, we were immediately surrounded by equally excited representatives of the governor of the islands. Our passengers quickly departed to separate destinations. My family was taken in tow by no less than five special agents of the governor and transported to our hotel. None of my family had been in this location, and we were in awe as we enjoyed the scenery en route.

Activities immediately were underway to assure the conference's success and the visitors' pleasure. Our daughters, Gayle and Julie, were caught up in many activities designed to entertain family members of the governors. I did not see either of the girls again until we were preparing to leave the islands several days later. My schedule was full, and Betty's activities were carefully orchestrated to blend in with those of other wives.

Several meetings of the Executive Committee were held as expected. Two principal subjects dealt with general revenue sharing and the Federal Highway Trust Fund. Several members of the president's cabinet addressed our group. The meetings were substantive, and the general arrangements for food and entertainment were memorable. I recall one private luncheon for the governors at which the press and staff were excluded. Seated at a table with several other governors, including Nelson Rockefeller of New York, I was surprised, then intrigued, as I watched the fabled Rockefeller reach out, take asparagus stalks from his salad plate, and deliver them to his mouth by hand. No fork was put in play. Later I questioned that conduct in relating it to my wife. To my amazement, she advised me that the governor's table manners were quite appropriate.

As time drew near to conclude the conference, everyone agreed it had been a memorable experience. At our final meeting prior to departure in the afternoon, a message was received from the White House inviting the National Governors Conference Executive Committee to a briefing on the nation's economy by President Nixon and members of his cabinet the following day in Washington. To ease the logistical problem, the president ordered his aircraft, Air Force One, to San Juan that afternoon to transport the committee to Washington. I was pleased with those prospects and immediately decided to participate. I was permitted one security person to accompany me, along with other governors and their aides.

Imagine my mixed emotions when I met Betty after the conference adjourned and explained to her what had occurred. While I regretted leaving her and the children, the awesome prospects of what lay immediately ahead made it easier to part company with the happy group that had journeyed together to the islands. Word quickly spread to the Tennessee news media, and I was even more pleased that we had invited them to travel with us. I was later told that, just prior to my family and friends boarding the aircraft for a flight back to Tennessee, an official car drove up and two of the Puerto Rican agents who had been responsible for Julie's and Gayle's safety presented Julie with a gunny sack containing two fighting cocks. A flurry of excitement followed, during which an effort was made by the commander and pilot of the aircraft to explain, first to Julie, why she couldn't accept the generous gift of birds and, second to the agents of the governor, that the rules of the day prevented the transport of such animals across governmental boundaries. The birds were a birthday gift to Julie, who no doubt had expressed her interest in such birds at some point. I was told that events soon became more normal and that our Tennessee group had a happy trip home. Betty was relieved that she did not have to make a decision regarding those birds.

Meanwhile, John White, my security man, and I were making plans to join others aboard Air Force One. It was a thrilling experience to drive up and see that magnificent aircraft gleaming in the sunlight. The words *The United States of America* on its fuselage never looked so beautiful. We were escorted aboard and assigned seats for the flight to Washington. I am sure John White, assigned to a different part of the airplane, was having many positive thoughts at that moment. Soon we were underway. As Air Force One lifted off the runway, my thoughts turned to Betty, the children, and our many friends aboard the National Guard airplane, which by then was lumbering through the sky headed toward Nashville. I wished they could have savored my feelings aboard the most important airplane in the world.

While in flight, a smartly uniformed member of the crew invited me forward to the president's conference room. Soon I was seated at an attractive round table in the company of several other governors. Each one of us was enjoying a first-time experience, and no one hesitated to express his awe. There was a variety of souvenirs available to take away. I was told a telephone on the table was available for me to make any call, anywhere, I might wish to make. I immediately took the phone in hand and placed a call to my secretary, Lucretia McDonald, at the capitol in Nashville. She had been advised of my change in schedule, but she was appropriately surprised when I spoke to her from Air Force One flying high over the Caribbean. It was a heady experience for me and other passengers.

I was told we would be landing at Andrews Air Force Base outside Washington. That would be another unique experience. I had always used Washington National Airport. As we were escorted off Air Force One, what should be awaiting each governor but a splendidly uniformed Marine Corps officer to serve as escort across the apron of concrete to a beautiful green Marine helicopter referred to as Marine Corps One. I was not prepared for that surge of excitement, but I adjusted. I was seated and strapped in across from another governor, and we lifted off and gained altitude, flying over the city and viewing sights I had never enjoyed before that time. We were advised by a crew member that the helicopter would land at the Pentagon where automobile transportation to the White House would be waiting. The Pentagon! I had never seen the place. Soon we two governors were seated in our limousine and rapidly weaving our way across the remaining distance to the White House. I would be less than honest if I failed to say that, in those moments, I began to hear the strains of "Hail to the Chief" in my mind. What an experience! I was feeling a surge of importance totally unwarranted but understandable.

The limousine breezed through the White House gates without the usual mandatory stop and identification procedure. We pulled up under a portico and were greeted by a very businesslike female aide.

We were directed down a hallway and to the left to directly enter the Cabinet Room. As I strode along as directed, I must again admit I was feeling very important. Upon entering the Cabinet Room, I noted the only person present was a familiar figure, the vice president of the United States, the Honorable Spiro Agnew, whom I had met on several occasions. I promptly said, "Hello, Mr. Vice President." His immediate response was, "Hello, Wendell!" When I heard the name Wendell instead of the expected Winfield, I was immediately deflated. A sensation of reality hit me, and I felt my knees buckle. I suddenly came back down to earth, stunned with the awareness that such an important man, whom I was approaching on an almost equal basis, didn't know my name! The wind suddenly left my sail, and I took my seat where I was quickly joined by others arriving.

What a buildup and what an unanticipated letdown! Later, I was slightly relieved to learn that Governor Wendell Anderson of Minnesota was behind me as I entered the Cabinet Room, and it was him to whom the vice president directed his hello. That helped me rationalize the situation, but it wasn't totally healing because what it told me was that the vice president didn't respond at all to my hello! I no longer heard "Hail to the Chief" in my mind, and that was as it should have been all along.

The governors received a thorough briefing on the state of the national economy from the president and several high-level advisers. After a short question-and-answer session, the president left, and we soon were on our separate ways out of the White House. I recall that, shortly after leaving the Cabinet Room and as I passed a stairwell, up the last few steps bounded a familiar face. It was Secretary of State Henry Kissinger, moving rapidly along with what appeared to be his personal dry cleaning slung over his shoulder. My, my! I had had a full day, and I was ready to return to Nashville. Colonel Pickron met us at the National Airport, and we were soon on our way to Nashville aboard the state's airplane.

A full calendar of events including more conferences, meetings, short trips, and endless appointments consumed our time as the year moved along. I received reports from Dr. Rachels that his committee studying our prospects for economic and community development was making progress. I was assured the completed report would be in my hands at year-end.

Ceremonial

In April I attended a dedication ceremony at one of the state's most unique parks. Fall Creek Falls State Park had received substantial federal funds under a program designed to enhance economic activity in depressed regions. New facilities and roads had been added. Governor Ellington deserved credit for the program, but I became the fortunate governor who cut the ribbon on opening day. I received undeserved compliments for an excellent addition to the state park system. Fall Creek Falls State Park soon thereafter became a place where my family and I could take refuge from the torrid schedule of events in Nashville. We used it often and continue to enjoy entertaining many friends there. Long walks, visits to Buzzard's Roost Overlook, fishing, good food, and blessed quiet, along with fun and games, made Fall Creek a special part of our lives.

Also in April, I traveled west to Pickwick Landing State Park in Hardin County. This trip was to dedicate a new golf course and additions to the lodge. As at Fall Creek Falls, it was a very special day when the governor paid a visit. I was directed to the first tee at the golf course where a large group had gathered. Local officials were present, as was my commissioner of conservation, responsible for our park system. After numerous appropriate remarks and requests for pictures to be made by the media, it was suggested that a popular musician, Porter Wagoner, and I be photographed hitting a few balls off the first tee. I had never met the famous Mr. Wagoner, but we quickly became comfortable and each of us hit golf balls. As we finished, some member of Wagoner's band shouted out that we should let Dolly hit a few balls. Porter chuckled and gave his approval. A petite blonde stepped forward, smiling and allowing as how she didn't know how to hit a golf ball. Quickly, help was offered, and in no time the little lady, dressed in a pink double knit suit and very high-heeled shoes, was flailing away at a golf ball. It was quite a sight to see. The audience howled, and the photographers snapped away. That was my introduction to Miss Dolly Parton, who was later to become a world-famous mega-star entertainer and champion for Tennessee.

Back at the capitol I was enjoying the newly refurbished office that had been converted from a large conference room in the governor's quarters. There was now room enough to receive reasonably large delegations of visitors. I had asked to borrow from the state museum a portrait of President Abraham Lincoln. It was hung prominently on the wall behind my desk, and I was pleased at how often Lincoln and I appeared jointly in newspaper photos. Among my most pleasant visitors were busloads of schoolchildren being introduced to their state capitol building. The young folks were such happy guests, and they seemed to enjoy seeing where a governor worked. Occasionally, a little tyke would lean close to my ear and let me know that his or her mother and daddy voted for me. Along with that statement would be a proud little smile.

A variety of delegations, too numerous to mention, came to my office unceasingly to receive proclamations and various awards. On one occasion the Dairymen's Association appeared for me to present a proclamation praising the value of milk. I was asked outside for photographs with the 1971 Dairy Princess. I met the Princess and was then introduced to a beautiful little Hereford calf. The calf was bashful and balked. The Princess was more cooperative. When all photos had been taken, the meeting concluded. As the calf was being led away, I asked if it was true, as I had been told, that the calf was a present for me. The answer was yes, but the assumption was that the governor would have no interest in the animal. I asked if they would take the beautiful little creature to the Residence because I wanted to give it to my daughter Julie. It was love at first sight. Julie named the calf Buckalena because it liked to run and buck. A convenient fenced-in area behind the garages was made to order. The two of them had a great relationship until, one year later, now a full grown cow, Buckalena was delivered to the Ellington Agricultural Center's grounds where she continued to enjoy a good life.

The days passed rapidly. Betty anticipated the coming Christmas season. She was anxious to have a memorable Christmas card representing the first family. She turned to a talented and successful Memphis artist, Dolph Smith. He responded in due time with a beautiful landscape in watercolor of the official Residence and grounds. That rendering graced the front of our official Christmas card and was well received across the state.

As we approached the end of my first year in office, I was satisfied that the administration was competently addressing the business of the government. I was particularly pleased with our legislative proposals, both those enacted into law and those that in the future would be dealt with by the second session of the 87th General Assembly. I was equally pleased with the performances of my staff and cabinet members. Having so little state government experience to guide them, each person was highly productive and ethical beyond reproach.

The legislature being no longer in session, I devoted a large amount of my time to getting ready for the second session. I believed that the economy would continue to flourish and that state revenues would permit positive adjustments in existing programs and new initiatives to be considered by both houses. Nineteen seventy-two would be a presidential election year. Plans were being made with our Republican Party leaders to be prepared. Ron Rietdorf and Chairman Kopie Kopald were fully engaged building our party across the state in anticipation of legislative and congressional races plus a presidential contest. I planned to campaign for legislative candidates where appropriate. It was a comfort to know the second session would be completed in the spring before campaigning began in earnest. Major legislative proposals on my agenda for the following year made it important that I not create excessive resentment with members of the other party.

Our First Christmas as the First Family

With the arrival of our first opportunity to celebrate the Christmas season as governor and first lady, we made the most of that occasion. We attended a number of parties in Nashville where we were warmly received by our new neighbors. A stately Christmas tree was in place in the Residence reception area. Decorations permitted the Residence to sparkle for the season. Presents in bright wrappings graced the tree, and all those in the immediate staff of the Residence were remembered. We hosted a gala Christmas party for members of my cabinet and their families. To our surprise and great pleasure, the cabinet members collectively gave Betty and me handsome wristwatches that we have treasured down through the years. It was a happy time for my entire family.

CHAPTER THIRTY

SECOND SESSION, 87TH GENERAL ASSEMBLY

Many Opportunities

In preparation for a productive second session, arrangements were made in January to take a large group of legislators aboard two chartered buses on a tour of state facilities and projects that were of special interest to us all. My idea was to try something unique to gain the attention of the lawmakers. Nothing of this nature had ever been attempted. There was ample publicity given to the project, and many members of the legislature signed up to participate.

On the appointed morning with two large buses fully loaded, following a press conference at which every legislator was given good media exposure, we began our journey. During the following two days, we visited a major mental health facility, sheltered workshops for mentally disabled and economically deprived people, a community college, a series of farm to market roads in need of major repair, dangerous automobile bridges, an interstate highway under construction, and a public school kindergarten class. Other sights and stops along the way were inspected. I spent time on each bus. The central thought on which the bus trip was based dealt with the dramatic change that had occurred in the important business of managing our state government. No longer would an all-powerful governor call every shot working with a legislative majority of his own party. The time had come for mutual understanding and cooperation in identifying problems and opportunities. Bipartisan unity was necessary if we were to maximize our potential to successfully govern. At the end of the second day as we returned to the capitol parking area, the number of legislators was much smaller than when we had started a day earlier. The tour was worth the energy and time spent. Although quite a bit of partisan grumbling was heard along the way, I was satisfied our trip together benefited all who participated. There was no shortage of opportunities to consider. By working together, many good things could be accomplished for the people.

State of the State, 1972

A major address to members of the press statewide was made on January 21 in keeping with traditions of the past. My remarks were upbeat, reflecting the optimism and sense of progress I felt based on a productive first year in office. The results of the study on controlling costs in state government were positive and substantial with approximately 40 percent of the report's recommendations having been implemented. We were developing strong central government management improvements in the areas of data processing, printing, motor vehicle management, and food service, among others. I noted major reorganization reforms that would be proposed to the General Assembly, among them a Department of Transportation, a new structure for governance of higher education, and major modifications in state planning that would offer a meaningful long-range development process.

In addition to bringing the news people up to date on progress across the broad range of state programs ongoing, I offered insights into the budget I would soon be presenting to the legislature. Two top priority items dealt with water pollution control and surface mining damage. Another excellent prospect was the creation of a Housing Development Agency that we felt would begin a process of overcoming the shortage of safe, decent, and sanitary housing in our state. A no-fault insurance program designed to halt the spiraling cost of automobile insurance and promote the prompt payment of claims was another initiative. I stated the obvious truth that state governments were entering a period of financial stress. Federal revenue-sharing proposals had fallen on deaf ears in the national Congress. I stressed the importance of federal government's continued confidence in the basic role of state and local governments to continue to be the dependable vehicles by which essential services are delivered to citizens.

I noted that the tax structure of Tennessee, both state and local, fell disproportionately on the poor, the elderly, and others on fixed income. Plans had been made to propose to the legislature authorization for me to appoint a tax reform and modernization study commission. The idea was to make an in-depth study of our state revenue system and to offer suggestions as to alternative means for obtaining necessary tax dollars on a more equitable basis than existed at the present time. I planned to ask Dr. Ed Boling, president of the University of Tennessee and a former commissioner of finance and administration under Clement and Ellington, to chair the effort.

I reviewed a number of accomplishments and many of my aspirations for progress in the ensuing years. My closing words reflected enthusiasm and desire to have the support and participation of those representing all the important news outlets that served our state. Nothing occupied a higher priority than action to build a better Tennessee.

The Second Budget Message, Fiscal Year 1973

On February 21 I addressed an assembly of both houses of the legislature. The centerpiece of my message was a proposed budget requiring no tax increases in order to be fully funded. I outlined my administration's priority program goals and noted the improvement funds necessary for their implementation.

My first year as governor had given me greater awareness of our mutual responsibilities, and I wanted to be certain the lawmakers knew that my first year had been a tremendous learning experience. My assembled cabinet, to a person, were moving into the new year with fresh insights, not only in their areas of expertise, but in the process of working cooperatively with legislators to achieve goals of mutual interest. We were a team poised to serve the people effectively and efficiently. I expressed my gratitude for advice and admonitions of members from both parties within the General Assembly.

I quickly acknowledged that we had not achieved all that we hoped for in the first year but that progressive action in the executive and legislative branches had enabled significant advances to be realized. In the areas of drug abuse, public kindergarten, improvements in our mental health facilities and correctional program, along with upgrading the state's pollution activities, we were able to demonstrate solid progress. Funds appropriated had enabled children in 248 classes across the state to attend public kindergarten. The new drug abuse act had given Tennessee one of the finest laws in the nation. At the current rate approximately seven thousand people would receive drug and alcohol treatment as a result of funds made available for fiscal 1972. We were surely moving in the right direction across all fronts. This was made possible by the legislature's willingness in the first session to seek added revenue.

I reported progress in the internal management of the government. Much of this was a direct result of the Study on Cost Control. The centralization of many administrative services was proving to be both effective and efficient. I indicated I would request authority to reorganize the present activities of the Highway Department, the Aeronautics Commission, and an urban mass transit unit into a Department of Transportation. I stressed the need for additional funds to support the planning and administration of a new Department of Economic and Community Development, involving the consolidation of multiple functions then spread too broadly across the governing process. A single administrative head of these services would be much more effective. I requested legislation creating a new governing body for regional universities and community colleges. A Board of Regents could assure balanced growth among the institutions and free the state Board of Education to focus essentially on kindergarten, elementary, and secondary education along with its responsibilities for vocational and technical institutes.

The budget message was all-inclusive, mentioning new initiatives and items of unfinished business in the current year. Most of government's activities involved providing services to the general population. The extraordinary needs of those deprived or distressed in society—the young, the old, the mentally ill, the criminal elements, those with special needs for social services such as citizens who were mentally disabled, blind, or deaf—demanded our particular concerns. In those areas I requested improvement budgets. The state Medicaid program was already consuming more dollars than those appropriated. Our University of Tennessee Medical Units in Memphis were in dire need of added funds for upgrading to meet accreditation standards. A well-thought-out program to expand the reach of medical education by adding to its capacity for clinical training of physicians in various areas of the state needed tax dollar support. The Tri-Cities area would benefit significantly from senior medical students training in that area in yet to be established satellite primary care centers and hospitals. Other areas of the state would likewise benefit. Additionally, I asked for money to establish a loan program for needy medical students with a plan to forgive the debt, provided the new physicians chose to locate in a medical shortage area of the state. Additional funds were needed for capital improvements in correctional facilities. I requested authorization for funds to initiate a system of regional correctional centers across the state, which would serve local government needs as well as those of the Department of Corrections.

Legislation would be submitted to improve occupational safety and health in the workplace. New dollars were requested to assist local governments in meeting environmental standards related to sanitary landfills. Mental health, certainly a high priority item of state responsibility, stood in need of capital funds for expansion and improvements. Our Tennessee roots remained firmly planted in the soil and should be nurtured by added funding for services in that sector with emphasis on dairy, food, and drug inspection programs. Our welfare services would be enhanced by new state dollars to be matched by federal funds in programs to care for displaced children. My message noted a directive sent to state agencies emphasizing employment opportunities for minorities.

The importance of our rapidly developing network of highways and interstate roads was stressed, and a request was made to employ innovative financing mechanisms to improve the rate of construction, repair, and means for reducing the death rate by auto accident.

It was my intention as a part of reorganization to create a Department of General Services that would incorporate the existing Department of Standards and Purchases, the Division of Surplus Property from the Department of Education, and the Divisions of Printing, Motor Vehicle Management, Personal Property Management, and Public Works from the Department of Finance and Administration. A new division of Food Service Management would be created as well. Howard Kesley, formerly a successful corporate executive, was the highly capable commissioner who would administer the new department. He was fortunate to have excellent personnel who remained to serve in my administration.

These recommendations and others were the heart of my message. I was grateful that the state economy had been sufficiently progressive to allow my requests and proposals to be positively dealt with. I felt it was a balanced approach to addressing problems and opportunities in the coming year. There were highlights within the otherwise routine message that would warrant the most serious consideration of the General Assembly.

My plans for fiscal year 1973 included requests for funds to implement the following priorities:

• For education, $2 million to continue expansion of the public kindergarten program, $1.6 million for special education, $7 million to support an average $200 annual salary increase under the Minimum Foundation Program, $0.4 million to establish a program of industrial training, and a $3 million capital bond authorization to expand and improve vocational education facilities.

• For higher education, a $14 million overall increase for various institutions, a $39.8 million capital improvements item, and an increase of $1.6 million for the University of Tennessee Medical Units.

• For the Department of Corrections, a $5 million capital authorization to initiate a system of regional corrections centers.

• For conservation, $100,000 for surface mining reclamation and $500,000 for staffing and support to open new state parks.

• For mental health, $2.8 million for program and staffing improvements at all mental health institutions, $2.8 million from current appropriations and $1.35 million for major maintenance and improvements at existing facilities, and a $5.5 million bond authorization for expansion and improvements in the community mental health and retardation centers.

• For the Department of Highways, an additional $3.5 million for bridge widening and replacement.

These were historically high dollar requests, and I expected challenges from various legislative committees. In some instances, specific dollar amounts were negotiated, but the overall dollar total was to be approved. We were living in demanding and changing times.

Total expenditures of funds from all sources, state revenues and reserves as well as federal funds, totaled nearly $1.4 billion. That figure represented an increase of approximately $150 million over the fiscal 1972 budget.

My second budget message, at its conclusion, was greeted with warm applause. Only time would reveal the degree of success that would be realized beyond the warmth of the moment. I was fully satisfied with the proposals contained in my message.

Results: Second Session, 87th General Assembly

Once again the administration staff people performed superbly, their efforts noticeably enhanced by the experience gained in the previous year. Republican legislative leaders effectively built bridges of understanding with members of the other party, learning to give without surrender in most instances and reaching acceptable compromises when necessary. Ralph Griffith played a key role by being an effective adviser to me and an agreeable intermediary with the news media. Only two of the state's major newspapers continued to manage their news and editorial policies on an adversarial basis. All other news outlets were highly professional with some going so far as to emphasize a friendly and supportive attitude. For that I was grateful because I tended to monitor what was printed and broadcast rather closely. M. Lee Smith, counsel to the governor, was increasingly talented in his very special area of responsibility.

The General Assembly granted a request for an additional $2 million to continue expansion of the kindergarten program. As a result nearly sixteen thousand additional students would be absorbed by our public school system in school year 1972–73. At five years of age, these children were rapidly growing away from their most critical formative years. Their needs were great.

My proposal for a no-fault automobile insurance program failed to receive adequate support. It was in conflict with another no-fault bill sponsored by two Democrat senators who were closely aligned with the general insurance business in the state and the Trial Lawyers Association. The opposing bill was passed. I exercised the veto and it was sustained. In a public statement I requested the legislature to take a closer look at my proposal for possible action in the next General Assembly. I was disappointed in the failure to gain the necessary support for what we offered.

Our Tennessee surface mining bill became law, opening the way for significant improvements in techniques used for surface mining of coal and reclamation. This was a major advance that would start a needed program to restore naturalness to mountain areas that had over many years been defaced and left with gaping wounds. The magnificent natural beauty of the state had been sorely treated, and it was a benefit to every Tennessean that it be healed.

The sum of $5 million was earmarked for capital funds to begin implementation of plans for a regional prison system. This progressive move was possible because of a federal matching funds program accessed through the national Law Enforcement Assistance Agency. The first two prison centers were to be located in Hamilton County and the Tri-Cities area. The central idea was to have facilities into which convicted first-time offenders, among others, could be placed. An ongoing state tragedy was that such first-timers often were sent to institutions far from home, thus making it practically impossible for family and community ties to be maintained. Young offenders were often cast into populations of seasoned, hardened criminals at existing prisons. Also, these new facilities were to serve nearby hard-pressed local government jails, which were overpopulated. It was a sound and progressive concept.

The General Assembly approved administration plans and provided funds to create a Department of Transportation, a Department of Economic and Community Development, a Department of General Services, and a state Planning Office within the governor's office. A state Board of Regents was authorized in response to a study and recommendations by a commission I appointed and chaired by Nelson Andrews of Nashville. Governance of higher education for regional universities and community colleges in Tennessee took a big step forward. In the process, a long festering competition between the University of Tennessee system, the regional college group, and the growing number of community colleges regarding funding was smoothed over, if not healed. The Commission on Higher Education, created during the last Ellington administration, had contributed positively to that situation prior to the establishment of the Board of Regents.

The legislature passed our proposal to issue $100 million in short-term notes by which acceleration of our highway development program could take place. Ninety percent of those notes would be retired with Federal Highway Trust Fund dollars available in the future. We also passed a proposed bill regulating the placement of highway billboards. This act passed despite intensive lobbying by the billboard industry. To have failed in the effort would have resulted in loss of 10 percent of Federal Highway Trust Funds. This was in keeping with the requirements of the Federal Highway Beautification Act.

A genuine sore spot for me and for Republicans generally was legislation passed to redistrict state legislative and congressional representation based on the federal census of 1970. Our state Constitution required such action each decade following a census. As a result of population changes in the decade of the sixties, Tennessee was forced to reduce our national congressional representation by one seat, leaving us with eight representatives rather than nine. The redistricting plans passed by a Democrat majority were clearly out of line with requirements of both the federal and the state constitutions. I vetoed the measures, but they were promptly overridden by a substantial majority in both houses. Every effort was made to prevent such capricious and unconstitutional gerrymandering. Regrettably, we failed! Congressman Dan Kuykendall, my close associate and friend, practically took up residence in my office, making every effort with legislators seeking to sustain my vetoes.

The federal Supreme Court landmark case, *Baker v. Carr*, compelled the state legislature to reapportion itself. That duty had been ignored for decades by the large Democrat majorities of the legislature. Now, forced to follow the law, the Democrat majorities resorted to gerrymandering. There were distinct differences between reapportionment requirements established by the Tennessee Constitution and those required by the federal Constitution. Tennessee's Constitution contained words that flew in the face of "one man, one vote." It was a highly complex set of circumstances to be dealt with. Time-consuming, expensive litigation leading to a Supreme Court decision seemed out of reach at the time. A sad result for Republicans was that the Democrat majority in redrawing districts would deprive Dan Kuykendall of his congressional seat at the next general election. Even more far-reaching would be the unfair influence on Republican state legislative election results in the future.

On a more positive note, a law sponsored by Representative Victor Ashe of Knoxville in the first session created an administrative procedure for recognizing natural areas of the state having outstanding scenic, biological, geological, and recreational values. In the second session, working closely with Ashe, conservationists, and legislators, several significant areas were classified under the Natural Areas Act of 1971. This assured the protection and preservation of valuable natural treasures in the state under the penalty of law. I was delighted with that outcome. Two foremost natural areas of our state were Savage Gulf and Radnor Lake. A tour of the Savage Gulf on horseback and by foot in the company of Alfred Adams and Mack Prichard, among others, had persuaded me that this remarkable land bordering on Fall Creek Falls State Park should be protected from private interests. Located near the border separating Bledsoe and Van Buren Counties, its virgin forests and land contours were unique. State funds were made available for the purchase. It pleased me to be involved in saving that valuable land. The legislature was most cooperative. Radnor Lake, a beautiful body of water, and surrounding land in Davidson County, was under threat from commercial residential developers. A concerted effort by private groups, local citizens, the Nature Conservancy, and state government made it possible for the property to be acquired by the state. This was a fine example of state government and private cooperation that resulted in all but the developers being highly satisfied with the outcome.

The second session adjourned with much having been accomplished. Ninety-five percent of the administration's priority legislation passed and became law. Seventy-three percent of additional administration proposals were approved. Pending legislation to be carried over and works in progress throughout my administration gave me reason to look forward to the following year. I enjoyed a growing sense of relief as the adjournment took place. The calendar year 1972 was memorable for many reasons. It was not only the planned events but frequently unexpected incidents that made my job interesting, rewarding, and often stressful.

A Pleasant Interlude

A standing tradition, of which I had been unaware, dealt with the governor's expected presence in New York City on the occasion of bond closings. I made plans to attend although the legislature was at the time in session. A large Tennessee delegation, including the state Treasurer Tom Wiseman and Secretary of State Joe Carr, was in attendance. Large capital outlays of the state were funded in part by the issuance of general obligation bonds. It was informative to meet the legal and financial experts who worked with our state people structuring these major financial transactions. A principal law firm employed by the Tennessee state treasurer's office was Mudge, Rose, Guthrie, Alexander and Mitchell. During our stay in the city our party was generously entertained. At one luncheon it was my pleasure to meet and visit at length with financier David Rockefeller, chairman of Chase Manhattan Bank and older brother to Governors Nelson Rockefeller and Winthrop Rockefeller.

While I was in New York, I was interviewed by a magazine reporter during lunch at the 21 Club. This posh restaurant was legendary in business and social circles. While seated for our meal and the interview, I glanced around and saw what I believed to be a familiar face at the rear of the room. I asked a waiter if that could be Captain Eddie Rickenbacker, the famous race car driver and World War I ace fighter pilot. The waiter did not answer but referred my question to the maitre d'. He confirmed that it was the legendary hero Ricken-backer. I asked him to deliver a note from me to the captain and, only because I was Governor Dunn, did he agree to do so. My note simply identified myself and requested that I would like to shake his hand. Just at that time, I was called away to the telephone to answer an important call from my office in Nashville. I was on the telephone in a booth for quite a few minutes discussing a legislative problem that had developed in my absence. When I emerged from the booth, standing there patiently was Captain Rickenbacker. I was embarrassed that the very important gentleman had been waiting to shake my hand as I had requested. I heaped words of praise on that American hero and did my best to show the deep respect in which I and many Americans held him. We soon parted. He was quite elderly at that time, and I felt he appreciated the attention I paid him. That chance meeting was the high point of my first visit to New York as governor.

A Sudden Shock

One day in early April as I was returning to my office from a lunchtime break at the Residence, local news received by the car radio suddenly got my attention. The news person reported that a resolution had just been introduced in the House calling for the impeachment of Governor Dunn. An added comment referred to my close relationship to a Memphis firm and a conflict of interest between the two of us. I immediately reversed course and returned to the Residence. I called my office and learned that a first-term legislator from Shelby County named Russell X. Thompson, Democrat, had introduced House Resolution 67. It was explained to me that the resolution called for an investigation, not for impeachment, because of an arrangement I had made with Percy Galbreath and Sons, Incorporated, of Memphis. This company was an agent for John Hancock Insurance Company of Boston, Massachusetts. John Hancock Insurance Company had financed the loan for construction of the apartment.

The basis for the resolution was that because the state government regulated licensed insurance companies, the governor was immediately suspect once evidence of a personal agreement benefiting either party was disclosed. I had, in fact, reached an agreement with friends at Percy Galbreath that was of personal benefit to me but had done so openly and confident that the arrangement was not a conflict of interest. The agreement provided for my occupancy of an apartment in a recently developed downtown apartment building on Main Street. We had leased our Memphis home and had no fixed location where we could rest during our frequent visits home. Jack Craddock of Percy Galbreath, a close friend who was acquainted with our circumstance, unexpectedly offered an apartment that was not occupied. Following the assassination of Martin Luther King in 1968, the building in question had stood virtually unoccupied because local unrest discouraged prospective tenants. We were offered the space, and after careful consideration and consultation with my legal staff, we accepted the offer on terms that called for my payment of a pro rata sum of money determined by a normal rental fee being divided by the number of any days of a particular month that we occupied the apartment. I could not afford full rent for each month, and the agreement required our exit from the space if full-time tenants were found. News of the arrangement was released from my office and gathered minor notice in a local newspaper. We enjoyed the convenience of the property, sparsely furnished, for several months. Then came the House Resolution.

To my regret, the resolution was interpreted by news media and some individuals as exposing a conflict of interest that warranted impeachment proceedings. It was embarrassing to me and some close associates in and outside government. I attempted to explain the situation. I denied any wrongdoing and called for an explanation by Representative Russell X. Thompson.

Eventually, I received a letter of explanation and apology from Representative Thompson. He delivered it in person. In the letter, and in our conversation, he expressed respect and confidence in my integrity. He had withdrawn his Resolution 67. He stated that his actions were an outgrowth of a visit with a prominent Memphis attorney and Democrat. Representative Thompson, who was unaware of my arrangement with Percy Galbreath, was urged by the prominent lawyer to introduce an impeachment resolution for the purpose of embarrassing me. The young, first-term legislator did just what was suggested. Now, he was in deep regret. To ease his conscience, Thompson offered an amendment to a pending bill that would deduct from the governor's official expense funds an amount equal to the total rental costs for the time we had used the apartment. I told him that what he proposed was not necessary. I accepted his apology. I regret not confronting the so-called prominent Democrat attorney who had instigated the affair. Thompson's public apology was noted by the news media, and the matter quickly blew over.

I will never forget the shock and dismay I felt on hearing of the Thompson resolution. As well as I can recall, that was the only instance during the four years as governor that my integrity was questioned.

Another National Governors Winter Meeting

The National Governors Association convened its annual meeting in Washington in February. Since 1972 was a presidential election year, there was much to discuss and speculate about. Nixon would seek reelection, and it was generally conceded his first term of service had earned him the right to be optimistic about its successful outcome.

Throughout the meeting governors were served lunch in private quarters in order to assure some privacy and freedom. During one luncheon I sat at a table with my fellow governors Jimmy Carter, Calvin Rampton, Ronald Reagan, and Nelson Rockefeller. It was a congenial group, and the various leaders were relaxed and comfortable in the private dining area. Two vivid memories remained with me. First, I noticed again Nelson Rockefeller grasping stalks of asparagus with his fingers and eating them without using a salad fork. The second impression was that Ronald Reagan was completely insensitive to his table mates regarding conversation. He monopolized it. He seemed to have an unlimited supply of anecdotes relating to his governorship in California. One story followed another as he made his points. He did not slow down long enough for any of the other governors to get a word or two into the mix. I sensed some frustration under the circumstances. Looking back, I believe Reagan's apparent insensitivity was really an insight into the depth of his convictions and the passion he felt. All his anecdotes were in reference to his philosophy regarding the role of government in the lives of citizens. His conservatism showed.

The final night of the governors' conference in Washington was once again the occasion for a formal state dinner hosted by President and Mrs. Nixon at the White House. Betty, as usual, was beautifully attired for the evening, and I wore the conventional tuxedo. At the appointed hour all governors and their wives had gathered at the White House. It was a splendid-looking group of people, and I was, as always, very impressed to be in the company of so many leaders from across the nation. Feeling somewhat more comfortable, I was relaxed in my attitude toward another introduction to the president of the United States. As Betty and I moved toward the Marine officer who was to present us to the president, a thought flashed through my mind. How silly it was the previous year, I remembered, when the president shook my hand while opening his mouth, pointing to his molar tooth, and then speaking my name. Surely, he would not do that again. Amazingly, as I took his extended hand and looked directly into his eyes, he repeated the same sequence. "Ah, yes, Governor Dunn." He opened his mouth and pointed to his teeth. I could hardly believe it! My response was somewhat muted, I am certain, consisting simply of a "good evening, Mr. President." Nothing more pertinent, such as "How are things in that great state of Tennessee?" or "I trust things are going well for you," came from his lips. It was a deflating moment for me, but the evening was otherwise very pleasant. I don't recall what the president had to say to his audience after dinner, but I will never forget his inane comment as we passed through the receiving line! He could have done much better!

A TVA Confrontation

During the late 1960s, the Tennessee Valley Authority started a dam construction project that required the impoundment of a portion of the Little Tennessee River in East Tennessee. That beautiful stream flowed out of the Smoky Mountains down through Blount County and joined the Tennessee River south of Knoxville. Betty and I had enjoyed an outing on the river early in my term, being hosted by people in the Department of Conservation. She and I caught rainbow trout and enjoyed a shore lunch that included our fresh catch.

I am certain that our outing on the river was planned to prepare me to confront the TVA's determination to add one additional dam to its extensive and complex system of waterways control. I admired the concerns of the conservationists who contributed so generously to the quality of life in our state. I was not a fan of the TVA. I considered the huge semi-autonomous agency to have strayed far from its initial mission. It seemed to me that the TVA, by then deeply involved in agriculture, education, water control, river navigation, and land management, was constantly looking to enlarge its influence. I felt it had long ago exceeded the bounds of its assignment, a New Deal concept that had considerable merit.

Aubrey Wagner, chairman of TVA and a powerful figure in the state and in the nation's capital, was pushing an agenda calling for the creation of a lake, a related industrial complex, and a recreational and residential resort. He saw it as an economic boon to the eastern region of the state. At his invitation, I joined Wagner on the TVA turbo-powered Gulfstream airplane for a fly-around view from the air of various agency installations, including the Little Tennessee dam site. I was impressed by what I saw but not persuaded regarding our differences.

I shared the views of many good people that the project would end access to Native American historical sites, old homesteads, beautiful, fertile lowlands, and a sportsman's paradise. Even though Senators Estes Kefauver and Howard Baker, Jr., had joined in support for the federally funded project, I was convinced that the Tellico Dam, as it was known, was not in the best interests of the state at large. It would have little, if any, effect on floodwater control. Over a lengthy period of time both sides attempted to make their cases. I issued a formal statement calling on TVA to abandon the project, and I gave my reasons. It fell on deaf ears. I made an appeal to Richard Nixon without result. The project was later challenged and delayed by the discovery of a small fish called the snail darter. No other location could be identified as a home for the unique little fish. It was claimed that impounding the waters of the river would destroy this rare creature. To my regret, the dam was completed years after my term ended. The project continues to be a subject of controversy. It has not lived up to the expectations by which it was well known to residents in that area of the state. I regret not being successful in stopping the development.

Brushy Mountain

In July the guards at Brushy Mountain State Prison in Petros, Tennessee, went on strike to express their dissatisfaction with their salaries and the decisions being made by prison administrators. There had been resentment because state policy prohibited the government from negotiating with organized labor. On one of my early post-election visits to the capitol I saw people with large signs walking the halls of the building. They were employees of the Corrections Department. Trouble had been brewing for some time. I felt some sympathy toward such people because I recognized how low state employee wages were at the time. A showdown on that matter would not be surprising, but the form it would take was anyone's guess. I was to find out.

A carefully orchestrated confrontation occurred at Brushy when the captain of the corrections officers cursed the warden. The leader of the guards was immediately fired. That resulted in the entire workforce of corrections officers going out on strike. It was an unusual emergency situation that resulted in Corrections Commissioner Mark Luttrell declaring his support for the action of the warden. The guards demanded that their captain be rehired, but they were refused. The matter was brought to my attention, and I ordered Claude Armour to staff the prison with Highway Patrol personnel. That facility was the state's maximum security resource. Negotiations went on for three days with neither side giving in. We offered to rehire all but two of the strikers. At the end of the third day, I directed Luttrell to inform the strikers that if they refused to return to work by the end of the seventh day of the strike, they would be fired. The guards refused to return to work, and at the end of the seventh day, 172 guards were terminated.

What followed was a tension-filled night. Secure transportation vehicles were rounded up, including some borrowed from the state of Georgia. The Highway Patrol officers under the direction of Claude Armour manned the prison. As darkness settled in on that seventh day, all prisoners were loaded on buses and moved off the remote, mountainous prison property. One hundred prison trustees and 175 hard-core convicted criminals were involved. Commissioners Armour and Luttrell were on the site. I was in telephone contact with Armour while this unusual transfer was taking place. The people to be moved were the most dangerous criminals in the state's prisons, and we were all concerned that there be no escapes. The loaded buses moved out onto the highway. As each vehicle passed through the small town of Petros, many drunken former prison guards lined the street, threw tacks and nails onto the pavement, and otherwise tried to obstruct what was taking place. The commissioner kept me informed throughout the night. His troopers did an outstanding job.

The next day, I was advised that some prisoners were moved to the Central Prison at Nashville, some to the women's prison, some to Turney Center (a medium security center) in Hickman County and Ft. Pillow in West Tennessee. Only one prisoner was unaccounted for: an elderly trustee who had aimlessly wandered off. He was recaptured.

Armour advised me that the most notorious prisoner at Brushy Mountain, the murderer of Dr. Martin Luther King, James Earl Ray, had simply been placed on the rear seat of the commissioner's car, properly manacled, and safely transported to the Central Prison. Thus ended one of the most gripping nights of my four-year experience as governor. That tense situation reminded me of action taken in Chattanooga in 1971 when I ordered units of the National Guard to patrol city streets to prevent looting and other violence. That was a carryover from Dr. King's assassination two years earlier and unrest concerning the war in Vietnam. It was the only occasion in which I was compelled to activate the Guard. The state troopers and Commissioner Armour with elements of his Highway Patrol did a fine job. I remained very much on edge until the streets were clear and quiet was restored in Chattanooga.

To adjust to the loss of Brushy Mountain prison, an old warehouse on the grounds of the Central Prison in Nashville was quickly renovated to house approximately two hundred minimum security prisoners. These convicts were referred to as trustees, and the system adapted to a major change in housing the state's felons.

The Brushy Mountain prison was an historical relic of state government. It was quite old and had been located in remote Morgan County originally for the purpose of requiring prisoners to mine coal. That activity ceased years ago. A study I had requested recommended that the prison be abandoned because of its remote location, the scarcity of a dependable workforce, and its worn-down physical conditions. With Brushy closed, our prison facilities were jam-packed. I directed that the prison remain open and limited personnel be employed to keep all utilities functioning. We needed the prison beds. I set a deadline of January 31 as the point after which active maintenance would cease. Regrettably, new guards could not be hired. At that time the old prison was completely shut down. I hoped the emerging regional jail facilities program would take some of the load off the other prisons, but that was yet to happen. The entire prison system was under great pressure. Mark Luttrell did an outstanding job managing a difficult situation. I recall receiving substantial criticism from Democrat legislative leaders and from some newspapers. For me it was a "seasoning" experience, and I did not regret my decision.

Cabinet Adjustments

A high moment for me had occurred when Memphis Superintendent of Schools E. C. Stimbert accepted my request to become a member of the new administration. He was popular in Memphis and highly regarded by both the *Commercial Appeal* and the *Press-Scimitar* newspapers. He would replace Howard Warf as commissioner of education. Mr. Stimbert fully understood my expectations of him as commissioner, particularly regarding kindergarten. I was pleased that six of the key commissioners joining me in my responsibilities were Memphians. After being shut out politically for sixty-four years, Memphis and Shelby County were poised to make a large contribution to a better Tennessee through the efforts of a new governor named

Dunn, a commissioner of corrections named Mark Luttrell, a commissioner of safety named Claude Armour, a commissioner of public health named Eugene Fowinkle, a commissioner of education named E. C. Stimbert, an adjutant general named Bill Smith, and a director of veterans affairs named Jack Mask.

Stimbert, as well as other commissioners, got off to what I considered to be an excellent start. As time passed, I would occasionally get a complaint from my staff assistant, Joe Hopper, regarding "E. C." as Joe called Stimbert. At the end of the first year, I was conscious of the fact that Stimbert and Hopper didn't get along at all. I heard complaints from both. I worked closely with Joe Hopper, and I understood the stress and strain he endured on a daily basis from a variety of sources, mostly political. Stimbert called me on at least one occasion to complain that Hopper was attempting to inject politics into the Department of Education and Stimbert resented that. I thought that strange, as Howard Warf had been the most politically oriented commissioner in state government that I had heard of. Frequently, in attempting to contact Stimbert, I was told that the Commissioner and Mrs. Stimbert were away attending a National Education Association meeting or were on a trip of some sort, far away from Nashville. He seemed to be absent quite often. I was becoming uncomfortable with the consistent unavailability of my commissioner when I needed to talk with him.

In November the matter came to a head. Hopper had all he could take of Stimbert's refusal to consider putting people to work whom he had recommended. The commissioner seemed to resent the obvious politics of placing fully qualified personnel with Republican connections in the Department of Education. I resented the fact that Stimbert resisted putting Joe Hopper's carefully evaluated nominees to work. He was unwilling to comply with my wishes. After serious consideration, I asked for a letter of resignation from the commissioner, and I received it. The news was not well received in Memphis, and my administration was criticized for injecting politics into a professional situation. That was an unfair way to state the case. The people I wanted hired were fully qualified. Another resentment I felt had to do with Stimbert's lack of enthusiasm for the kindergarten program. He obviously did not share my commitment. I experienced many painful moments as I read editorial criticism from Memphis regarding my decision to fire Stimbert. Nevertheless, I had no alternative. I was fortunate to replace him with Benjamin Carmichael, former city superintendent of schools at Chattanooga. The new commissioner was sworn in and proceeded to perform his job immaculately. Joe Hopper was pleased and so was I. Mr. Stimbert left feeling deep resentment. I had concluded that the gentleman did not understand the logic and necessity of rewarding good people properly qualified to serve. I knew that politics could not be totally ignored. I also sensed that Stimbert, during his service as superintendent of Memphis schools, had enjoyed a close working relationship with Howard Warf, the former state commissioner. That relationship probably added to the circumstances leading to my action.

Many months later, I received a personal call from George Barnes, the Shelby County superintendent of schools. He was a highly respected individual who was very popular. He said he called to compliment me for having fired Stimbert. He said that Stimbert's popularity in Memphis was based on the fact that he was riding on the coattails of Ernest Ball, the city superintendent of schools who had preceded Stimbert in Memphis. Ernest Ball was a good man whom I had known because he was Dr. Prichard's patient in my dental office. Barnes's words were music to my ears and gave me a great sense of relief. I had grieved considerably for taking such drastic steps with E. C. Stimbert. Mr. Barnes received my sincerest thanks for the phone call. He could not know the profound sense of relief I felt. I wished he had publicly expressed that opinion nearer the time of my drastic action. By the time he called, the furor over firing Stimbert had passed.

Earlier in the year I was advised by my commissioner of finance and administration, Russell Hippe, that he desired to step down from his post. I had sensed some frustration on Hippe's part in the demanding job serving as the administration's gatekeeper and close adviser on all matters pertaining to the expenditure of state funds. I honored his request and accepted his resignation with thanks for his good service. He was replaced by a talented young man named Ted Welch, a protégé of my good friend and supporter Dortch Oldham. He came highly recommended by Oldham who had worked closely with Ted at the Southwestern Corporation of Nashville. Ted stepped in and proceeded to become an outstanding commissioner.

Neither of the rather sudden changes in key leadership positions had been expected, and I felt grateful to have had access to such outstanding replacements as Carmichael and Welch.

The Pending 1972 Nixon Campaign

Quite by accident I learned that U.S. Attorney General John Mitchell had designated Senator Bill Brock to be Tennessee chairman of the campaign to reelect the president in 1972. This news came as a big surprise to me. As governor of the state, I was the titular head of the Republican Party. I had assumed party leadership and worked closely with Chairman Kopie Kopald and his assistants. The month was April, and I felt sure appointment of a chairman for Nixon was not far off. I was not willing to accept Mitchell's decision to appoint the junior senator, much less the affront of not being consulted in the matter. People close to Brock were notified that it was imperative we discuss the matter as soon as possible.

A meeting soon took place at the City Club in downtown Nashville over lunch. I stated firmly that I would be glad to co-chair the Nixon campaign in Tennessee with the junior senator and that nothing else, other than my assuming full chairmanship, would be acceptable. Brock had little choice but to accept my offer, and he did so. Senator Baker was not present at the meeting, but I was confident he would find the arrangement satisfactory.

Nixon won the state in November. I don't recall that Bill Brock and I took any joint action supporting Nixon during the campaign. Brock was an aggressive player who had developed a good relationship with John Mitchell. I did not appreciate his attempt to pre-empt me. Representing the president, Mitchell had attended my inauguration. I was fully prepared to take my case to him if necessary, but I was relieved not to have to do so. There was no other statewide election in 1972. I spent quite some time on the campaign trail for Nixon and other Republican candidates. Unfortunately, we did not achieve our long sought-after goal of gaining control of either the state House or Senate, but an honest effort was made. Democrats continued to control both houses of the legislature by substantial majorities. Richard Nixon was reelected president of the United States by the largest majority of popular votes ever recorded in a presidential election until that time. To my great regret Congressman Dan Kuykendall fell victim to the partisan gerrymandering of Tennessee congressional districts. The vote was along racial lines, and Dan was defeated by Memphian Harold Ford.

Rounding Out the Year

The year 1972 was filled with a relentless series of events including meetings, speeches in and out of state, and social engagements. Political campaigning within the state for Richard Nixon and many legislative candidates required numerous trips by automobile and airplane. Whenever I flew on the state aircraft to attend a purely partisan political function, we were careful to reimburse the state from party funds available for such purposes. Even though the airplane cut travel time, I experienced many late-hour arrivals home, often quite tired physically.

I took advantage of every opportunity to be supportive of my commissioners as they administered their departments and took on new initiatives. Commissioner Bob Smith and his engineers in the Department of Transportation had broken through natural barriers that prevented the completion of Interstate 40 on the Cumberland Plateau. At a point near Crab Orchard earth and rock slides had made highway construction impossible. By employing large collections of limestone crushed rock contained in mesh wire netting, they had succeeded in stabilizing the foundation for a segment of the interstate that had not been completed. It was a major technical breakthrough and gained national attention and acclaim. I was extremely proud of the accomplishments.

I worked with Commissioner Ben Gibbs in the Labor Department seeking public acceptance of federal guidelines regarding occupational safety. An Occupational Safety and Health Act, OSHA, passed by the U.S. Congress required implementation state by state. This was a complicated and many-faceted undertaking that Commissioner Gibbs successfully put in place across the state. While the act was heavily bureaucratic and loaded with regulations, the results were safer work environments throughout Tennessee.

Commissioner of Health Dr. Eugene Fowinkle occasionally requested my involvement in various state initiatives at local or regional health departments. A significant undertaking involved the development of rural health clinics in an effort to bring services to areas typically deprived of professional healthcare services. Statistics on dietary concerns and services for prenatal care indicated that the state could do much to improve the quality of life and health of many Tennesseans in rural areas. I was fortunate to inherit Fowinkle from the Ellington administration, and I made the most of his services. He was outstanding in his work.

I worked with Commissioner Claude Armour as he restructured the Department of Safety and dealt with a state Highway Patrol that had too long been plagued with political consideration as a major part of personnel advancement. Professionalism was the order of the day, and I was proud to visibly demonstrate my support of that approach throughout the ranks of the department. It was among the more enjoyable features of my job. I could not have wished for greater loyalty and friendship than those I received from Claude Armour. The state had never been served by a higher degree of professionalism than that offered by Armour.

We spent considerable time identifying prospective corporate investors for the state. Among our successes was S. C. Johnson and Son, Inc.'s development of its first plant outside the state of Wisconsin. The company chose the city of Cookeville and created many new employment opportunities in the plant constructed there. The Trane Corporation located a large plant near Clarksville. The Trane management group gave our economic development personnel credit for their decision to choose Tennessee. R. R. Donnelley Corporation of Chicago selected Gallatin as the site for a major printing facility and provided hundreds of jobs for Tennessee workers. Texas Instruments chose Johnson City as the location for a major plant. Numerous other such decisions were made throughout the four years of my term, bringing much satisfaction to me personally while adding substantially to employment statistics statewide. During our four years billions of dollars were invested in new plants and existing plant expansions.

Three separate governors' conferences were among the various organizations to which the governor was expected to give his time. They were the National Governors Association, the Republican Governors Association, and the Southern Governors' Association. During my term I served on the Executive Committee of the National Governors

Association and as chairman of the Republican Governors Association. Of the three, I found the Southern Governors' Association to be the most enjoyable. The group met once each year, always choosing a site that boasted a holiday-type environment. At each meeting, our hosts always treated guest governors to lavish arrangements regarding housing. In addition, efforts were made to present each visiting official family with gifts that were produced locally. The most memorable of the gifts we received was an electric golf cart that was presented during the festivities and shipped to our Residence at the end of the conference. Our daughter Julie assumed command of that little vehicle and made many tracks around the ten acres on which the Residence was located.

During the year, I was selected to chair an organization called the Education Commission of the States. Tennessee had been, and continued to be, supportive of that commission. The organization was dedicated to the advancement of higher education and focused its attention on state colleges and universities. Among its many good works was a fund created to provide tuition dollars to college students who qualified. The chairman was expected to travel extensively, and I found myself in various cities and on numerous college campuses during my period of service.

A popular project and one that was heavily represented by professional lobbyists was the Tennessee-Tombigbee Waterway Development program. This expensive undertaking had a long history of being promoted in the national Congress as a sound expenditure of taxpayer dollars. An official authority was created by Congress to promote the effort. Major federal funding took place at the outset of my administration. In my activities related to this authority I was joined by Alabama Governor George Wallace and Mississippi Governor Bill Waller. On one occasion we three governors met to formally break ground for the first of many locks that would be constructed along the Tombigbee River. Those waters flowed out of Tennessee into Mississippi and eventually Alabama. This was a major, somewhat controversial project that had been promoted by state and federal advocates for decades. It was entirely federally funded. Governor Wallace had to use a wheelchair, having suffered gunshot wounds from an attempted assassination several years earlier. It was obvious that he was in pain during the ceremonies, and I was impressed by his determination to carry out his duties. The groundbreaking went well.

Our social activities after legislative adjournment were somewhat limited because of the press of official duties. However, Betty and I were treated to a wide variety of gatherings in which we were privileged to meet many new friends, often outside the realm of partisan politics. Our friendship with Minnie Pearl and her husband, Henry Cannon, flourished. Tennis games and parties at our Residence and in her home were always welcomed distractions. Often Minnie had prominent celebrity guests in her home, and we were always included in her efforts to properly entertain them. Getting to know such stars as Burt Reynolds, Kaye Starr, and Jim Nabors, among many others, was a delightful experience for us. Such people were good for the Tennessee economy, especially in music publishing and recording. We were happy to be parts of such activity.

There was no shortage of invitations from prominent citizens across the state. Leading attorneys and major banking personalities made their presence known and offered warm hospitality. I appreciated every bit of that. Occasionally, I would chuckle to myself, remembering how few such stalwart citizens I saw during my long campaign in 1970! That was just the nature of the "game" of politics.

Betty and I were grateful that our children had settled into reasonably normal lives in Nashville. Julie was enrolled at Oak Hill Elementary School where she made many new friends. Our daughter Gayle was a student at Harpeth Hall. She was happy to have been selected to be a cheerleader for Montgomery Bell Academy. There, football games were a highlight of her life. We found many of our most enjoyable days to be those we spent at Fall Creek Falls State Park, often just with family members, but occasionally with friends. The unique place treated every visitor with scenic beauty, privacy, and a totally relaxed environment. It was certainly good for both Betty and me. Each of us, when in Nashville, found ourselves so busy and concentrated on such a variety of responsibilities that there was little time to relax. Fall Creek Falls was very therapeutic.

Our son, Chuck, was a frequent visitor but also busily engaged getting his college education at Washington and Lee University in Lexington, Virginia. During one conversation he mentioned to me that he had been stopped by the Tennessee Highway Patrol for excessive speed as he drove back to school in Lexington. He made sure I knew that he did not identify himself as the governor's son and dutifully paid his fine for driving too fast. I thanked him for that! He enjoyed staying in what he called the "Red Room" at the Residence during his visits and while he was in school recess. For summer work he obtained a job with a local company's construction crew. He mentioned that one fellow worker happened to ask him what his dad did. Chuck replied that his dad worked for the state. He handled himself well. In our last year as first family he took up residence in the apartment behind the Residence during his first year at Vanderbilt's School of Law. I have remained so grateful that our children dealt with their unusual circumstances as well as they did.

There was no letup in activities as Thanksgiving and Christmas seasons rolled around. My wife was busy making the Residence a warm and welcoming home. The state prison personnel who worked within the building and on the grounds were generally well behaved and friendly. They were treated with respect, and every effort was made to show them our appreciation. One afternoon Betty stepped into the hallway outside her office and discovered one of the prisoners near a refrigerator with a bottle of champagne in his hand. Someone had left a rear hallway door unlocked. The man had discovered that fact and had climbed a back stairway to the second floor, opened the refrigerator, and removed the bottle. Betty demanded that he put the bottle back and get downstairs immediately. Fortunately, that was exactly what he did, and the confrontation was brief. It could have been a dangerous situation for my wife but, thankfully, nothing happened.

My attention was directed toward legislative initiatives we planned for the upcoming session of the General Assembly in January 1973. Intense planning and preparation occupied considerable time in November and December.

CHAPTER THIRTY-ONE

FIRST SESSION, 88TH GENERAL ASSEMBLY

Better Prepared to Govern

One of the most interesting activities following the general election took place beginning on the first Tuesday in January 1973 when the new General Assembly convened to organize and prepare for the busy months ahead. The state Senate, one-half of its membership having been elected in November, proceeded to reelect John Wilder to be Speaker and lieutenant governor. The House of Representatives, with Jim McKinney as Speaker for the previous two years, engaged in a close reelection contest that McKinney lost to Representative Ned McWherter of Dresden. I was relieved to know that the previous Speaker had lost his seat of power. While I didn't know what sort of leader the new Speaker would be, I was satisfied he would not match the hostility and brashness that had been practiced by McKinney and directed toward me and my administration. The Democrats remained in control of both houses, and although I remained optimistic about future progress, I realized it would be a session in which partisan politics would play its role.

The organizing session of the legislature then adjourned and reconvened on the fourth Tuesday in February. This was my third opportunity to work formally with the two bodies, and I anticipated a productive session. Following the practice we established two years earlier, the first lady and I hosted a seated dinner for members and their guests. We had erected a large tent covering the patio and portions of the yard at the Residence in order to accommodate the entire group. The event was well received and, I believe, imparted the feeling of "togetherness" that I hoped would carry over to many of the major issues to be addressed in the upcoming session.

With two years' experience under our belts, Betty and I felt more comfortable on that special occasion with the legislature. She had become completely competent in her management of the Residence, a professional chef had been employed, frequent visitors were commonplace because we had opened our fine home to visitors two days a week and our trained docents were helpful, the handsome wrought iron fence surrounding the property was in place, and many unique historical furnishings had been added to the décor. It was a pleasant "get acquainted" evening for all concerned.

The Budget Message, Fiscal Year 1974

On January 11, I presented my third budget message to a joint first session of the 88th General Assembly. In addition to legislators of both houses, my personal and my official families were present along with members of the state Supreme Court, the media, and visitors in the galleries.

Opening remarks included my belief that the 88th would become a landmark General Assembly because the legislative and executive branches of state government had an opportunity to put unequaled material resources together with carefully developed legislative proposals to work for the good of all Tennessee citizens. The state was enjoying unprecedented economic progress, and we were using every agency of state government in attempting to extend to each person a better standard of living. It was a splendid time for progress. I said that while we were four million in numbers, we were not four million strong. Many, many deficiencies existed across the broad gamut of social and physical circumstances in which we found ourselves. Joblessness, underemployment, health challenges, disabilities of aging and physical infirmities, addictions to drugs, crime, and education shortcomings challenged us. Every legislative district and each community deserved careful evaluation and consideration by the state. As long as there were unmet needs, our jobs would not be completely done.

I stressed the need to maintain our existing tax structure in order to have an adequate funding base on which to build our programs and initiatives. For the first time in a number of years, revenues were available to finance construction requirements, including the Department of Transportation, without increasing our state indebtedness. That would not be good news for the bond attorneys of New

York City. I shared the encouraging news that revenue collections for the next fiscal year should exceed the current year's budget by $140 million. I urged members not to view those dollars as surplus because there existed needs where each one could be soundly applied.

I requested significant improvements across the board for public education, an area where funding shortages had been historical realities. I urged full funding to complete the coverage of kindergarten for 100 percent of our eligible youngsters. Among the many items covered, I stressed the importance of focusing on medical education and medical personnel placement in areas where great shortages existed. In addition to increasing the number of Tennesseans studying medicine at Vanderbilt and Meharry, there was a need to develop clinical training centers for senior medical students in Knoxville, Tri-Cities, and Jackson. A demonstration program of primary healthcare centers would provide a model for better distribution of healthcare personnel across the state. There was a serious shortage of physicians in every rural area.

Fair compensation for state employees was a matter of high priority. In addition, expanded services to the mentally ill were required, an increase in grants of public assistance to the aged, disabled, and blind was needed, and care for children released from juvenile institutions without adequate supervision or housing was essential. The state had a primary responsibility to make provision for basic human needs, and limited resources were available.

A major request dealt with our correctional institutions and the pending crisis the state faced. Many prisons were old and inadequate with inmate populations exceeding capacity. It was necessary to begin decentralization of the large institutions and move toward community-oriented programs. It was clear that obstacles would be encountered in the process. I requested the means to fund regional correctional centers in Upper East Tennessee and Hamilton and Shelby Counties. A federal matching fund program would be an integral part of the effort.

The newly created Department of Economic and Community Development was the centerpiece of my administration's efforts to radically alter the state's approach to jobs and prosperity. We were in direct competition with bordering sister states that had demonstrated successfully new opportunities in economic growth and community development. We had to compete on an equal footing, and new funding for our efforts was essential. That request was clearly laid out with stress on the need for a highly competent commissioner.

A severe housing shortage had long confronted many of our citizens. I recommended the establishment of a state Housing Development Agency to assist low- and moderate-income families in securing decent housing. Such a state agency would not only allow more Tennesseans to purchase homes under tight money conditions, but the activities of the agency would create new jobs and income for many citizens. I was convinced that this constructive response to a basic need for adequate housing would be a boon to our society. I strongly urged the General Assembly's cooperation in the matter.

The program I outlined provided a balanced approach to meeting the needs of our citizens. Our sound financial condition permitted us to make many improvements. Recent studies had indicated that our tax system was highly regressive. Lower income families were contributing more than their fair share of earnings toward financing the business of the public.

In an effort to ease the tax burden on some citizens, I proposed a novel approach known as the circuit breaker, a means by which a family falling below a certain level of income automatically became qualified to be compensated for a portion of property and sales taxes paid. Several states were using partial circuit breaker systems. The one I proposed would be more comprehensive. It was estimated that 250,000 low-income families would receive some tax relief under the proposal. The cost to the state would be minimal, and local governments would incur no cost.

Environmental preservation was emphasized as a continuing responsibility. I noted in particular the problems of Reelfoot Lake in which silt from the deforested hills to the east had reduced the lake area from its original 40,000 acres to only 18,000 acres. In addition, we had a prime opportunity to preserve pristine lands through the Natural Areas Law. These and other environmental considerations ranked high on my list of priorities.

My message pointed up the needs, opportunities, and obligations we public officials had the privilege of addressing. Before us lay an opportunity to harmonize a variety of interests and thereby strengthen our nation as we built a better Tennessee. I was satisfied with what I had laid before my fellow public servants.

State of the State, 1973

The Tennessee Press Association was a receptive and interested audience for my address on January 19, 1973. I had given my budget message eight days earlier to the General Assembly. Reaction to that presentation was mixed, depending on who was reacting. The Democrat leadership was basically positive pending the legislative messages that would accompany what we would offer. There were combative elements within that party that I could only shrug off and disregard. The press was generally supportive, and I appreciated a number of encouraging editorial commentaries. Ralph Griffith did a good job of gathering media comments across the state, and I could not resist reading various opinions.

My remarks to the Press Association were prefaced by the observation that I was pleased with our progress but at the same time distressed by my awareness of the many needs yet to be met—so many lives yet to be positively touched by resources of the state to which many turned out of necessity.

I wasted no time detailing the advances that had been achieved by the exhaustive businessmen's study on controlling costs within state government. More than three hundred of the report's recommendations had been addressed in efforts to make government responsive, practical, and effective. The creation of a Board of Regents for higher education, the new Department of General Services that allowed us to consolidate basic support services and purchasing procedures, more centralized administrative services through finance and administration, and other administrative improvements were brought to the audience's attention.

I reviewed the advances made and remaining needs in public education. Emphasis was placed on the work being done in the Department of Public Health to focus on prevention in prenatal care, obstetrical services, nutrition, immunizations, dental therapy, and hygiene. The broad range of challenges in mental health, corrections, and environmental protection was outlined. I took some pleasure in observing that our highway construction projects were at an historic high level of development and intensity. I reminded one and all that the largest single number of projects under contract at any one time was achieved the previous August, totaling in excess of $324 million.

The Department of Economic and Community Development was my final topic. I wanted to emphasize the importance I attached to this initiative. With an economy more dynamic than ever in our history those people needed to know that the solid agricultural-industrial foundation we had to work with was in the earliest stages of its potential for growth. A new state Planning Office had been charged with the preparation of a comprehensive development plan that would impact the multitude of plant sites, farm to market transport needs, and urban-rural balance that was the envy of many other states. Such progressive action, I stated, would enable us to continue to move away from government by crisis toward government by expectation. The people of our state deserved no less in visions of the future from its political leaders.

I concluded by pointing out that much, much more could be said about what lay ahead. There was, indeed, a healthy climate of confidence in Tennessee. In such a climate a great deal could be accomplished.

Results: First Session, 88th General Assembly

Following its introduction, my proposal for a circuit breaker mechanism to give modest tax relief to those on whom the state tax burden fell most unfairly was met with significant resistance. I was disappointed that many Republican legislators saw the proposal as a welfare measure outside their philosophy of conservative governing. Democrat legislators characterized the bill as negligible relief. I argued that the price of a pair of shoes or a warm jacket loomed large in the eyes of many Tennesseans who would have welcomed any relief they might receive. I engaged many lawmakers one on one in conversations without success and, with great regret, saw the bill die in the House and Senate Finance Committees.

After careful study, I vetoed a controversial non-administration measure that would have prevented bank holding companies' de novo entry into our state. Later in the year I requested my staff to study our banking structure and offer recommendations for my consideration. As a result of the study, with my encouragement a Tennessee Bankers Association committee offered a compromise on the issue, and it was enacted in the second session of the 88th General Assembly. Our bill calling for a Department of Banking became law, and I appointed Hugh Sinclair of Memphis its first commissioner. The new department was assigned regulatory duties previously carried out by the Department of Insurance.

Across the board in public education substantial progress was made. My administration requested and received funds to fully implement for the first time a new higher education funding formula developed by the Higher Education Commission. This measure went far toward reducing the tensions among our college and university leaders regarding state financial support. Based on a study by the state Board of Education, I recommended that the Tennessee Preparatory School located in Nashville be phased out and replaced with family-style unit facilities. The bill failed primarily because of local opposition by Davidson County legislators who wanted to maintain the historic old institution. Later, funds were appropriated to demonstrate the community concept. Funds to extend the kindergarten program to all five-year-olds were requested for the 1973–74 school year. Only two-thirds of the requested appropriation was approved. As a result approximately 39,000 children attended 1,670 state-supported kindergarten classes in the next school year. I was frustrated with the unwillingness of the Democrat majority to grant full funding. It meant a large segment of our five-year-old children would be deprived of that valuable early education experience.

A Democrat initiative produced a bill directing the Department of Education to conduct a statewide survey to determine a method to expand vocational and technical education programs for high school and post–high school learners. The bill required that the expanded program be available within a certain distance of every Tennessee student by school year 1977. A companion bill required the state to issue a $136 million general obligation bond funding mechanism to implement the intent of the bills. I found the first bill acceptable but felt compelled to veto the funding portion as premature and an unnecessary addition to the state's bonded indebtedness at that time. Because of the mileage proximity requirement, additional new schools would have to be built. The question was, how many? My action was attacked by the original sponsors, and promises were made to override the veto in the second legislative session. We subsequently offered an alternative funding plan that was rejected. The veto was overridden in the second session. This was a good example of political expediency overruling sound management of the government's resources.

Capital Punishment

A U.S. Supreme Court decision in 1972 ruled that capital punishment as administered in some states, including Tennessee, was unconstitutional. The decision was based on the court's conclusion that, while capital punishment as such was not unconstitutional, its use could not be left completely to the discretion of the jury. Our state laws accepted the verdict of a jury as sufficient. That procedure had been historically applied in our state. I was compelled by the higher court decision to commute all death row inmate sentences to life imprisonment. Believing, as I did, in the soundness of capital punishment as an ultimate penalty for certain heinous crimes, I regretted the action I was compelled to take.

In the 1973 legislative session my administration submitted a capital punishment bill designed to comply with the Supreme Court decision. The legislation called for mandatory death penalties for certain crimes. It was passed, and I signed it. However, due to a drafting error, the bill was declared unconstitutional by the U.S. Supreme Court. The error was later corrected by a new law passed in 1974. No one was executed by the state during my term in office.

That Supreme Court decision resolved an extraordinary situation I inherited from the governor I succeeded. On the day of my inauguration Governor Ellington had confidentially given me a letter he had received years earlier from Shelby County Criminal Court Clerk J. A. Blackwell. Mr. Blackwell on December 13, 1966, had received the letter from its author, Shelby County Trial Judge W. Preston Battle. Judge Battle's message was written by hand on plain paper. He requested that the letter be placed in the hands of the sitting governor. It was obviously a heartfelt expression of his belief that a fatal miscarriage of justice was in the making and his effort to be certain justice prevailed in that particular case.

Judge Battle had presided at the trial of a group of men accused of rape in Shelby County. According to the judge's letter, the assistant attorney general representing the state, Mr. Jewett Miller, in his closing argument to the jury waived capital punishment for all defendants except two. The jury, however, chose to convict five defendants and assign the death penalty. Battle then overruled a motion for new trial, thereby accepting and adopting the verdict of the jury as to the guilt of five defendants.

Later, in what clearly was a reflection on his earlier denial of a new trial—and I quote the letter, "I have given this case long, hard, deep thought"—the judge, as thirteenth juror, stated his opinion that only two of the five convicted men should receive the death penalty. He specified those two. He recommended that each of the remaining three sentences be commuted to ninety-nine years' imprisonment. Just prior to writing the letter, Judge Battle had signed a bill of exception in that criminal case that would lead to appeal in a higher court. In effect, he reversed his earlier ruling denying an appeal. He stated that "knowing the uncertainty of human life," he was writing the letter and requesting it be turned over to the then governor of Tennessee after action by the appellate court in the event of his death or incapacity.

This dramatic event demonstrates the human qualities that cannot be separated from the criminal justice process. Judge Battle was determined to alter what he most deeply believed was a severe mistake in that trial. The story also points to the power ultimately vested in the state's governor as the final arbiter in some matters. I believe the state's appellate courts had not heard an appeal in that case. The matter was resolved by the decision of the U.S. Supreme Court regarding capital punishment as it was then practiced. The judge's letter became no longer significant. I retained it in my personal papers.

The Jet Age

One day as I sat in our state airplane waiting for takeoff from an airport in Alabama, I glanced out the window and saw a pure jet airplane bearing, in large letters on the fuselage, the name "University of Alabama." I asked Colonel Bill Pickron, my pilot, if the plane I saw was actually the property of the university. His positive answer led me to ask if the state of Alabama also owned a pure jet airplane. He replied that it did. On returning to my office, I questioned whether other sister southeastern states used jet aircraft, and I learned all but one state had that aircraft capability. I decided Tennessee should have that same resource for logical reasons, among them being competitive with other states.

In my budget request for the first session, I included a $400,000 sum earmarked for the purchase of a jet airplane. Under previous administrations a used aircraft had never been purchased. My ally in seeking legislative approval was Democrat state Representative Ed Murray of Winchester. He was an avid pilot and understood the potential value to the state a pure jet would offer. He was also a respected leader in the legislature, and his support assured passage of my proposal. With Colonel Pickron's expert guidance a Lear 21 pre-owned pure jet airplane was purchased for use by the governor and other state officials. We thus increased the state aircraft fleet by one and enhanced the ability to transport persons on state business.

The airplane became one of the most controversial subjects during my first three years in office. I was criticized by some legislators and news people for purchasing an unnecessary luxury. Such talk was politically motivated and totally wrong. The airplane was commonly referred to as "Governor Dunn's private jet." I was fully satisfied that its use for my travel and for the purpose of efficiently moving industrial development prospects in and out of the state fully justified its acquisition. For example, prospective investors could be picked up in New York or New Jersey, flown to Tennessee, shown one or more factory building sites, then transported back home by mid-afternoon. The jet was small and fast. Someone remarked that instead of getting in the craft, a passenger just sort of put it on. My comment was, perhaps so, but then you didn't have to wear it very long! As far as I was concerned, the benefits of the machine far outweighed the criticism.

A unique feature of the new airplane was suggested by my wife, Betty, who is a licensed private pilot and knew the jargon and procedures necessary for airplane identification. She suggested that the official registration of our new airplane be one zero echo charley. The alphabetical prefix was n. Following its official registration, the Learjet was always easily identified over the radio waves as November ten echo charley or November ten-e-c. We appreciated her good idea.

Creation of the Department of Economic and Community Development had been one of our major accomplishments in 1972. I requested the Industrial and Agricultural Development Commission to appoint a search committee to take the next big step by seeking a highly qualified person to become the commissioner of the new department. By November they had located such a person: the regional director of the Federal Economic Development Administration stationed in Atlanta. His name was Dr. Pat Choate. He agreed to move to Tennessee if we could meet his salary expectations. He requested a minimum salary of $50,000. I sought the legislature's approval. Unfortunately, law stipulated that the salary for that position was to be no more than that of my highest paid commissioner. The commissioner of public health was paid $39,500, the absolute limit. I attempted to supplement that figure with outside funds to meet the requested $50,000. I will note here that the governor's salary at the time was $30,000! I was advised by the state attorney general that any supplement of the salary from private sources would be unlawful. The salary was eventually set at $39,500, and Pat Choate graciously agreed to accept his new challenge at that level. Partisan controversy surrounded the entire proceeding, and it was a distasteful matter only made palatable by Dr. Choate's acceptance. He was to fulfill my greatest expectations, and for that the entire state should be deeply grateful. Economic and community development in our state began to assume new and historic proportions.

In the 1970 census of housing we learned that 21 percent of the state's 1.3 million dwelling units were substandard. I recommended that the General Assembly create a state housing agency. I proposed that a Tennessee Housing Development Agency would have power to create new sources of mortgage money and would be responsible for providing the means for qualified citizens to purchase or rent safe, sanitary housing. Persons in the lower and moderate income groups, if inclined to do so, would be better able to afford acceptable housing.

When first proposed, the concept drew opposition from the state's mortgage bankers and various savings and loan associations. Fortunately, good judgment prevailed, and the bill was passed and signed into law. The program continues to be highly successful, and all involved in its creation should take pride in that fact.

The highly partisan power play to embarrass me and limit my freedom to select a future Supreme Court justice as had been the practice during the existence of the Modified Missouri Plan became a bill that reached my desk as expected. The Democrat-controlled legislature proposed to remove Supreme Court justices from the plan. The lower appellate courts were not affected. In part, that action was based on my earlier attempts to fill a vacant Supreme Court position. My response was to veto the bill because it created a dual system for the filling of appellate court vacancies. I reasoned that if the Modified Missouri Plan embodied in the 1971 act was desirable as the method for filling appellate court vacancies, then it should be retained. Were it not so, it should be repealed in its entirety. Any attempt to override my veto would take place in the next session of the 88th General Assembly. The heavy hand of partisan politics was in action.

In the first session of the 88th General Assembly I vetoed 24 bills. One veto message dealt with the General Appropriations Act, Senate Bill 75. I approved the act subject to reductions and changes in certain items it contained. The Republican and Democrat leadership in both houses had studied my proposed budget document intensively in consultation with my office, and several amendments strengthened the program for fiscal year 1974 in a number of important ways. Regrettably, many individual legislators, in disregard of the careful study and recommendations of their own committees, sought and obtained amendments that inflated appropriations far out of proportion to revenues that we would have available. Their disregard of the financial soundness of the state was remarkable in view of the prohibition in our Constitution against budgeting in the red. We were not to spend more than we had. The total of non-budgeted appropriations vetoed was $65 million. Legislative reaction would not take place until the second session of the Assembly.

A memorable meeting had taken place in my office in mid-July 1972. It set in motion a series of events that has stood the test of time and served the people of the state very well. I was visited by a small but very impressive delegation of ladies one afternoon. In the group were Mrs. E. Bronson Ingram, Mrs. Irwin Eskind, and Mrs. Pat Wilson. These women, all of whom I had met at various times, were on a mission with real merit.

Martha Ingram advised me that earlier conversations in the Nashville community had focused on a venue for a performing arts center and certain real estate in the city had been targeted. That particular real estate failed to materialize. Nashville's Mayor Briley had shown no interest in the concept. Federal funds for the Tennessee

Bicentennial Celebration were forthcoming, I was advised, and there was strong interest in learning if the state might consider including, physically, a performing arts center in plans for a new office building slated to be constructed on the site of the Andrew Jackson Hotel in downtown Nashville. Emphasis was put on the idea of a public-private partnership using federal and state funds for construction and private funds to endow maintenance of a center.

I was impressed with the idea, with the vision and determination of Martha Ingram, Annette Eskind, and Anne Wilson. I agreed to pursue the concept and spoke to my commissioner of finance and administration, Ted Welch. Mrs. Ingram and her associates targeted Ned McWherter after he became Speaker of the House in 1973, and gained his support for, as Mrs. Ingram put it, jacking up the new state office building and putting a performing arts center under it. The concept soon took form, and in March of 1973 I attended a dinner held by the Advisory Board of the Tennessee Performing Arts Foundation, which helped the concept become a reality.

Today the Tennessee Performing Arts Center is an almost legendary reality brought about by the hardworking private citizens who raised the necessary funds for endowment and sold the idea so thoroughly to private donors and to state officials. Mrs. Ingram, at that time an active board member of the Kennedy Center in Washington, provided the essential leadership that such a successful undertaking required.

By any reasonable measure, the first session of the 88th General Assembly came to a successful conclusion, and the legislators adjourned. Priority legislation proposed by my administration consisted of 33 bills. Of these, 24 bills were passed, which was a 72 percent success rate. Left pending for the second session were 9 bills. The work of Republican leaders Tom Jensen, Tom Garland, and Houston Goddard, among others, was outstanding. They, along with other Republican legislators, "carried the water" throughout the session with energy and effectiveness.

Contemplating the final session during my last year as governor and being described in the press as a "lame duck," I had much to think about. Several issues of importance were in the process of developing into full-blown political time bombs. The issues were essentially regional in nature. So-called bloody Highway 11 West in East Tennessee, the evolving showdown on a stand-alone medical school in Johnson City, the regional prison needs that affected the entire state, the long-standing conflict over extending Interstate Highway 40 through Overton Park in Memphis, and growing discomfort among Democrats at the capitol in Nashville with the existing mechanism for choosing members of the state Supreme Court—these composed the major issues that would have to be dealt with.

Another Mid-Winter National Governors Association Conference

In February 1973, Betty and I joined the nation's other governors and first ladies in Washington for our third annual conference. This was another interesting meeting during which we heard presentations by many of the Nixon administration representatives. This was the first year of Nixon's second term. Small group conferences and pleasant gatherings with our country's top leaders were stimulating and informative. It was a good time for governors to share individual state concerns with powerful Washington decision makers.

The president had electrified the world by making an historic trip to Communist China. The timing of that journey meant that he would not be present to personally welcome the governors during that conference. Frankly, I was somewhat relieved that the White House dinner would be held at another location in his absence. I could not erase memories of the first two such occasions at which the president had greeted me and shown me his molars as a means of letting me know he knew who I really was! Although it seemed inconceivable to me, I would not have been surprised, had he been present, if he had pulled the same stunt. I had teased Betty by commenting that, if the president pulled that stunt on me again, I was prepared to ask him what he did when he saw his proctologist! The formal dinner was hosted by Vice President and Mrs. Spiro Agnew. It was a fine occasion, and the group was entertained by singer Frank Sinatra. The third National Governors Association Conference in Washington soon was a matter of history.

Earlier, in January, we had attended the presidential inauguration. That was a splendid event with all the trappings of such an occasion, and we enjoyed it. Having participated in the Republican National Convention held in Miami the preceding summer, a tumultuous event in which outlandish demonstrations by unruly protestors on the streets were commonplace, we were very pleased with the relative composure that characterized Nixon's second inauguration. The lamented Vietnam conflict was being resolved by the withdrawal of our armed forces under Nixon's direction, the economy was healthy, and the president was enjoying great popularity.

Betty and I had attended the president's first inauguration in 1968. Our party of six, including the Alex Danns and the Harry Wellfords, had journeyed first to the eastern shore of Maryland for a visit to Alex Dann's beautiful family farm. It was an old, historic setting, and Alex amused us with his special stories concerning Revolutionary War days in that area. We journeyed on to Washington where we joined the large gathering of Republicans anxious to witness the swearing in of our president. It was an exciting time in the lives of our little group of devoted Republican workers. Now, attending Nixon's second inaugural as a sitting governor and first lady, there was no doubt which of the two circumstances was more appealing from a comfort and convenience point of view. However, our experiences there in an official capacity took absolutely nothing away from the pleasures we vividly recalled of our earlier inaugural trip with close friends.

A Tennessee Hero Returns

On a blustery day in March I joined Mayor Beverly Briley and other Nashville leaders, along with a large gathering of citizens, at a ceremony on the Davidson County courthouse steps welcoming the return home of an illustrious Tennessee fighting man and patriot. U.S. Navy Commander William P. Lawrence had just returned from nearly six years of captivity in a North Vietnam prison. He and his co-pilot had been shot down while on a mission and had been captured in June 1967. He had endured torture and deprived living conditions, surviving, he stated, by memories of his family and state.

During those years of isolation, Commander Lawrence maintained his composure by writing poetry. On the day of his welcome home, copies of his poem "Oh Tennessee, My Tennessee" were distributed to the audience. Later, by legislative resolution, the poem was adopted as the official poem of the state. I offered brief remarks of welcome and appreciation on behalf of all Tennesseans. Spending a brief time with the brave naval pilot, so recently released from his Vietnamese captors, was an experience I will always treasure. Bill Lawrence was later promoted to the rank of vice admiral and served as superintendent of the U.S. Naval Academy at Annapolis.

A Trip to Remember

In April Betty, Gayle, and I flew to New York City to attend a Republican Governors Association (RGA) spring meeting. We, along with other Republican governors and their families, were to be hosted by Governor and Mrs. Nelson Rockefeller. Our son, Chuck, was engrossed in school at Washington and Lee University and could not join us. Our daughter Julie did not accompany us for reasons I cannot recall.

At that time only thirteen Republicans served as governors of their states. Our meetings would therefore be somewhat more intimate than were the gatherings of all state governors. The Rockefellers proved to be extraordinary hosts, and the three days our group was together in New York were quite memorable.

Our first gathering was a dinner party in the Rockefeller New York City home. It was located in a high-rise apartment building overlooking Central Park. I will always remember vividly being impressed by the objects of art adorning the walls as Betty and I were ushered into their living quarters. The paintings were beautiful, and other items were attractively located throughout the space. The governor was a well-known art collector and expert in the subject. His tastes were most impressive.

A delicious dinner was served to the group seated in the handsome dining area. I was seated immediately to Mrs. Happy Rockefeller's left. She was a delightful conversationalist. At a point late in the evening, Happy leaned over and, somewhat confidentially, said to me, "You know, Governor, John Mitchell tells me he 'owns' Tennessee. He is very fond of your state." I was taken aback by her remark and recall that I made some comment as to my appreciation that Mitchell and his wife had attended my inauguration representing President Nixon. From that unusual comment by our hostess I trust our conversation moved on to other topics. She did not elaborate on what she had said, but I couldn't dismiss the attorney general's reference to our state in such unusual terms. Later, I concluded that the "ownership" reference must have related to the fact that John Mitchell, when a senior member of the law firm Mudge, Rose, was quite involved in handling the legal matters pertaining to the occasional issuing of general obligation bonds for the state of Tennessee. Nothing else seemed to make sense. It was interesting to me how an apparent offhand remark by the gentleman to his friend Happy found its way to the ears of a Tennessee governor.

The next day in New York consisted of a plenary session of the Governors Association. The wives and children were lavishly entertained in the city while we governors discussed matters relating to government and political matters. We were addressed by several prominent business executives and government officials.

The last day of the meeting found our group being bused to the Pocantico Hills estate built in 1912 by John D. Rockefeller, which had become the home of Nelson Rockefeller. We took tours of the magnificent home overlooking the Hudson River. The ladies were treated to a separate luncheon while we governors had our meal at the table of the famed oil tycoon John D. Rockefeller. It was an impressive setting at which to conduct business affairs of the association. To my delight and surprise, a favor was placed at each lunch setting. The favor was a handsome wristwatch engraved with our host's name and the date. Each governor's wife was favored with a beautiful Steuben glass trout mounted on a pedestal in an action mode with a gold artificial fly lure fixed to its lower lip. Remarkable. And quite extravagant. A true Rockefeller touch!

The final event of the RGA meeting hosted by the Rockefellers took place at the Metropolitan Museum of Art. The affair was a formal dinner. My two ladies, Betty and Gayle, were beautifully dressed for the occasion, and I can't imagine the museum being decorated for the occasion more dramatically. It was a striking event, and we were entertained lavishly. It was certainly true to the form of everything else that had occurred during our visit. One interesting note is that our daughter was assigned a fine-looking young man who was a Rockefeller aide to serve as her personal aide for the evening. Gayle certainly enjoyed herself and would later be thrilled to learn that the young man was George Pataki, a future outstanding governor of New York.

I met Governor Pataki in 2004 in Nashville, and we enjoyed recalling that special evening. We returned from New York greatly impressed with the Rockefellers and the hospitality of New York.

A Supreme Dilemma

With the first session of the 88th General Assembly adjourned and freed from the intense demands on my time during the legislative session, I found little relief because of several major problems only the governor could attempt to resolve. One significant situation was tied to an event that had its beginning in June 1972. A Supreme Court vacancy unexpectedly occurred. For the first time in recent history a Republican governor was charged with the task of appointing a justice of the state's highest court. The result was that a flood of conflict and partisan bias among judicial, legal, and legislative interests in the state was to take place merely because a Republican occupied the statehouse.

Historically, the duty of the governor was to appoint a successor to fill any vacancy occurring in our justice system. The so-called Modified Missouri Plan had been introduced in the first session of the 87th General Assembly with the encouragement of Tennessee lawyers as a merit selection plan designed to upgrade the quality of state appellate court judges. Upon its passage by both houses, I signed the bill into law. My impression was that the plan was intended to eliminate awkward campaigning across the state supported by financial contributions opening the door to questions of partiality and favoritism. The age-old question of "politics" was thus to be, if not answered, at least negated. At the time of its passage, there were thoughtful comments regarding the Missouri Plan's constitutionality, but no challenge was made.

On June 19, 1972, the sudden death of Supreme Court Justice Larry Creson of Memphis, who represented the Western District of the state, triggered a series of actions under the law that ultimately led to contentious legal wrangling and ill will. My duty under the rules of the Modified Missouri Plan was to officially declare that a vacancy existed. I followed the steps outlined in the new law by requesting three names from the recently appointed Appellate Court Nominating Commission and from those names, or from another list of names to be submitted in the event I required further candidates for consideration, select one individual whom I would appoint to fill that vacancy on the court. Major complications arose.

Although the death occurred more than thirty days before an August 3 primary election, the newly enacted merit selection law required that three names be submitted to me within a certain time. That certain time would be consumed by the eleven-member commission identifying desirable candidates, conducting interviews, and making a proper selection to present to the governor. Five days before that time expired, the Nominating Commission submitted three names for my consideration. I chose from among those names that of Thomas F. Turley, Jr., of Memphis, a Republican. The law required that I make the appointment and issue a commission verifying my action. The newly appointed justice would then stand for up or down approval by the voters in the upcoming August 3 primary election.

The duty requiring the governor to act in such a circumstance was made impossible by virtue of the timing of the unfortunate death and the requirements of the merit selection law. As fate would have it, across the state all ballots and voting machines had already been prepared for the election. There was no means by which the name of my choice to fill the court vacancy could be added to the ballot as required by law. Additionally, absentee voting had already taken place, and ballots for U.S. military personnel voting absentee had also been previously mailed. It was impossible to include a new name for voter consideration at the August 3 election. To further complicate matters, Mr. Turley, then a sitting U.S. district attorney, stated that he could not accept appointment until September 1. Clearly, the governor and the state judiciary faced an impossible dilemma in attempting to follow the law.

To make matters even more difficult, in an ugly act of partisanship, Memphis attorney and Democrat Robert Taylor announced that he would be a write-in candidate for the Supreme Court vacancy on August 3. I issued a statement to the effect that Taylor was not eligible.

Several days prior to the Election Day of August 3, I was visited on a highly confidential basis by Chief Justice of the Supreme Court Ross Dyer. We discussed the dilemma at length, following which the Chief Justice advised me in greatest confidence to wait until September 1, at which time I should appoint Thomas Turley and issue a commission to that effect. Justice Dyer assured me that such action on my part was the best possible choice I had and that he was certain the Supreme Court would not challenge my action. Regrettably, that proved to be poor advice. His action in that matter would lead the Chief Justice later to excuse himself from participating in a subsequent Supreme Court decision that settled the entire matter to the satisfaction of no one concerned.

The names of both Robert Taylor and Thomas Turley were submitted by a number of voters as "write-ins" at election time. Taylor received a greater number of "write-ins" than did Turley, but their total vote was a minor fraction of the more than half million cast. In an act that I considered highly irresponsible, Secretary of State Joe Carr issued a certificate of election on behalf of Taylor. The Supreme Court determined that neither candidate was eligible under the law. That nullified Carr's partisan certificate of election for Taylor. However, those actions precipitated a flood of litigation, which spilled over into the next year.

During the ensuing year, the phrase "Taylor versus Turley" became a commonplace reference. The Modified Missouri Plan was found to be unconstitutional by the high court, but this point was glossed over in the principal finding that neither candidate Taylor nor Turley was eligible for the office because the true function of the Missouri Plan was to accept or reject, not vote for, a particular person.

Continuing efforts by the court to resolve the matter resulted in a conclusion being reached that, in fact, there had been no election and therefore the governor could proceed to fill a vacancy that continued to exist. So advised, I made a request of the Appellate Court Nominating Commission that they submit three names for my consideration. By that time, Thomas Turley had withdrawn from consideration. I chose to appoint Memphis attorney William H. D. Fones, a political independent whom I held in high regard. Justice Fones eventually became Chief Justice Fones and served with distinction.

Thus, a unique series of events that captured the attention of legal minds across the state as no other problem had in recent times were resolved. Timing was the culprit that created an impossible legal situation in which the human weaknesses of incumbent justices of the Supreme Court were revealed and the inexactness of carefully contrived state law was shown to be defective under certain circumstances. Equally evident in the case was a determination on the parts of Democrat leaders to put every obstacle possible in the path of a Republican governor conducting the business of the government. It was a painful time for me, and I was relieved to see the important matter of a vacancy on the state Supreme Court resolved at last. Apparently, the earlier court finding that the Missouri Plan was unconstitutional was disregarded. Those events would not mark the end of partisanship and the Supreme Court's ineptness, however.

Opportunities requiring me to administer the myriad administrative duties of the office consumed the remaining months of the year. Public appearances, the reception of various delegations of visitors in the capitol, appointments to boards and commissions, attendance at other governors' conferences, visits to state prisons, hospitals, and regional offices, and local events assured the swift passage of days. Among my more pleasant duties was that of welcoming groups representing new business and industrial investments in our state. State and national economic conditions were healthy, and Tennessee was benefiting from substantial growth in tax revenues.

Memphis Shines

At the annual Republican Governors Association meeting in 1972 I was nominated to succeed Virginia Governor Linwood Holton as its chairman when his term expired in 1973. This was an unexpected honor and responsibility. As the chairman-elect, I had the duty of arranging for the 1973 RGA meeting, which would be held somewhere in Tennessee in the fall. I lost no time advising my wife and staff that a busy time in planning and preparation for that event lay ahead. We enthusiastically set about thinking through the many details that would be involved, among them the major decision regarding the most desirable location to accommodate visiting state governors, their associates, interested participants, RGA staff, and members of the media. Nothing of that nature had ever occurred in our hometown, so we chose Memphis as the site.

The Holiday Inn Corporation, founded in Memphis, had an elegant facility named the Holiday Inn Rivermont located high on a bluff in the city. It would be the ideal location at which to host the conference.

My first lady and my director of communications, Ralph Griffith, immediately became the key leaders in managing the preparation that would take place in the months ahead. Betty took charge of selecting individuals, mainly in Memphis and Nashville, with whom she would work. Among her most worthy selections was that of Anna Morrow, who was the wife of Robert Morrow, a Memphis industrialist. Anna Morrow was a remarkable lady, highly popular in Memphis circles, and well known for her artistic and civic activities. Anna helped Betty select others who enthusiastically joined in the effort. An official Host Committee was formed. As the months elapsed leading up to the convening of the conference, a capable team of volunteers came together to see that our conference was a memorable success.

With help from Nashville friends in particular and working with my staff and personnel from the RGA office in Washington, D.C., the Memphis people did an outstanding job of making sure that our visitors from across the nation would enjoy a productive and enjoyable visit to Tennessee's Queen City.

The dates of Sunday, November 18, through Tuesday, November 20, were confirmed. The many details of preparing for such an event were put in the hands of others, among them the staff of the Republican Governors Association. The work required to bring all events together was demanding and time consuming. The people of Memphis were thrilled with the opportunity to put our city's best foot forward. Everyone was excited over the anticipated presence of Governor and Mrs. Ronald Reagan of California and Governor and Mrs. Nelson Rockefeller of New York, among the many other prominent political leaders who would be present.

I invited all governors to arrive a day early to join me for a trip to Jackson, Mississippi. Our Tennessee Vols football team was to play my alma mater, the University of Mississippi, on Saturday afternoon prior to the beginning of our Memphis meeting. Tennessee was favored to win. Governors Ronald Reagan, Jack Williams, and Kit Bond accompanied me, and we were most graciously hosted by Mississippi's Governor Bill Waller. Regardless of Mississippi's reputation for southern hospitality, Ole Miss defeated Tennessee 28 to 12.

Our carefully planned conference went off like clockwork. On Sunday the various delegations representing sixteen of our nation's nineteen Republican governors began to arrive. Each party had a special host and hostess composed of well-known Memphians who gave generously of their time. That evening, a reception and dinner took place aboard the Schlitz Corporation's *Schlitz Belle*, a facsimile of a large riverboat. It was a unique setting and quite a hit with all those present. Memphis entertainer Rufus Thomas performed his popular song, the "Funky Chicken." Several out-of-state visitors viewed the performance in awe, we were told.

Monday morning a plenary session of the governors convened. The principal issues before us related to a growing energy crisis based on gasoline shortages nationwide and the Watergate investigation by Congress. A resolution was pending in the U.S. Congress regarding the declaration of an energy emergency. There was serious consideration being given to gasoline rationing. Earlier in the year, with the crisis impending, I had appointed a capable Nashville businessman named Carroll Kroeger to head up a Tennessee Office of Fuel Allocation, which was created by executive order. He was doing a good job in preparing fuel suppliers to be ready for rationing if that was the federal government's decision.

Speakers for the morning session included U.S. Interior Secretary Rogers C. B. Morton and national pollster George Gallup. At noon, a luncheon for local Republican leaders and precinct workers was held. Six of our visiting governors spoke to this group, praising them for their grassroots political work. It was a fitting tribute to fine people.

The afternoon session consisted of various reports from committees and further discussions regarding the energy crisis and the ongoing events surrounding the Watergate mystery. That situation was consuming much of the Congress's attention and creating a huge distraction for the Nixon administration. A resolution was offered and adopted complimenting Richard Nixon on his many accomplishments and encouraging full disclosure of all details surrounding Watergate. During that session we were advised that the White House had requested time the next day when President Nixon wished to appear before the group of governors. That news quickly altered the nature of our conference and created an air of expectation reflected by all participants. Governor Holton, the chairman, quickly offered a resolution to welcome the president, and it was approved.

The black-tie state dinner planned for Monday night was a resounding success. Following a large reception and dinner, the speaker, House Minority Leader Gerald Ford who by then was the vice-presidential designee to replace Spiro Agnew, gave an excellent address praising the governors, commenting guardedly on the Watergate question, and reviewing various national issues. Ford's speech was followed with entertainment offered by Johnny Cash, his wife, June, members of her family, and his band. The show was a smash hit with all in attendance. I was very grateful for Mr. Cash's generous contribution to the conference.

Tuesday's session involved routine association business, including the selection of Governor Kit Bond of Missouri as chairman-elect. At this same meeting Governor Holton turned the gavel over to me, and I chaired the remaining moments. The previous day I wrote three brief personal notes to governors asking them to serve on my Executive Committee. Governor William Milliken of Michigan sent a note back graciously accepting. Governor Robert Ray of Iowa did the same. Governor Ronald Reagan wrote back, "H— yes!" I kept that note! The meeting was adjourned. Events were timed so that governors could exit to the front of the hotel where arrangements had been made to welcome the president.

Memphis had done herself proud. It was a shining moment for that great city. Tours of interesting sights, host couples exerting every effort to make their special guests comfortable, golf outings, and interesting Tennessee-produced gifts all contributed to the pleasures that were received and gratefully acknowledged. The Host Committee chaired by Anna Morrow had done its work to perfection.

The Nixon Visit

Exactly on time, the presidential motorcade arrived at the Holiday Inn Rivermont to be welcomed by a crowd of approximately four thousand citizens. It was a warm and friendly greeting, marred only slightly by several sign bearers demanding answers to Watergate. The president and his lovely wife, Pat, were officially welcomed, after which he responded with words of thanks to the people assembled. They were then led into the hotel where arrangements had been made for the governors' wives to entertain Mrs. Nixon with a luncheon. I vividly recall a glimpse of Betty seated with Pat Nixon in a swing facing each other while photographers took many pictures.

The president was ushered into a fairly small conference room where he, along with all governors, sat surrounding a handsome wooden table. The only governor not present was Ronald Reagan, who had left early Tuesday morning to return to California for urgent reasons. As RGA chairman, I initiated the discussion by welcoming the president. I thanked him for coming to our meeting. The previous week he had met with a group of Republican senators to give them assurance regarding his Watergate problem. I told him that our group of governors, as chief executives of governments, could relate to him based on our mutual responsibilities to lead and be forthright. I further stated that his presence was deeply appreciated.

My comments were brief. I remarked that I had encountered difficulty in the past in attempts to speak directly with the president and that we all valued the occasion to have direct conversation. He frowned, reached over, patted my leg in an expression of sympathy, and then accepted my invitation to address our group.

Nixon's voice was very subdued as he began his remarks. I noticed several governors leaning forward in order to hear his words. He said that this was a stressful time and mentioned reasons why that was so. He then proceeded to comment on the national economy's good condition, his ongoing discussions with Russia's Leonid Brezhnev, the national energy crisis, and other matters. As he continued, the president's voice grew stronger, his energy seemed to surge, and he began to assume the role of the person he was. Watergate became the chief topic. He apologized to the group for any discomfort and concern the controversial situation may have posed for any one of us.

The president spoke for ten or twelve minutes. The core of his message was that he would survive the congressional inquiry and that the matter would be resolved. He emphatically assured the group that there were no more "bombs" to go off or "shoes" to be dropped. He was referring to prior revelations, including the big one having to do with secret tapes that had been made throughout his time in office for his personal use. The tapes had become the major issue in the Watergate investigation. He had been directed by the attorney general to surrender certain of the tapes to a senatorial committee. A subpoena had been issued. Nixon had staunchly refused to release the tapes, claiming that it was his duty to protect the power of executive privilege for the office of the president. At the time we met with him the tapes had not been turned over as requested.

His presentation was followed by questions from the governors. It was interesting to me that the president sat unaccompanied by staff or attorney. The questions were frank and to the point. I recalled those of Governor Tom McCall of Oregon. He was no fan of Nixon, and his questions were unvarnished. At the conclusion of the questions and answers, our guest once again emphatically stated that he would survive the ordeal and that we could be assured there would be no more "surprises."

The meeting adjourned, and the group of governors accompanied the president to his limousine. At a news conference shortly after the official party had departed, I, along with two other governors, addressed questions from the major networks that had set up cameras for the occasion. Our general consensus was that the president had put to rest any doubts we may have had and that we had been assured he would survive the investigation. He assured us things would return to relative normalcy. We repeated our support for the president. By that time, our RGA Conference had concluded.

Imagine my shock the following evening when a news broadcast revealed that one of the tapes subpoenaed contained an eighteen-and-one-half-minute gap. The president's longtime secretary, Rosemary Woods, claimed that the gap was caused by her foot hitting a pedal attached to a recorder from which she was transcribing that tape. The timing was critical to the Senate's investigation because the tape was recorded only several days after the Watergate break-in had occurred. Investigators believed that section of the tape would have revealed Nixon's management of the attempt to cover up the break-in. Richard Nixon must have been aware of the flawed tape when he met with us. Although he managed to survive additional months in office, I am confident the highly questionable tape played a major role in his subsequent resignation from office. I was, to say the least, disappointed.

The Good Times

The fall season of 1973 was a busy time. Much energy had been required for the Memphis RGA Conference. A new football season brought many opportunities to visit various college campuses and enjoy the sport. The University of Tennessee was scheduled to play the Military Academy at West Point, and my family was invited to attend and be hosted by the commandant of the Academy. Among the pleasures of the trip to the Academy was my privilege to review the cadets marching on the famous Plain, standing at attention with the commandant. Our daughter Gayle was a guest at the commandant's residence while we stayed in a nearby hotel. She was treated elegantly and enjoyed a date with a cadet officer. The high point came on Saturday afternoon when the Vols won their game. It was a grand experience for my family.

Betty enjoyed her position as first lady and opportunities that often resulted from that prominence. In the fall of 1973 she learned the movie star Burt Reynolds was in Nashville for several days to record an album. He was the house guest of Buddy and Sue Killen, friends we had met through Minnie and Henry Cannon. Betty called Sue and invited the Killens and their guest to our Residence for a country dinner and tennis, which had earlier been planned for Sunday afternoon with the Cannons. A grand time was spent eating a delicious country dinner prepared by Betty and playing tennis. In addition, we enjoyed watching a professional football game on television. Burt Reynolds was a delightful guest. He had brought with him his lady friend, Miss Dinah Shore. We were thrilled to have Dinah, a Tennessee girl, join us. It was a memorable day, and Reynolds was an excellent tennis player. At the end of our last set when he and Dinah had defeated Betty and me, Reynolds leaped from his side of the court across the net and gave Betty a big hug. She liked that. Later, he gave his warm-up suit to our daughter Julie. It was a special occasion.

Several days later I received a call from Reynolds. He explained that he was under contract with NBC television to produce three late night one-hour TV special shows, one of which he had already done. He further explained that, after spending the afternoon with us at the Residence, he had dreamed that evening of producing a show at the Residence featuring some of our most popular country music performers. I agreed that he had a good idea and that I could approve it. Within a matter of weeks, arrangements had been made, and the special TV show was well on its way.

A large staff of NBC technicians, directors, and others set themselves in place at the Residence one evening after doing quite a bit
of preliminary filming in and around Nashville. Cameras and power
lines were in abundance. It was a big production, and it would be a
fine event to showcase our capital city. Betty and I invited a number
of friends to come over and witness the activity.

The entertainment portion of the show was filmed at the Residence.
Guest performers included Minnie Pearl, Glen Campbell, Bobby
Goldsboro, Dolly Parton, Charlie Rich, Dinah Shore, Porter Wagoner,
Jim Nabors, and others. Betty, Julie, and I were also featured. The
program was filmed with all participants sitting around in the state
drawing room of the Residence laughing, joking, being informal,
and performing. It was quite an evening.

The Burt Reynolds special from the Governor's Residence was
presented to the public by NBC and its sponsors. I felt it was worth
the effort and time spent assisting in the production. It certainly
presented our state in a favorable light to millions of viewers. Once
again I was proud of my wife for being on her toes.

As Christmas approached we enjoyed the experience of sharing
our official Residence with many visitors and entertaining various
groups. The Christmas tree and other decorations were splendid. It
was very satisfying to Betty and me to host visits by members of our
family. Relatives from Mississippi, Alabama, Memphis, and Dyersburg
always enjoyed their time with us since they were treated with such
kindness by the good people on the house staff. We enjoyed many
happy moments together. Demands on my time for official duties
relented only near Christmas Day and at the New Year's celebration.

Betty and I learned from our next door-neighbors, Sarah and
Henry Cannon, that we had been invited to fly to California as
guests of entertainer Jim Nabors. We had all become acquainted
during his visits to Nashville to record various albums. Once aboard
the airplane for the flight west, we had quite a treat. It was not long
after being airborne that most passengers discovered the presence of
our celebrity friend, Minnie Pearl. She became the center of attention
and proceeded to entertain one and all with her hilarious comedy
routine. It was a quick flight not soon to be forgotten by all aboard.

We were met at the Los Angeles air terminal by Jim Nabors
and swiftly transported to his beautiful home in the Bel Air suburb.

To our amazement, Jim insisted that Betty and I occupy his master bedroom suite. He proudly showed the four of us his extensive wardrobe that filled two very large adjoining rooms. That evening we attended a dinner party hosted by a friend of Nabors. Seated to my left was actor Carroll O'Connor, who was more widely known as Archie Bunker. He was a highly intelligent conversationalist who has become identified as television's greatest actor. In the course of our talk, he minced no words in telling me that he believed Richard Nixon was a crook. I defended the president, only to recall later that Mr. O'Conner was closer to the truth than I.

The next evening, after a day of sightseeing, we prepared for Jim's Christmas party. As his guests arrived, Minnie Pearl, Henry, Betty, and I stood near the host who was welcoming his visitors. It was clear that we were the guests of honor! We were in the midst of a swarm of movie stars and other Hollywood celebrities. When singer-songwriter Burt Bacharach and his wife, Angie Dickinson, came through the door, I thought Betty would swoon. When Jim introduced my first lady to Burt, he gave her a big kiss. I've never heard the end of that moment! The number of popular movie stars at that party was impressive. It was a gala evening. Some of the guests gathered around a piano being played by musician Paul Weston while his wife, Jo Stafford, stood by, and we sang old, familiar songs. The next day we returned to Nashville, somewhat heady from finding ourselves on a first-name basis with so many interesting people. We were grateful to Jim Nabors. To me, he will always be Gomer Pyle.

My First Lady

It was satisfying for me to pause occasionally and observe my wife as we engaged in various activities that came along. She had surely progressed in confidence from the days when an appearance before any group, such as a Sunday school class, caused her pulse rate to quicken. Two examples taken from notes she had recorded serve well to make my point.

One of my most special days at the Governor's Residence came when I received a call from the Easter Seals Camp asking if they could bring the children for a tour. I was amazed when

493

the vans drove up and out came children with crutches, wheel chairs and one child was carried in because he was missing arms and legs. They were happy and smiling and obviously excited over being there. I put on my best smile, invited them in and proceeded to point out all the beautiful furnishings and shared some of the history. The children were interested but what they really wanted to know about was "Minnie Pearl." I whispered to the trooper to call Minnie to see if she could possibly slip over for a few minutes. Luckily, Minnie was at home. She came right over in time to share juice and cookies and some pretty funny stories about Grinder's Switch. One of life's greatest lessons I learned from Minnie right then and there. She asked them to give her a gift! A look of wonderment came over their faces. She said she knew that they had been to camp and had learned some songs and would they share some of them with us. Needless to say they proudly sang their little hearts out, happily knowing that they had given something of themselves to Minnie and me.

And then,

The Governor's Residence was an awesome place to live. State Troopers, servants, secretaries, people in and out constantly, but we managed to make it as much like home as we could. We love celebrating birthdays so when Winfield had his "first" birthday there, we decided to have a beautiful dinner party in the state dining room and invite our close friends, among them a future governor and first lady, Lamar and Honey Alexander. We set that long table with a lovely tablecloth that came almost to the floor, china, crystal and so forth, and, of course, planned for a birthday cake to be brought out at the end of dinner. It was fun to be with our friends but I noticed an unusual amount of giggling and knowing glances among our guests. I had no idea at the time that our youngest daughter, Julie, then 10, was under that table "tweaking" our guests' toes and whispering that they not give her away. Can you imagine Winfield's surprise, when ready to blow out the candles, Julie jumps out from under the table singing "Happy birthday, Daddy!!"

Betty entertained many groups of visiting ladies with such stories, and they loved it. She was always poised and the confidence showed. What a teammate!

As the new year approached, my thoughts were drawn toward the challenges and opportunities that my final year as governor would bring. Major issues mentioned earlier loomed large. They were the long-standing Overton Park I-40 controversy in Memphis, efforts to build regional prisons, the growing problem of how to deal with a free-standing medical school in Johnson City, the completion of I-81 in East Tennessee as it related to bloody Highway 11 W, and continued partisan struggles over the selection of Supreme Court judges. None of these had diminished in the intervening months from legislative adjournment and the start of the new year. Beyond those pressing issues were the presentation of a forward-looking budget and the necessary legislative efforts to implement my recommendations. Additionally, it was to be an election year during which a new governor and legislature would be chosen by the people. A second term for me was prohibited by the Constitution. My last session would be a busy time, and I looked forward to the opportunities.

CHAPTER THIRTY-TWO

SECOND SESSION, 88TH GENERAL ASSEMBLY

No Letup

The legislature convened in a mood to get its work done and then look immediately to the demands of the 1974 election year. Its members were veterans of a productive session the year earlier, and each individual was prepared to move quickly into action. Chief among the Democrat priorities was garnering the necessary simple majority to override a number of my vetoes and legislating changes in the Modified Missouri Plan to thwart a Republican governor's opportunity to appoint new members of the Supreme Court. The Republican leaders, Tom Jensen of the House and Houston Goddard of Maryville (who had replaced Garland as the Senate leader), remained steadfast in their commitment to assist the administration in every possible way. The political pot was boiling.

State of the State, January 9, 1974

By an earlier resolution, the legislature requested that the governor forego his annual address to the newspaper editors and publishers. Rather, my invitation was to deliver that message to a joint meeting of both houses. This was a first in recent history, and I welcomed the opportunity to make an extra presentation to our lawmakers. There was much, outside the constraints of a budget message, to speak about.

I thanked the members for their invitation. Then, recognizing a confused and restless world and our highly complex American society, I noted with satisfaction that our armed forces were returned from Southeast Asia. I lamented the political scandal and abuse of authority in high places within our federal government and the erosion of our dollars because inflation was a growing reality. Growing unemployment figures were in evidence. The era of cheap energy was at an end, and the excesses in spending public tax dollars were sobering considerations. And yet, I felt that no previous generation of Americans was more willing to acknowledge our shortcomings and to correct them than was ours. It was a time of change and challenge in which we Tennesseans had a major role to play.

The core message I delivered centered on three major concerns that touched the lives of Tennesseans every day. They included the current and prospective economic climate of our state, perceived social attitudes of our citizens influenced by government policy, and the role of the state in meeting its responsibilities to govern.

During the previous three years, we had experienced steady improvement in our economy. Per capita earnings were at their highest levels in history, more people were at work, and record numbers of dollars had been invested through business and industrial growth. On the horizon, however, were signs of uncertainty with the national economy. On the supply side were clear signs that materials and products for growth were increasingly difficult to obtain. Predictions reached a consensus that the nation should not be surprised at moderate growth or slight recession in the year ahead. For Tennessee, because of its diversified economy and lack of dependence on any one industry or product, the state should do better than the nation as a whole. We could expect our unemployment rate to remain one to two percentage points below the national average. In turn we should anticipate future state revenues to be adequate in the coming year for continued growth.

I suggested we keep in mind that the progress of our people could not be measured by material growth alone. We were progressively a more tolerant people regardless of race, religion, or lifestyle. Through our Tennessee churches and community groups and as individuals, we remained ready to lend helping hands. We were convinced that every public facility should be available to all citizens, and we insisted that every young person should have access to whatever public education he or she could absorb. We were frustrated by and fearful of an increasing rate of violent crimes. We were convinced strong punishment was necessary, including the death penalty for certain crimes. We remained dedicated to the neighborhood concept for public schools and deeply regretted the failure of the federal courts to see the negative effects of forced busing. In every sense, Tennessee remained a work in progress supported by a people, young and old alike, who found ourselves with great opportunity to seek health, happiness, and prosperity through our own industrious efforts and a concerned, effective state government.

My speech contained many references to the progress that had been made and the concerns that still existed. In public education, mental health, public health, modernization of our criminal justice system, transportation, economic sufficiency, and a fair and adequate system of taxation there was progress yet to be made and challenges yet to be met. Far beyond my tenure and perhaps those of legislators present, efforts and opportunities for happy and productive lives for all our citizens should remain the concerns of one and all.

I closed by expressing my respect and appreciation for the members of the Assembly. I pledged cooperation in every possible way as they received my next and final budget message for fiscal year 1975. They would soon be debating the merits of proposals to meet serious needs. I wished them well.

The Budget Message, Fiscal Year 1975

My budget message to the 88th General Assembly outlined the administration's priority program goals for the new fiscal year and improvement funds necessary for their implementation. Considerable success had been achieved during the past three years, and the foundation that had been laid by previous leaders in recent years had been significantly strengthened. My words were optimistic, yet laced with numerous reminders that our Tennessee society faced serious unmet needs.

I requested a total appropriation of $2.1 billion, which represented a $210 million increase over the previous year's budget. That overall request represented a 10 percent increase. More than $500 million of the budgeted expenditures represented federal funds. These significant figures reflected the tax increases I requested in 1971 plus a growing and vibrant Tennessee economy that had produced adequate revenues for each year of my service as governor.

I emphasized that my administration had been frugal as it worked to make sure Tennesseans received a dollar's worth of service for every dollar they paid into the state treasury. We showed savings in each budget period and were able to redirect much needed dollars into programs where compelling needs were met. Assuming the legislature continued the temporary one-half cent sales tax, I could assure a sound base for many essential programs in the year ahead.

The program I proposed stressed my belief that education, jobs, and transportation ranked at the top among our most vital concerns. Education consumed approximately one-half of all state taxes. Significant issues in education resulted in strong disagreement between me and the Democrat-dominated Assembly. A major case was represented by their insistence that a $136 million bond issue be enacted to fund the vocational education legislation passed the previous year. It would be at least another year before those funds would be called on. It was not necessary to add that figure to our total bonded indebtedness. My request for their reconsideration would fall on deaf ears or, better put, partisan ears. I was focused on teachers' salary increases, money for higher education with emphasis on medical training, and demand for operating funds for newly opened community colleges. Those were priority items. Another priority for me was completion of adequate funding to give every child a public school kindergarten head start.

The Department of Economic and Community Development was off to a strong start, and added funds were necessary to maintain its momentum. We had developed specific programs for reaching our objectives that included assisting communities to increase capacity to grow. We needed to sharply accelerate industrial development efforts by both domestic and foreign investors. The horizon was bright with opportunity for well-ordered industrial expansion and commercial growth. A major emphasis was put on promoting tourism.

I stressed the obvious fact that our transportation system was the lifeline of our state. The completion of the interstate highway system had been frequently compromised by the untimely flow of Federal Highway Trust Funds. A previous authorization of short-term notes assisted our efforts by allowing us to move consistently forward in construction with added money. I requested authorization for another round of such notes to pre-finance and accelerate building the remainder of the interstate system.

The balance of the message addressed my continued interest in state park development, surface mining supervision, local mass transit aid, state worker salary increases, an effective capital punishment law, no-fault automobile insurance, worker's compensation law revision, stronger drunk-driving laws, and the real energy crisis that was upon us.

I felt a hallmark of my administration would be our constant emphasis on changes in the way our state did business. We set a tempo and selected a course that the people found acceptable. The experience of the past three years had demonstrated the willingness of Tennesseans to accept change when that change meant true progress. My travels across the state and discussions along the way reinforced my belief that our people expected a responsive and a responsible government. While it was impossible to meet every call for service, it was possible for state government, through its elected leaders, to make progress based on common sense and available resources. With that, my message was concluded.

Results: Second Session, 88th General Assembly

The last session was perhaps the most contentious of the four I experienced. Hard-core Democrat leaders were spoiling for issues and events that would discredit my reputation as a successful governor, and they had ample grist for their mill. Evidence of that fact could be seen in the number of vetoes I was compelled to issue. There were a total of 23 veto messages sent to the secretary of state including the General Appropriations Bill that contained line item objections to various programs and appropriated sums that I felt to be undesirable or unnecessary.

In the 87th General Assembly we had a 96 percent success factor in passage of priority legislation and an 80 percent success factor on all administration legislation. The 88th General Assembly gave us a 61 percent success factor for priority legislation and a 78 percent success factor overall. I was proud of the quality legislation various departments of the administration proposed and equally proud of the work done by my staff in pushing those items we felt essential for the kind of government we were promoting. Serious differences of opinion flavored the atmosphere of those three months, and they certainly brought into play the process by which free people and the democratic process of governing is carried out.

The session was not without its more affectionate moments. Betty and I were invited to a joint meeting of the Assembly in March at which time she was presented a beautiful sterling silver tea service with a handsome platter containing her engraved name and the dates of our time of service. Gracious words were spoken regarding the manner in which she had conducted herself as the state's first lady. A resolution appropriately signed accompanied the gift. We were deeply touched and attempted to respond with the gratitude we felt toward such a warm gesture. The gift remains a treasured keepsake in our family.

Another token of appreciation occurred when a joint resolution from both chambers officially designated the attractive nature center building at Fall Creek Falls State Park to be named the Betty Dunn Nature Center. Proper signage was put in place at the facility, and we have, down through the years, taken great pride in visiting the center on occasion.

An improvement request was passed by the legislature enabling all five-year-olds who so desired to attend state-supported kindergartens. That additional sum assured that my campaign pledge made in 1970 to provide a statewide kindergarten for every Tennessee child would become a permanent reality.

A highly emotional issue had surfaced in 1973 resulting from an incident involving a male student at Middle Tennessee State University in Murfreesboro who was charged with abusing a female student while both were residents in the same dormitory building. The issue of co-educational dormitories created much interest and debate in the 1974 session. A 1973 bill introduced legislation that would prohibit housing of male and female students in the same dormitory of any institution of higher education chartered by the state. Such a law, if enacted, would have caused major disruptions in a number of colleges and universities, among them Vanderbilt University, Fisk University, the University of Tennessee at Knoxville, and the UT Medical Units at Memphis. Substantial shifting of students and new construction costs became major concerns. The bill failed in committee but was reintroduced in the 1974 session and passed both houses. I received urgent pleas by representatives at the highest levels from among the universities that would be adversely affected. I felt it was my duty to veto the bill and did so, citing a lack of objective data to indicate its need and expressing a general sense of confidence in Tennessee's college students. An effort to override the veto failed in the Senate and was not attempted in the House.

Another issue that had grown in intensity had to do with state savings and loan associations. Legislation had been proposed in 1973 to provide interim regulatory authority to deal with antiquated and inadequate statutes pointed out by that industry. Nothing developed at the time, but in 1974 my administration offered a comprehensive savings and loan regulatory bill after much study of the subject. My bill was defeated in a Senate committee, but a non-administration bill that we were able to strengthen eventually was enacted into law. It was a major step forward for the financial community.

Other matters that characterized the intense nature of the session included the following. We introduced a bill to substantially increase the penalties for driving while intoxicated. Rather heated exchanges between me and several legislators, whom I felt were obstructing priority business, eventually led to the bill's failure in both Calendar Committees of the legislature. However, we were able to amend a Habitual Offenders Act to accomplish the strengthening DWI provisions. A Senate joint resolution requiring withdrawal of a 1972 state ratification of an Equal Rights Amendment became quite an emotional issue. We heard much from various women's organizations. The repeal passed both houses but languished on questions of constitutionality. My bill to comply with a Federal Emergency Highway Energy Conservation Act requiring states to reduce maximum automobile speed to 55 miles per hour passed. A bill sponsored by a senator, which had the effect of reducing penalties for excessive speed, also passed and came to me. I vetoed the bill, but it was overridden.

A "sunshine" law dealing with the Watergate mood and addressing open meetings, lobbying activities, campaign finance, ethical practices, and conflicts of interest was enacted. It was later ruled unconstitutional by a Chancery Court. Because the legislature failed to enact meaningful ethics legislation, I, along with the press and general public, severely criticized that shortcoming. An administration bill patterned after a Florida no-fault law, as well two additional bills on the subject, each died in the Senate Commerce Committee. This was a major disappointment to me.

The final legislative session of my term was somewhat controversial but by no means unproductive. Many, many housekeeping details proposed by my various commissioners consumed considerable time. New initiatives that related to the Governor's Cost Control

Study were required to receive the approval of the legislature. Significant steps were taken to improve the efficiency with which government business was conducted. Members of the General Assembly who were facing reelection were anxious to get pet projects for their districts approved by the governor's office. When adjournment time arrived, it was welcomed by one and all.

To Japan

I had accepted an invitation to attend the annual meeting of the Japanese-American Governors Conference in Japan along with ten other governors. I was to represent my state and nation in the meeting, which alternately took place in the United States and Japan. This would be my first and only official visit to a foreign country, and I was anxious to make contacts that might lead to future business relationships.

On April 7, 1974, Betty and I flew to Tokyo where we were met by Japanese representatives and joined by other governors as they arrived. For just short of two weeks we were entertained by our Japanese counterparts, governors of various prefectures across the nation. The hospitality was overflowing and enjoyable. One uncertainty arose as we traveled by bus to various destinations. Not unlike the fabled Keystone Cops of early Hollywood, an assistant to the bus driver would suspend himself out the bus open door, blowing a whistle in an attempt to clear our way through congested traffic. It was humorous but somewhat dangerous for all concerned. We stayed in the finest hotels and learned to drink warm sake chased by beer and served by geishas.

I called on C. Itoh, son of the founder of the then world's largest trading company. My introduction was through Kemmons Wilson of Memphis, founder of Holiday Inns. Our group met with the founder of the Toyota Motor Company, a Mr. Toyoda. I found it interesting that he spelled his last name with a d instead of the t in his company name. We were given an insiders' glimpse of the National Diet of Japan and met Prime Minister Kakuei Tanaka. The day before we were to return to America, the six governors still in our group were notified that we were to be received by Emperor Hirohito and his Empress. This was unexpected and highly unusual.

Our group was transported by bus across the moat that separates the official palace in Tokyo from the city proper and ushered into a modern building that was the residence of the infamous Emperor. After being introduced, the wives joined the Empress in a small circle while the governors met in the same fashion with the Emperor. When my turn formally came to speak with Hirohito, our subjects were hydroelectric power as represented by the world-famous Tennessee Valley Authority and ichthyology, the Emperor's favorite hobby. It was an interesting meeting. I have spoken about that encounter with a number of Japanese acquaintances. On more than one occasion I have been asked to extend my hand for another handshake as the listening party realized that my hand had actually touched the hand of the Emperor. We returned to our homeland weary but grateful for an unusual experience.

Back home and reflecting on the most recent legislative session, three major controversies that were met head-on deserve special comment. They were the proposed free-standing medical school in Johnson City, the Interstate 40 planned route through Overton Park in Memphis, and the opposition to developing two regional prisons in East Tennessee.

The Medical School Controversy

The most divisive and contentious political issue I had to deal with occurred in the second session of the 88th General Assembly when those bodies created the East Tennessee State University Medical School to be located in Johnson City. My ultimate veto of that proposal was intertwined with Democrat determination to deprive me as a Republican governor of my duty to choose three members of the state Supreme Court. Other controversial interests also played a part. In a monumental series of trade-offs with little regard for the best interests of the state at large, members of the legislature achieved their aims, to my great disappointment.

The idea for creating an additional school of medicine in Upper East Tennessee began to take root in the mid-1960s. A number of influential citizens of the area, primarily physicians, felt that a second medical school would be the answer to an acknowledged shortage of physicians throughout the region. At that time three schools of medicine existed. The University of Tennessee College of Medicine in Memphis, Vanderbilt School of Medicine, and Meharry School of Medicine served to educate MDs. Of the three, only the University of Tennessee was a responsibility of the state. Long deprived of attention and adequate services from their state government, residents of Upper East Tennessee felt their interests in obtaining a school for medical education were fully justified. There was no question regarding the shortage and distribution of physicians. However, that situation existed not only in the East but throughout the rural areas of the state in general.

I was fully aware of the existing attitudes in the upper eastern reaches of our state that it had been a political stepchild during the many years of Democrat domination in the governor's office and legislature. I had chosen commissioners of transportation and conservation who were from that area to demonstrate my determination to right old wrongs. Plans for highway and interstate construction in the Tri-Cities area were underway, and new attention to state park opportunities was a priority.

A 1970 study by the newly created Tennessee Higher Education Commission (THEC) stated the obvious regarding a statewide physician shortage. It recommended five major steps. They included providing more financial support for the UT College of Medicine, producing a supply of physicians that matched the national average of such numbers, developing a group of regional training centers for senior medical students by the University of Tennessee Medical School in hospitals across East Tennessee, expanding our UT School of Medicine by forty students along with limiting out-of state-enrollment, and recommending that the state contract with Vanderbilt University and Meharry Medical College to support the admission of ten additional in-state students per year at each school. This was a major study approved by the Ellington administration. The state authorized the development of clinical training centers for senior medical students, interns, and residents at Knoxville, Tri-Cities, Chattanooga, and Jackson. Those were moves in the right direction, but in my case, regrettably, the entire subject would become totally politicized and a matter of intense personal discomfort and frustration to me as events unfolded.

In 1971 the second medical school idea began to become a movement with the passage in the U.S. Congress of the Teague-

Cranston Bill. This legislation called for the creation of eight medical schools to be built in partnership with Veterans Administration hospitals around the country. Johnson City was the home of a VA hospital and seemed to members of the movement to fit perfectly into their plans for a medical school. The legislationcalled for the federal government to provide a majority of the capital outlays and operational costs for six years. Congressman Jimmy Quillen, quite naturally, embraced the idea and was a co-sponsor of the bill. He was instrumental in seeing that the legislation was fully funded in spite of severe reservations from the Nixon administration due to budgetary concerns.

Congressman Quillen and the strong Upper East Tennessee legislative delegation wasted no time letting me know how important it was to them that the General Assembly authorize the creation of the second school of medicine in order to qualify for federal funds. Fresh on the scene as a new governor, I was quick to recognize their interests, and I agreed to give the entire question my most serious consideration. I felt a strong obligation to study the matter not only because of the obvious needs to be met in medical education but also because that strong Republican area of the state had played a large part in my efforts to be elected.

My attention to the medical school issue was dwarfed by the vast number of projects that were immediately in need of my attention. I was fully aware of the THEC study and recommendations. The idea of senior clinical centers with emphasis on family practice made sense to me. I realized that the medical shortage existed throughout the state. The limited funds to which the state had access to meet all its needs remained a primary challenge for me. I knew that the proposed federal funding under Teague-Cranston was restricted to the early years and that a completely new medical school would become the full financial responsibility of the state in a short time.

Near the end of 1971, there was a clear division of interests across the board regarding a second free-standing medical school. The Higher Education Commission and a large legislative delegation were invited to Johnson City to view the proposed site and the VA hospital. The most dramatic outcome of that visit was an opinion shared by all visitors that the people supporting the second school concept were totally committed to a new school. Officials in higher education across the state, as well as legislators outside the upper eastern reaches, felt the recommendations of THEC were the most practical solutions. As for me, considering my duty to the state at large as contrasted to my desire to please my East Tennessee friends and colleagues, there was no easy way out. I requested that another totally impartial study be undertaken to examine the logic and feasibility of a second medical school.

The study, to be headed by Dr. William Willard of the University of Kentucky, was commissioned. The expert consultants involved in the study were approved by supporters of the new medical school. At the conclusion of an in-depth investigation that included consideration of the state at large, its existing medical education facilities, and its needs in general, the study recommended that no second state-supported school should be built. The consultants further suggested that if a second school were to be created in the future, that school should be located in Knoxville. I took the position, after deepest consideration of all the facts as I knew them, that the study's findings were appropriate and that I would be guided by them.

The study was reported in early 1972. It was at that time, to quote my chief legal counsel Lee Smith, a native of Johnson City, that "all hell broke loose!" The subject of a second medical school became the most emotional issue with which I had to deal during my administration. Upper East Tennessee legislators from that time forward became susceptible to political "horse trading" to a degree that was hard to measure. I am confident they wanted to support their Republican governor where possible, but they were totally adamant when any subject regarding their vote could be influenced by the question of the second medical school. Throughout the years 1972 and 1973 the debate and "horse trading" rolled on.

Between legislative sessions late in 1973, I continued to experience the repercussions of my resistance to the new medical school. Messages received and personal pleas from people I respected were intended to persuade me to change my position. I learned that Senators Baker and Brock, neither having any direct responsibility for the question but politically very much aware of what was happening, had shifted their earlier positions in opposition to the school to support for the project. I decided that I needed to go in person to Johnson City and make my case before an assembly of citizens who held steadfast to their objective.

Before a large audience on the East Tennessee State University campus, I made my case. In essence it was that I fully realized the need for more medical doctors, especially for family practitioners. The bottom line for me was that there was a less expensive way to solve that problem, one that could be better afforded by our state in which so many unmet needs remained unfunded. I stressed that my respect for the people in the Tri-Cities area, as well as my appreciation for them, was such that I felt compelled to come to them in person rather than to issue a press statement. I wanted the people to know I was totally sincere in attempting to lead with the concerns of the entire state at the forefront of my thinking.

The audience was courteous but cold. They were such good people. The movement had become, for many, an obsession, a crusade. I persuaded no one to my point of view. The only bright spots for me were an editorial by John M. Jones, publisher of the *Greeneville Sun* newspaper, that supported the logic of my position and messages from two prominent physicians in the area who confidentially expressed their support.

More than once Congressman Quillen reminded me that I had, prior to my election while traveling with him during the campaign, promised that I would support a free-standing medical school if I were elected. My response always was that I could not remember making such a commitment. Throughout my campaign I had been careful not to commit to anything or anyone regarding any matter over which I had no knowledge. Bone weary and often near exhaustion during those campaign days, I can imagine, but not recall, that a promise to give every consideration would have been as far as I could go. Once more, Congressman Quillen and I disagreed.

A third study was requested, and its results were made public in February 1974. It was sponsored under contract by East Tennessee State University at Johnson City. The consultants involved were headed up by Dr. William Harlan, director of the Clinical Studies Program at Duke University. Dr. D. P. Culp, president of ETSU, and the legislative delegation from that area were unrelenting in their efforts to realize their dream. The report was the result of an exhaustive effort that went into great detail as to feasibility, funding, staffing, and administration for a new school. The report essentially became a plan of action for supporters of the school. It recommended the creation of a new medical school. If any fuel was needed to intensify the emotional flames created by this major controversy, the Harlan report was that fuel. Those who favored the plan poured it on. I maintained my position based on the THEC report and confirmed by the Willard study.

Democrat members of the legislature clearly saw opportunities to capitalize on the divisions that had been created within Republican ranks. Aware that I would be required by law to appoint three justices to the state Supreme Court in 1974, the Democrat leaders were apparently convinced I would appoint only Republicans to the state's highest court. Black legislators were focused on overriding my veto of a redistricting bill based on the 1970 census that would have made reelection of Congressman Dan Kuykendall impossible. It was strongly suggested by the majority leadership that blacks support an expected medical school veto before any effort was made to override my veto on redistricting.

Republican legislators determined to have a medical school were persuaded to override my veto of the redistricting bill. No matter that an opportunity existed for the first time to see Republican judges appointed to the state's high court, they were also persuaded to support a Democrat proposal to remove the Supreme Court justices from the Missouri Plan. That legislation was passed and then was vetoed by me. The override came by a substantial majority. A more blatant swapping of votes based on regional interests rather than the interest of the state at large could hardly be imagined.

I spent the early days of the second session of the 88th General Assembly seeking to firm up an overriding support for my position. By a close vote the state Board of Regents adopted a position opposed to the second school. I met with countless legislators in attempts to persuade them to support me. Members of my cabinet joined in the effort. It was a difficult time, and I soon arrived at the point where I felt some compromise of the matter was my best hope of controlling future costs in medical education for the state.

After in-depth discussions, the Board of Regents and THEC joined me in offering a proposal for a combined medical education program involving the University of Tennessee and East Tennessee State University. We recommended maintaining and expanding the basic science medical training program at the school in Memphis and assigning students to a senior clinical training program at ETSU from which an MD degree would be granted upon completion. It was felt that students completing their education in Upper East Tennessee would be inclined to settle and pursue their professions there. It was predicted to be an expensive compromise, but not as expensive as creating a full-blown medical school with its many attendant expenses in years to come. The compromise fell on deaf ears.

The second medical school supporters were rewarded when the medical school bill passed both houses in February 1974 and came to me. With great regret I vetoed the bill, which was then overridden by both houses by substantial majorities. In spite of efforts to reach a compromise that could conserve taxpayers' dollars in the future, the bill contained everything the original concept for the second school required.

The long battle was over, and I willingly bowed to the wishes of the legislative majority. The advocates for the second school were naturally overjoyed, but unfortunately for me, the bitterness and rancor that my position created for many of them were to linger for years to come. When the final budget numbers were presented to me later on, I fully supported the early funding for the school and stated my hope that it would become the finest medical school possible.

All the regrets I felt in not supporting the desires of a people that had long been overlooked and shortchanged were somewhat softened by my personal belief that I did the right thing. Upper East Tennessee benefited substantially from major commitments made and followed through regarding state highway and interstate road development. Great strides forward were realized in business and industrial growth. I remain satisfied that my administration had served that area of the state well.

Interstate 40 and Overton Park

U.S. Highway 51 North connects Memphis with Mississippi to the south and Kentucky to the north. For many years I had traveled that two-lane highway with Dr. Frank Prichard, my father-in-law, to visit his farm in Dyer County. In past years that roadway had often served as a political item when electioneering produced many a promise to four-lane the important connector that followed the Mississippi River through the communities of Millington, Covington, Ripley, Dyersburg, and Union City. When elected governor, I quietly pledged to make that important connector road a four-lane reality. With Commissioner Bob Smith's help, every mile was under contract when I left office. The work was completed during the next administration. It was a major economic boon to Memphis and that entire western area of the state, particularly the town of Dyersburg.

Highway 51 North was a snap because I had complete authority in the matter. Overton Park and Interstate 40 through Memphis, however, were a huge headache for me. I was not prepared mentally at the beginning of my administration for what lay ahead, but I soon became intimately acquainted with the problem that 342 popular acres of park land represented.

Overton Park is a Memphis treasure located in midtown. It is the home of the Memphis Zoo, the Brooks Memorial Art Gallery, a nine-hole golf course, and other attractive features. It became a major item of controversy when the U.S. interstate highway system's plan for Tennessee included a route that would require passage directly through the park. A large segment of the population took issue with the plan to go through the park, and in 1957 a petition opposing infringement on the park was signed by 10,000 Memphis citizens.

Throughout the 1960s, plans continued to be made by federal and state officials to use the park as the most practical route to continue developing I-40, by that time being constructed from its origin in North Carolina to its termination in California. I was aware in those years that local opposition existed, although city of Memphis and state officials strongly supported the route as first developed. The disputed segment through the park was 4,900 feet in length, but that relatively small segment was part of a 3.7 mile section that would be affected one way or another.

By the year 1969, location and design approvals from three federal highway administrators and two secretaries of transportation had encouraged the state to spend $14 million of taxpayer money for engineering, utility adjustments, and right-of-way acquisition to complete a 3.7 mile section of I-40 making that important interstate whole in the Memphis area. Private residences had been purchased and families were uprooted and moved to new locations, while twenty-six acres of right-of-way through Overton Park were acquired at a cost of $2.2 million. Everything was in order to move ahead. At that point, serious troubles for the program occurred.

A group called Citizens to Preserve Overton Park filed suit against the state and the federal Bureau of Public Roads. By 1972, as I was well into my term of office, the litigation was directed by the court to Secretary of Transportation John Volpe to make a final route determination. The secretary requested that an appropriate statement be prepared followed by a public hearing.

The statement and the public hearing took place over time, and in January 1973 the findings were forwarded to Secretary Volpe with a request that he approve the proposed use of land from Overton Park. This was done with my approval on recommendation from Commissioner Bob Smith. The secretary responded that based on the information provided him, he could not agree that the park route was the only feasible choice. Further extended and complex litigation and court action followed. The secretary was determined to let the lawsuits proceed. Our Department of Transportation formally re-evaluated every possible alternate route and concluded there was none.

Various schemes were submitted in an effort to minimize any harm to the park. A cascade of appeals and petitions from citizens, public officials, and civic groups was offered. My final appeal ended with the statement that I strongly agreed with the conclusions and recommendations of a final report offered in concert with the state and local government. The matter was appealed to new Secretary of Transportation Claude Brinegar by letter from Commissioner Smith in June 1974. Three possible schemes were outlined, including a proposed partially depressed roadway with noise barriers, a fully depressed roadway with partial tunnel, and a fully depressed roadway with a full tunnel. The matter was remanded to the courts.

What an irony, I thought. A Republican governor, two Republican senators, a U.S. secretary of transportation appointed by a sitting Republican president of the United States—all unable or unwilling to get a firm directive to proceed with a project that was clearly in the public interest.

The issue remained in contention several years beyond my administration. In 1981 the I-40 park segment was officially deleted by the state. By that time Interstate 40 had been routed to the north onto I-240. It became I-40 again at the Memphis-Arkansas bridge. I believe the failure of the planned route through downtown Memphis contributed substantially to a lessening of economic vitality in that important area of the city.

Regional Prisons

Among my earliest impressions of the grinding demands that fell on my shoulders was that of the conditions prevalent in the state Department of Corrections. Recently constructed prison facilities including the medium security complex at Only, Tennessee, and the Tennessee Prison for Women in Nashville had eased a housing problem for our growing prison population. Wages paid for correctional personnel were totally inadequate. Brushy Mountain Prison, the maximum security facility at Petros in Morgan County, was a hotbed of unrest because of low wages. My first budget requested substantial salary increases for all state employees with emphasis on corrections and mental health. Commissioner Mark Luttrell had his hands full.

An opportunity to use matching funds under the federal Law Enforcement Assistance Act existed. The state could build a series of minimum security prisons to house first offender convicts and serve as backup resources to county jails. One of the great faults in our correctional system was that young first-time criminals were placed in our main prison in Nashville, usually far removed from their families. Such situations usually put the troubled person, often convicted on a drug charge or auto theft, out of reach of family. To add to the problem, these young people were housed with hardened criminals of every type. Regional prisons would keep offenders closer to their homes. Family members could stay in touch, provide a more constructive climate for rehabilitation, and serve as a resource for overcrowded and inadequate local jails. The entire concept made sense, and I quickly asked Commissioner Luttrell to make plans by identifying desirable sites for consideration.

My 1973 budget message requested initial funding to locate three regional prisons in Memphis, Chattanooga, and Upper East Tennessee. Statistics showed these were the areas most in need of such facilities. Federal guidelines required that the prison be located in close proximity to a community. The existence of civic groups, libraries, and medical resources that could serve the prison population was strictly called for. Those requirements ruled out any prospective site located in remote areas with minimum populations. The concept made sense, but the reality of public attitudes toward prisons and the criminals they contained was something we were to learn a great deal about.

Memphis proved to be an ideal location for a regional prison. Shelby County had adequate land available, and local officials were quick to buy in to the plan. Commissioner Luttrell had complete cooperation, and development was begun in short order.

Chattanooga proved to be an entirely different situation. State personnel spent hours and days working in that area to locate a desirable site. An effort was made to sell local officials on the idea of a regional prison. The effort was a complete failure. The county judge, a man named Frost, was uncooperative. Public opinion was definitely opposed to the creation of "a jail" run by the state. We stretched the interpretation of federal guidelines in an effort to find an acceptable building site. Local state representatives and senators who had voted for the legislation were of no help. They tested the political waters regarding the subject and quickly backed off. Chattanooga was eventually removed from our plans.

Luttrell chose Johnson City as the location for an Upper East Tennessee regional prison. There, and in other communities of the area, he experienced the same resistance. Elected officials and community leaders quickly learned that public opinion leaned strongly against the thought of a collection of criminals being housed nearby. Eventually, corrections personnel turned to Morristown, a community that could be described as bordering on the region we were interested in serving. Following presentations to local officials and civic groups, including the Chamber of Commerce, an agreement was reached, and a site selection process was begun. The mayor of Morristown was cooperative, and a site was selected and purchased. The development process was soon underway.

The Morristown site adjoined land owned by a woman who became alarmed at the idea of a regional prison being located close to her property. Shortly after the land purchase was completed, the woman's son began to stir public opinion against the idea. As the project of construction got underway, strange things began to happen in the community. Groups in opposition, inflamed by the adverse rumors circulated by David Miller, the property owner's son, began to have meetings throughout the community. Outrageous stories were spread about the horrors of such a state facility, crosses were burned on the property of citizens who supported the prison, and ditches were dug across the roadway that construction crews were using. Over a period of many months in 1974 one incident following another inflamed public opinion, and support began to wane. Commissioner Luttrell made a valiant effort to send positive messages regarding the benefits that would result from a regional prison. New jobs would be created, young people in trouble with the law would be given many advantages while serving their sentences, and the public would be the beneficiaries. The tide would not be turned, it appeared. The mayor had a change of heart and declared his opposition to the project after having first welcomed it. David Miller, leading the opposition, became such a folk hero that he was elected a state representative in November 1974.

During the Democrat and Republican primaries of 1974, it was rumored that candidates for governor were promising that, if elected, the prison project would be ended. By that time the prison structures were in an advanced stage of being built. I was assured by my commissioner that everything possible was being done to move the project along. There was little I could do aside from supporting state officials who were involved. Although no personal violence occurred, tempers were flaring to the point that it was necessary for me to assign state troopers to the construction site to prevent ditches from being cut across the roads leading to the property.

This sad story drew to a close when I left office. My successor killed the project that was near completion. The contractor, a Kingsport company, was forced into bankruptcy, and Morristown, an otherwise fine Tennessee community, failed to reap the many benefits that a new regional prison would have brought. Of the three locations most in need, only the Memphis facility was built. No doubt the state would experience critical days ahead in contending with an inadequate corrections system. I was deeply disappointed. I am certain that, had I had more time in office, the prison would have been completed and would today be a valued resource for Morristown and Tennessee.

CHAPTER THIRTY-THREE

IN THE FINAL ANALYSIS . . .

Wrapping It All Up

The various and sundry duties of the governor of Tennessee were such that there was little or no time for boredom to set in during my concluding months in office. There seemed to be no letup in demands for the presence of the governor at functions large and small across the state. I tried to respond positively to as many invitations as time would permit. Governors' conferences, whether national, regional, or partisan, required not only my attendance but also preparation in advance. Three major conferences were scheduled for the remaining months of my service. Routine public relations duties and a wide range of administrative responsibilities kept me and my staff busy.

Several key personnel changes took place midyear. Ted Welch, who had served so effectively as commissioner of finance and administration, submitted his resignation. It was my good fortune to have Gerald Adams, a longtime employee of the department, accept appointment as the new commissioner. He did an outstanding job during the remainder of my term. Hal Carter, my choice from the beginning to serve as commissioner of insurance, also submitted his resignation. He was replaced by Roy Bess, a longtime employee of the department. Dale Young, my loyal executive assistant, decided to return to his law practice in Maryville. Earlier, I had said a fond farewell to Bill Russell, my friend from the days of the Ramp Festival. He had worked as assistant commissioner of conservation and had carried a lot of political water, so to speak, for me. Bill Russell, along with Joe Hopper, had given me immeasurable relief from the political pressures that were constantly being brought to bear at the governor's office.

Political considerations at that time were getting a lot of attention. Events had occurred at the national level that would affect the fortunes of the Republican Party for years to come. In the Watergate matter

Richard Nixon failed to use the good judgment he had demonstrated on so many occasions. We had a new president named Gerald Ford and a vice president named Nelson Rockefeller. Our nation had been tormented by the failed thinking of a president who believed he was above the law. The Watergate burglary and attempted cover-up were disasters, not only for the party and its representatives, but also for the country at large.

Although we were deeply hurt by Nixon's misjudgment, Betty and I were anxious to support the Republican cause at every opportunity. In 1974 she devoted much of her time and energy to entertaining busloads of Republican ladies from around the state with lunch at the Residence. I received many invitations to make appearances for our Republican candidates for the legislature. Three well-known Republican leaders had, by late spring, announced their intentions to seek the party's nomination for governor. They were Lamar Alexander, Dortch Oldham, and Nat Winston. Since all were my good friends, and because I felt I should stay neutral in the primary race, I spent no time on the campaign trail. I did help in as many legislative races as possible.

Alexander won the primary race in August and ran against Congressman Ray Blanton in the general election. Blanton had run against Howard Baker for the Senate in 1972 and lost. He had a statewide organization in place. Having an existing organization in place, having the Watergate controversy to chew on, and having a sitting Republican governor who had made the people of heavily Republican Upper East Tennessee unhappy made the political situation for Blanton very favorable. He won his race and became the governor-elect. I was disappointed that our Republican candidates did not fare well in the election results, but I realized that the political winds of the time did not favor us.

During the governor's race I made several speeches in support of Alexander and pulled no punches in stating why I thought he was the better choice. I met only one time with the newly elected governor before he was sworn in. It was quite evident that I was not on his list of favorites, and I could understand his feelings. I had made it clear during the election that he wasn't the leader that Tennessee needed. Our purpose in meeting was to set in motion the transition of power. With Leonard Bradley's help, I was confident we would measure up to the standard set by Buford Ellington. I made one personal request of Blanton. I wanted my devoted friend and aide, Captain John White, to be treated fairly as he settled back into some role in the Department of Safety where he could continue to work toward retirement. He agreed to that. To my great disappointment and disgust, John White was treated poorly, demoted in rank, and assigned to menial duties. It was an indication of the kind of conduct that was yet to come in the Blanton years.

After the legislature adjourned, in addition to meeting the daily demands of my office, I began to seriously think about life after the governorship. I stayed in close touch with friends from Shelby County who had been so important in helping us to be elected and who continued over the years to be supportive. I had several discussions regarding my future after leaving office. I made a decision not to return to my dental profession. Several conversations led me to believe there were opportunities in both Memphis and Nashville to become involved in the corporate business world, and that appealed to me. My financial circumstances were such that I knew respectable compensation would be absolutely necessary for me to see to all my family's needs. The question of how I would use whatever skills I might bring to the business world was given much thought as the remaining months of my term played themselves out.

My friend Jack Massey talked seriously with me about a relationship with Hospital Corporation of America. HCA was a young company, founded in 1968 by Massey; Thomas Frist, Sr., MD; his son, Tom, Jr.; and the Hooker brothers. Its mission was to own and operate community hospitals profitably throughout the nation. Mr. Massey, chairman of the company, offered me a position on the board of directors and the possibility of a full-time relationship in some capacity. I devoted much time to a decision in the matter, realizing that, to become so connected, would require that Betty and I remain in Nashville. Our daughters had spent four formative years in Nashville and were very happy. Our son spent most of my four years as governor away at college. My wife and I knew we would, as matters of conscience, have serious remorse in not returning to the wonderful city that had given us so much. It was a difficult decision, but I honestly felt the future opportunities offered me in Nashville justified not returning to Memphis permanently. We decided to accept the relationship with Hospital Corporation of America.

A beautiful gesture took place in Shelby County on December 10. The Cook Convention Center in downtown Memphis was the location. To my great surprise, the special guest for the evening in which Betty and I would be honored was Governor Mills Godwin of Virginia. It was quite an event in which Betty, Chuck, Gayle, Julie, and I were reminded of the love and respect that we had somehow earned over the years from the people of Memphis. Our dear friend Kopie Kopald had played a major role in planning the Winfield Dunn Appreciation Day. We were greeted and treated royally by a large group of friends on an occasion we will never forget. We all agreed that the most recent four years had, indeed, flown by. That wonderful evening at the Cook Center, along with a special dinner the Memphis Chamber of Commerce had held in our honor after my election in 1971, will remain forever among my most prized memories.

At the time I felt that the public was satisfied with the performance of the Dunn administration, but I continued to be anxious regarding certain issues. Those included the medical school ill will that existed in Upper East Tennessee, the public unrest regarding the regional prison under construction in Morristown, and dissatisfaction because Interstate 81 was not yet ready to absorb huge volumes of traffic then struggling along on Highway 11. As soon as ribbons were cut opening I-81, the longed for relief on Highway 11 came, and I was greatly relieved. I could not shake off the disappointment I felt because so many controversial issues focused on the great Republican area of East Tennessee. I knew they would someday be grateful for the massive highway development that Bob Smith and I had set in motion. Sadly for me, those ribbons would be cut by others in later years.

As Christmas neared, it was obvious that Betty's attention was focused on preparing to physically move from the Residence. We enjoyed our last Christmas as the first family as much as we had enjoyed our first, but the mind-sets all around were quite different. Gone were the moments of titillation and excitement as new friends and new experiences were showered down on us. By this time, we had earned veteran status, and we knew rather well what to expect from one moment to another. Many, many boxes had to be packed, and decisions had to be made regarding our adjustment once again to private life.

The inauguration of the new governor had been designated to take place on January 18 of the new year. We made our plans accordingly and decided we would leave the Residence in time for the new occupants to get settled before the inauguration, just as Governor and Mrs. Ellington had so thoughtfully done for us.

We continued to enjoy the privileges that come with being the first family. Brief trips with friends to various sites were a welcomed change. Our friendships with Minnie Pearl and Henry Cannon were pleasant and rewarding. Good friend Jim Nabors invited us to visit him at his home in Hawaii to celebrate the New Year, 1975, and we accepted. We flew to Oahu and were warmly welcomed to his home at the foot of Diamond Head. In addition to seeing the beautiful sights, we had the pleasure of meeting many well-known celebrities.

Helen Reddy was a very popular singer whom we enjoyed. Steve Lawrence and Eydie Gorme were favorite entertainers whom we were thrilled to meet at a party on New Year's Eve. As Helen Reddy finished her performance at the party, the doors to the large room opened, and in stepped a small figure clothed in a white blanket. Everyone's attention was riveted on the new arrival who, with a large wooden staff in his hand, appeared to be Father Time. Suddenly, he dropped the staff, shed the blanket, and stood there naked except for what appeared to be a diaper. It was Sammy Davis, Jr. The audience roared with pleasure, and the small, skinny entertainer did his thing. It was quite memorable. After a good visit with our host Jim Nabors, we returned to Nashville, Minnie to continue to perform at the Grand Ole Opry and other venues, while my first lady and I began to make preparations to leave what had been our grand, rent-free home for the past four years.

Some Heartache

During our time at the official Residence, we followed the age-old tradition of using domestic help selected from the population of the state prison. Because previous Democrat governors had followed that tradition, I knew it would be difficult, if not impossible, to get legislative approval for a Republican governor to increase the Residence budget allowance sufficiently to add private domestic staff. Some inmates selected for work at the Residence were serving life sentences for murder, and others were serving sentences for robbery. By the time they came to us, they had earned merit for good conduct. We easily adjusted to the presence of these men and, with a few minor exceptions, felt very comfortable with their presence and work. We had, in fact, developed friendships with a number of the prisoners because they were kind to us and well behaved.

As my term of office neared its conclusion, the time came for me to have a farewell meeting with each one of these inmates. I chose to do so individually rather than as a group. I had heard stories of past governors who had exercised their power of pardon and parole to grant freedom to their favorites among the prisoners assigned to the Residence. I personally felt that such action would be an abuse of my legitimate power based on personal preference rather than respect for the law and its application to those who had been convicted for its violation. There was some room for me to be considerate of individual prisoners based on their good conduct and recommendations from the Board of Pardons and Paroles. Where it was possible for me to reduce the time remaining to be served by individual prisoners, I did so. I did not choose to simply cut their time served to zero and grant immediate release. It was obvious that rumors had led many of these prisoners to believe I might do that.

I met with each man in the parlor room opposite my Residence office. Sitting there, man to man, telling each one that I was limited in what I could do to help shorten their time in prison was one of the most difficult chores that befell me as governor. Each conversation was sheer agony for me. I visited with all the prisoners in one afternoon. As we spoke, on more than one of those faces I could see eyes welling up with tears. I must say that I could not hold back tears of my own. It was a hard time for all of us, but I finished the chore, satisfied that I had done the right thing.

So Long, Farewell

Our good-byes were said in a variety of settings. The staff that assisted me and others in the administration was told good-bye with deep feelings of appreciation on my part. The younger members of our team had worked their hearts out. Annie Hill and Mary Jane Creel were the senior members who provided stability and good advice countless times. A good-bye gathering of my cabinet members was an emotional event. I was so proud of the high marks of excellence in public service these fine people earned. To my knowledge, there was never a hint of misconduct or impropriety during our four years of service, and that was more valuable to each of us than any other one accomplishment.

I knew, deep within my most serious moments of reflection, that our administration had set a new benchmark for others to match. With all due respect to those who had served in the past, I was convinced that no single four-year period of Tennessee state government had seen the level of energy and devotion to duty that had been provided by the first Republican administration to serve in fifty years. We had literally made history by changing the ways things were done, by reforming major state responsibilities, by bringing in fresh, new faces and new ideas to serve the state, and by demonstrating ethical conduct beyond reproach.

We as a family had been spoiled to some extent by the incredible respect and kindnesses extended to us for four years. I recalled Governor Ellington admonishing us not to change when we came in so that we wouldn't have to change again when we went out. He said the time would pass swiftly, and he was correct. There would be big changes in our lifestyles, and each family member was prepared as much as possible for those changes. We would once again be responsible for our own housing, transportation, and security after four years of freedom from those duties. I would have to polish my shoes, keep my automobile clean, and find my way around the city of Nashville. Betty would no longer have a private secretary or housekeeper. Our daughters would have to adjust to driving themselves wherever they wished to go. Chuck would be required to make the least adjustment. He had remained somewhat independent of routine life in the Executive Residence but certainly enjoyed his time there. Frankly, each one of us looked forward to a return to a more normal lifestyle. I certainly looked forward to privacy that I had not experienced for four years. For each of us, the time had come to move on.

We physically moved out of the Residence during the second week of January 1975. Once again, Betty assumed the details of that chore and carried it off without a hitch. While I attended to the duties of my office she was rising at 6:00 a.m. making decisions about packing boxes of belongings. Eventually, we settled down in a private residence, each of us having made his or her personal adjustments. Our state trooper security personnel were required to make some adjustments as well. There was much less space in our new quarters to accommodate their presence, and those fine gentlemen spent considerable time on duty sitting in parked cars outside our new home.

A Proper Closure

On the morning of January 18, my family and I were driven to the War Memorial Building within the capitol complex to participate in the official inaugural activities for a new governor. It was a rainy day, making it necessary to conduct the official business of the inauguration indoors. After all those involved, including both houses of the legislature, appropriate members of the judiciary, and the soon-to-be first family were in place, the ceremonies commenced. As was historically and legally the precedent, the Senate Speaker, John Wilder, gaveled the audience to silence and officially called the proceedings to order. Shortly thereafter I was introduced to make my brief, parting remarks as follows:

> *Mr. President Wilder, Speaker McWherter, Governor Blanton, Mr. Chief Justice, members of the 89th General Assembly, respected public servants, ladies, and gentlemen:*
>
> *The 21st book of the Old Testament, Ecclesiastes, makes a very practical as well as a poetic reference to the various seasons or times in our lives when we experience living at its fullest. Today is such a time for me and my family—it is a time of happiness, a time of thanksgiving, and a time of appreciation.*
>
> *We are happy because we have fulfilled our official commitment to the people of our state to the best of our abilities. We are thankful for the hundreds of our fellow citizens from every area who have involved themselves in Tennessee's destiny as they participated in their state government. We are filled with appreciation for the support and guidance of the general assembly which has assured the progress of our state during my term of office.*

Four years ago, great numbers of good people gathered in this capital city to support a family from Memphis which had embarked on a new and unusual adventure in public service. Today, we gather to celebrate the beginning of such a journey for a new family of proud Tennesseans.

I join the 89th General Assembly in extending my sincere best wishes to the new first family of Tennessee, and its first citizen, the governor. I know it is the heartfelt wish of every thoughtful citizen that he succeed in his endeavors—that he realizes his hopes and dreams for Tennessee.

Finally, as I depart from a labor of love, I take this opportunity to renew the expression of my grateful appreciation to the people of Tennessee. I do so for myself, for Mrs. Dunn, and for our children. Four years as your governor have given me an awakened sense of values and an increased respect for my heritage. I will always be grateful.

Thank you.

Shortly after I finished my remarks, we were escorted to our cars and driven to our new residence in West Nashville. As we exited the shiny black Lincoln Town Car leased by the state for the chief executive, we said good-bye to our security personnel. In an instant, we had been transported far beyond the doors of a state vehicle. We had been transported back into the status of regular citizens from whence we had come four years earlier. Each of us realized that our lives would never be quite the same as while we were the first family, but neither would they be quite the same as they were before we undertook our great adventure. And so it has been, down through the years.

I have had the privilege of watching new governors and first families come and go. It has been most interesting to observe those people assume the awesome responsibilities Betty and I, along with our children, experienced. Most of my successors have distinguished themselves and served the people well. Our state has moved ahead, and it remains a wonderful place to call home.

I take satisfaction in knowing that many of the major initiatives undertaken during my administration have borne and continue to bear positive results for the taxpayers of our state. I believe state employees and public school teachers were energized and motivated by reasonable salary increases. I have no doubt the executive branch of state government was the beneficiary of reorganization and modernization efforts to gain more efficiency from every tax dollar. I continue to see positive results in public kindergarten, in the Tennessee Housing Development Agency, in the new business and industrial investments and jobs created through the good work of the Department of Economic and Community Development, in our colleges and universities, and in major highway development. It is also clear that much remains to be done to improve the opportunities for life and good fortune in our state.

My successors have had the option to seek consecutive four-year terms. I had no such option. I sincerely believe additional time for one governor to serve could be beneficial to the state. My strong recommendation is that a governor of Tennessee be elected to serve one six-year term with no option for immediate reelection. That period of time would favor the completion of initiatives undertaken. An added benefit might be that the incumbent would not be distracted by reelection considerations. The fact that I could not seek immediate reelection gave me freedom from basing any of the difficult decisions I had to make on whether or not the decision might affect my potential to be reelected. Perhaps a constitutional amendment to that effect will be proposed in the future. A single six-year term for a governor of Tennessee makes good sense.

The year 1970 was a pivotal one in the ongoing chronicle of Tennessee state government. No single political effort, to my knowledge, had benefited from such unselfish volunteerism and the devotion of so many ordinary citizens as had my race for the governorship. Our neighbors and friends in Memphis and Shelby County made the difference. They assured my victory in a difficult primary campaign. They gave us the opportunity to make a contribution. We started with nothing but an idea and a logical argument stating clearly the political wisdom of finding a way to add the untapped, independent political thinking of West Tennessee voters to the dependable Republican voter strength of the East. The timing was right, and so, from a standing start, we began to feel our way and good things happened. It was not an easy victory, but it was a victory and I sincerely hope the people were the beneficiaries.

Finally, in reflecting on the interesting and sometimes tumultuous political events that changed the life of each member of my family, my profound good fortune continues to be the fact that Providence led me to marry Miss Betty Prichard of Memphis, Tennessee, on December 30, 1950. Among her many gifts to me are my Tennessee citizenship, three superb children who conducted themselves beautifully as members of the state's first family, a lifetime of companionship and vivid memories of a shining, sparkling, competent wife, mother, and devoted Tennessee first lady. She surely won the hearts of the people. She will always be remembered as the lovely, warm, and talented lady she remains to this day. All that happened would not have happened without her.

INDEX

Armour, Claude A. (supporter), 291-293, 425, 454-455, 461-462
  appointed commissioner of safety, 364-365, 423, 461
  member of Ellington administration, 363-364
Arnold, Sammy (pharmacist), 175
Ashe, Victor (state senator), 206, 447-448
Ashley, J.D., 182
Aswumb, Gwen (friend), 24, 46, 48, 77, 91, 112
Atkins, Chet, 340
Austin, Richard (neighbor), 310
automobiles
  low license tags highly sought after, 391-395

B

Bacharach, Burt (singer-songwriter), 493
Baird, Linden, 192
Baird, William D. (state senator)
  meets Dunn and wears red suspenders, 384
Baker, Howard, Jr., (senator), 45, 52, 53, 54, 56, 63, 65, 66, 74, 76, 85, 93, 95,
  102, 108, 115, 119, 153, 223, 276, 277-278, 285, 302-303, 388, 426,
  453, 518
  attends Dunn inauguration, 354
  Dunn encounters on campaign trail, 162
  elected to the U.S. Senate, 64
  and gubernatorial primary (1970), 143, 223
  offers up suggestions for campaign staff, 254-255
Baker, Howard, Sr., (U.S. congressman), 46
Baker, Lamar (congressional candidate), 221, 265-266, 277, 283, 285, 302
  wife Sue, 277
Baker v. Carr (Supreme Court case), 447
Ball, Ernest (city superintendent of schools), 458
Ball, Zimri, 186
Ballou, Carl (supporter), 131
Barlow, Jack (country music singer/songwriter), 271-272
Barnes, George (superintendent of schools), 458
Barnett, Frank (campaign staffer), 377
  administrative assistant, 365, 370, 385
  general election campaign, 259, 280
  pre-inauguration, 325
  transition team member, 331, 353
Barret, Paul (banker), 59
baseball
  Blues Baseball Stadium campaign event, 286-287
Bass, Ross (U.S. senator), 63

E

Hooker, Tish (wife of John Jay)
  makes campaign appearance at luncheon, 301
Hopper, Joe Neal (administrative assistant), 365, 370, 385, 422-423, 457, 517
Hospital Corporation of America (HCA), 519
Humphrey, Hubert (presidential candidate), 76
Humphreys, Raymond, 85-86, 88, 112 177, 178, 204, 219, 253
  general election campaign, 255
Hurst, Julius (school superintendent), 172

I-J
Ingram, E. Bronson (businessman), 406
  wife Martha, 476-477
Itoh, C. (Japanese businessman), 504
Jackson, Andrew (president)
  portrait painting purchased for Executive Residence, 428-429
James, Bob (Shelby County Party Chair), 33-34, 39, 41-42, 46, 48, 50-51,
  57, 77, 91, 99, 102, 104, 107, 112, 139, 141, 178, 219
  chairman of the County Republican Executive Committee, 45
James, Pat (wife of Bob), 33, 41-42, 43, 55, 102, 140, 142
Jarman, Maxey (gubernatorial candidate), 93, 98, 127-128, 145, 160,
  172, 182, 187, 194, 198, 200-201, 204, 214, 226-228, 233-234, 237,
  244, 246-247, 257, 274, 319
  asks Dunn to not run for governor, 96-97, 105-106
  campaign upset following loss in primary, 244
  chairs Governor's Study on Cost Control, 399-404
  commenting on runoff law for primaries, 204
  Dunn's assessment of, 146-147
  Dunn's criticism of during primary, 213, 222
  levels charges against Dunn campaign, 223
  poll results for primary, 205, 208
  poster falling to floor during event, 230
  primary election vote totals, 239
  support for Bobby Kennedy in 1968, 222, 234
Jarman, Sarah Mac (wife of Maxey), 202
Jenkins, Bill (gubernatorial candidate), 127-128, 136, 145, 160, 170, 172, 178,
  182, 185, 187, 198-199, 200, 216, 229, 233-234, 237, 303
  commissioner of conservation, 364, 366
  conflict of interest, article charging him with, 206
  Dunn's assessment of, 146-147
  gracious in loss, 246-247
  speaker of the house, 92-94, 98
Jennings, Dick & Virginia, 183, 230, 263
Jensen, Tom (representative), 477, 497

attends Dunn inauguration, 354
  legislative point man for the House, 379, 418
John Birch Society, 18
Johnson City (TN), 79-82, 83
Johnson, Dorothy "Happy" (party colleague), 78
Johnson, Doyle (airplane pilot), 65
Johnson, J.D. (dentist), 221
Johnson, Joe, 284
Johnson, Lyndon Baines (president), 21, 56, 65
Johnson, Victor (businessman), 406
Jones, Carl, 230, 283
Jones, Ed (congressman), 176
Jones, John M. (newspaper publisher), 184, 229, 283
Jones, "Skeet" (auctioneer), 187, 215
  wife Jean Jones, 187, 215
Jones, Snowden (party colleague), 91
Judd, Walter (U.S. congressman), 23-24

K

Kefauver, Estes (U.S. senator), 20, 45, 51, 63, 453
Kennedy, John F. (president), 47, 67, 76, 275
Kennedy, Robert F. "Bobby", 275
Kesley, Howard, transition team member, 331, 353
  appointed to head new department, 443
  commissioner of standards and purchasing, 373
Kesley, Roger, transition team member, 331, 353
Kilday, Iula, 184, 229
Kile, Jim, 318
Killen, Buddy and Sue, 491
kindergarten 412, 439, 441. *See also* public education
  budget requested for implementation, 418-419, 444, 445
  campaign theme, 220-221, 294-295
  commitment for funding for all students, 467, 500, 502
  initiative for, 403
King, Martin Luther, Jr., (civil rights leader)
  assassination of, 287, 292, 450, 455
King, Tom "Tommy" (businessman), 270, 286-287
King, Warren (consultant), 353, 398
Kissinger, Henry (secretary of state), 435
Knoxville and Knox County (TN), 149
  gubernatorial primary and, 152-156, 158-162
Kopald, S.L. "Kopie", 78, 103, 107, 112, 219, 253, 438, 459
  appointed chairman of the state Republican party, 388-389

Y
York, Clyde (Tennessee Farm Bureau head), 72
Young, Brigham (pharmacist), 183
Young, W. Dale (attorney), 191, 377
   executive administrative assistant, 365, 370, 422-423
   general election campaign, 259-261, 264
   returns to private practice, 517